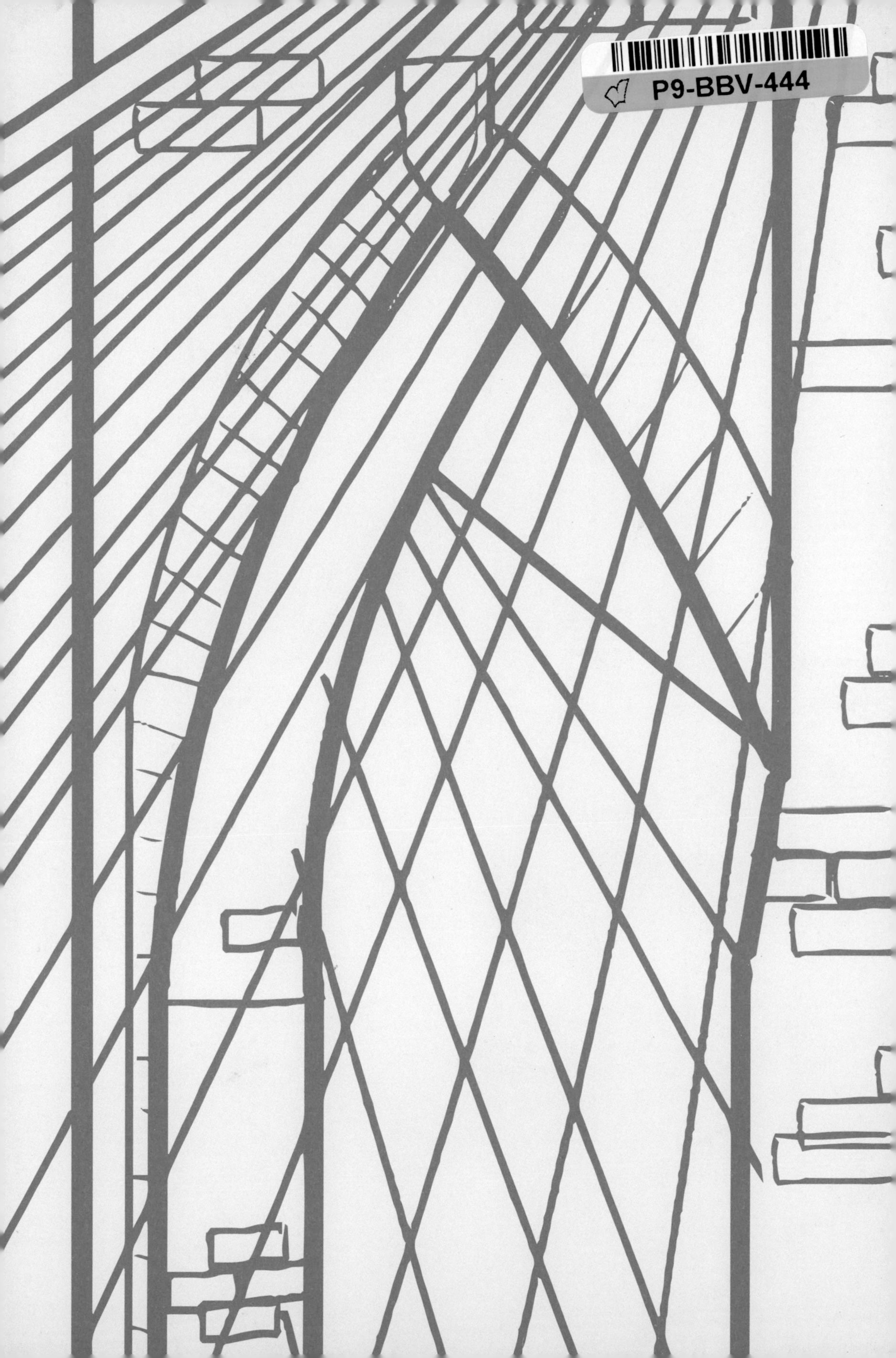

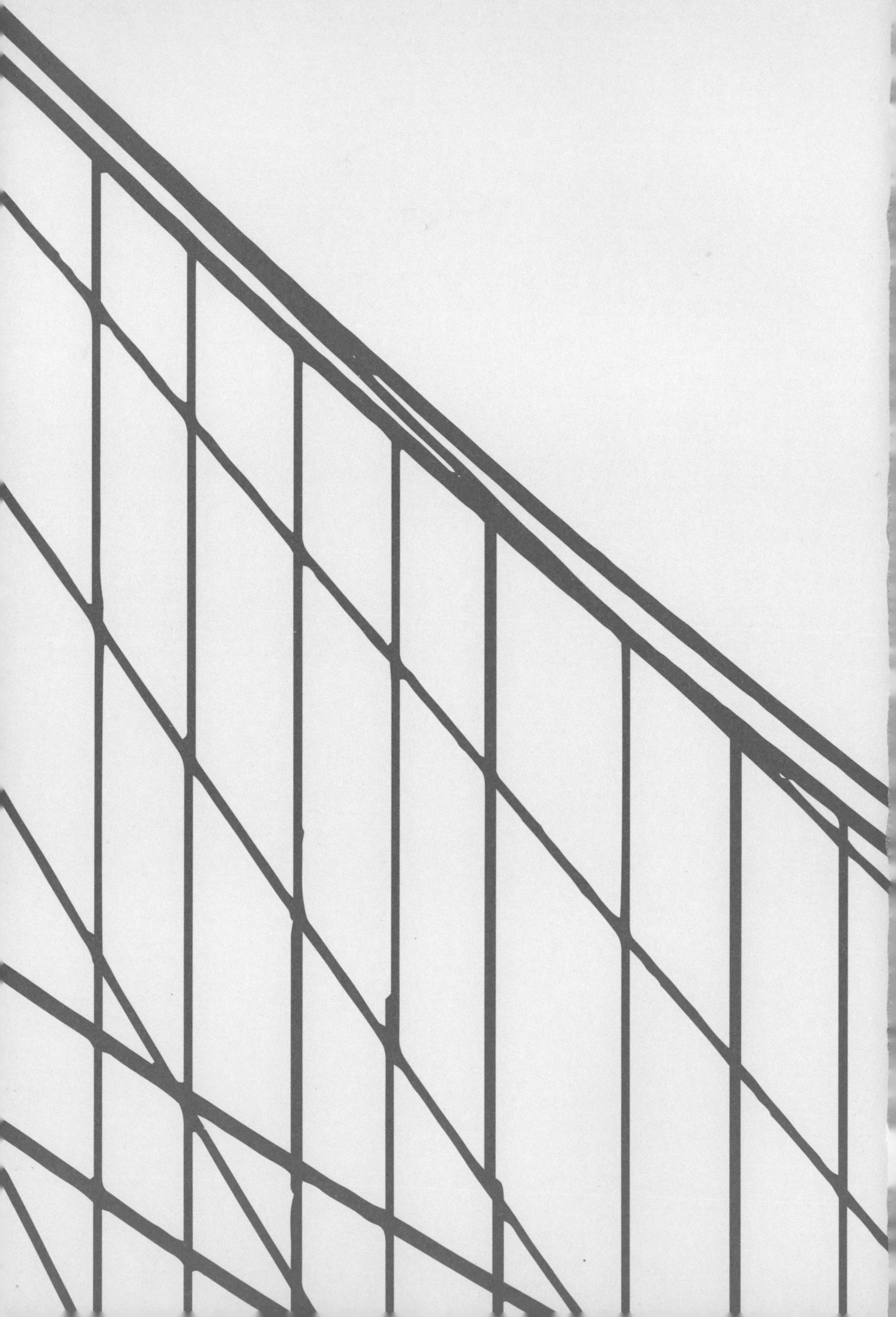

By **PETER J. TOMASI**

Illustrated by **SARA DUVALL**

THE
BRIDGE

How the Roeblings Connected Brooklyn to New York

Coloring by **GABRIEL ELTAEB** and **JOHN KALISZ**   Lettering by **ROB LEIGH**

ABRAMS COMICARTS
New York

To my wife, Deborah, and son, Alexander,
bridges across tranquil and troubled waters forever
—PT

Thanks to my family for their never-ending support
—SD

Editor: Orlando Dos Reis
Project Manager: Charles Kochman
Designer: Pamela Notarantonio
Managing Editor: Samantha Hoback
Production Manager: Alison Gervais

Cataloging-in-Publication Data has been applied for
and may be obtained from the Library of Congress.

ISBN: 978-1-4197-2852-5

Printed and bound in China

10 9 8 7 6 5 4 3 2 1

Abrams ComicArts books are available at special discounts when purchased
in quantity for premiums and promotions as well as fundraising or educational
use. Special editions can also be created to specification. For details, contact
specialsales@abramsbooks.com or the address below.

ABRAMS The Art of Books
195 Broadway, New York, NY 10007
abramsbooks.com

Preface

My name is Peter J. Tomasi, and I'm trying to sell you a bridge.

The Brooklyn Bridge, actually.

I am a native New Yorker, born and raised in Washington Heights, and I have to be honest here: It was the George Washington Bridge, *not* the Brooklyn Bridge, that first made an indelible impression on me. You see, our apartment windows looked out at the looming gray steel that leaps across the Hudson. The bridge was there in the morning, afternoon, and evening, noticeable from what seemed to be every street corner of my old neighborhood—its beacon visible from my bedroom, turning again and again; a soothing nightlight that put me to sleep each and every evening.

Living in the shadow of the GW bridge put me on a collision course with John and Washington Roebling, and, as we'll learn, Emily Roebling's Brooklyn Bridge, because it led me to walk across all the connecting bridges of Manhattan as a teenager and learn who, what, where, when, and why these beautiful works came into being; to discover just what kind of person sits and sweats at a drafting table and dreams up these wonders. Obviously, given my book, it's the Roebling story that grabbed me the hardest and never let go.

The Roeblings and the construction of the Brooklyn Bridge is one of those quintessential American stories that no one really seems to know about. The average person on the street has no idea what went into this massive undertaking, what physical and emotional limits had been pushed to the breaking point, how a wife took on the duties of her ailing husband and was a big factor in helping make the bridge a reality. This epic story, in my mind, cries out to be seen by American and foreign readers alike, that we honor the names of visionaries such as the Roeblings, who left something of true, lasting value behind, and not just the next Serial Killer, Drug Kingpin, or Dirty Politician story that promotes a lack of morals, ethics, and self-interest.

I was chomping at the bit to be true to history and to the Roeblings, trying to find the right balance between drama and detail. A balance between taking liberties with true events, while also boiling them down and compressing the story into a manageable page count.

So, after countless hours immersed in books and old issues of *Harper's Weekly*, the *Brooklyn Eagle*, the *New York Times*, etc., and time spent at the Rensselaer Polytechnic Institute in Troy, New York, coupled with countless walks and photos of the amazing span itself at all hours and all seasons of the year, it was time to get my butt in the seat and my fingers busy on a keyboard.

But I couldn't.

When it came right down to it, I was scared of actually starting my passion project for one simple reason: It suddenly felt too big. I was scared of screwing it up.

So I kept coming up with reasons not to start it. Writer's block and procrastination demons sat on my shoulders, and I let quite a bit of time slip by.

Then I woke up to a blue morning.

September 11, 2001.

A city, a country, a world, changed forever. Blood and terror. Souls lost and lives altered. Roiling clouds of pulverized bodies, steel, concrete, paper, and smoke blowing unbelievingly through the canyons of lower Manhattan.

My Manhattan.

The Manhattan I was born in, grew up in, schooled in, partied in, loved in, hated in, married in, and on that day, worked in, now possessed a Ground Zero.

A week later, after finally stepping away from the TV, I stepped up to my laptop. I had to write this for my own peace of mind. I didn't care if anyone ever read it, I just needed to do it.

The Roeblings and the Brooklyn Bridge is a story of construction, not destruction. Of perseverance and dreams. Of sacrifice and loss. The kind of story the world needs more of, especially now. Not only do Americans need to be reminded what was accomplished in the past, but we need to see how that knowledge can help us build toward a better future.

Upon finishing the script, I decided to start my adventure with the Roeblings and the Great Bridge with a visit to Cold Spring Cemetery (I live only forty minutes from the burial grounds). I stood in front of the subtle, yet distinguished, grave markers of Washington and Emily, and said a silent prayer for those two amazing souls. I look forward to leaving a copy of this book—beautifully illustrated by Sara DuVall, colored by Gabriel Eltaeb and John Kalisz, and lettered by Rob Leigh—at the Roeblings' graves, hoping we've done justice to their life and their story.

I'd like to end this little ditty with the opening quote from David McCullough's *The Great Bridge*. It's from 1883 by Montgomery Schuyler and beautifully sums up all the yapping and blabbing I've done here:

"It so happens that the work which is likely to be our most durable monument, and to convey some knowledge of us to the most remote posterity, is a work of bare utility; not a shrine, not a fortress, not a palace, but a bridge."

Peter J. Tomasi
New York
July 2017

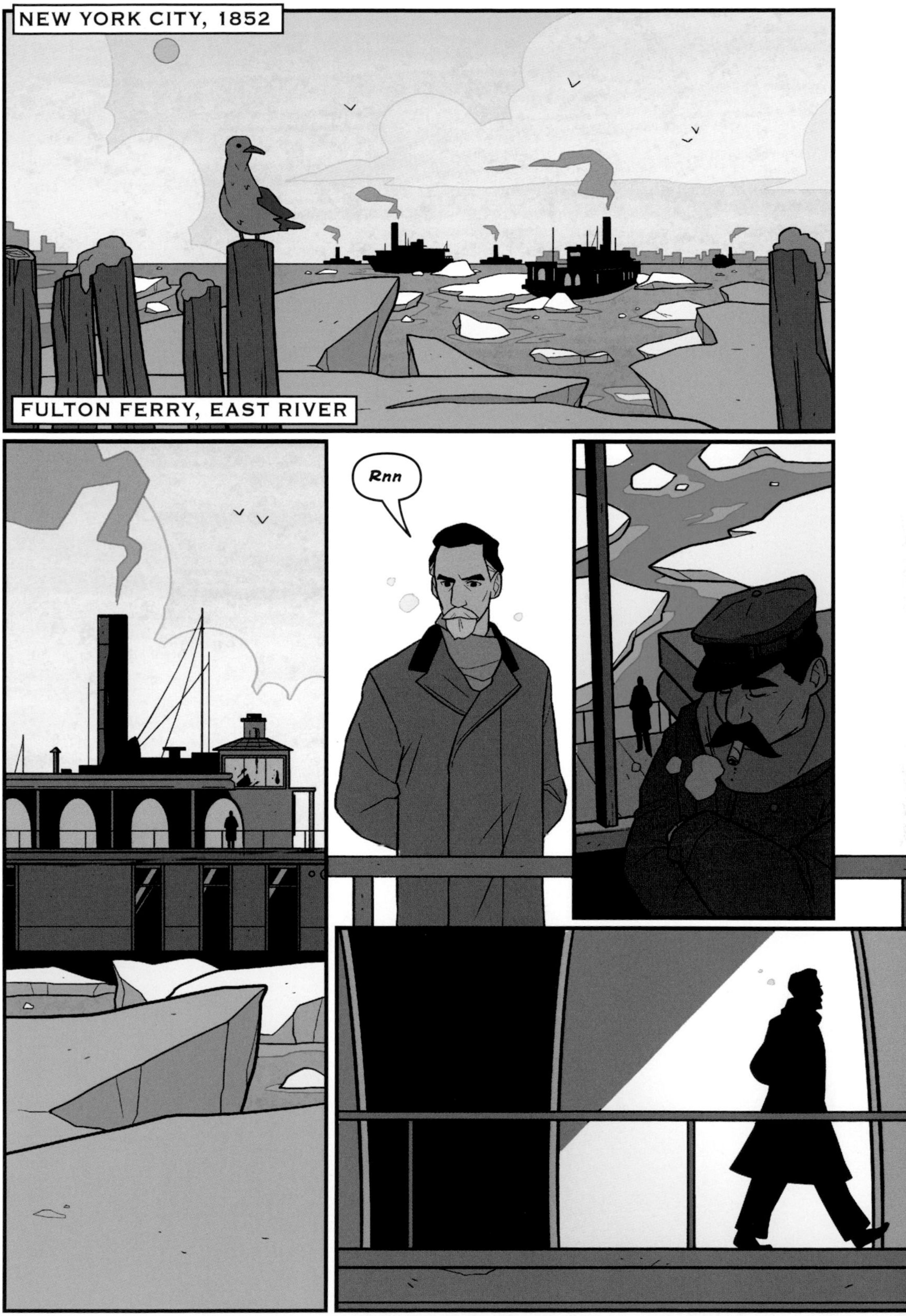
NEW YORK CITY, 1852
FULTON FERRY, EAST RIVER
Rnn

YOUR PAD, WASHINGTON.

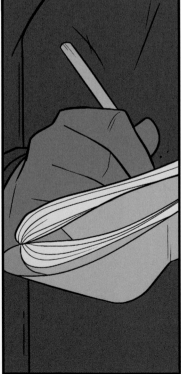

GO UP TO THE WHEELHOUSE.

SEE THAT THE FERRY CAPTAIN GETS THIS.

YES, DA.

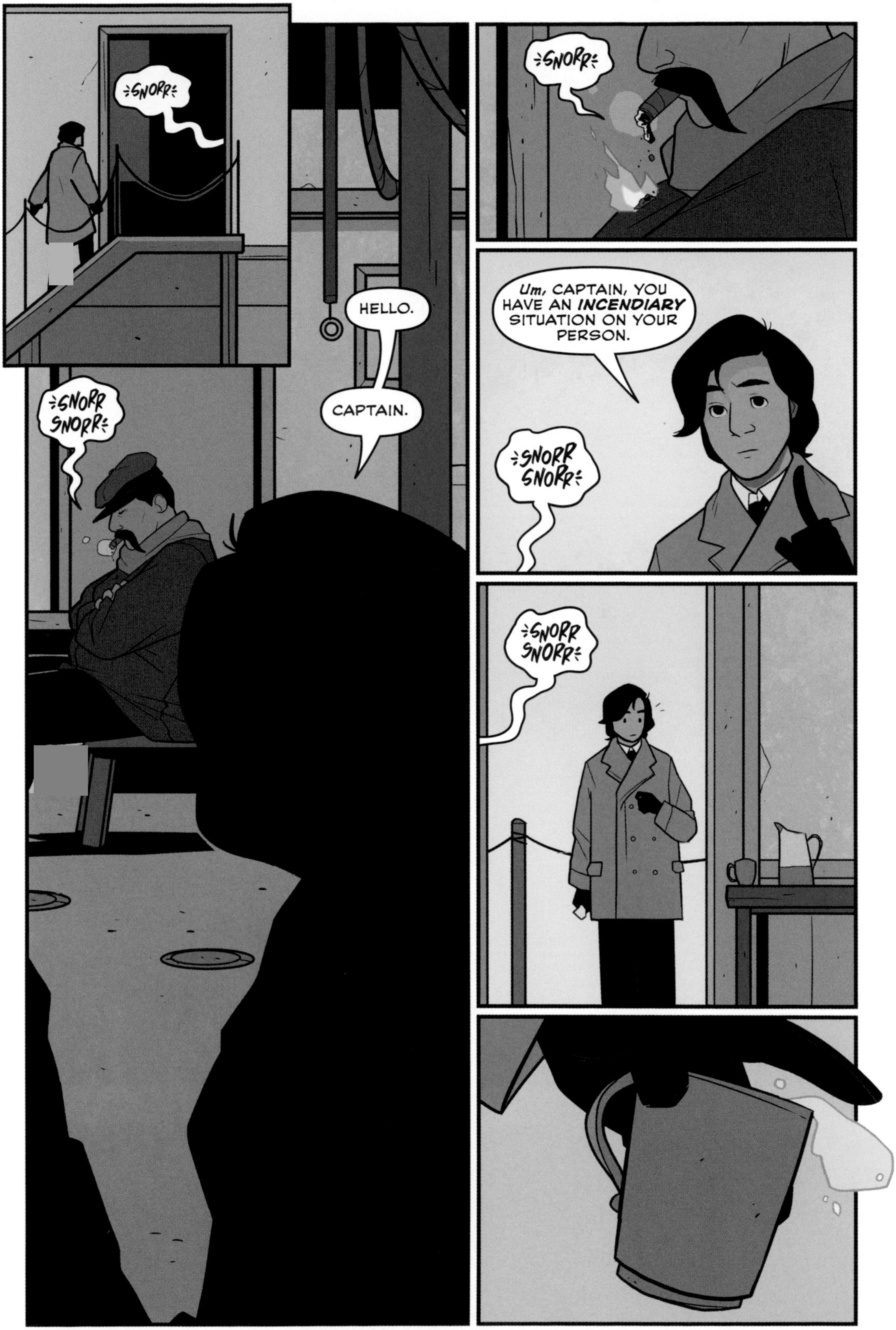
SNORR
HELLO.
CAPTAIN.
SNORR SNORR
SNORR
Um, CAPTAIN, YOU HAVE AN INCENDIARY SITUATION ON YOUR PERSON.
SNORR SNORR
SNORR SNORR

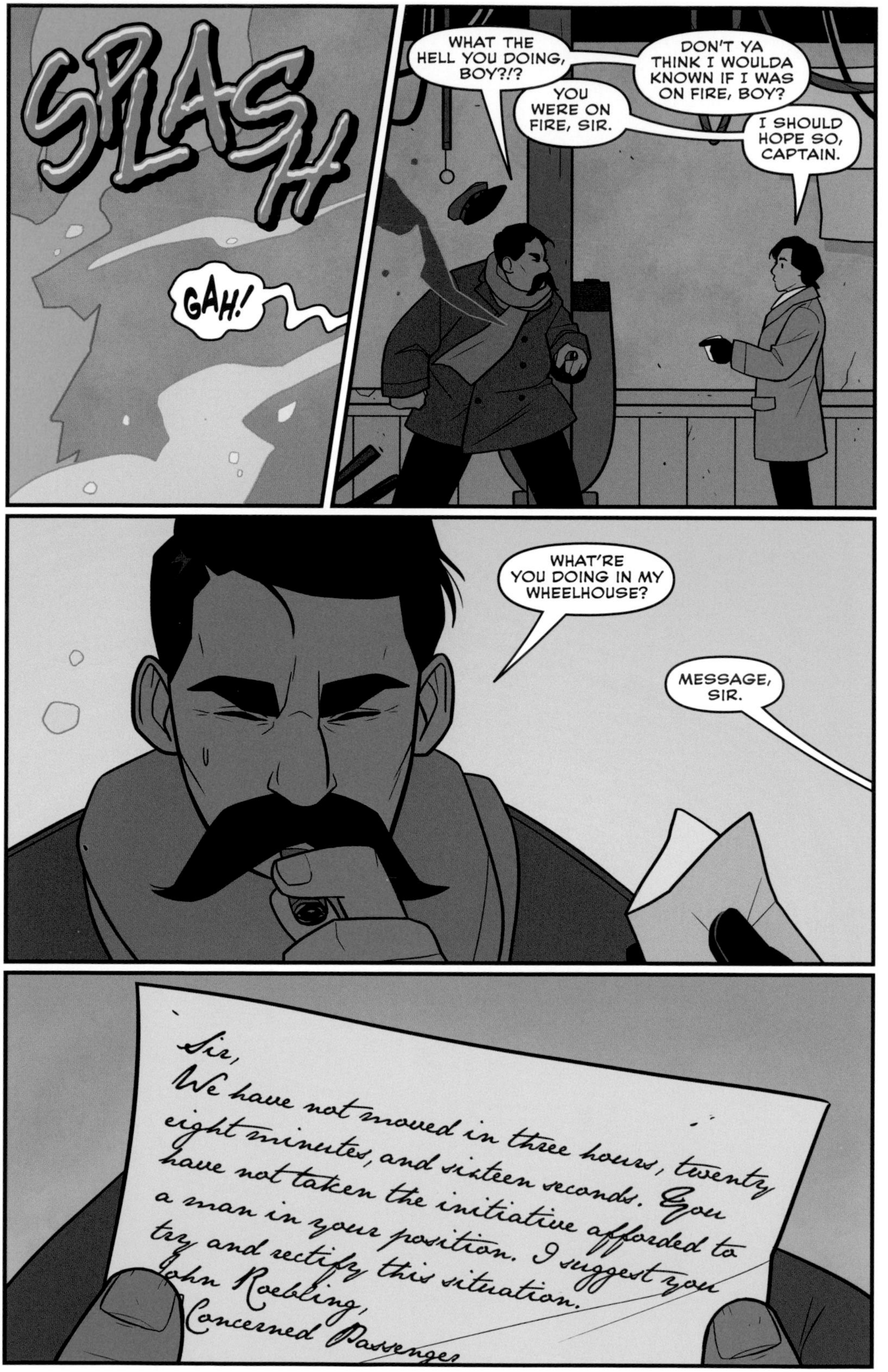
SPLASH
GAH!
WHAT THE HELL YOU DOING, BOY?!?
YOU WERE ON FIRE, SIR.
DON'T YA THINK I WOULDA KNOWN IF I WAS ON FIRE, BOY?
I SHOULD HOPE SO, CAPTAIN.
WHAT'RE YOU DOING IN MY WHEELHOUSE?
MESSAGE, SIR.
Sir,
We have not moved in three hours, twenty eight minutes, and sixteen seconds. You have not taken the initiative afforded to a man in your position. I suggest you try and rectify this situation.
John Roebling,
Concerned Passenger

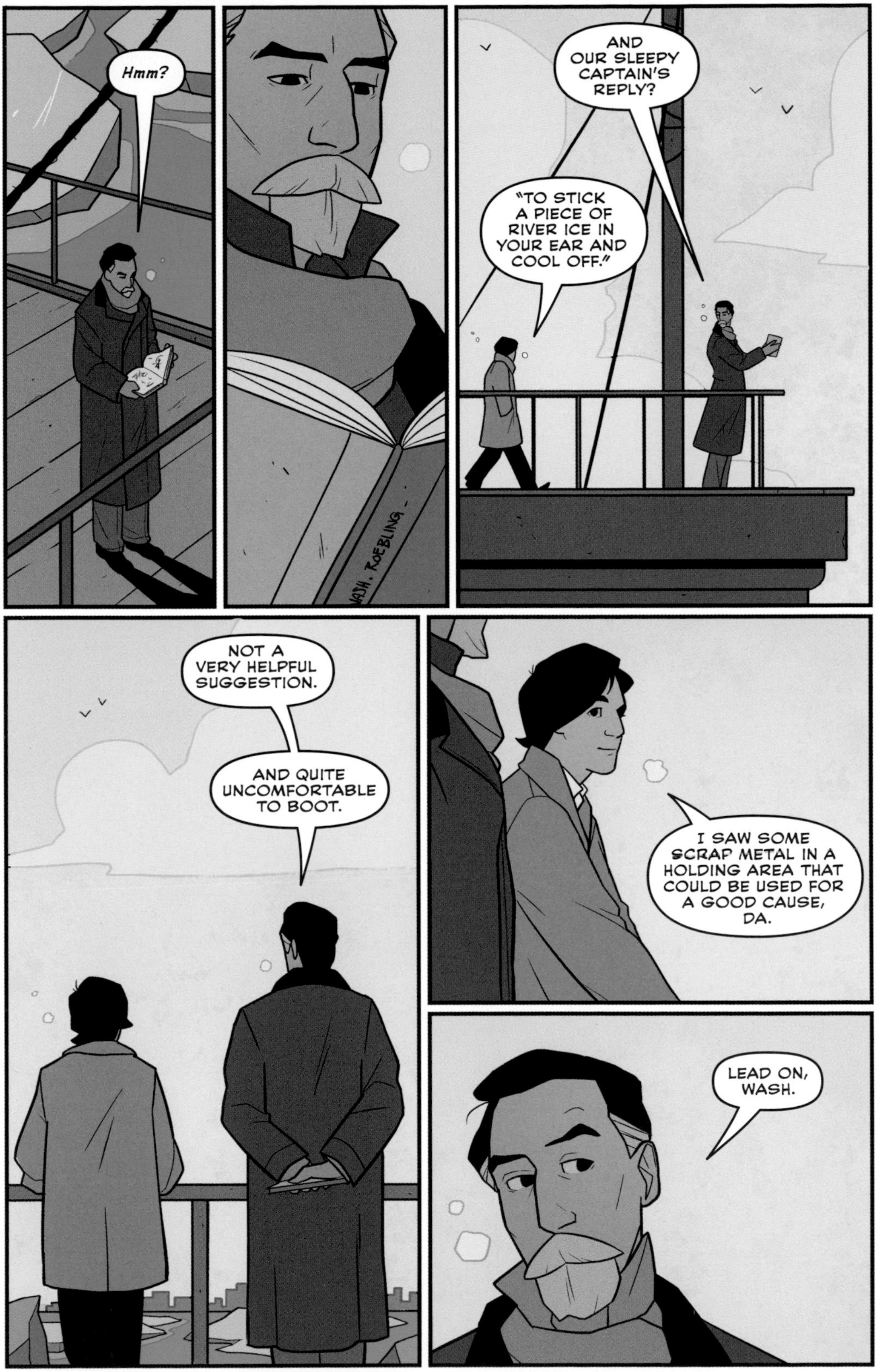
Hmm?
WASH. ROEBLING
AND OUR SLEEPY CAPTAIN'S REPLY?
"TO STICK A PIECE OF RIVER ICE IN YOUR EAR AND COOL OFF."
NOT A VERY HELPFUL SUGGESTION.
AND QUITE UNCOMFORTABLE TO BOOT.
I SAW SOME SCRAP METAL IN A HOLDING AREA THAT COULD BE USED FOR A GOOD CAUSE, DA.
LEAD ON, WASH.

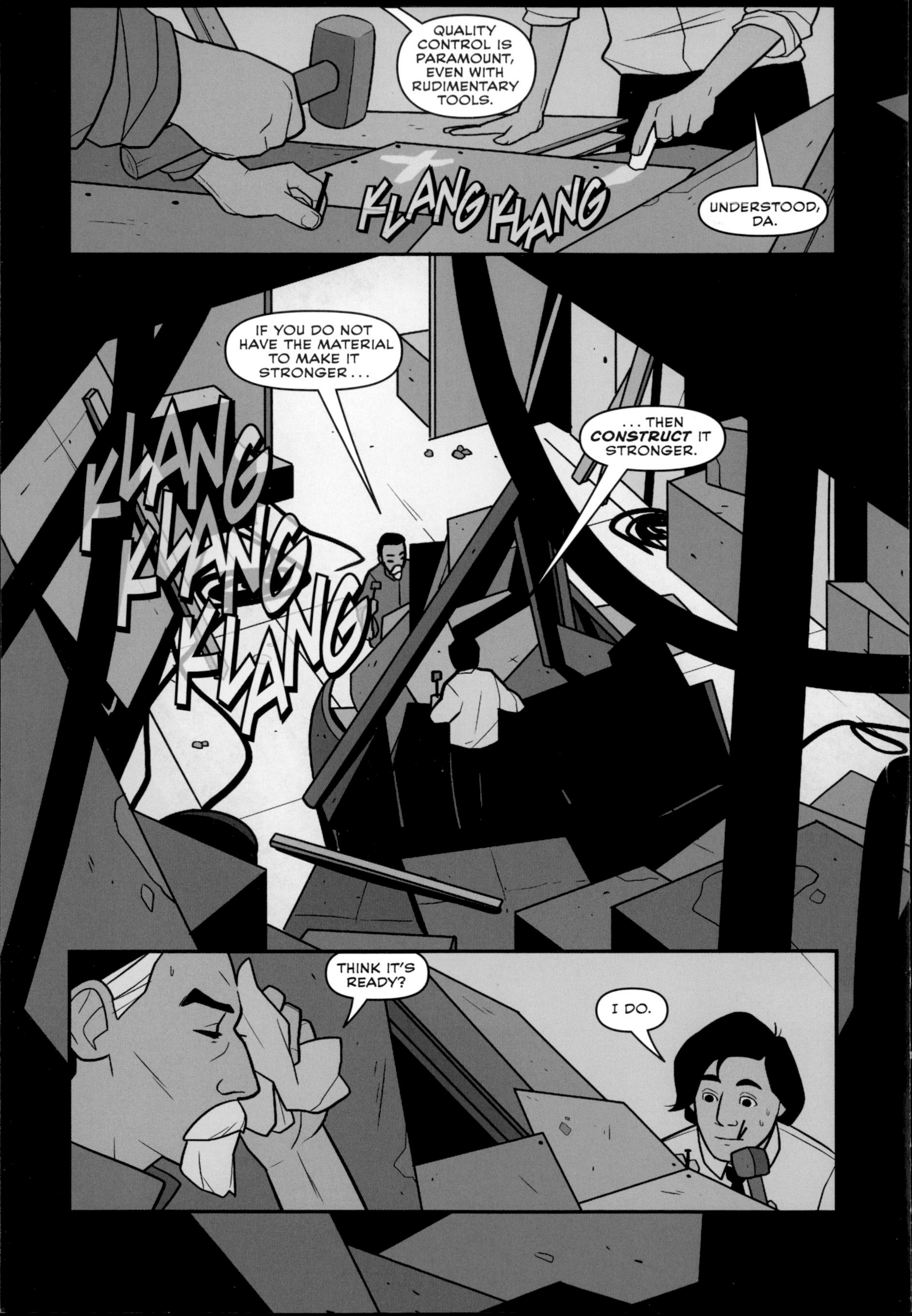
QUALITY CONTROL IS PARAMOUNT, EVEN WITH RUDIMENTARY TOOLS.
KLANG KLANG
UNDERSTOOD, DA.
IF YOU DO NOT HAVE THE MATERIAL TO MAKE IT STRONGER . . .
KLANG KLANG KLANG KLANG
. . . THEN CONSTRUCT IT STRONGER.
THINK IT'S READY?
I DO.

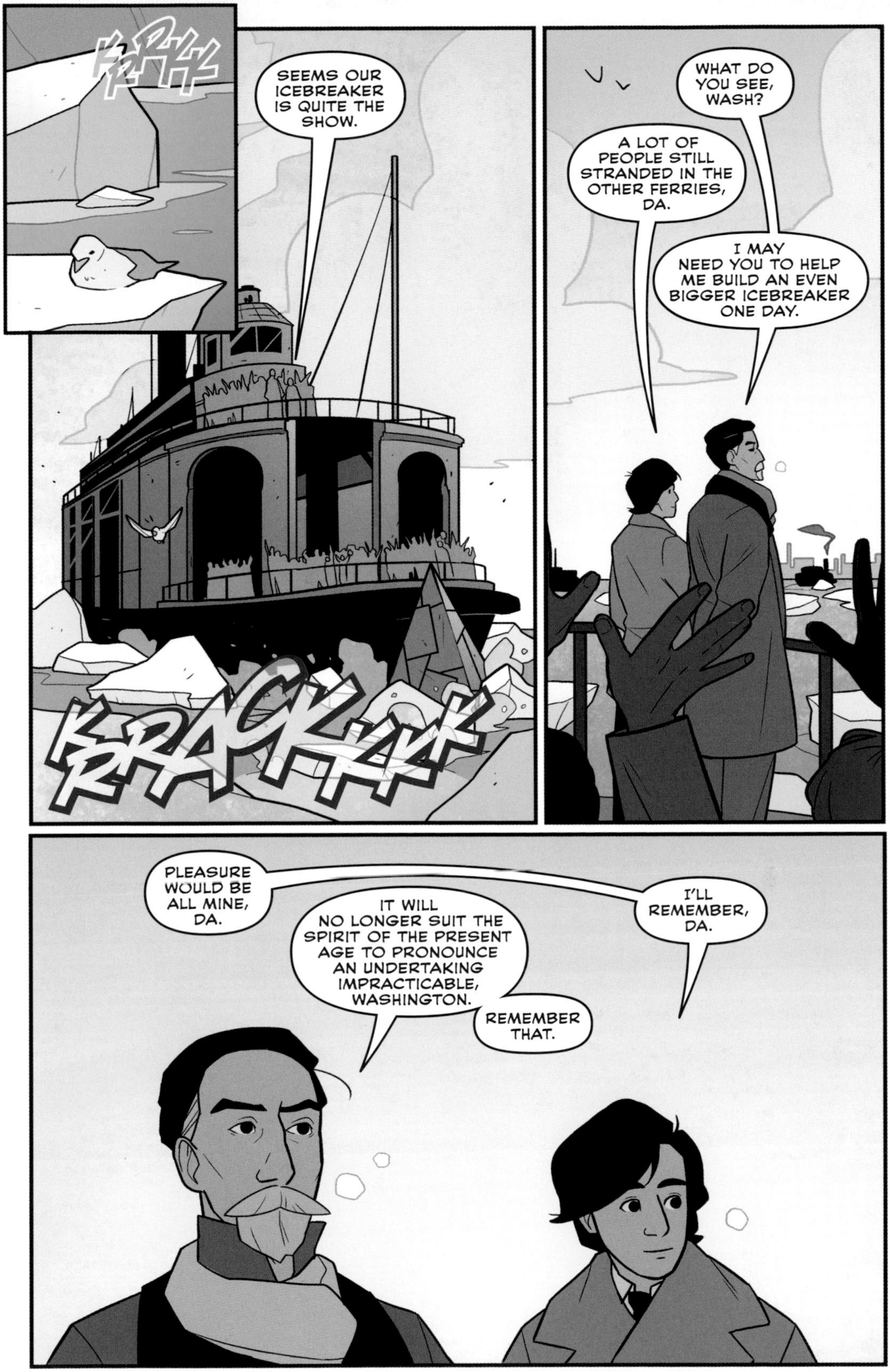
KRRKK
SEEMS OUR ICEBREAKER IS QUITE THE SHOW.
KRRACKAKK
WHAT DO YOU SEE, WASH?
A LOT OF PEOPLE STILL STRANDED IN THE OTHER FERRIES, DA.
I MAY NEED YOU TO HELP ME BUILD AN EVEN BIGGER ICEBREAKER ONE DAY.
PLEASURE WOULD BE ALL MINE, DA.
IT WILL NO LONGER SUIT THE SPIRIT OF THE PRESENT AGE TO PRONOUNCE AN UNDERTAKING IMPRACTICABLE, WASHINGTON.
REMEMBER THAT.
I'LL REMEMBER, DA.

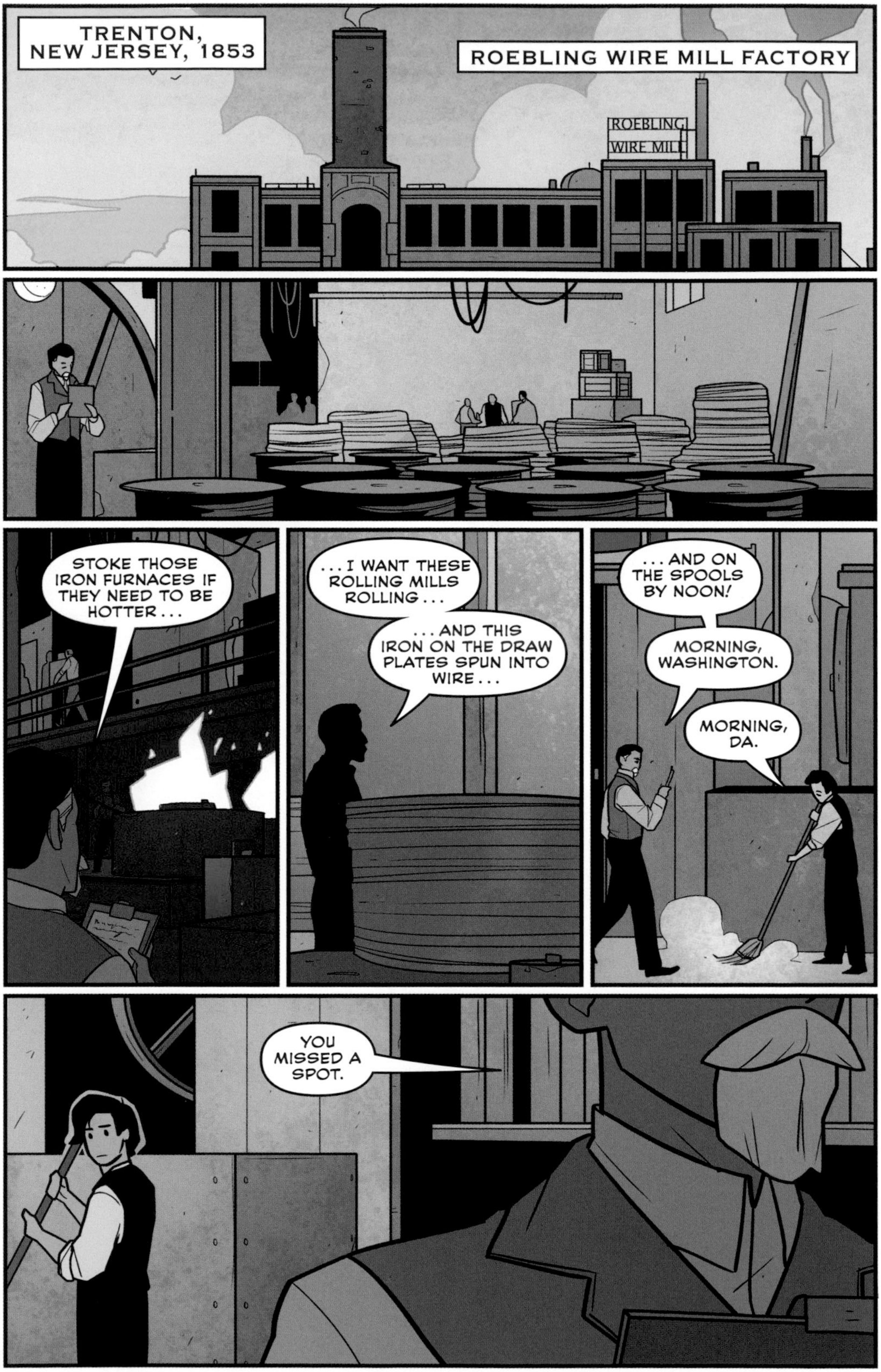
TRENTON, NEW JERSEY, 1853
ROEBLING WIRE MILL FACTORY
ROEBLING WIRE MILL
STOKE THOSE IRON FURNACES IF THEY NEED TO BE HOTTER...
...I WANT THESE ROLLING MILLS ROLLING...
...AND THIS IRON ON THE DRAW PLATES SPUN INTO WIRE...
...AND ON THE SPOOLS BY NOON!
MORNING, WASHINGTON.
MORNING, DA.
YOU MISSED A SPOT.

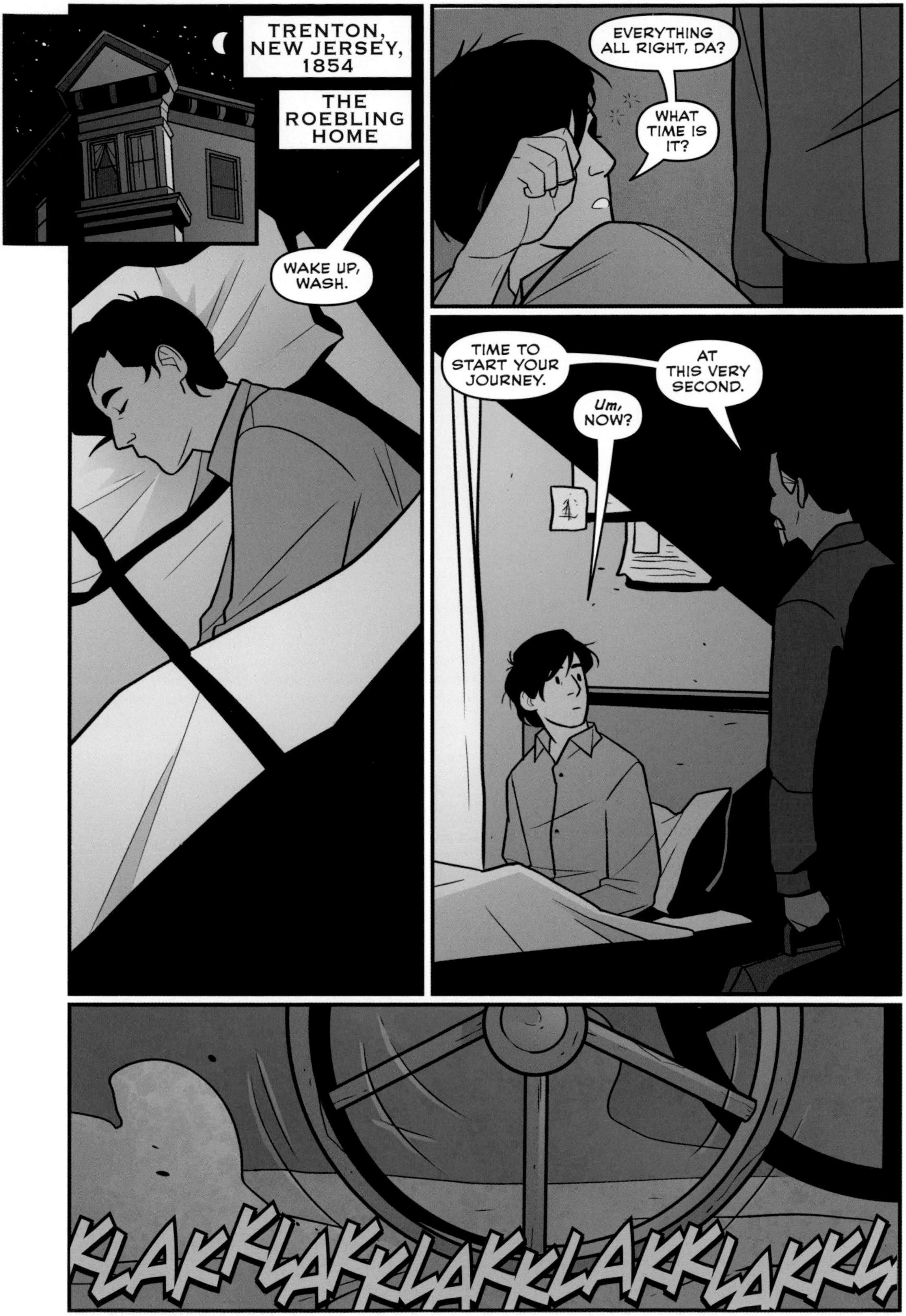
TRENTON, NEW JERSEY, 1854
THE ROEBLING HOME
WAKE UP, WASH.
EVERYTHING ALL RIGHT, DA?
WHAT TIME IS IT?
TIME TO START YOUR JOURNEY.
AT THIS VERY SECOND.
Um, NOW?
KLAKKLAKKLAKKLAKKLAKKL

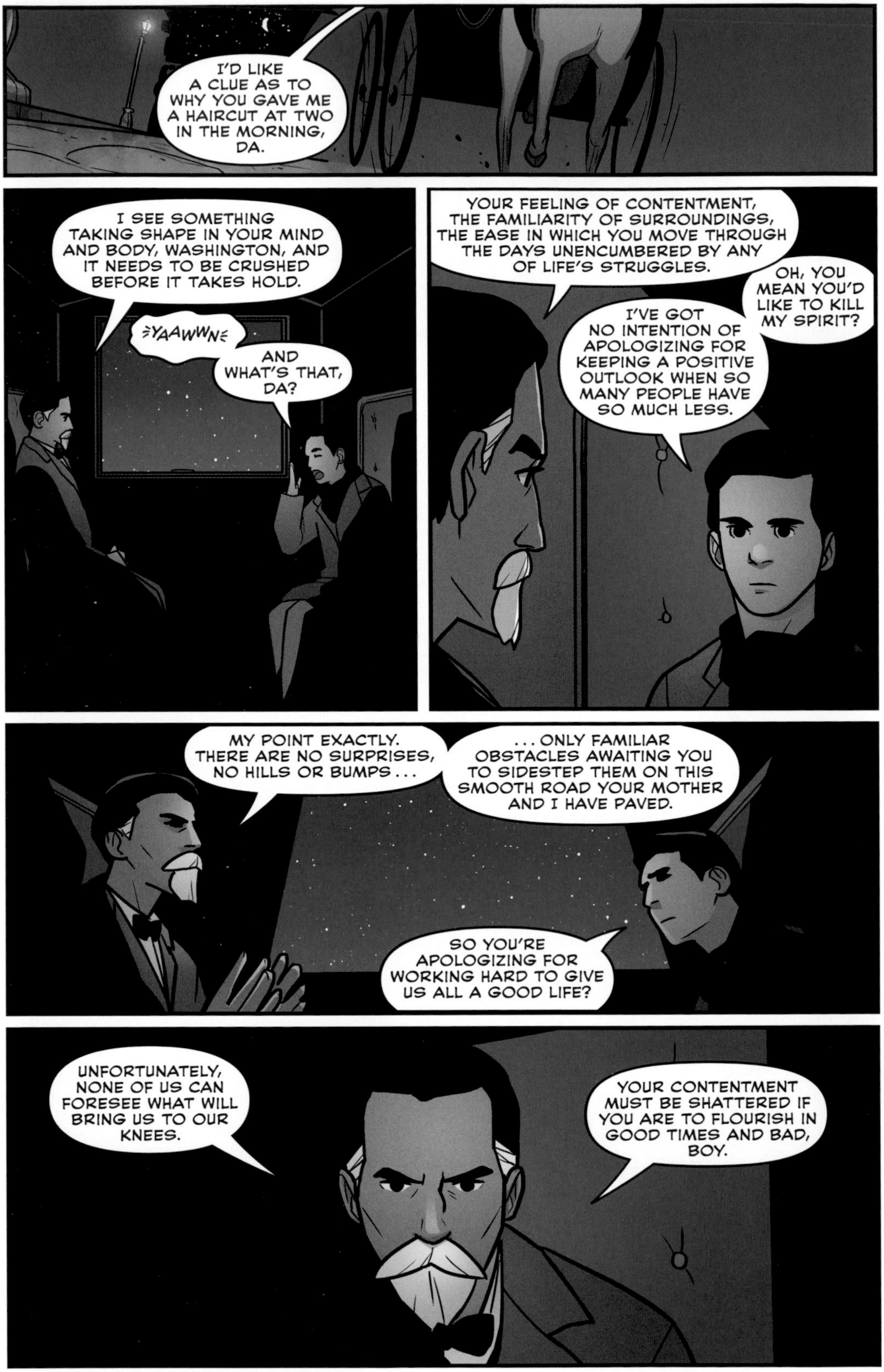
I'D LIKE A CLUE AS TO WHY YOU GAVE ME A HAIRCUT AT TWO IN THE MORNING, DA.
I SEE SOMETHING TAKING SHAPE IN YOUR MIND AND BODY, WASHINGTON, AND IT NEEDS TO BE CRUSHED BEFORE IT TAKES HOLD.
YAAWWN
AND WHAT'S THAT, DA?
YOUR FEELING OF CONTENTMENT, THE FAMILIARITY OF SURROUNDINGS, THE EASE IN WHICH YOU MOVE THROUGH THE DAYS UNENCUMBERED BY ANY OF LIFE'S STRUGGLES.
OH, YOU MEAN YOU'D LIKE TO KILL MY SPIRIT?
I'VE GOT NO INTENTION OF APOLOGIZING FOR KEEPING A POSITIVE OUTLOOK WHEN SO MANY PEOPLE HAVE SO MUCH LESS.
MY POINT EXACTLY. THERE ARE NO SURPRISES, NO HILLS OR BUMPS . . .
. . . ONLY FAMILIAR OBSTACLES AWAITING YOU TO SIDESTEP THEM ON THIS SMOOTH ROAD YOUR MOTHER AND I HAVE PAVED.
SO YOU'RE APOLOGIZING FOR WORKING HARD TO GIVE US ALL A GOOD LIFE?
UNFORTUNATELY, NONE OF US CAN FORESEE WHAT WILL BRING US TO OUR KNEES.
YOUR CONTENTMENT MUST BE SHATTERED IF YOU ARE TO FLOURISH IN GOOD TIMES AND BAD, BOY.

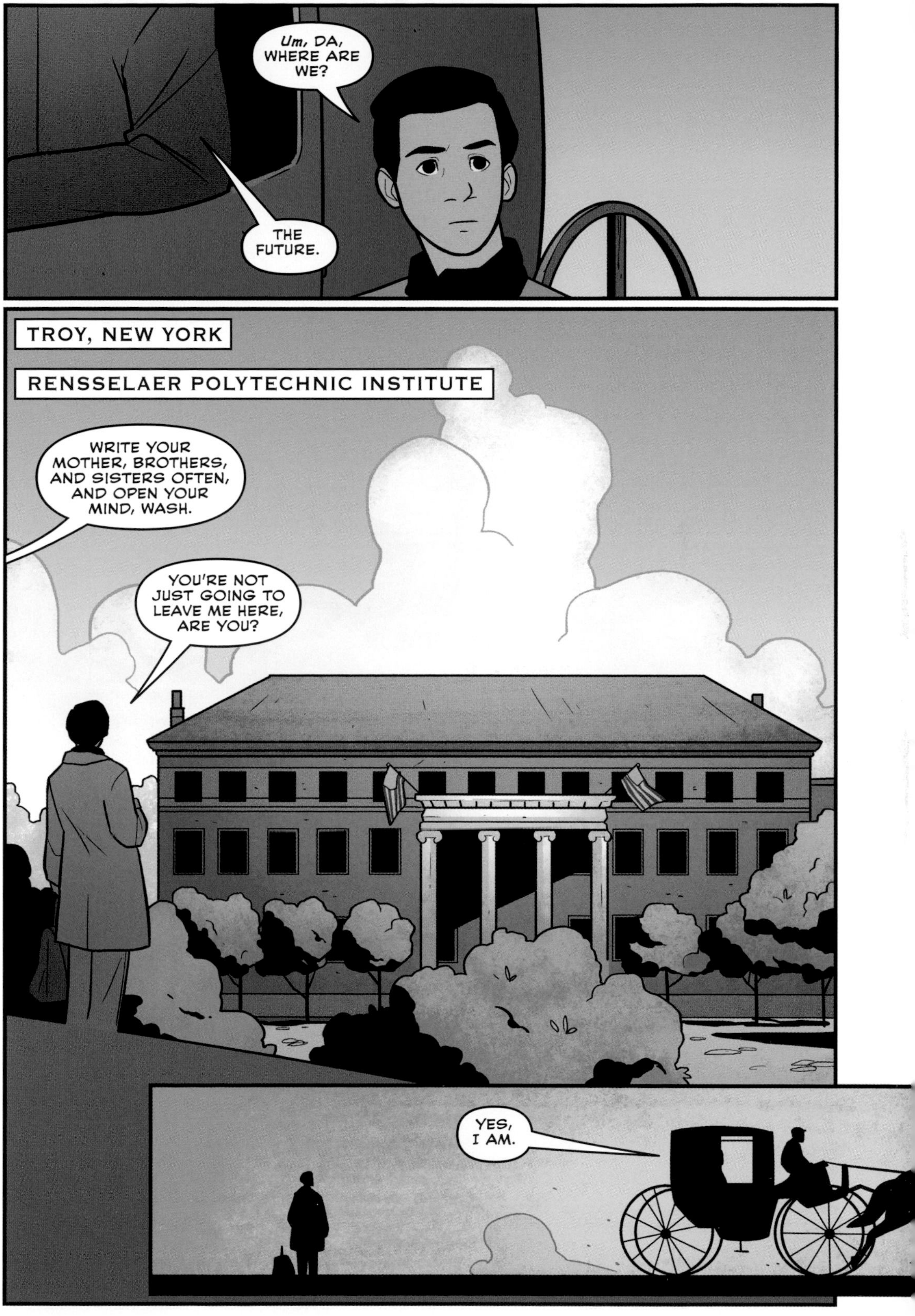

Um, DA, WHERE ARE WE?
THE FUTURE.
TROY, NEW YORK
RENSSELAER POLYTECHNIC INSTITUTE
WRITE YOUR MOTHER, BROTHERS, AND SISTERS OFTEN, AND OPEN YOUR MIND, WASH.
YOU'RE NOT JUST GOING TO LEAVE ME HERE, ARE YOU?
YES, I AM.

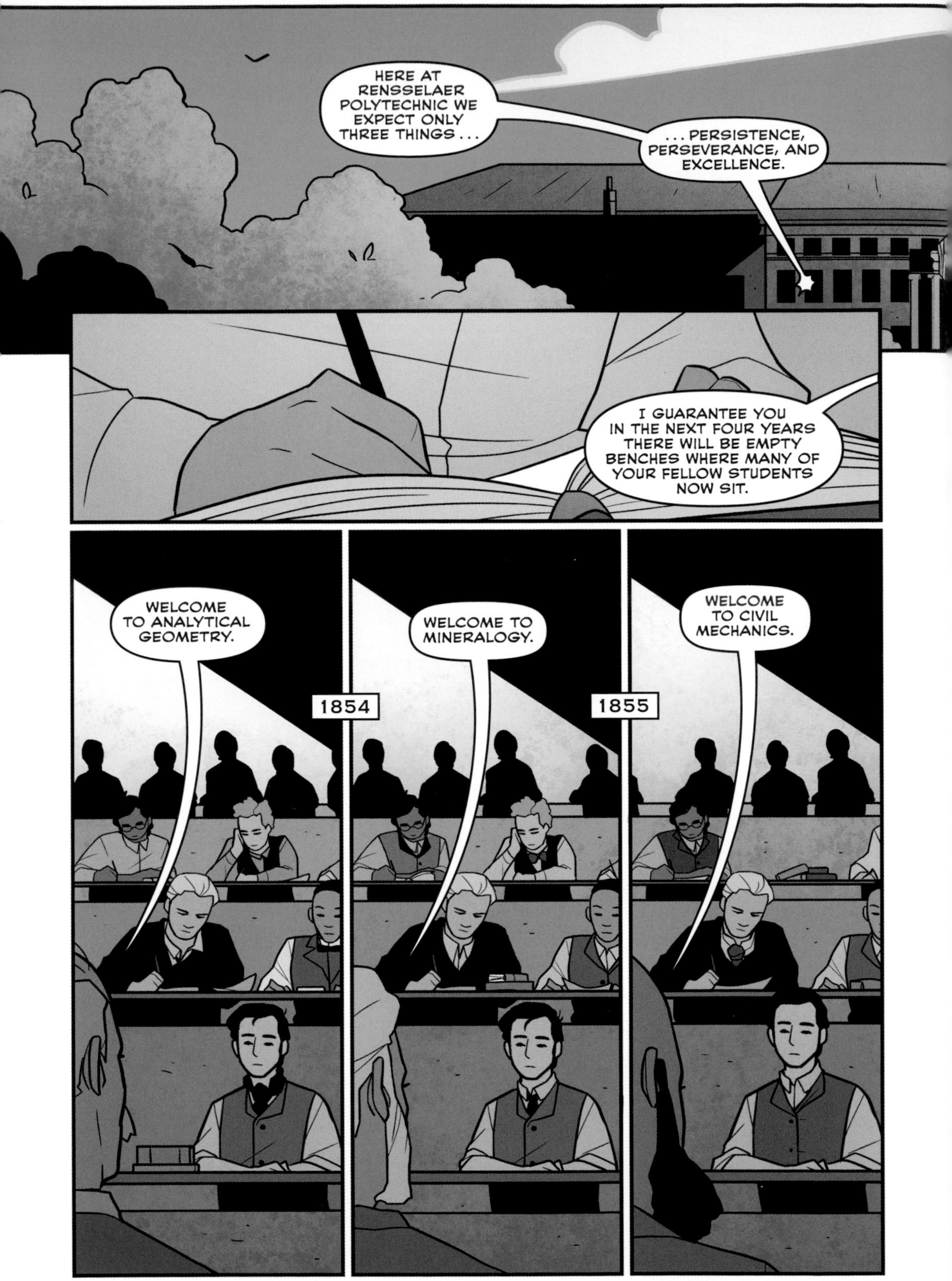
HERE AT RENSSELAER POLYTECHNIC WE EXPECT ONLY THREE THINGS . . .
. . . PERSISTENCE, PERSEVERANCE, AND EXCELLENCE.
I GUARANTEE YOU IN THE NEXT FOUR YEARS THERE WILL BE EMPTY BENCHES WHERE MANY OF YOUR FELLOW STUDENTS NOW SIT.
WELCOME TO ANALYTICAL GEOMETRY.
1854
WELCOME TO MINERALOGY.
1855
WELCOME TO CIVIL MECHANICS.

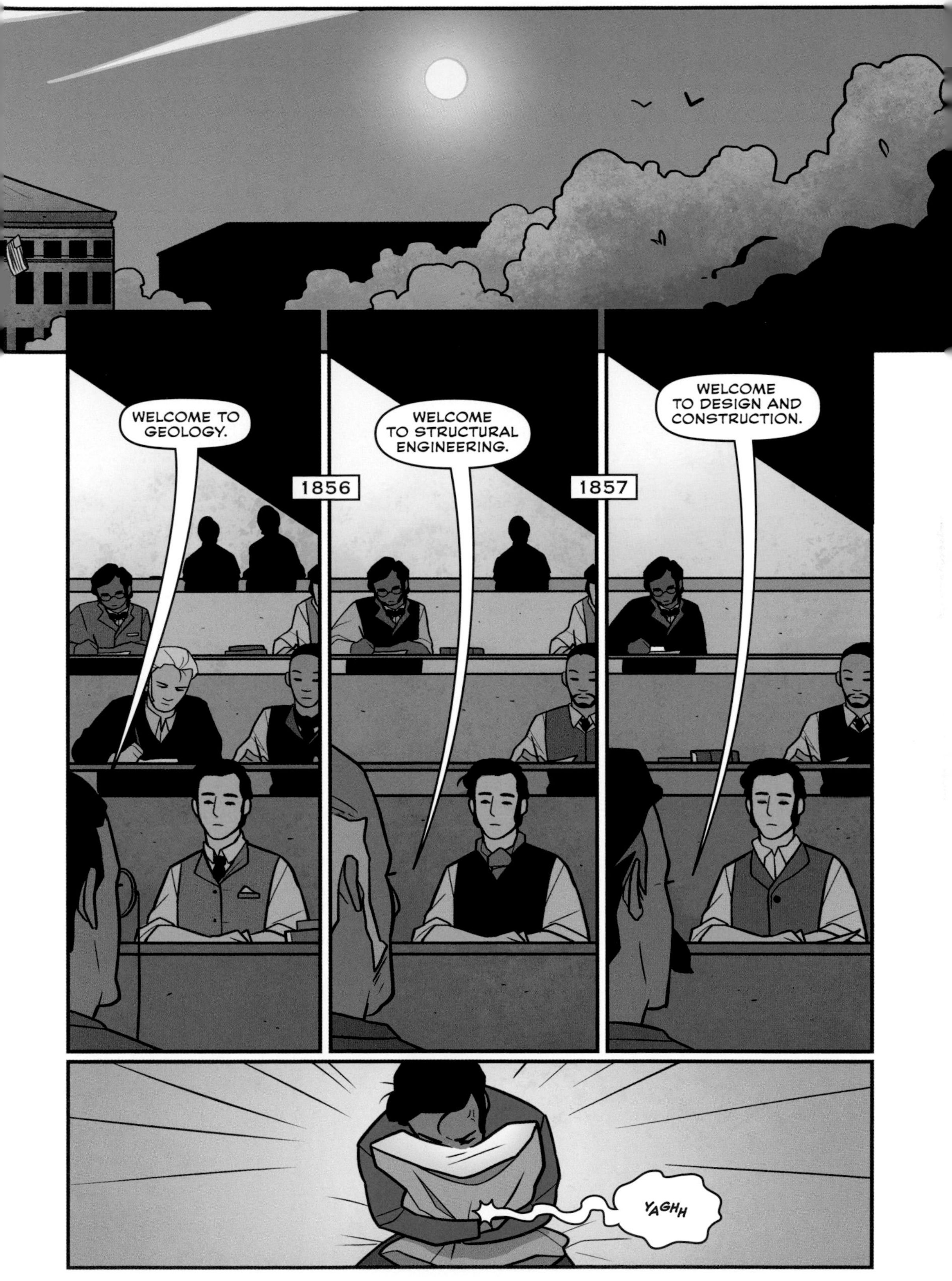
WELCOME TO GEOLOGY.
1856
WELCOME TO STRUCTURAL ENGINEERING.
1857
WELCOME TO DESIGN AND CONSTRUCTION.
YAGHH

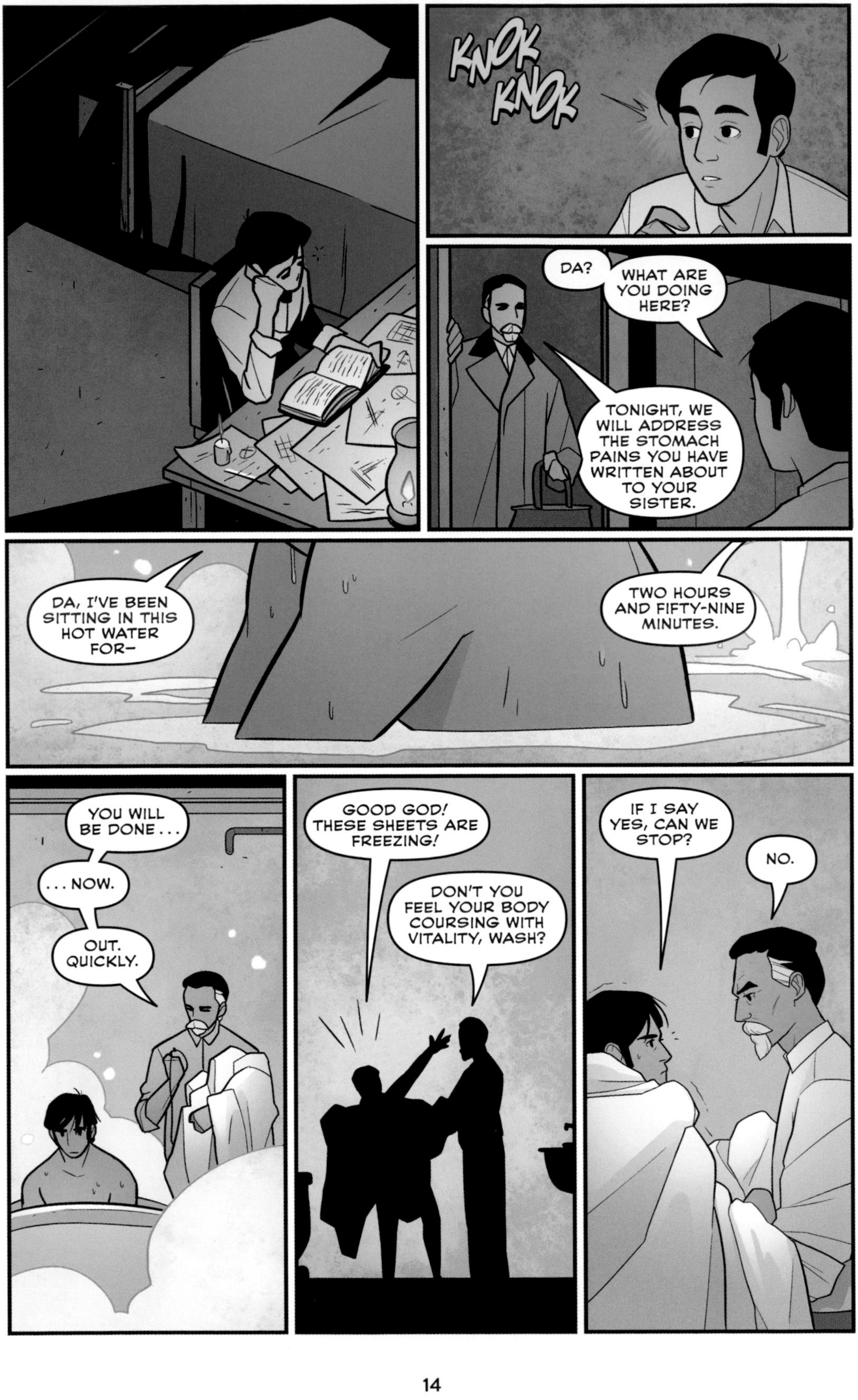
KNOK KNOK
DA?
WHAT ARE YOU DOING HERE?
TONIGHT, WE WILL ADDRESS THE STOMACH PAINS YOU HAVE WRITTEN ABOUT TO YOUR SISTER.
DA, I'VE BEEN SITTING IN THIS HOT WATER FOR–
TWO HOURS AND FIFTY-NINE MINUTES.
YOU WILL BE DONE . . .
. . . NOW.
OUT. QUICKLY.
GOOD GOD! THESE SHEETS ARE FREEZING!
DON'T YOU FEEL YOUR BODY COURSING WITH VITALITY, WASH?
IF I SAY YES, CAN WE STOP?
NO.

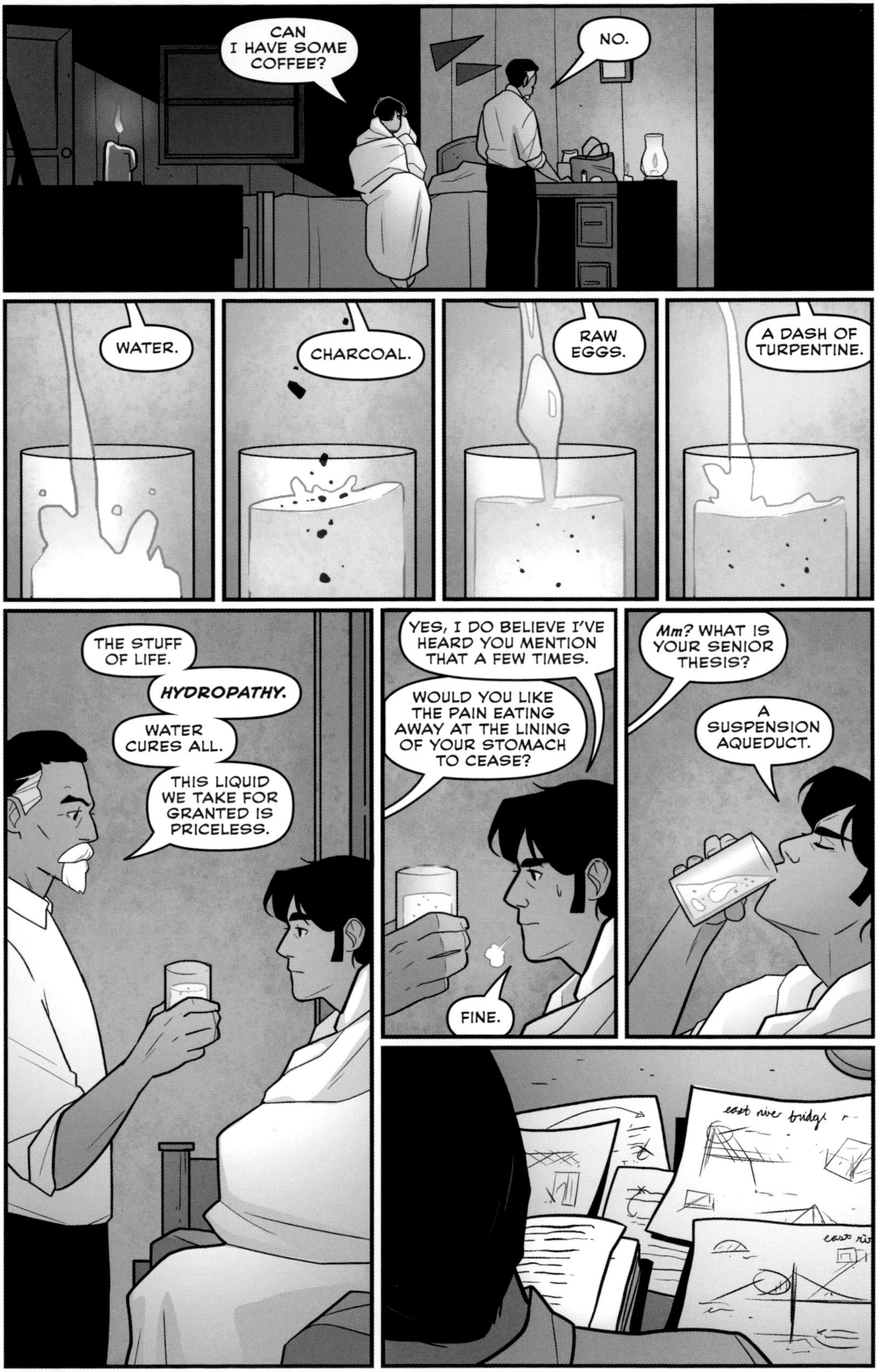
CAN I HAVE SOME COFFEE?
NO.
WATER.
CHARCOAL.
RAW EGGS.
A DASH OF TURPENTINE.
THE STUFF OF LIFE.
HYDROPATHY.
WATER CURES ALL.
THIS LIQUID WE TAKE FOR GRANTED IS PRICELESS.
YES, I DO BELIEVE I'VE HEARD YOU MENTION THAT A FEW TIMES.
WOULD YOU LIKE THE PAIN EATING AWAY AT THE LINING OF YOUR STOMACH TO CEASE?
FINE.
Mm? WHAT IS YOUR SENIOR THESIS?
A SUSPENSION AQUEDUCT.
east river bridge

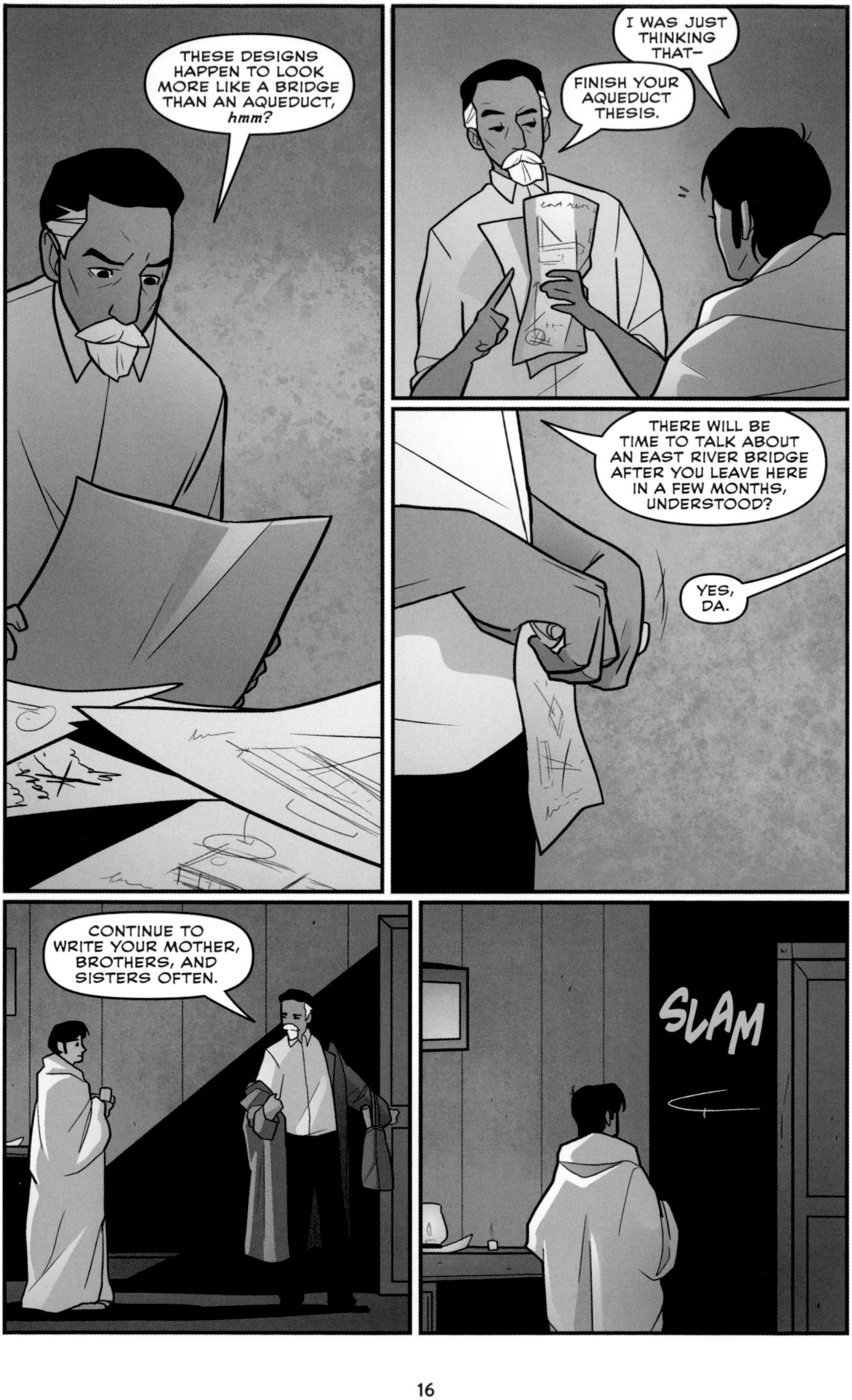
THESE DESIGNS HAPPEN TO LOOK MORE LIKE A BRIDGE THAN AN AQUEDUCT, *hmm?*
I WAS JUST THINKING THAT—
FINISH YOUR AQUEDUCT THESIS.
THERE WILL BE TIME TO TALK ABOUT AN EAST RIVER BRIDGE AFTER YOU LEAVE HERE IN A FEW MONTHS, UNDERSTOOD?
YES, DA.
CONTINUE TO WRITE YOUR MOTHER, BROTHERS, AND SISTERS OFTEN.
SLAM

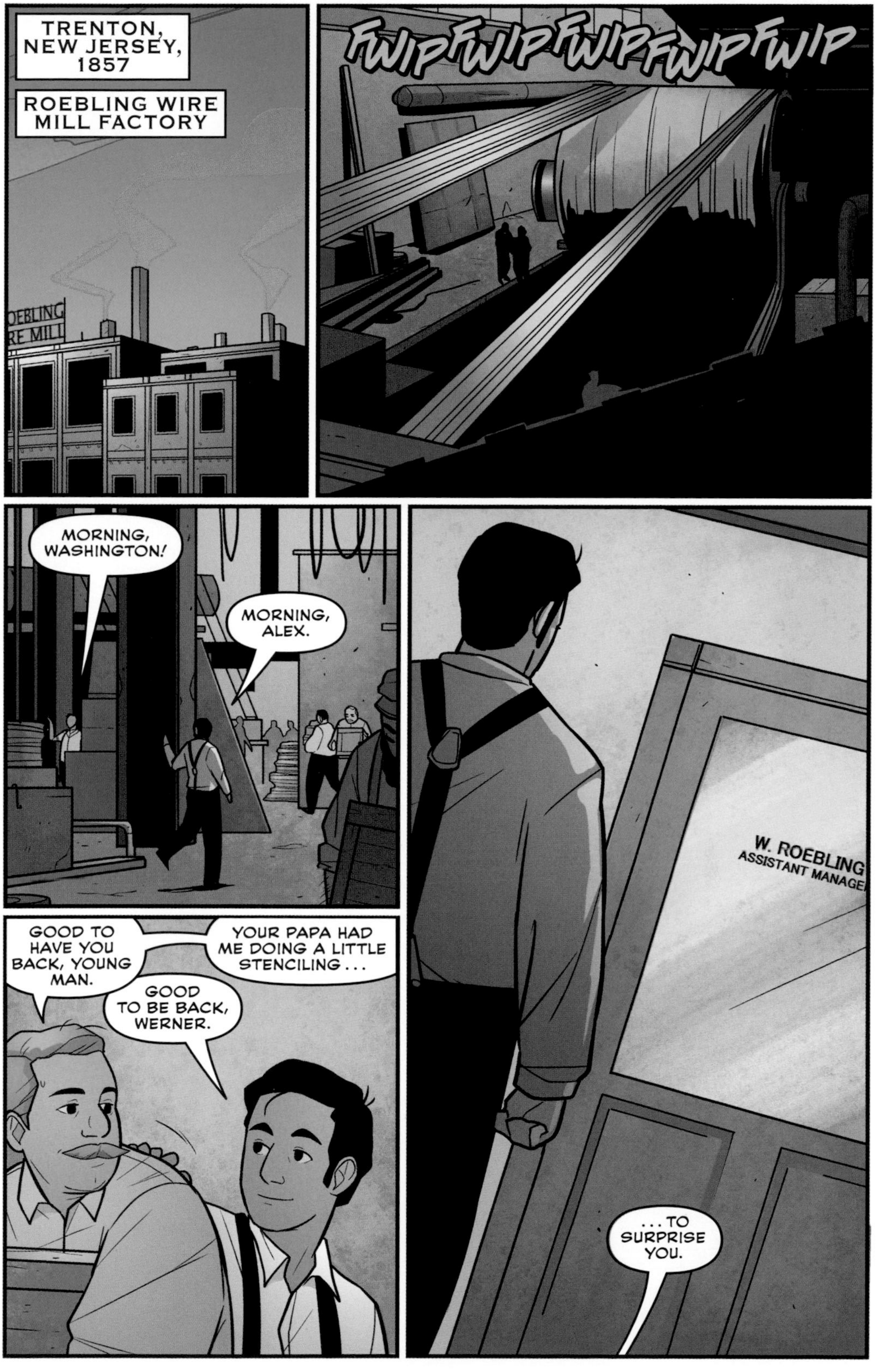
TRENTON, NEW JERSEY, 1857
ROEBLING WIRE MILL FACTORY
FWIP FWIP FWIP FWIP FWIP
MORNING, WASHINGTON!
MORNING, ALEX.
GOOD TO HAVE YOU BACK, YOUNG MAN.
GOOD TO BE BACK, WERNER.
YOUR PAPA HAD ME DOING A LITTLE STENCILING . . .
W. ROEBLING
ASSISTANT MANAGE
. . . TO SURPRISE YOU.

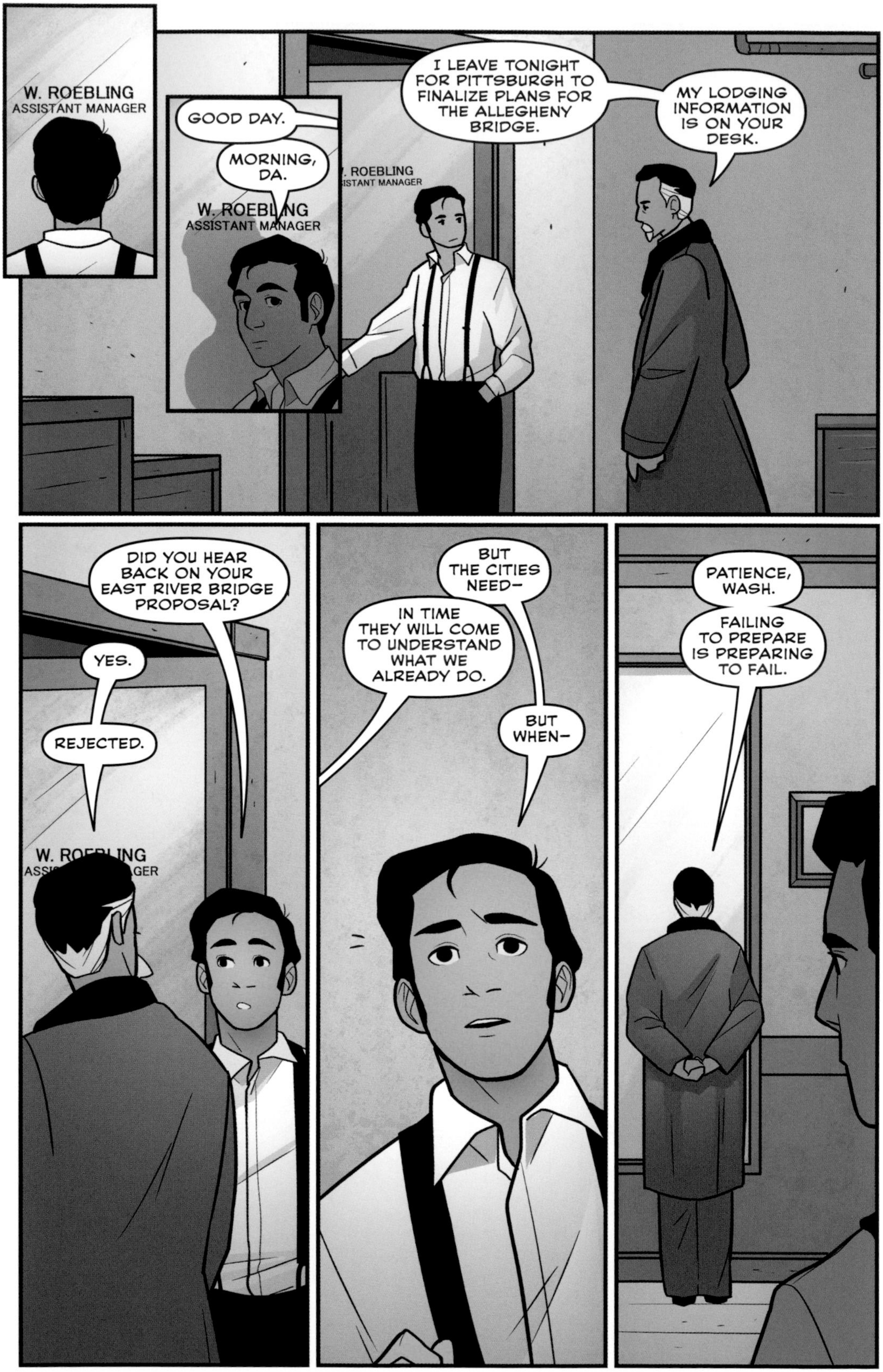
W. ROEBLING
ASSISTANT MANAGER
GOOD DAY.
MORNING, DA.
W. ROEBLING
ASSISTANT MANAGER
I LEAVE TONIGHT FOR PITTSBURGH TO FINALIZE PLANS FOR THE ALLEGHENY BRIDGE.
MY LODGING INFORMATION IS ON YOUR DESK.
DID YOU HEAR BACK ON YOUR EAST RIVER BRIDGE PROPOSAL?
YES.
REJECTED.
W. ROEBLING
BUT THE CITIES NEED–
IN TIME THEY WILL COME TO UNDERSTAND WHAT WE ALREADY DO.
BUT WHEN–
PATIENCE, WASH.
FAILING TO PREPARE IS PREPARING TO FAIL.

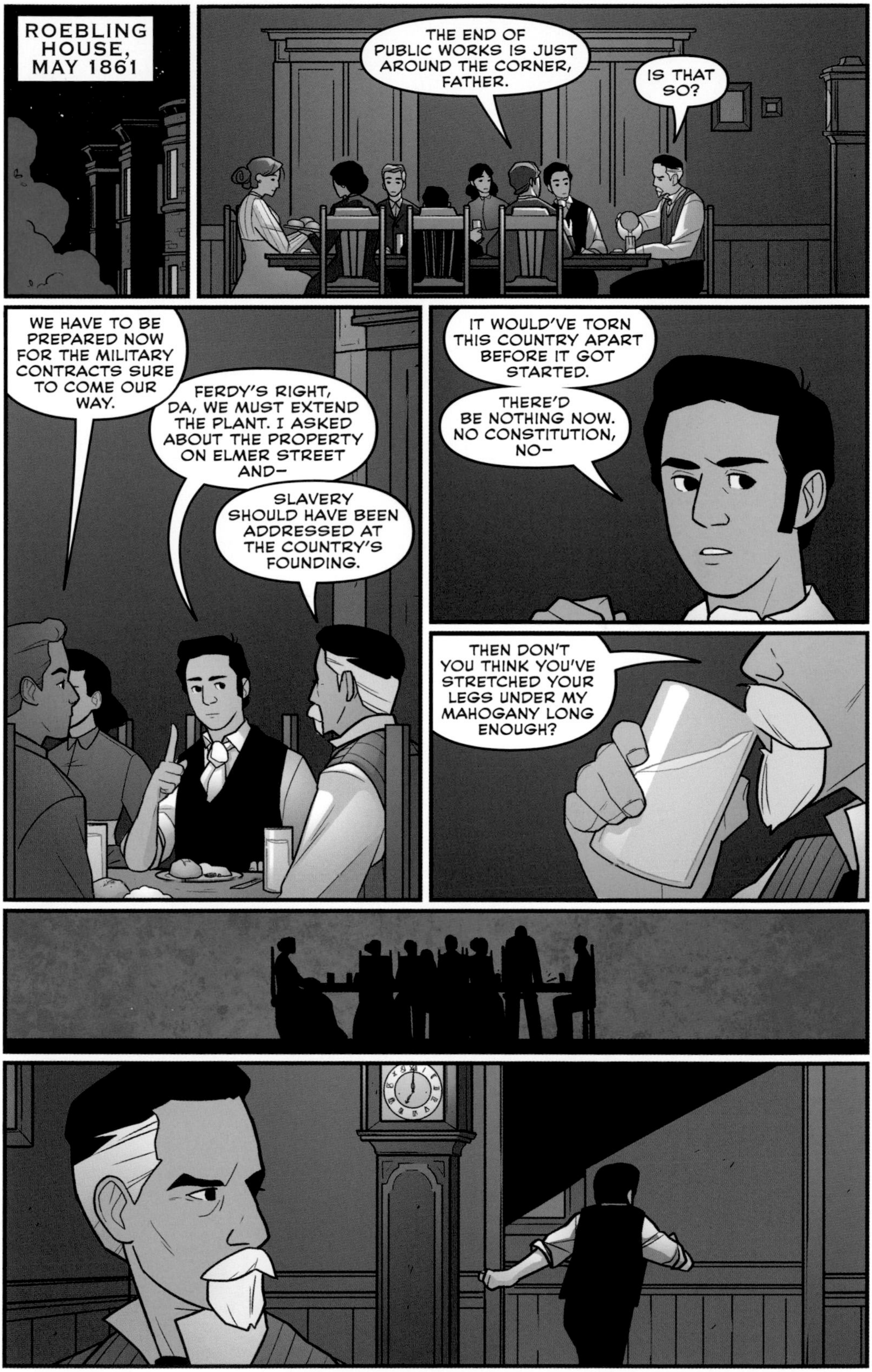
ROEBLING HOUSE, MAY 1861
THE END OF PUBLIC WORKS IS JUST AROUND THE CORNER, FATHER.
IS THAT SO?
WE HAVE TO BE PREPARED NOW FOR THE MILITARY CONTRACTS SURE TO COME OUR WAY.
FERDY'S RIGHT, DA, WE MUST EXTEND THE PLANT. I ASKED ABOUT THE PROPERTY ON ELMER STREET AND—
SLAVERY SHOULD HAVE BEEN ADDRESSED AT THE COUNTRY'S FOUNDING.
IT WOULD'VE TORN THIS COUNTRY APART BEFORE IT GOT STARTED.
THERE'D BE NOTHING NOW. NO CONSTITUTION, NO—
THEN DON'T YOU THINK YOU'VE STRETCHED YOUR LEGS UNDER MY MAHOGANY LONG ENOUGH?

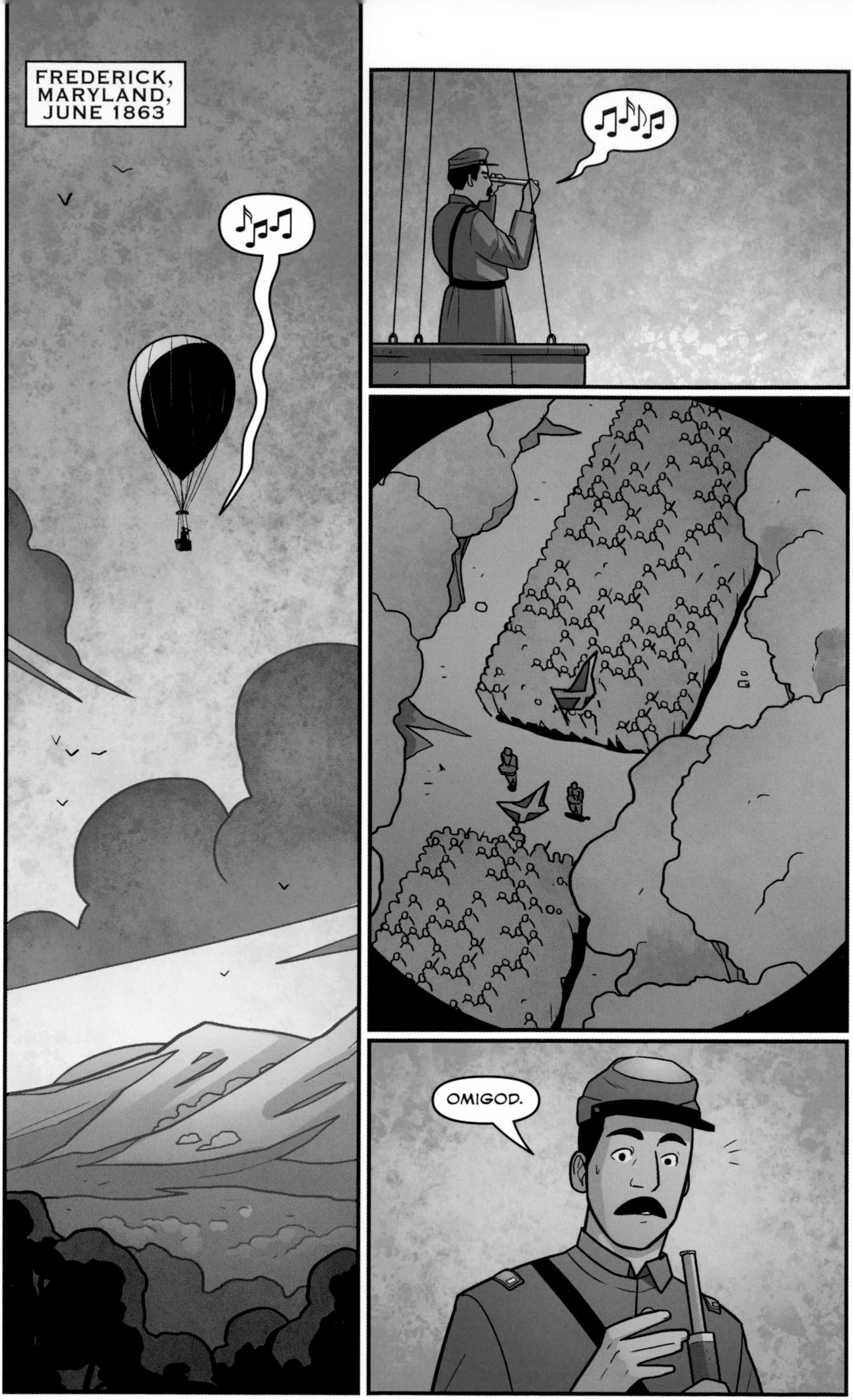
FREDERICK, MARYLAND, JUNE 1863
OMIGOD.

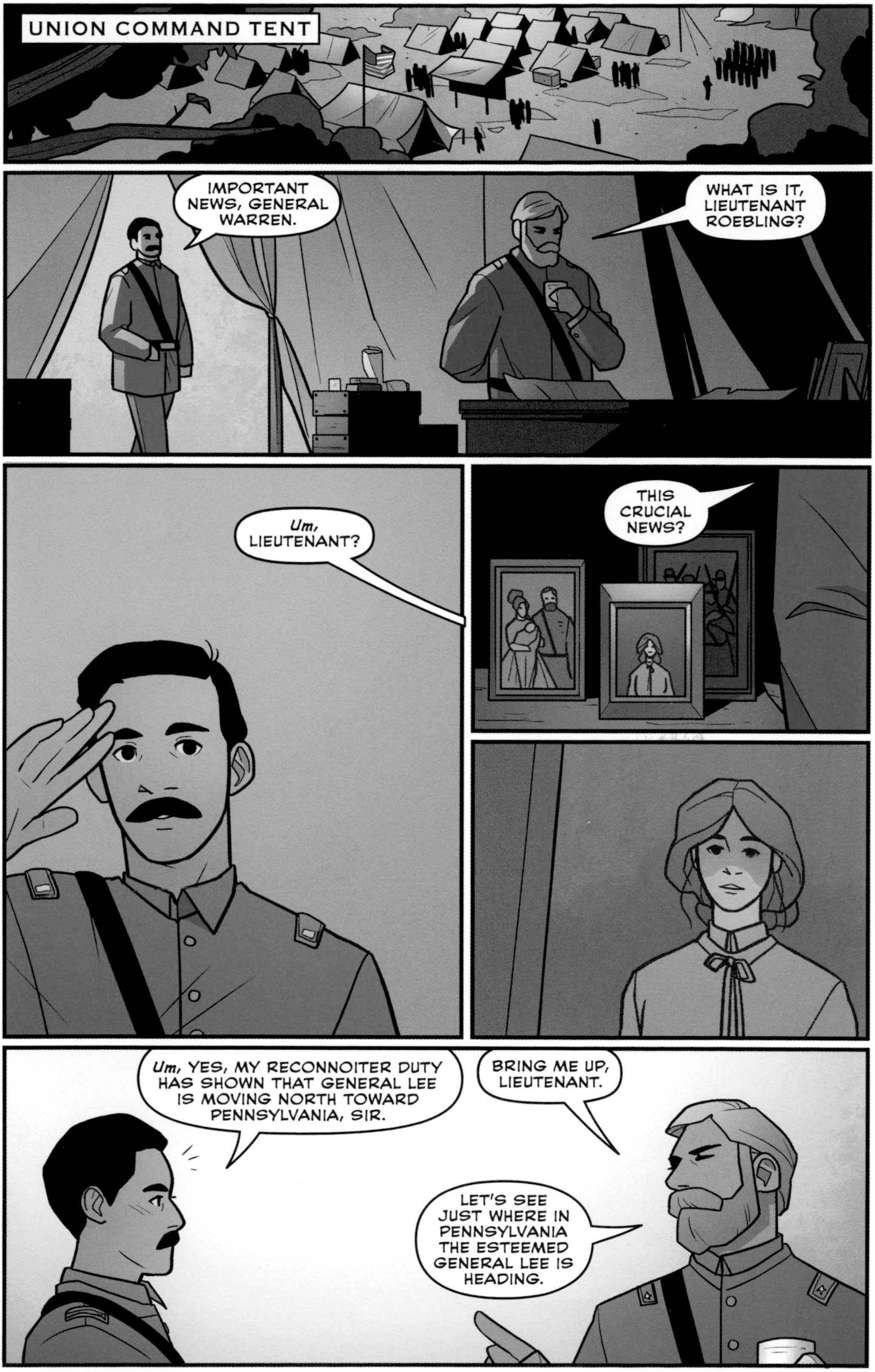
UNION COMMAND TENT
IMPORTANT NEWS, GENERAL WARREN.
WHAT IS IT, LIEUTENANT ROEBLING?
Um, LIEUTENANT?
THIS CRUCIAL NEWS?
Um, YES, MY RECONNOITER DUTY HAS SHOWN THAT GENERAL LEE IS MOVING NORTH TOWARD PENNSYLVANIA, SIR.
BRING ME UP, LIEUTENANT.
LET'S SEE JUST WHERE IN PENNSYLVANIA THE ESTEEMED GENERAL LEE IS HEADING.

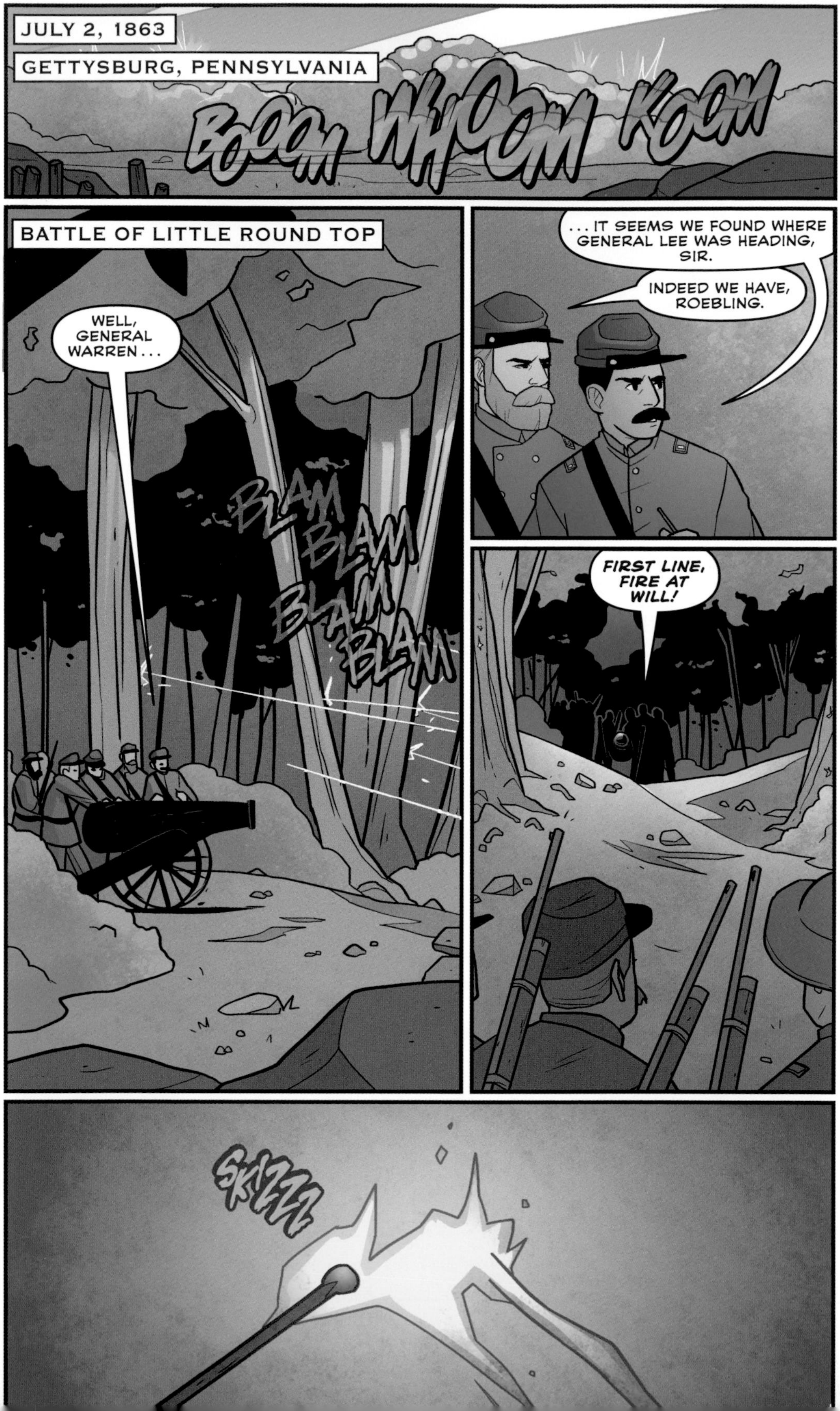
JULY 2, 1863
GETTYSBURG, PENNSYLVANIA
BOOOM WHOOM KOOM
BATTLE OF LITTLE ROUND TOP
WELL, GENERAL WARREN . . .
BLAM BLAM BLAM BLAM
. . . IT SEEMS WE FOUND WHERE GENERAL LEE WAS HEADING, SIR.
INDEED WE HAVE, ROEBLING.
FIRST LINE, FIRE AT WILL!
SKIZZZ

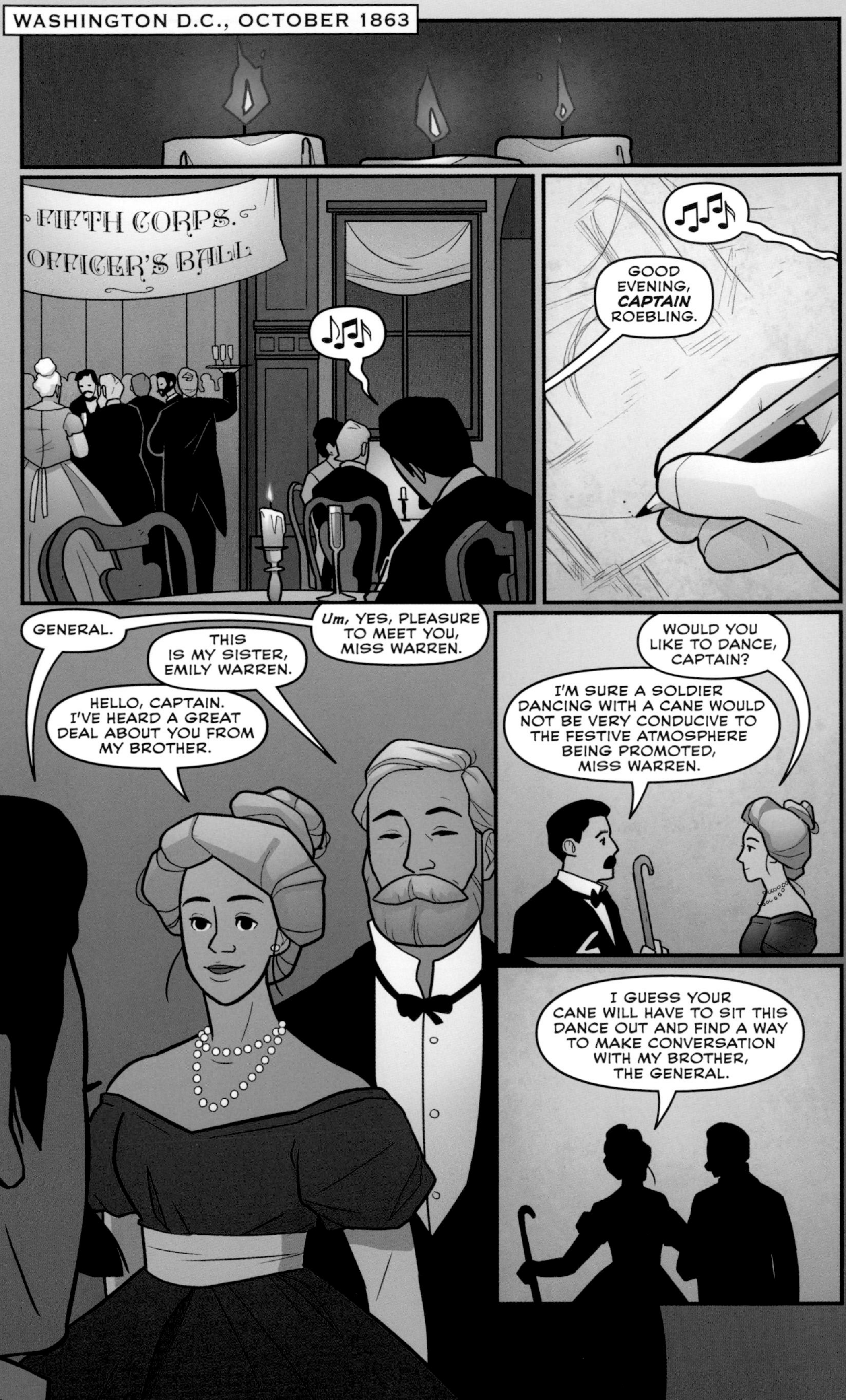
WASHINGTON D.C., OCTOBER 1863
FIFTH CORPS. OFFICER'S BALL
♫♫
♫♫
GOOD EVENING, *CAPTAIN* ROEBLING.
GENERAL.
Um, YES, PLEASURE TO MEET YOU, MISS WARREN.
THIS IS MY SISTER, EMILY WARREN.
HELLO, CAPTAIN. I'VE HEARD A GREAT DEAL ABOUT YOU FROM MY BROTHER.
WOULD YOU LIKE TO DANCE, CAPTAIN?
I'M SURE A SOLDIER DANCING WITH A CANE WOULD NOT BE VERY CONDUCIVE TO THE FESTIVE ATMOSPHERE BEING PROMOTED, MISS WARREN.
I GUESS YOUR CANE WILL HAVE TO SIT THIS DANCE OUT AND FIND A WAY TO MAKE CONVERSATION WITH MY BROTHER, THE GENERAL.

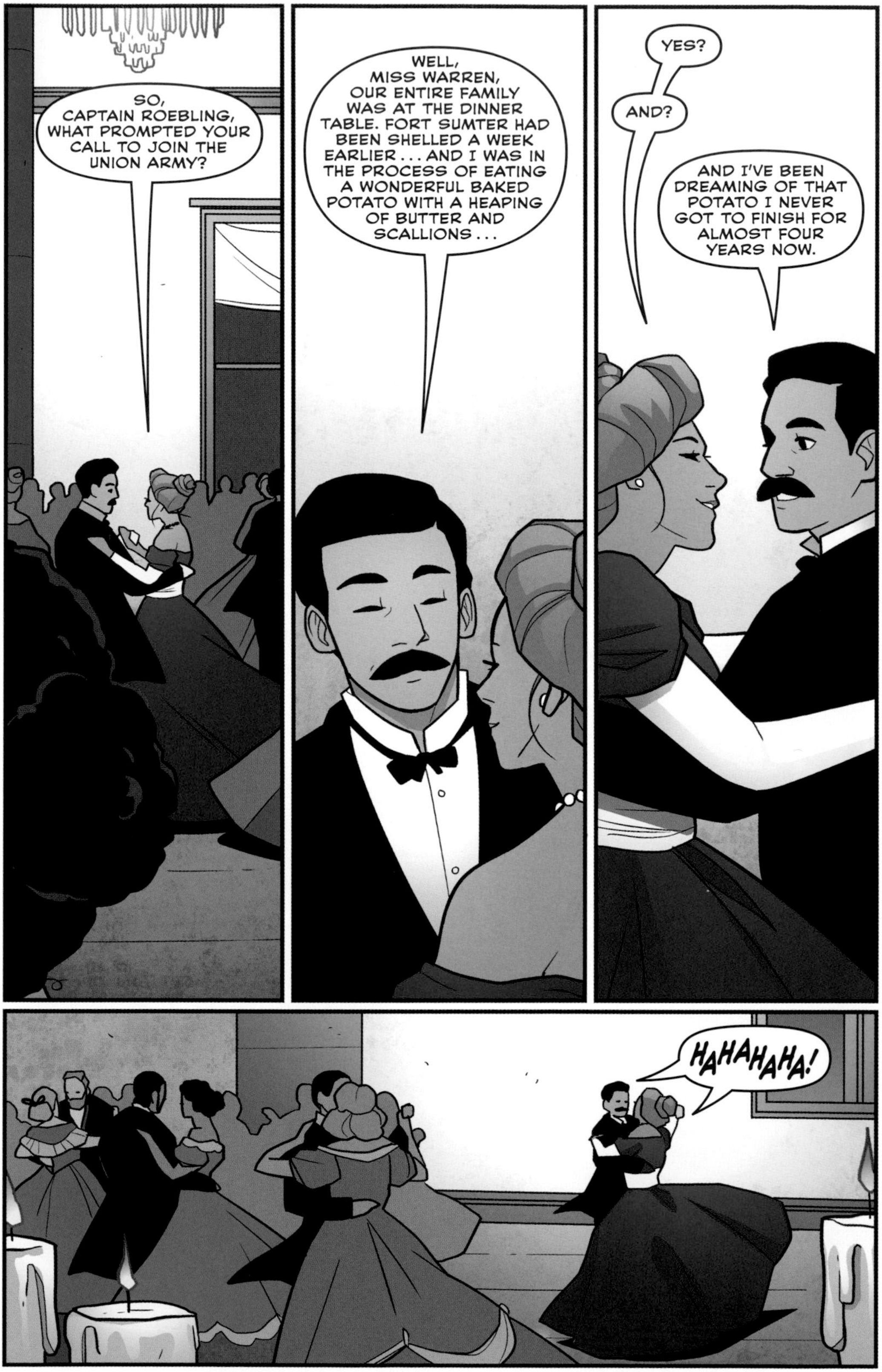
SO, CAPTAIN ROEBLING, WHAT PROMPTED YOUR CALL TO JOIN THE UNION ARMY?
WELL, MISS WARREN, OUR ENTIRE FAMILY WAS AT THE DINNER TABLE. FORT SUMTER HAD BEEN SHELLED A WEEK EARLIER . . . AND I WAS IN THE PROCESS OF EATING A WONDERFUL BAKED POTATO WITH A HEAPING OF BUTTER AND SCALLIONS . . .
YES?
AND?
AND I'VE BEEN DREAMING OF THAT POTATO I NEVER GOT TO FINISH FOR ALMOST FOUR YEARS NOW.
HAHAHAHA!

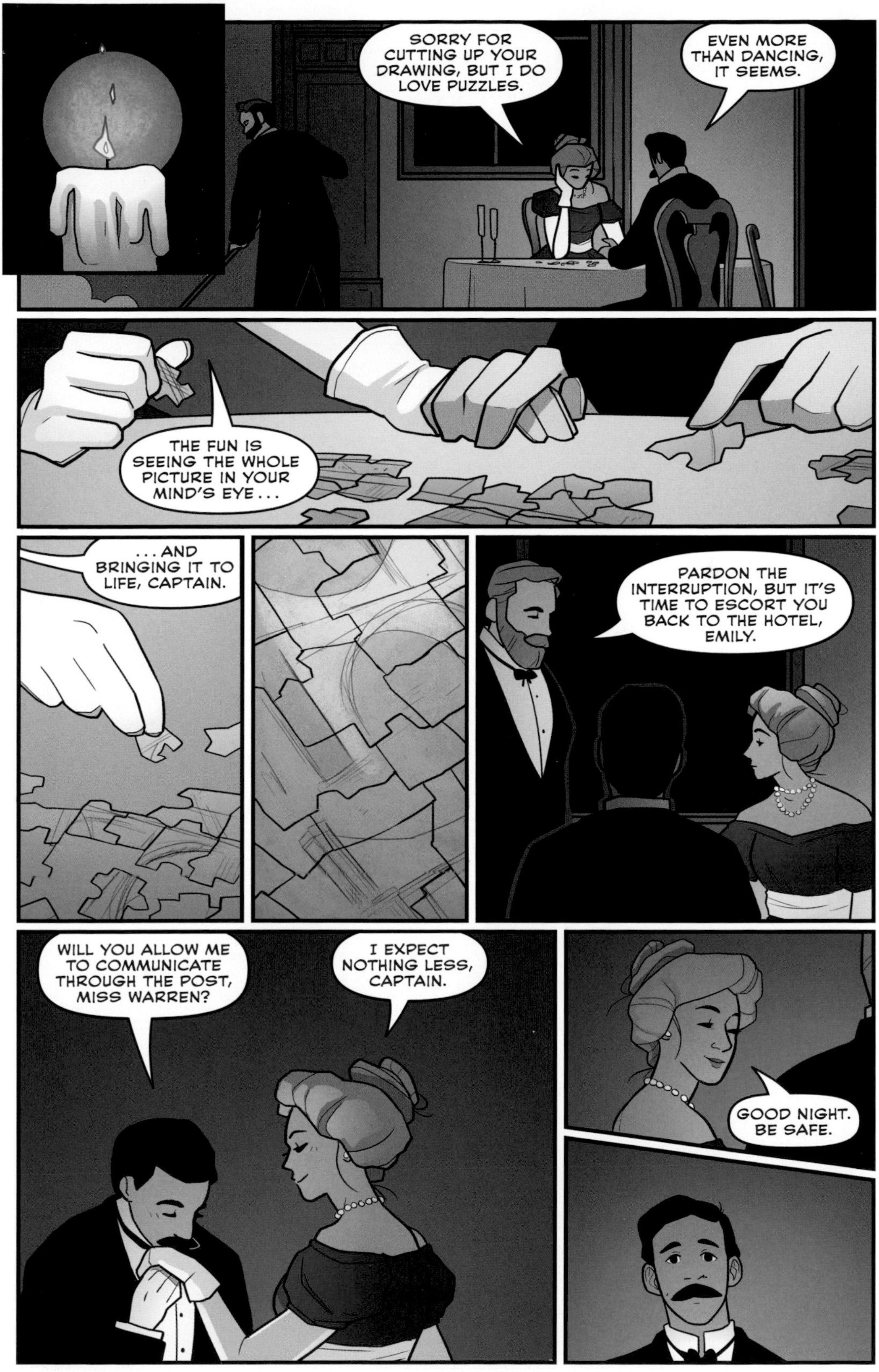
SORRY FOR CUTTING UP YOUR DRAWING, BUT I DO LOVE PUZZLES.
EVEN MORE THAN DANCING, IT SEEMS.
THE FUN IS SEEING THE WHOLE PICTURE IN YOUR MIND'S EYE . . .
. . . AND BRINGING IT TO LIFE, CAPTAIN.
PARDON THE INTERRUPTION, BUT IT'S TIME TO ESCORT YOU BACK TO THE HOTEL, EMILY.
WILL YOU ALLOW ME TO COMMUNICATE THROUGH THE POST, MISS WARREN?
I EXPECT NOTHING LESS, CAPTAIN.
GOOD NIGHT. BE SAFE.

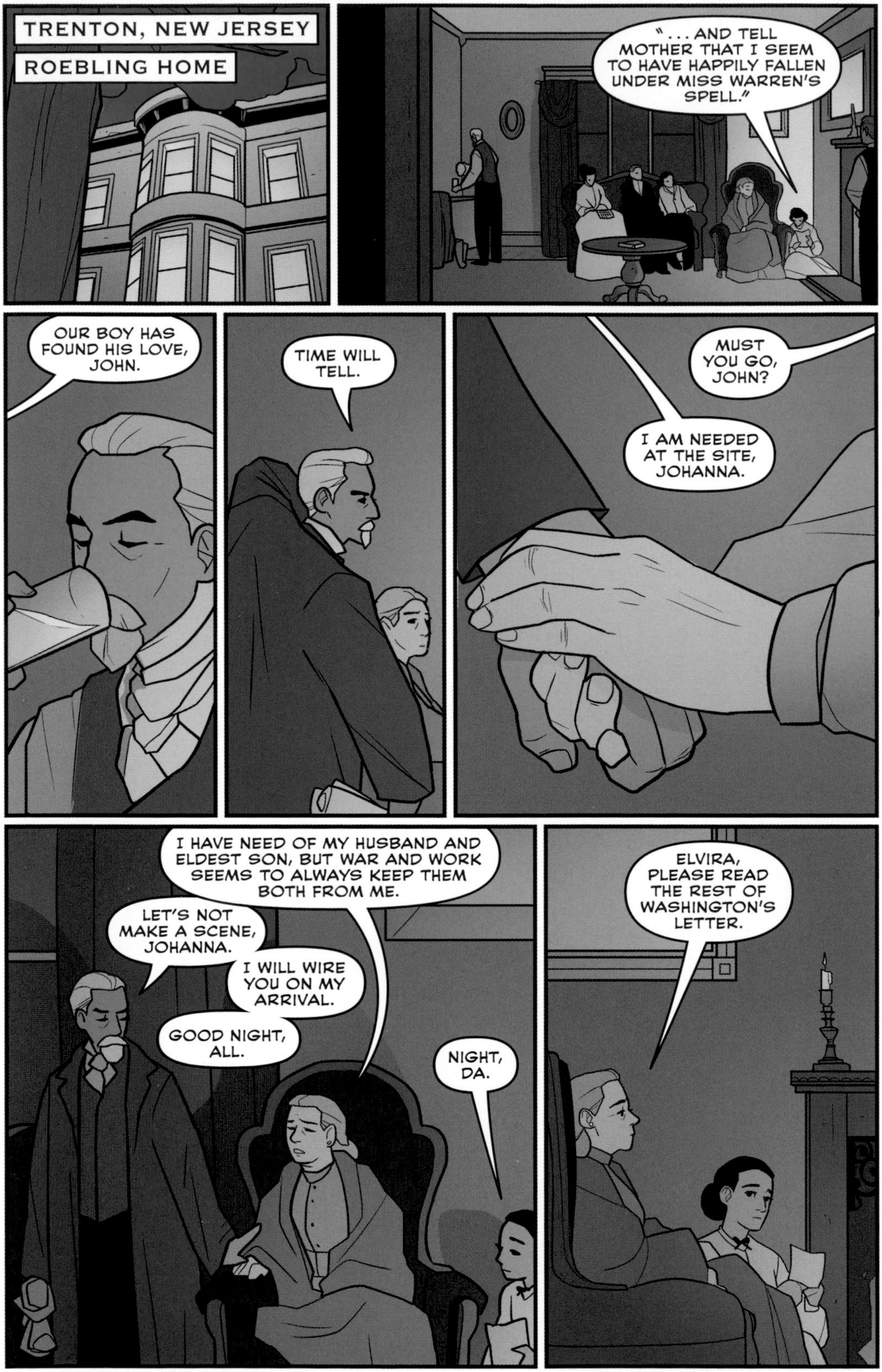
TRENTON, NEW JERSEY
ROEBLING HOME
"... AND TELL MOTHER THAT I SEEM TO HAVE HAPPILY FALLEN UNDER MISS WARREN'S SPELL."
OUR BOY HAS FOUND HIS LOVE, JOHN.
TIME WILL TELL.
MUST YOU GO, JOHN?
I AM NEEDED AT THE SITE, JOHANNA.
I HAVE NEED OF MY HUSBAND AND ELDEST SON, BUT WAR AND WORK SEEMS TO ALWAYS KEEP THEM BOTH FROM ME.
LET'S NOT MAKE A SCENE, JOHANNA.
I WILL WIRE YOU ON MY ARRIVAL.
GOOD NIGHT, ALL.
NIGHT, DA.
ELVIRA, PLEASE READ THE REST OF WASHINGTON'S LETTER.

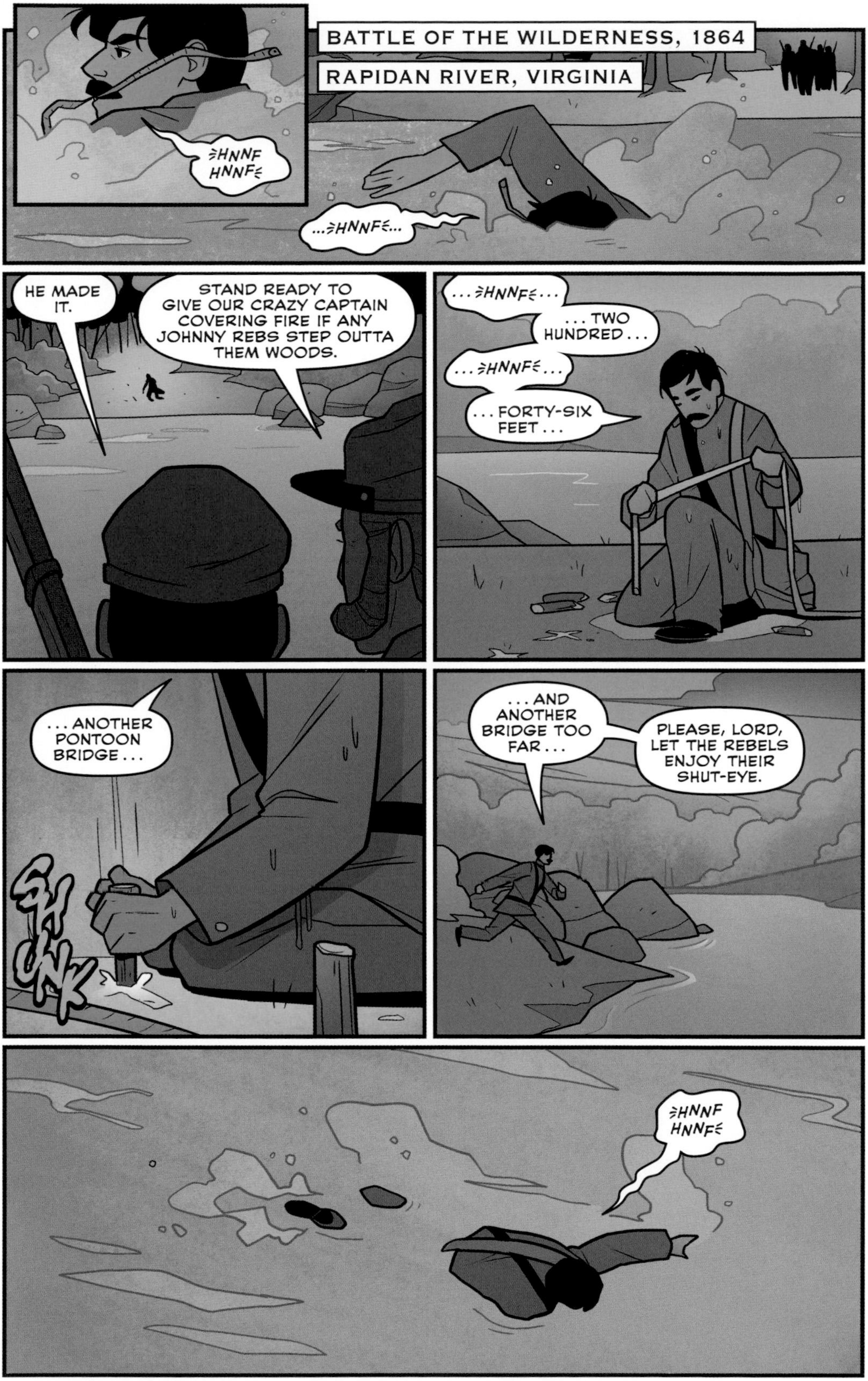
BATTLE OF THE WILDERNESS, 1864
RAPIDAN RIVER, VIRGINIA
≡HNNF HNNF≡
...≡HNNF≡...
HE MADE IT.
STAND READY TO GIVE OUR CRAZY CAPTAIN COVERING FIRE IF ANY JOHNNY REBS STEP OUTTA THEM WOODS.
. . . ≡HNNF≡ . . .
. . . TWO HUNDRED . . .
. . . ≡HNNF≡ . . .
. . . FORTY-SIX FEET . . .
. . . ANOTHER PONTOON BRIDGE . . .
. . . AND ANOTHER BRIDGE TOO FAR . . .
PLEASE, LORD, LET THE REBELS ENJOY THEIR SHUT-EYE.
≡HNNF HNNF≡

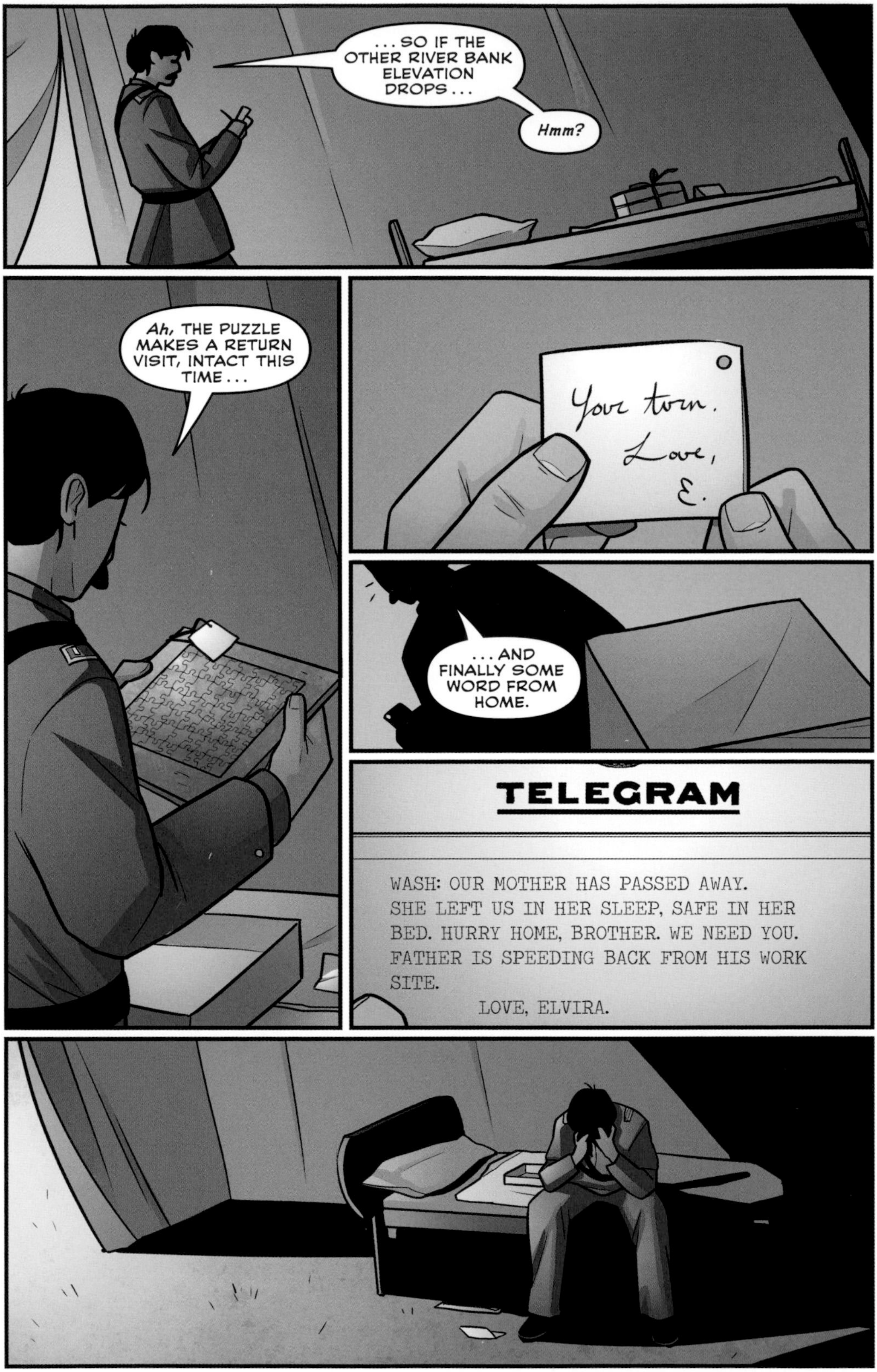
...SO IF THE OTHER RIVER BANK ELEVATION DROPS...
Hmm?
Ah, THE PUZZLE MAKES A RETURN VISIT, INTACT THIS TIME...
Your turn. Love, E.
...AND FINALLY SOME WORD FROM HOME.
TELEGRAM
WASH: OUR MOTHER HAS PASSED AWAY. SHE LEFT US IN HER SLEEP, SAFE IN HER BED. HURRY HOME, BROTHER. WE NEED YOU. FATHER IS SPEEDING BACK FROM HIS WORK SITE.
LOVE, ELVIRA.

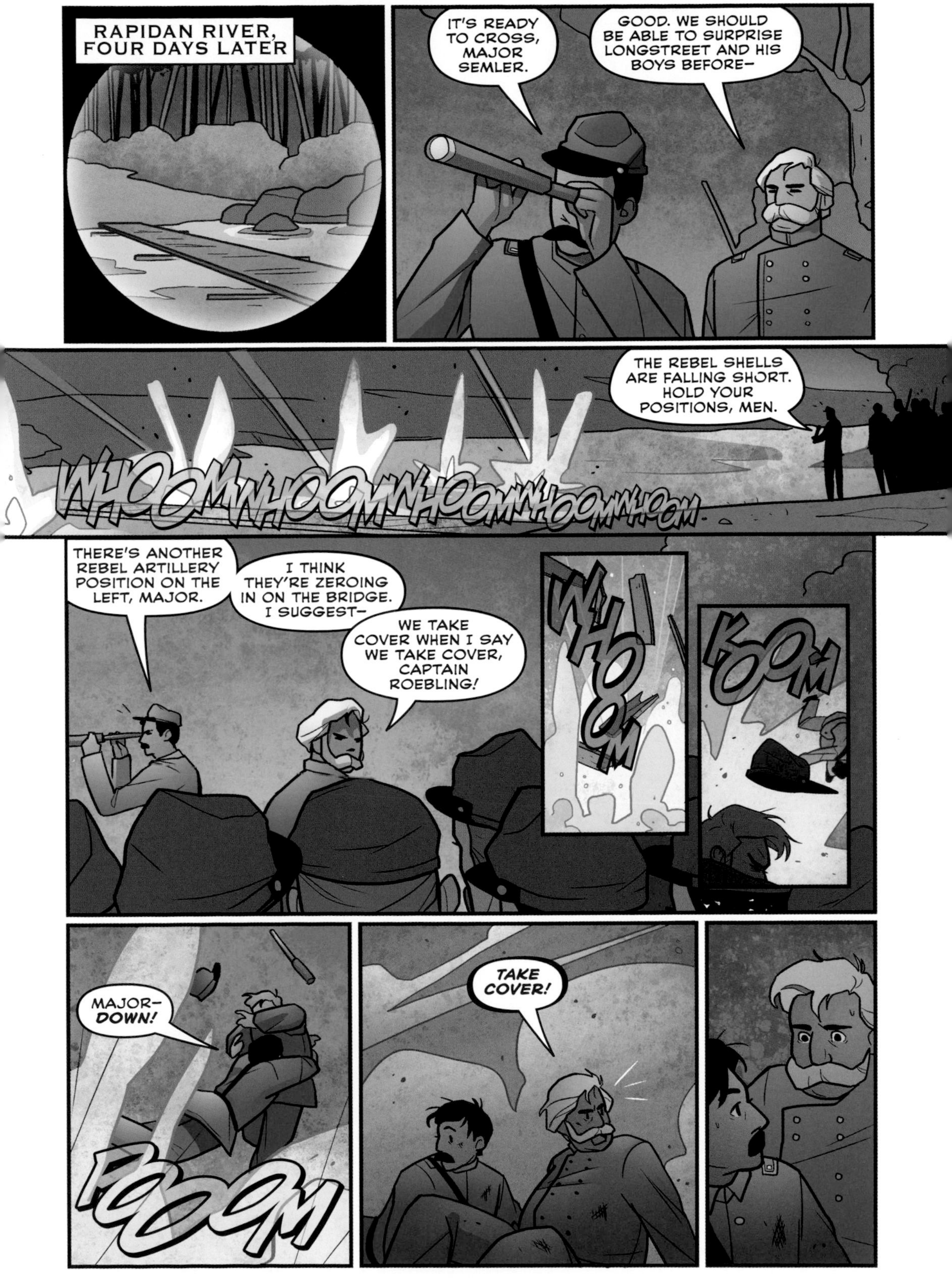
RAPIDAN RIVER, FOUR DAYS LATER
IT'S READY TO CROSS, MAJOR SEMLER.
GOOD. WE SHOULD BE ABLE TO SURPRISE LONGSTREET AND HIS BOYS BEFORE–
THE REBEL SHELLS ARE FALLING SHORT. HOLD YOUR POSITIONS, MEN.
WHOOMWHOOMWHOOMWHOOMWHOOM
THERE'S ANOTHER REBEL ARTILLERY POSITION ON THE LEFT, MAJOR.
I THINK THEY'RE ZEROING IN ON THE BRIDGE. I SUGGEST–
WE TAKE COVER WHEN I SAY WE TAKE COVER, CAPTAIN ROEBLING!
WHOOOM
KOOM
MAJOR– DOWN!
POOOM
TAKE COVER!

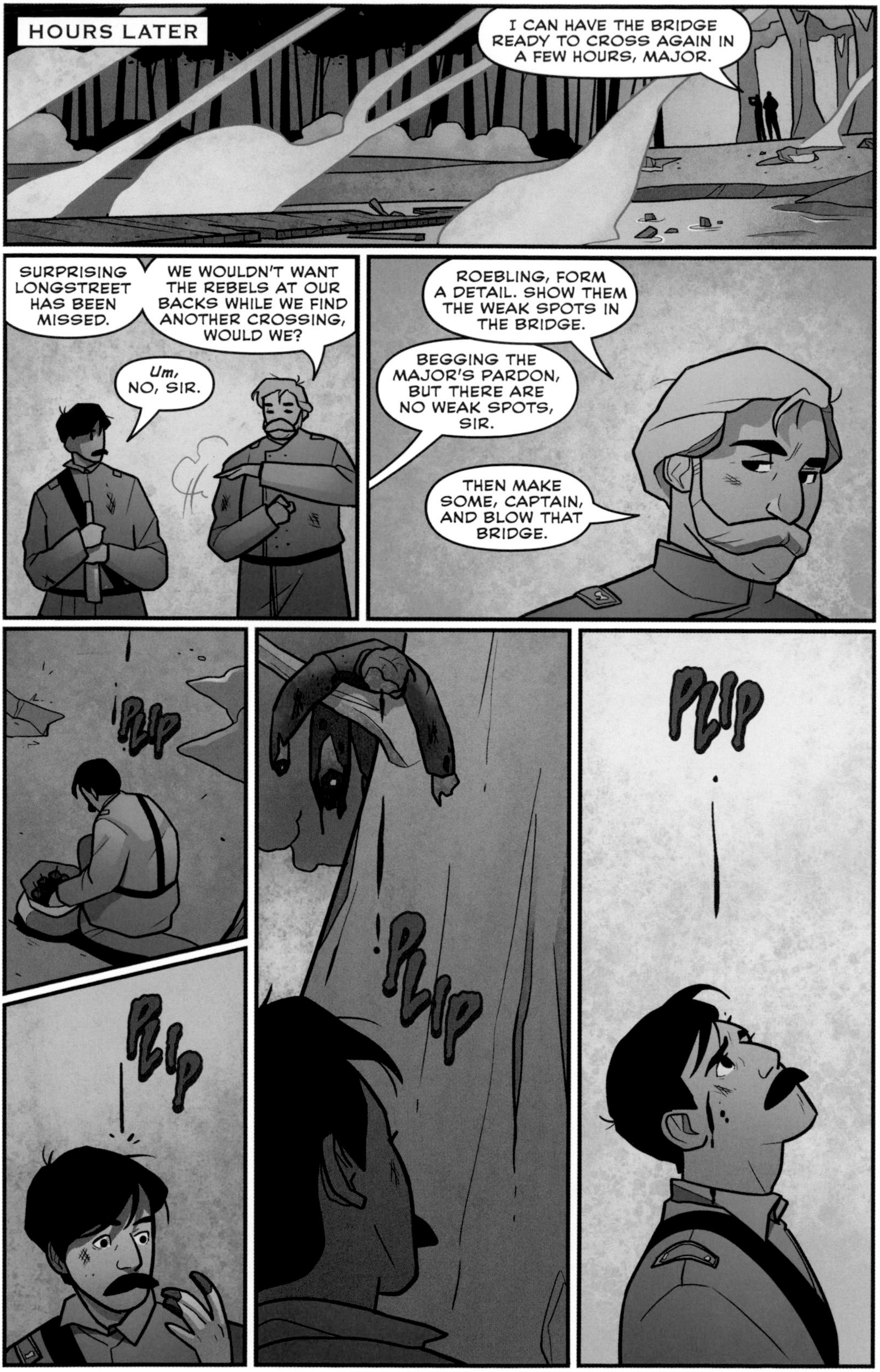
HOURS LATER
I CAN HAVE THE BRIDGE READY TO CROSS AGAIN IN A FEW HOURS, MAJOR.
SURPRISING LONGSTREET HAS BEEN MISSED.
WE WOULDN'T WANT THE REBELS AT OUR BACKS WHILE WE FIND ANOTHER CROSSING, WOULD WE?
Um, NO, SIR.
ROEBLING, FORM A DETAIL. SHOW THEM THE WEAK SPOTS IN THE BRIDGE.
BEGGING THE MAJOR'S PARDON, BUT THERE ARE NO WEAK SPOTS, SIR.
THEN MAKE SOME, CAPTAIN, AND BLOW THAT BRIDGE.
PLIP
PLIP
PLIP
PLIP

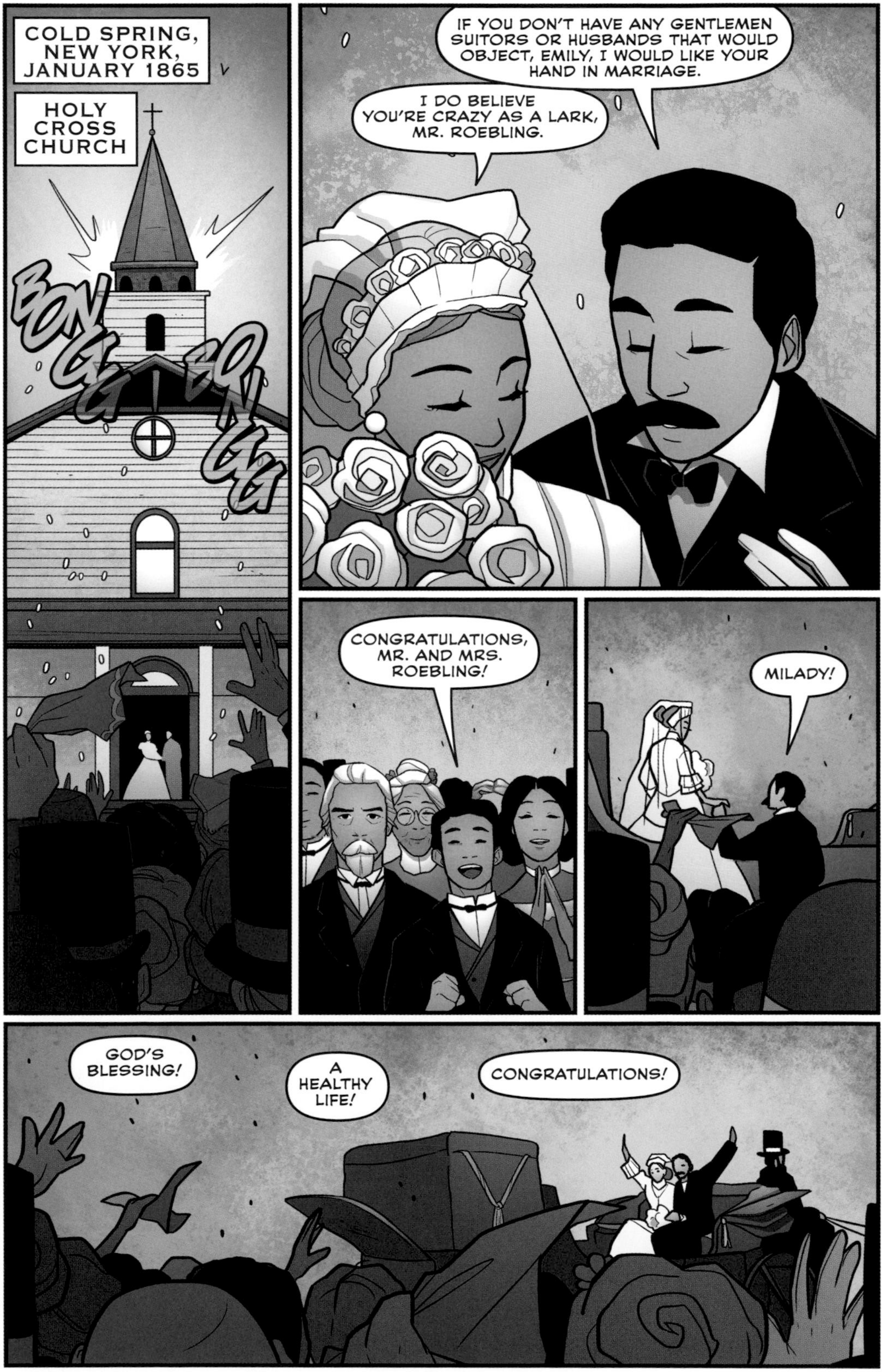
COLD SPRING, NEW YORK, JANUARY 1865
HOLY CROSS CHURCH
BONG
BONG
IF YOU DON'T HAVE ANY GENTLEMEN SUITORS OR HUSBANDS THAT WOULD OBJECT, EMILY, I WOULD LIKE YOUR HAND IN MARRIAGE.
I DO BELIEVE YOU'RE CRAZY AS A LARK, MR. ROEBLING.
CONGRATULATIONS, MR. AND MRS. ROEBLING!
MILADY!
GOD'S BLESSING!
A HEALTHY LIFE!
CONGRATULATIONS!

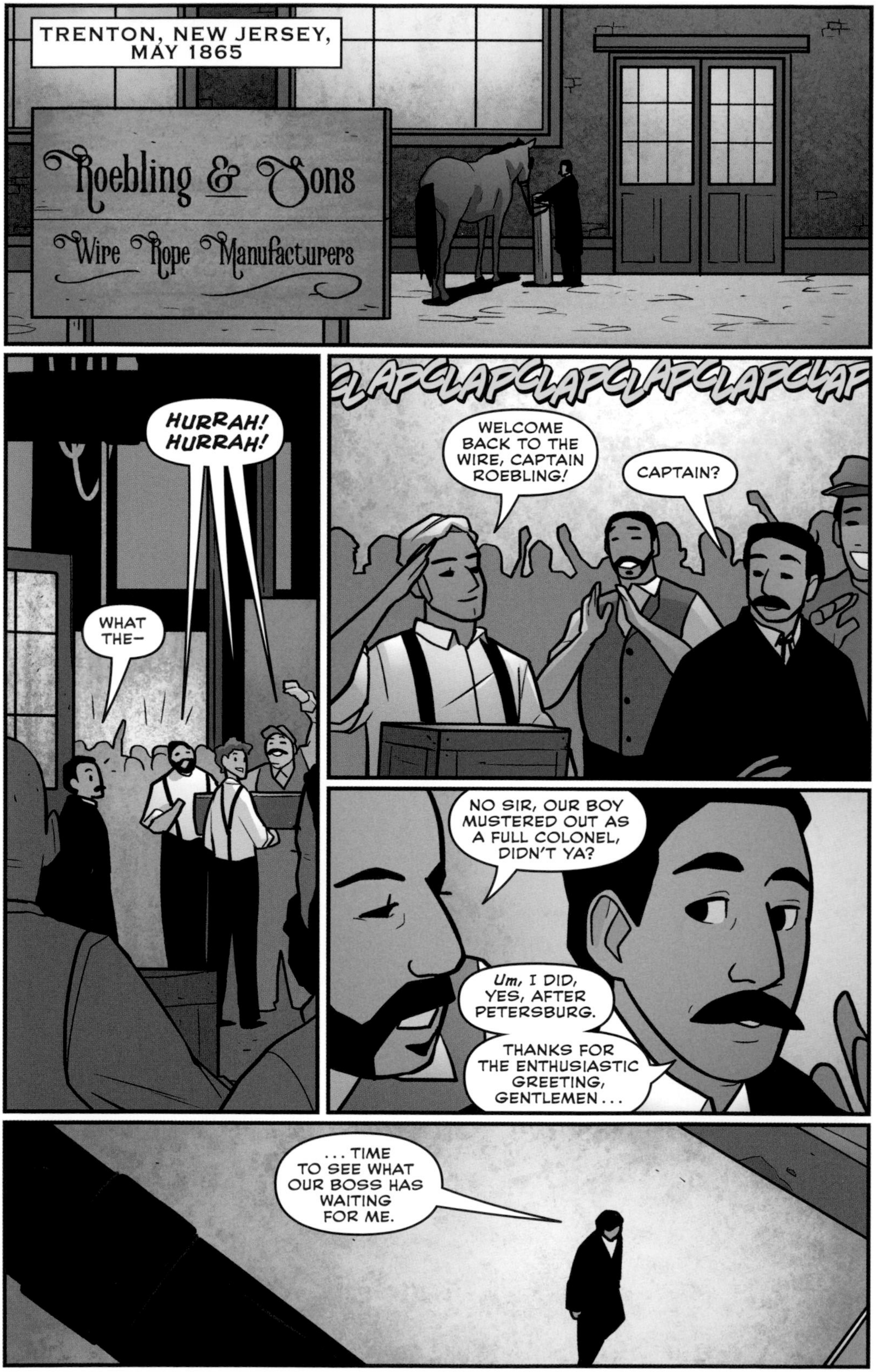
TRENTON, NEW JERSEY, MAY 1865
Roebling & Sons
Wire Rope Manufacturers
HURRAH! HURRAH!
WHAT THE–
CLAPCLAPCLAPCLAPCLAPCLAP
WELCOME BACK TO THE WIRE, CAPTAIN ROEBLING!
CAPTAIN?
NO SIR, OUR BOY MUSTERED OUT AS A FULL COLONEL, DIDN'T YA?
Um, I DID, YES, AFTER PETERSBURG.
THANKS FOR THE ENTHUSIASTIC GREETING, GENTLEMEN . . .
. . . TIME TO SEE WHAT OUR BOSS HAS WAITING FOR ME.

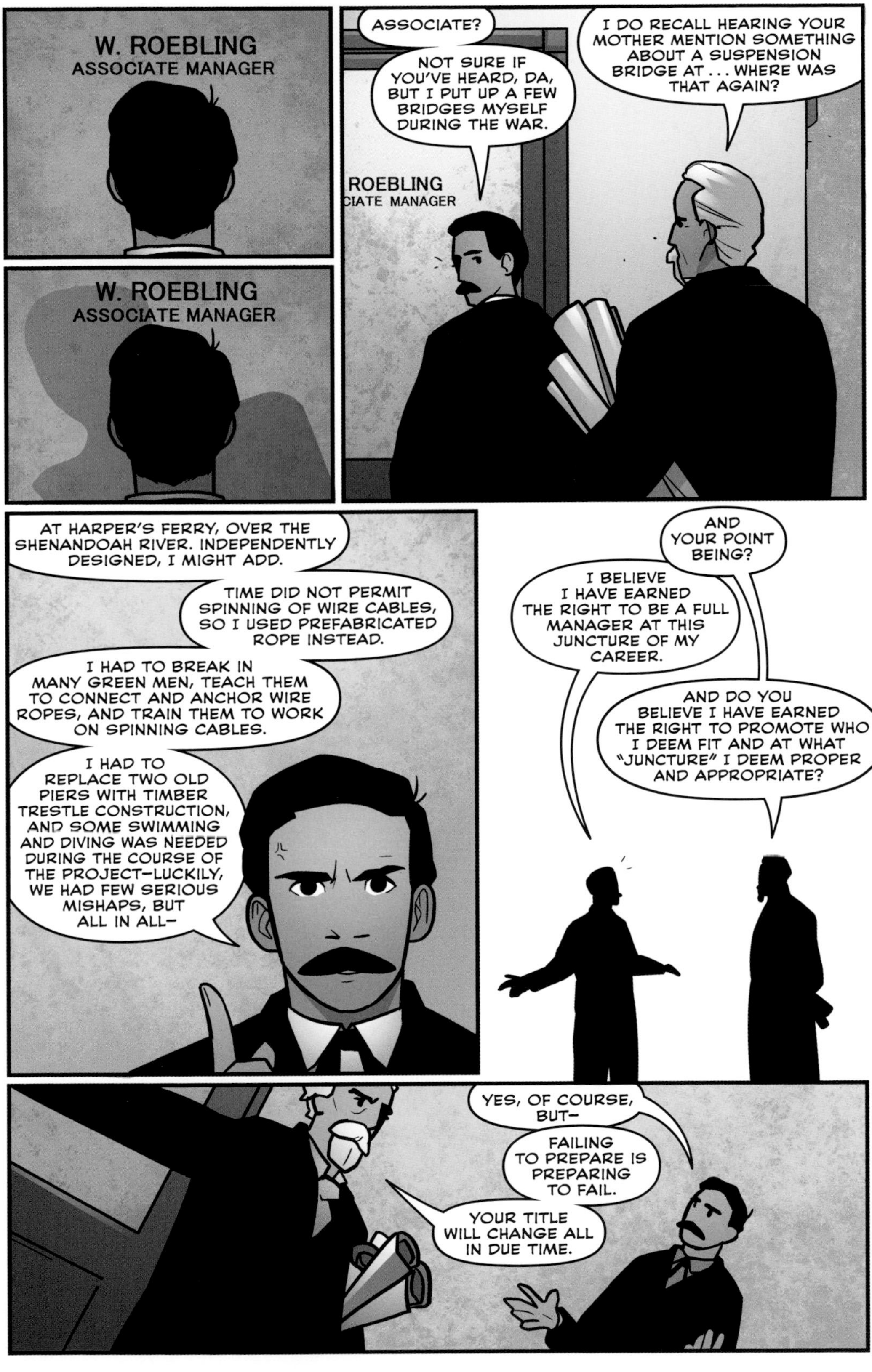
W. ROEBLING
ASSOCIATE MANAGER
W. ROEBLING
ASSOCIATE MANAGER
ASSOCIATE?
NOT SURE IF YOU'VE HEARD, DA, BUT I PUT UP A FEW BRIDGES MYSELF DURING THE WAR.
ROEBLING
CIATE MANAGER
I DO RECALL HEARING YOUR MOTHER MENTION SOMETHING ABOUT A SUSPENSION BRIDGE AT . . . WHERE WAS THAT AGAIN?
AT HARPER'S FERRY, OVER THE SHENANDOAH RIVER. INDEPENDENTLY DESIGNED, I MIGHT ADD.
TIME DID NOT PERMIT SPINNING OF WIRE CABLES, SO I USED PREFABRICATED ROPE INSTEAD.
I HAD TO BREAK IN MANY GREEN MEN, TEACH THEM TO CONNECT AND ANCHOR WIRE ROPES, AND TRAIN THEM TO WORK ON SPINNING CABLES.
I HAD TO REPLACE TWO OLD PIERS WITH TIMBER TRESTLE CONSTRUCTION, AND SOME SWIMMING AND DIVING WAS NEEDED DURING THE COURSE OF THE PROJECT—LUCKILY, WE HAD FEW SERIOUS MISHAPS, BUT ALL IN ALL—
AND YOUR POINT BEING?
I BELIEVE I HAVE EARNED THE RIGHT TO BE A FULL MANAGER AT THIS JUNCTURE OF MY CAREER.
AND DO YOU BELIEVE I HAVE EARNED THE RIGHT TO PROMOTE WHO I DEEM FIT AND AT WHAT "JUNCTURE" I DEEM PROPER AND APPROPRIATE?
YES, OF COURSE, BUT—
FAILING TO PREPARE IS PREPARING TO FAIL.
YOUR TITLE WILL CHANGE ALL IN DUE TIME.

SO, DO WE CONTINUE WASTING ENERGY ON EMOTIONAL MATTERS, OR DO WE GET BACK TO WORK THAT MAY SOMEDAY LEAVE A STAMP UPON THE AGES?

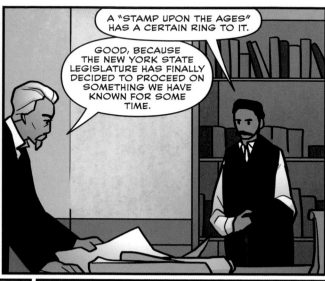

A "STAMP UPON THE AGES" HAS A CERTAIN RING TO IT.

GOOD, BECAUSE THE NEW YORK STATE LEGISLATURE HAS FINALLY DECIDED TO PROCEED ON SOMETHING WE HAVE KNOWN FOR SOME TIME.

AS I NOTICED IN YOUR SKETCHBOOK, YOU HAVE BEEN CONCENTRATING MORE OF YOUR EFFORT ON THE CAISSONS. THAT IS WISE, BECAUSE WITHOUT A STRONG STEM THE FLOWER WILL WILT.

OUT WITH IT, DA. SPINNING NEWS IS NOT ONE OF YOUR STRENGTHS.

THE TIME HAS COME TO COMBINE OUR EFFORTS ON THE EAST RIVER BRIDGE. I HAVE BEEN INVITED TO NEW YORK CITY TO PRESENT A PROPOSAL.

WHEN DO YOU LEAVE?

TOMORROW.

IT'S TIME TO EXPAND THE WIRE WORKS, DA. OUR ORDERS HAVE TRIPLED IN THE PAST FEW MONTHS . . .

. . . AND IF YOU DO MANAGE TO BE CHOSEN FOR THE EAST RIVER BRIDGE, ONLY OUR WIRE CAN MEET THE HIGH STANDARDS THAT WILL BE REQUIRED.

THE WIRE FACTORY WILL MAKE US QUITE RICH IF WE LET IT, AND WITH A CHANCE TO PURCHASE THIRTY ACRES AROUND THE MILL AT A REASONABLE PRICE, IT MEANS I NEED TO BE IN TRENTON WHILE YOU'RE AT THE BRIDGE SITE.

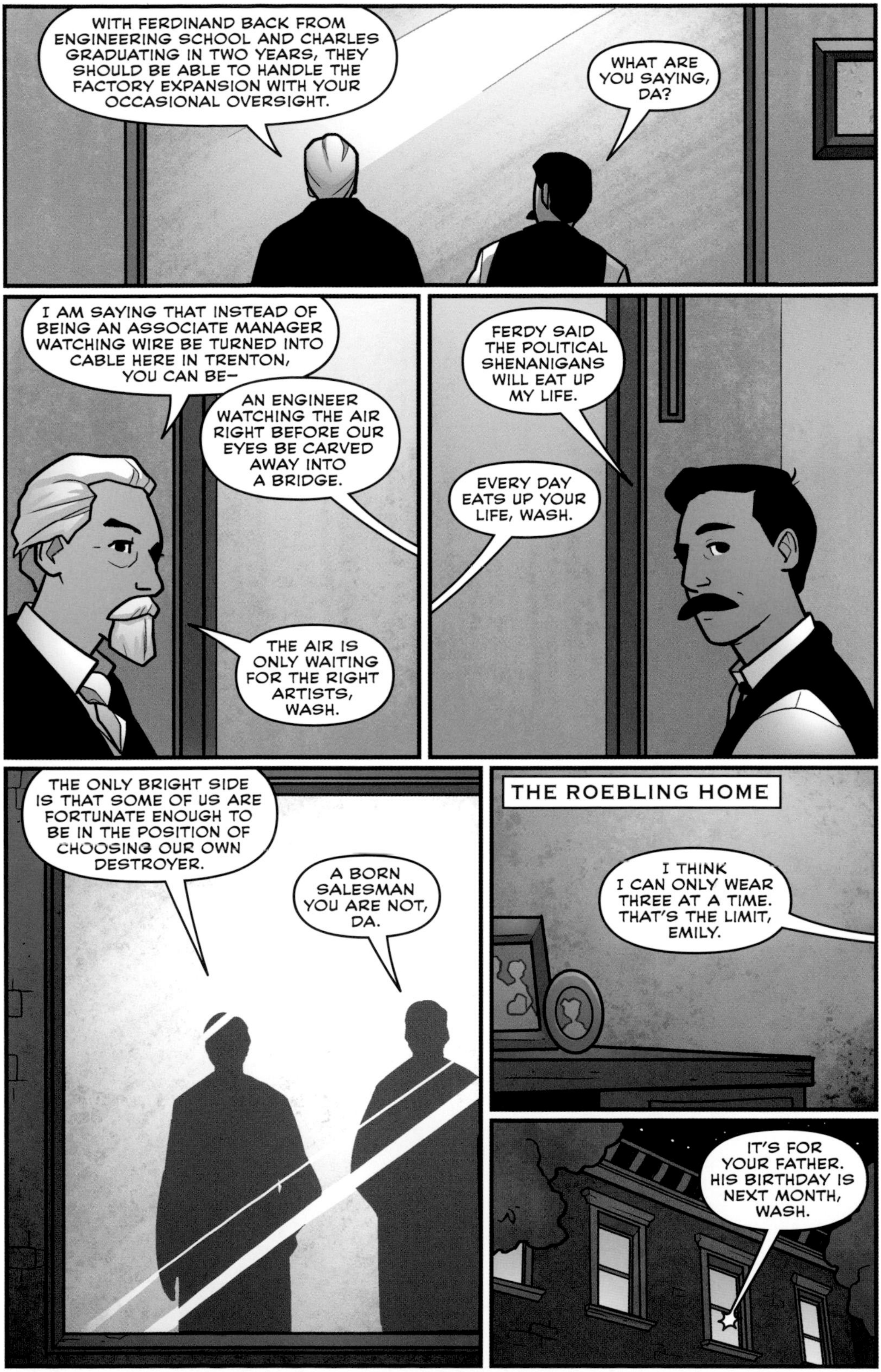
WITH FERDINAND BACK FROM ENGINEERING SCHOOL AND CHARLES GRADUATING IN TWO YEARS, THEY SHOULD BE ABLE TO HANDLE THE FACTORY EXPANSION WITH YOUR OCCASIONAL OVERSIGHT.
WHAT ARE YOU SAYING, DA?
I AM SAYING THAT INSTEAD OF BEING AN ASSOCIATE MANAGER WATCHING WIRE BE TURNED INTO CABLE HERE IN TRENTON, YOU CAN BE—
AN ENGINEER WATCHING THE AIR RIGHT BEFORE OUR EYES BE CARVED AWAY INTO A BRIDGE.
THE AIR IS ONLY WAITING FOR THE RIGHT ARTISTS, WASH.
FERDY SAID THE POLITICAL SHENANIGANS WILL EAT UP MY LIFE.
EVERY DAY EATS UP YOUR LIFE, WASH.
THE ONLY BRIGHT SIDE IS THAT SOME OF US ARE FORTUNATE ENOUGH TO BE IN THE POSITION OF CHOOSING OUR OWN DESTROYER.
A BORN SALESMAN YOU ARE NOT, DA.
THE ROEBLING HOME
I THINK I CAN ONLY WEAR THREE AT A TIME. THAT'S THE LIMIT, EMILY.
IT'S FOR YOUR FATHER. HIS BIRTHDAY IS NEXT MONTH, WASH.

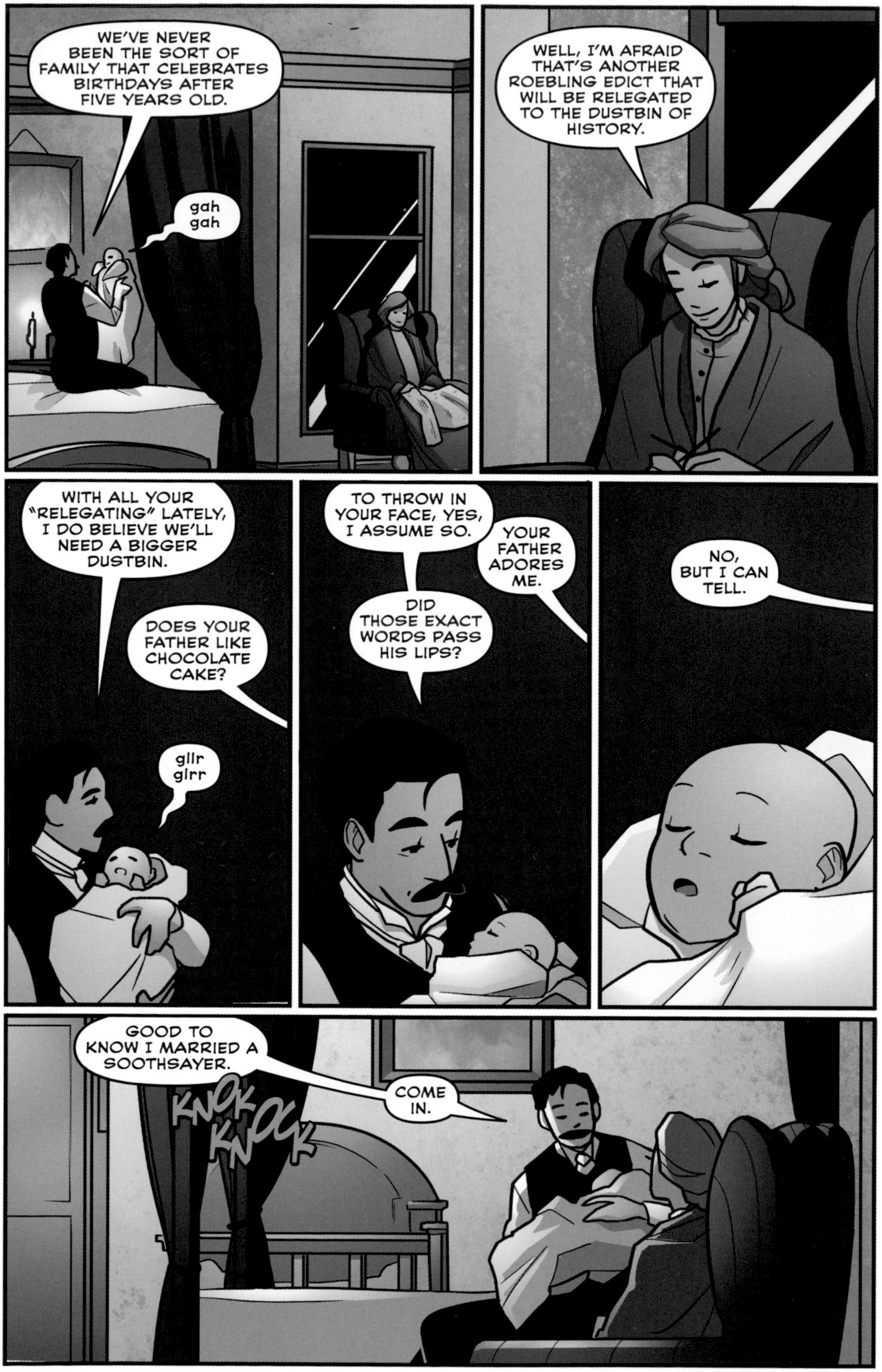
WE'VE NEVER BEEN THE SORT OF FAMILY THAT CELEBRATES BIRTHDAYS AFTER FIVE YEARS OLD.
gah gah
WELL, I'M AFRAID THAT'S ANOTHER ROEBLING EDICT THAT WILL BE RELEGATED TO THE DUSTBIN OF HISTORY.
WITH ALL YOUR "RELEGATING" LATELY, I DO BELIEVE WE'LL NEED A BIGGER DUSTBIN.
DOES YOUR FATHER LIKE CHOCOLATE CAKE?
gllr glrr
TO THROW IN YOUR FACE, YES, I ASSUME SO.
YOUR FATHER ADORES ME.
DID THOSE EXACT WORDS PASS HIS LIPS?
NO, BUT I CAN TELL.
GOOD TO KNOW I MARRIED A SOOTHSAYER.
KNOCK KNOCK
COME IN.

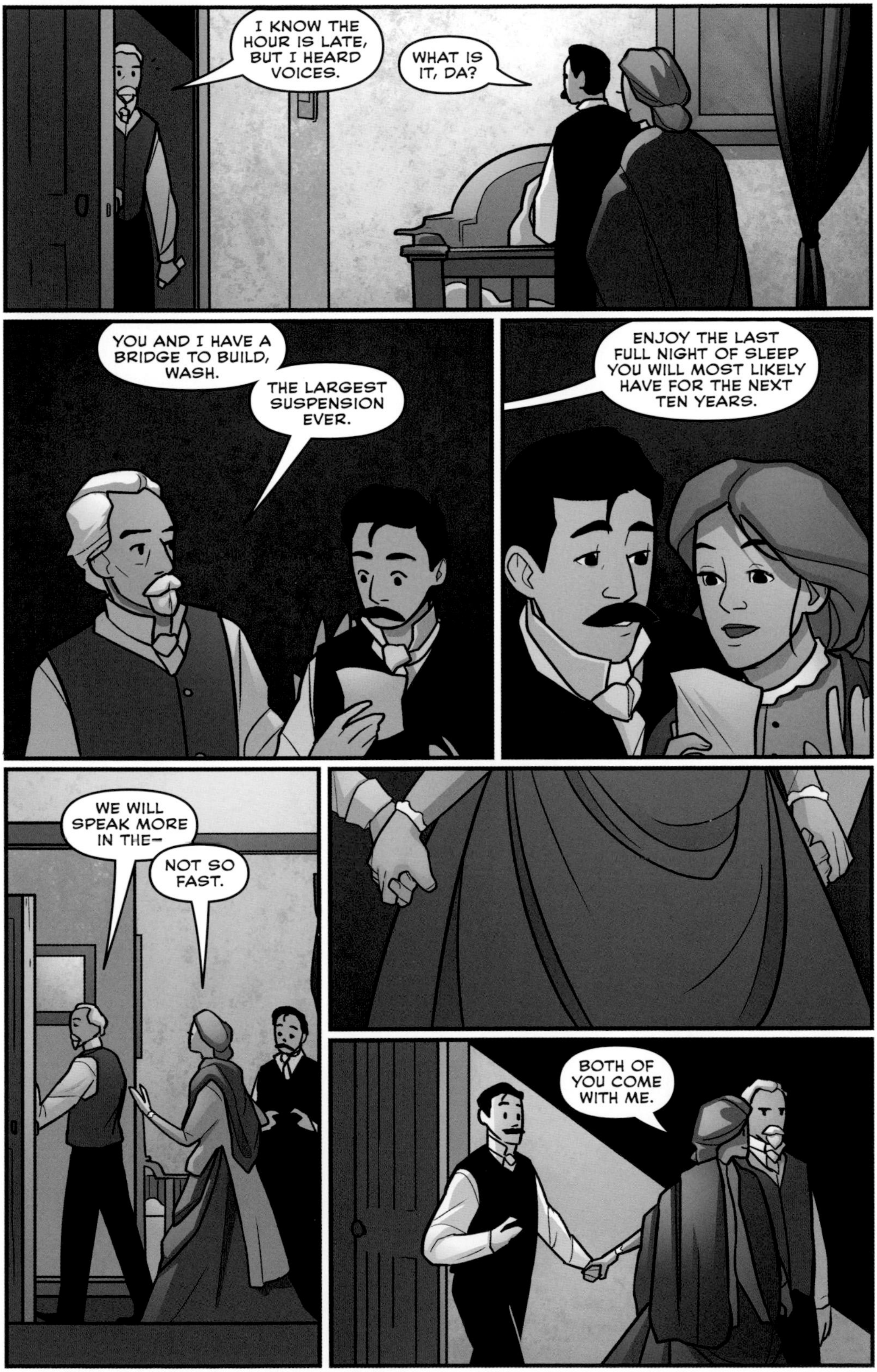
I KNOW THE HOUR IS LATE, BUT I HEARD VOICES.
WHAT IS IT, DA?
YOU AND I HAVE A BRIDGE TO BUILD, WASH.
THE LARGEST SUSPENSION EVER.
ENJOY THE LAST FULL NIGHT OF SLEEP YOU WILL MOST LIKELY HAVE FOR THE NEXT TEN YEARS.
WE WILL SPEAK MORE IN THE—
NOT SO FAST.
BOTH OF YOU COME WITH ME.

DON'T EITHER OF YOU MOVE.

WHAT IS YOUR WIFE DOING?

EMILY.

WHAT IS *EMILY* DOING?

I HAVE NO IDEA.

WATER AND WINE.

HERE'S TO A DREAM REALIZED FOR THE ROEBLING FAMILY.

AND HERE'S TO NEW YORK.

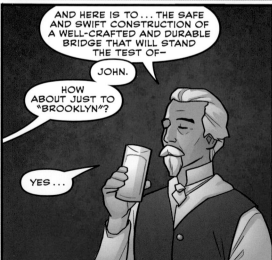

AND HERE IS TO . . . THE SAFE AND SWIFT CONSTRUCTION OF A WELL-CRAFTED AND DURABLE BRIDGE THAT WILL STAND THE TEST OF—

JOHN.

HOW ABOUT JUST TO "BROOKLYN"?

YES . . .

. . . TO BROOKLYN.

38

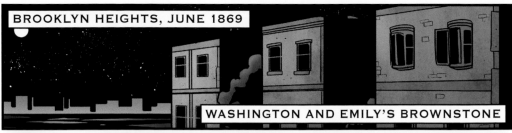

BROOKLYN HEIGHTS, JUNE 1869

WASHINGTON AND EMILY'S BROWNSTONE

...CAN'T SLEEP, *hmm?*

NOT A WINK.

I SWEAR, I CAN SEE IT STANDING THERE LIKE IT'S ALREADY DONE. CAN YOU SEE IT TOO, EM?

I *DO* SEE IT, WASH. IT'S GOING TO BE SPECTACULAR.

IS IT ME, EM, OR ARE THE CITIES MOVING FARTHER APART?

IT'S JUST YOU...

...GOOD NIGHT.

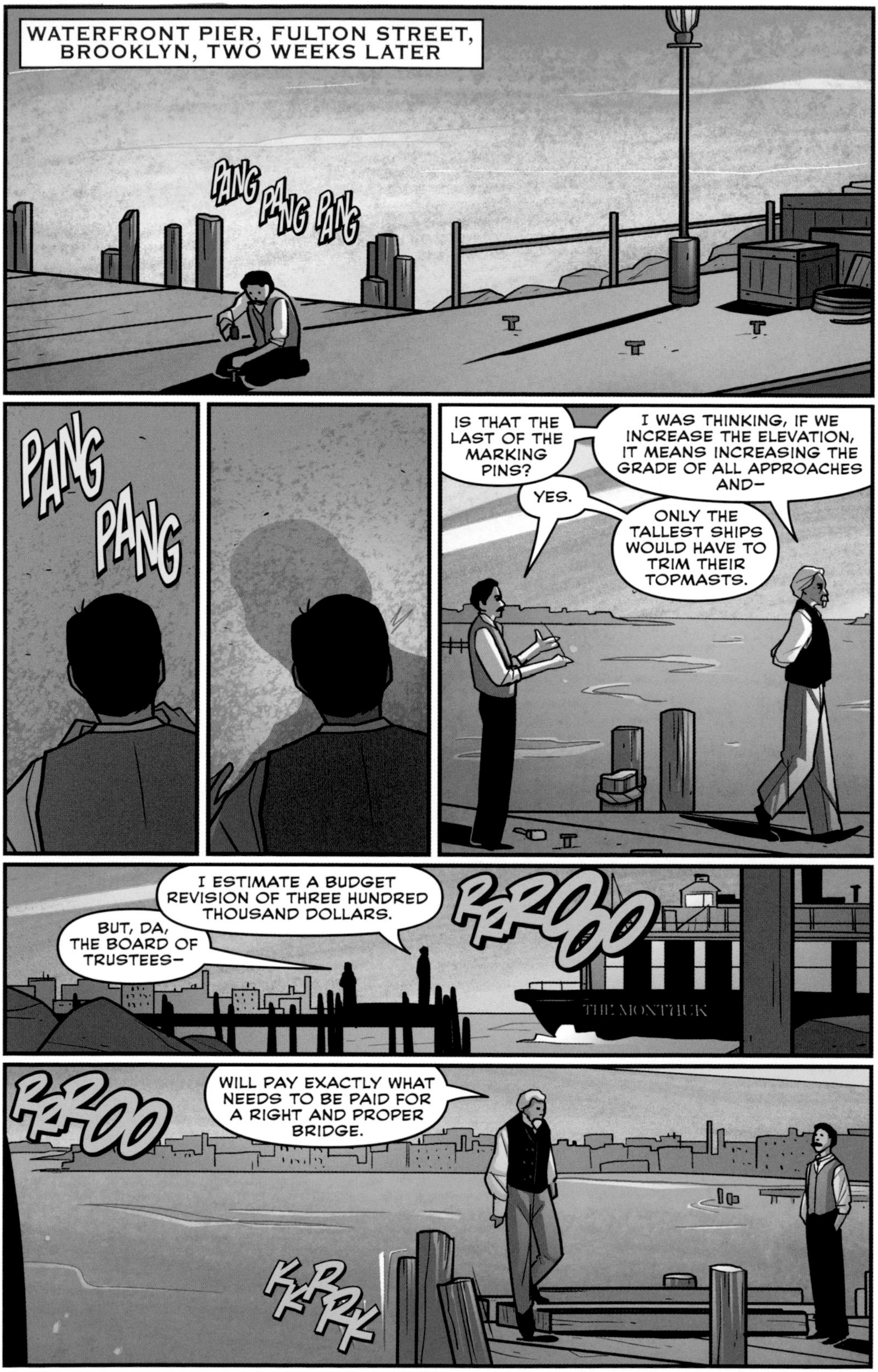
WATERFRONT PIER, FULTON STREET, BROOKLYN, TWO WEEKS LATER
PANG PANG PANG
PANG PANG
IS THAT THE LAST OF THE MARKING PINS?
YES.
I WAS THINKING, IF WE INCREASE THE ELEVATION, IT MEANS INCREASING THE GRADE OF ALL APPROACHES AND—
ONLY THE TALLEST SHIPS WOULD HAVE TO TRIM THEIR TOPMASTS.
I ESTIMATE A BUDGET REVISION OF THREE HUNDRED THOUSAND DOLLARS.
BUT, DA, THE BOARD OF TRUSTEES—
RRROOO
THE MONTAUK
RRROOO
WILL PAY EXACTLY WHAT NEEDS TO BE PAID FOR A RIGHT AND PROPER BRIDGE.
KKRRK

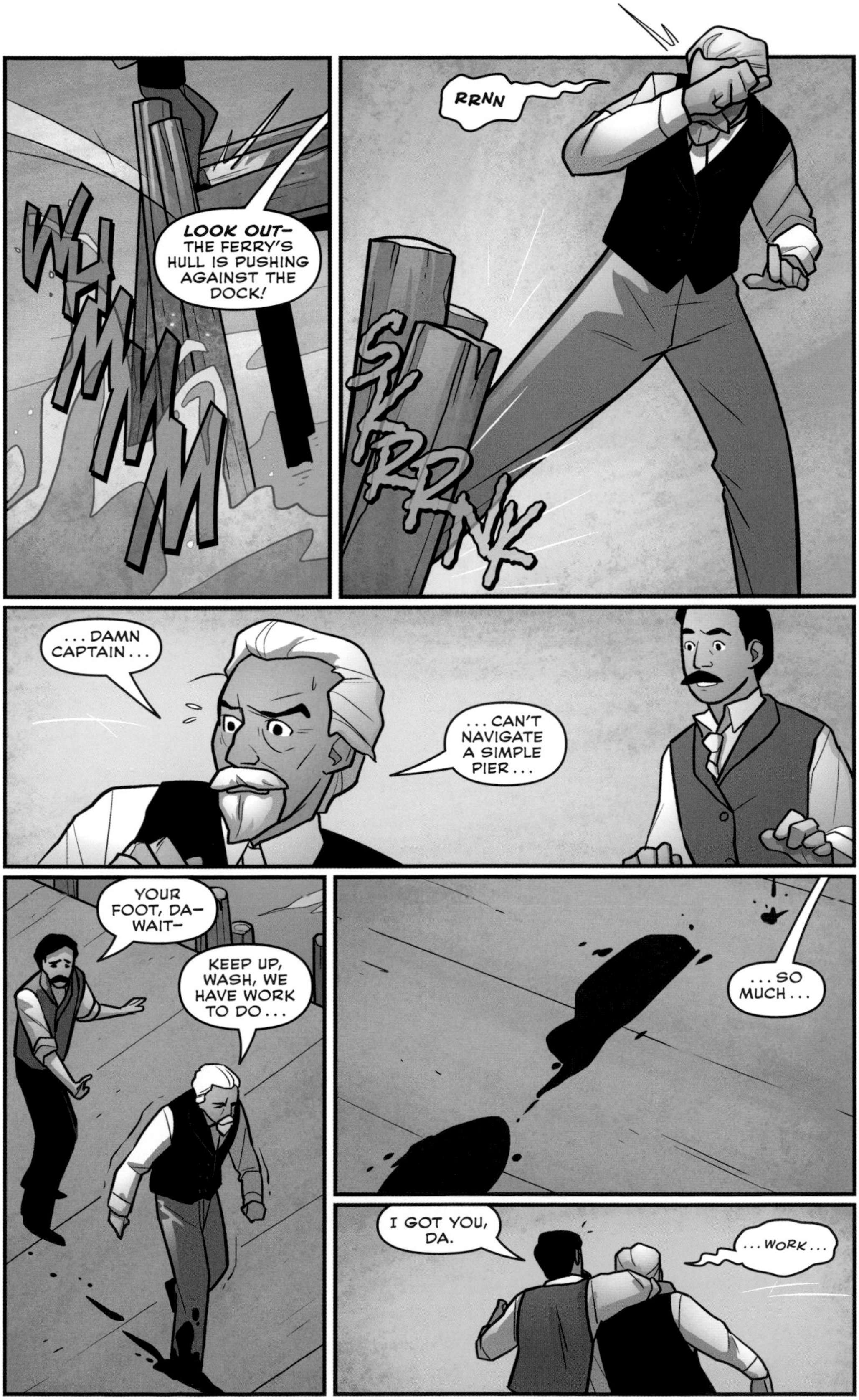
WHMMMM
LOOK OUT– THE FERRY'S HULL IS PUSHING AGAINST THE DOCK!
RRNN
SKRRNK
. . . DAMN CAPTAIN . . .
. . . CAN'T NAVIGATE A SIMPLE PIER . . .
YOUR FOOT, DA– WAIT–
KEEP UP, WASH, WE HAVE WORK TO DO . . .
. . . SO MUCH . . .
I GOT YOU, DA.
. . . WORK . . .

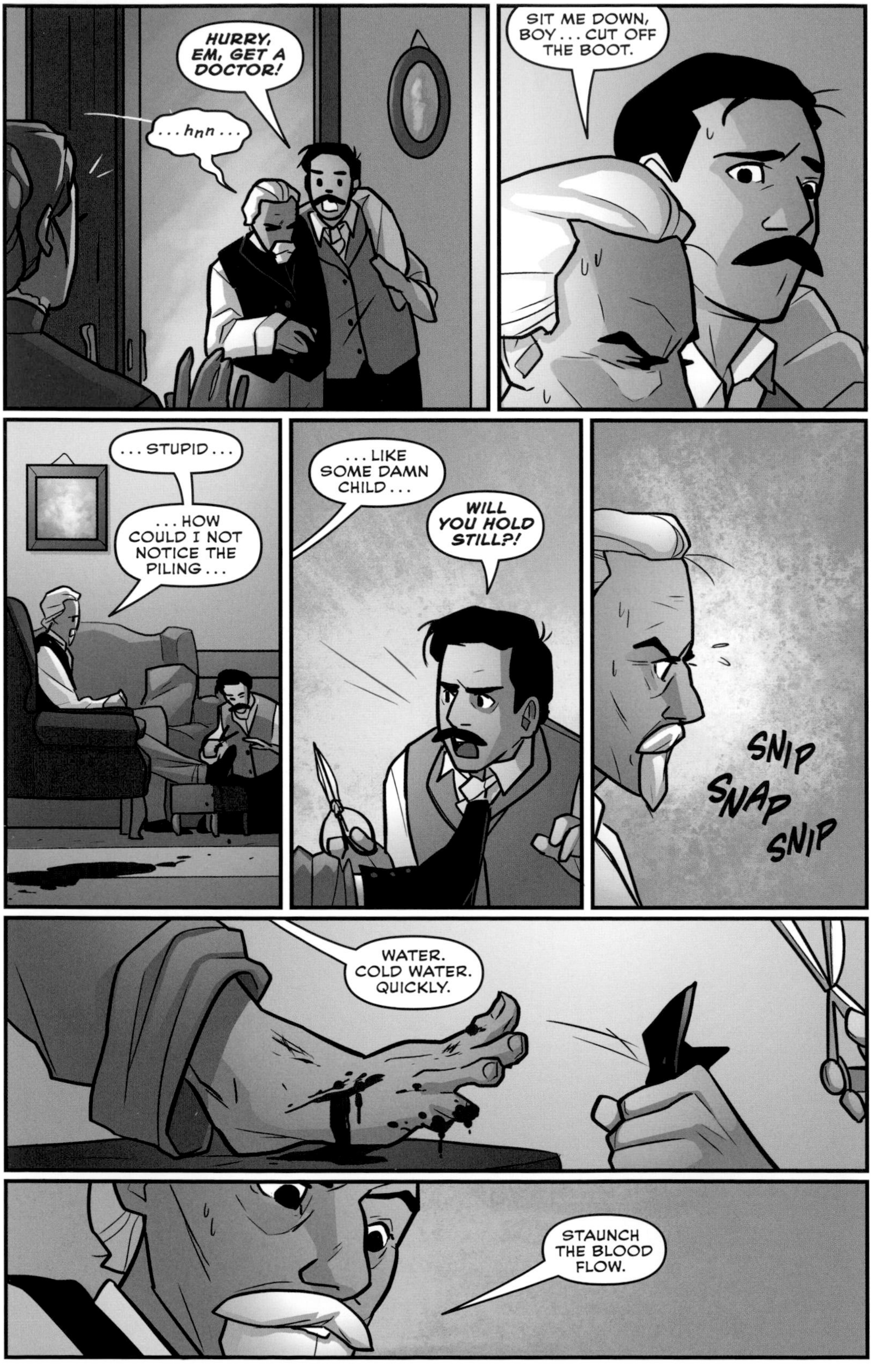
HURRY, EM, GET A DOCTOR!
...hnn...
SIT ME DOWN, BOY... CUT OFF THE BOOT.
...STUPID...
...HOW COULD I NOT NOTICE THE PILING...
...LIKE SOME DAMN CHILD...
WILL YOU HOLD STILL?!
SNIP
SNAP
SNIP
WATER. COLD WATER. QUICKLY.
STAUNCH THE BLOOD FLOW.

THANKS FOR COMING SO SOON, DOCTOR McCULLOUGH.

EXAMINE AWAY, DOCTOR.

OMIGOD... JOHN...

NOTHING TO GET EXCITED ABOUT, EMILY.

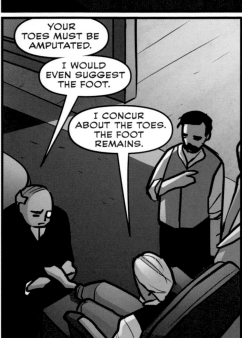

YOUR TOES MUST BE AMPUTATED.

I WOULD EVEN SUGGEST THE FOOT.

I CONCUR ABOUT THE TOES. THE FOOT REMAINS.

NGGH

I INSIST ON NO ANESTHETIC.

WHEN THE SURGERY IS OVER I WILL BIND THE WOUND AND TREAT IT MYSELF.

LET'S GET THIS DONE. PLENTY OF WORK AWAITS.

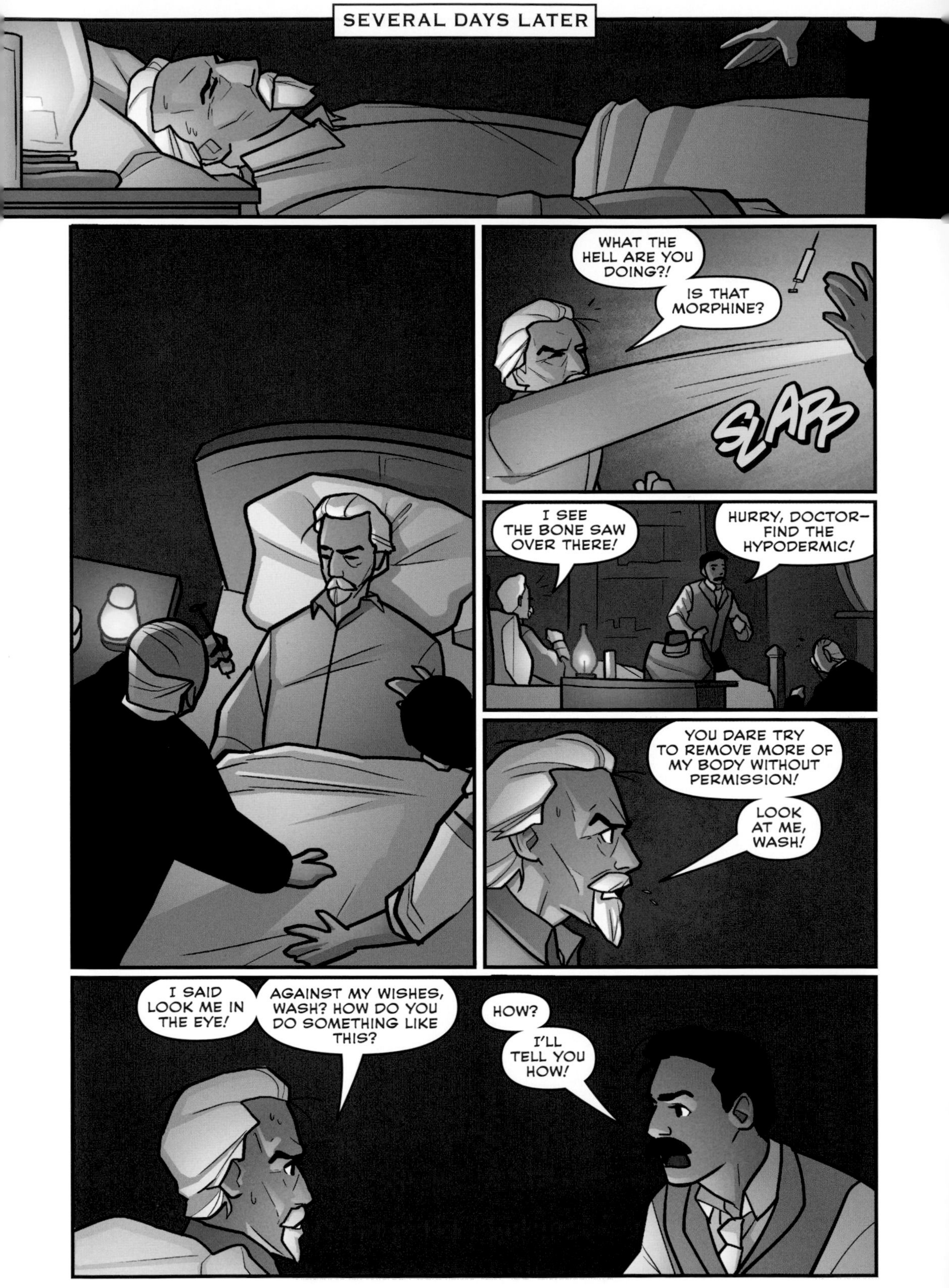
SEVERAL DAYS LATER
WHAT THE HELL ARE YOU DOING?!
IS THAT MORPHINE?
SLAPP
I SEE THE BONE SAW OVER THERE!
HURRY, DOCTOR— FIND THE HYPODERMIC!
YOU DARE TRY TO REMOVE MORE OF MY BODY WITHOUT PERMISSION!
LOOK AT ME, WASH!
I SAID LOOK ME IN THE EYE!
AGAINST MY WISHES, WASH? HOW DO YOU DO SOMETHING LIKE THIS?
HOW?
I'LL TELL YOU HOW!

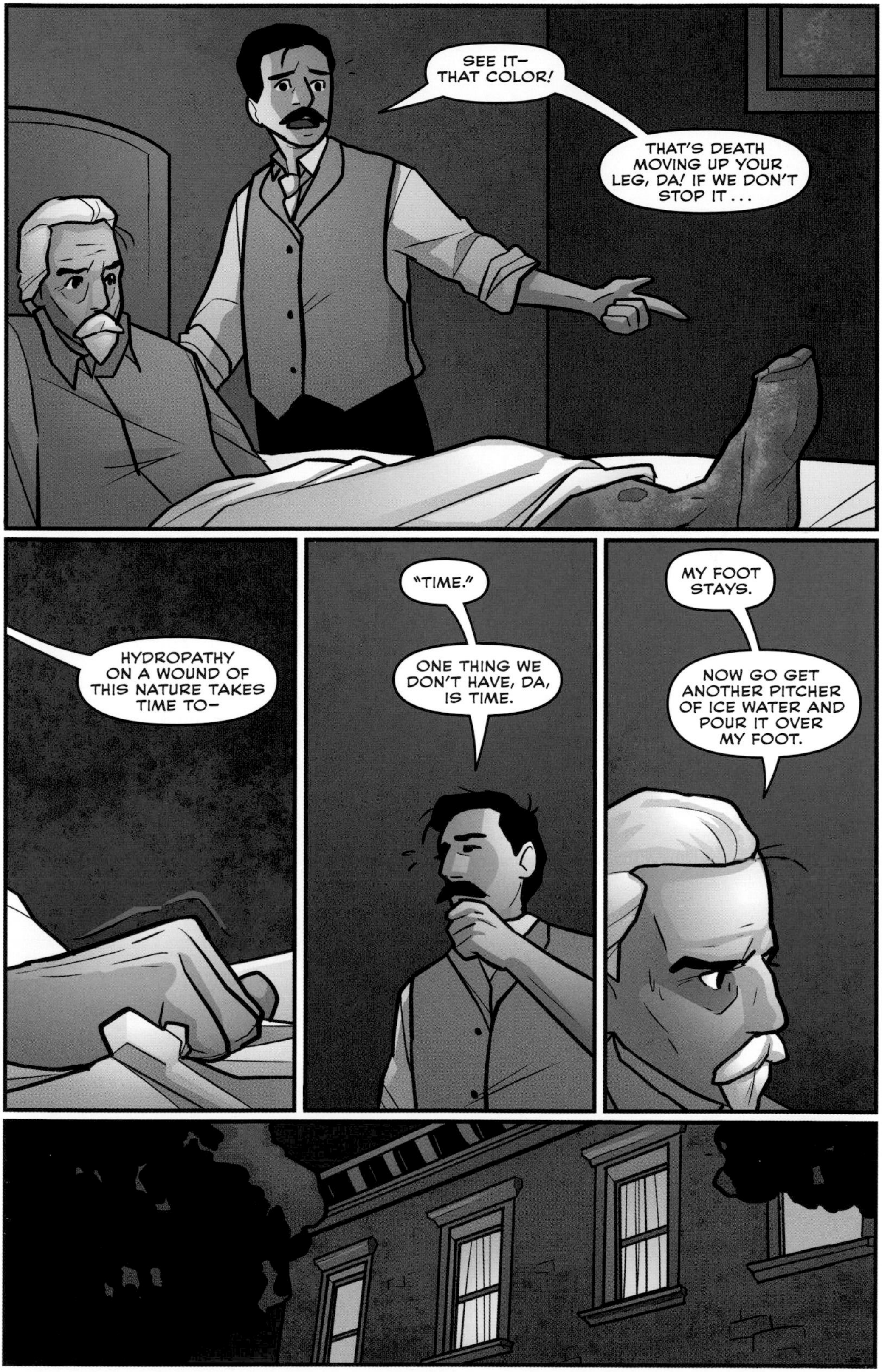
SEE IT—
THAT COLOR!
THAT'S DEATH MOVING UP YOUR LEG, DA! IF WE DON'T STOP IT . . .
HYDROPATHY ON A WOUND OF THIS NATURE TAKES TIME TO—
"TIME."
ONE THING WE DON'T HAVE, DA, IS TIME.
MY FOOT STAYS.
NOW GO GET ANOTHER PITCHER OF ICE WATER AND POUR IT OVER MY FOOT.

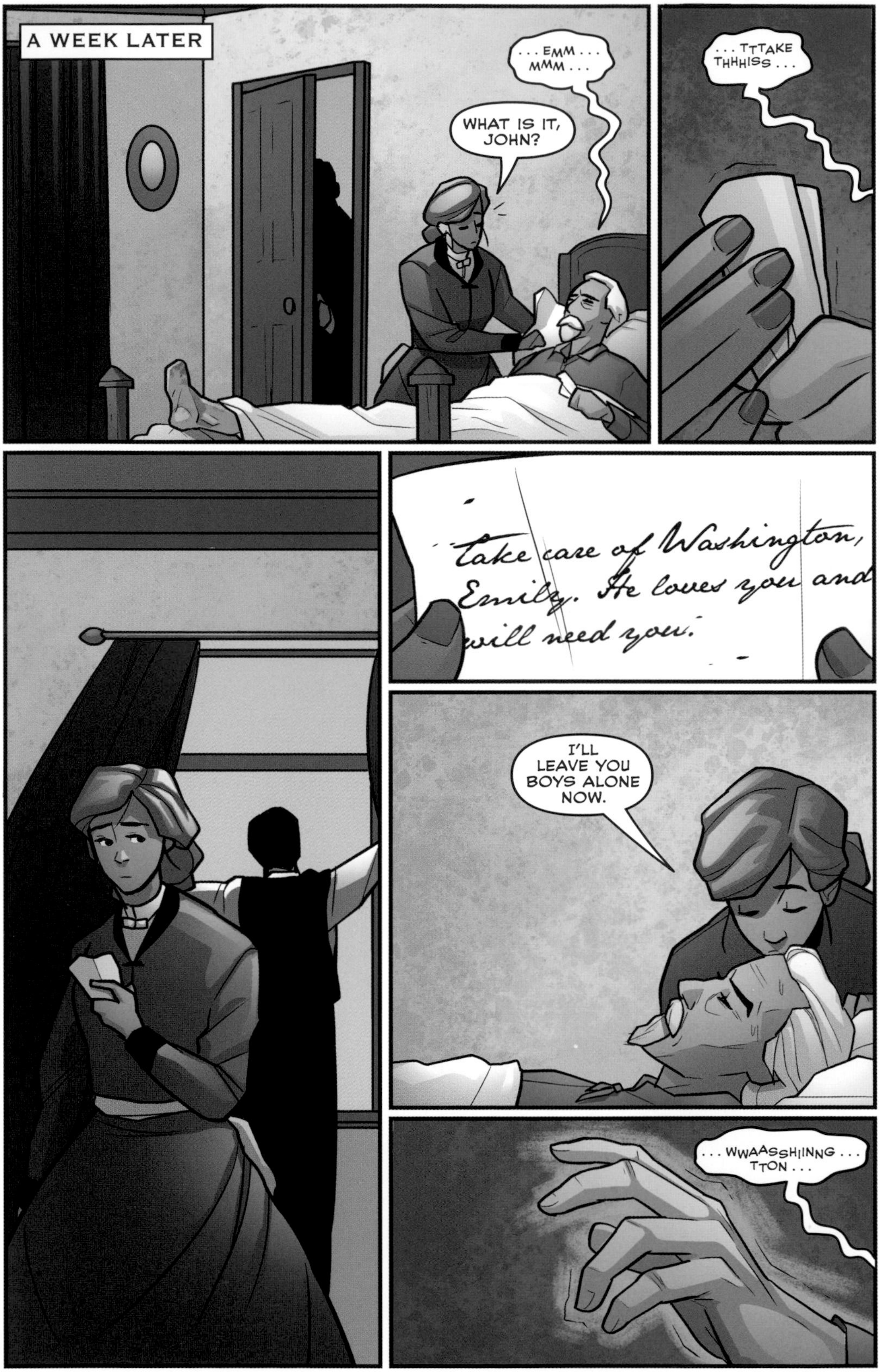
A WEEK LATER
. . . EMM . . . MMM . . .
WHAT IS IT, JOHN?
. . . TTTAKE THHHISS . . .
take care of Washington, Emily. He loves you and will need you.
I'LL LEAVE YOU BOYS ALONE NOW.
. . . WWAASSHIINNG . . . TTON . . .

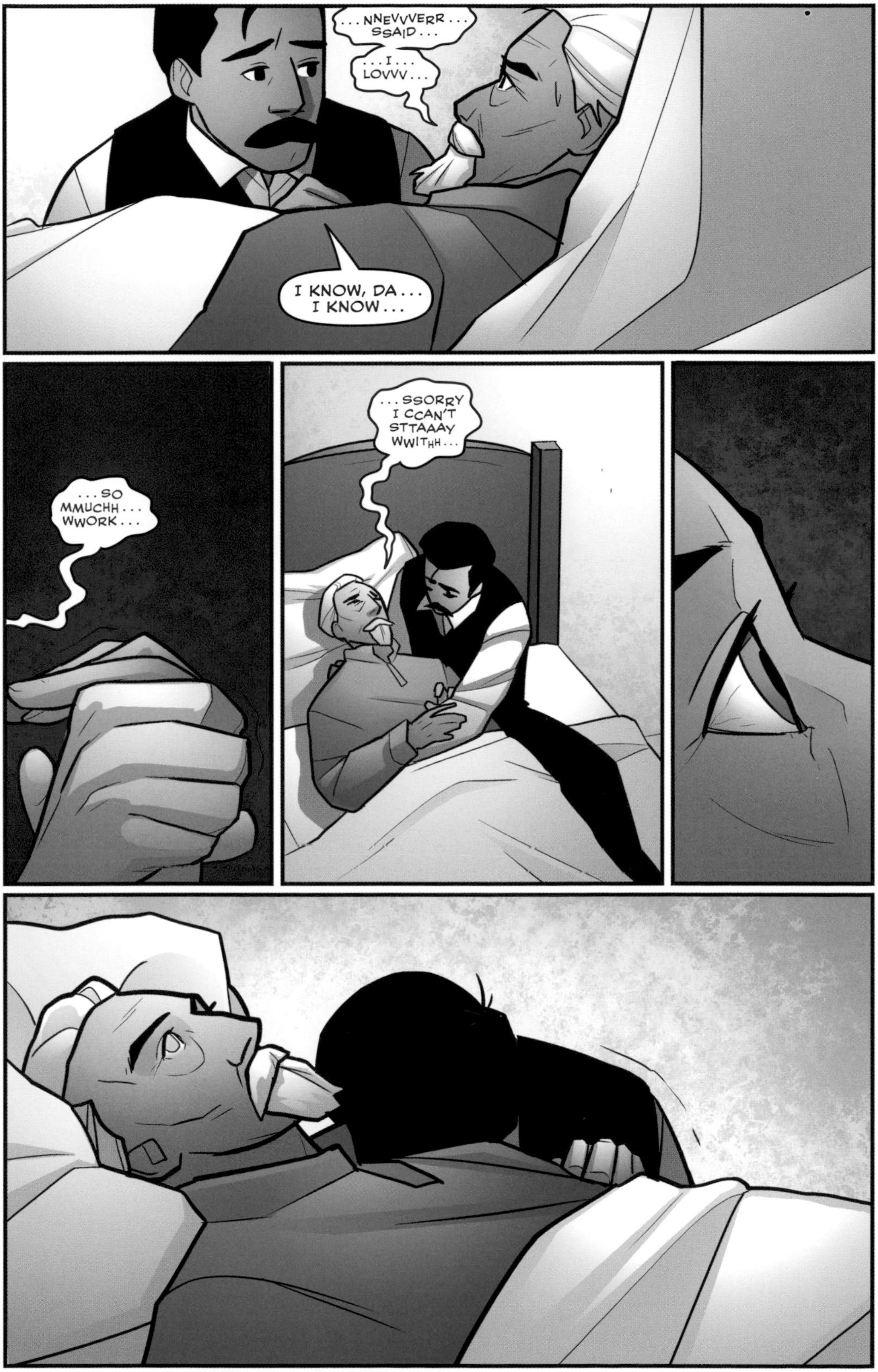
...NNEVVVERR... SSAID...
...I... LOVVV...
I KNOW, DA... I KNOW...
...SO MMUCHH... WWORK...
...SSORRY I CCAN'T STTAAAY WWITHH...

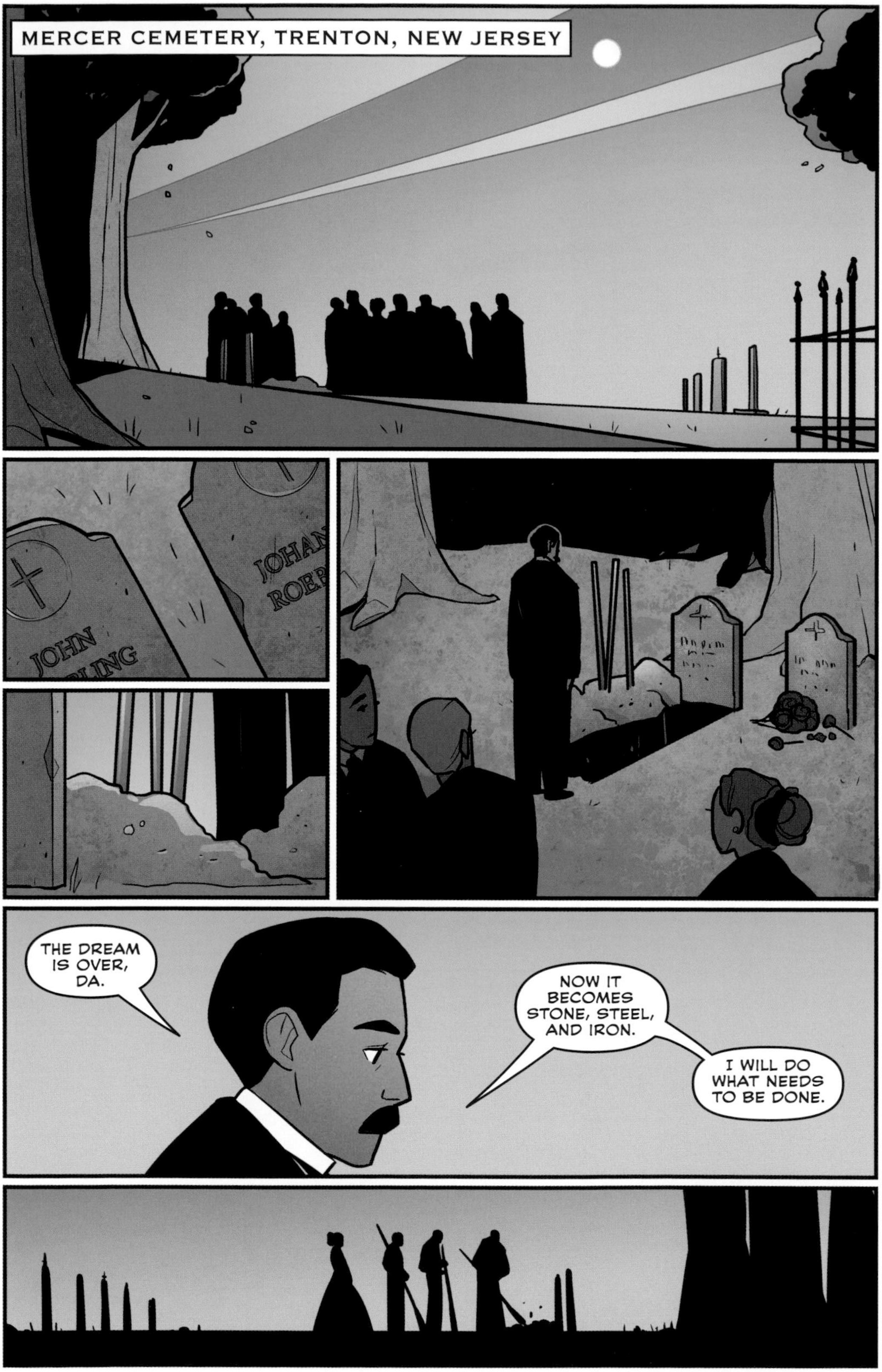
MERCER CEMETERY, TRENTON, NEW JERSEY
JOHN
JOHAN ROEB
THE DREAM IS OVER, DA.
NOW IT BECOMES STONE, STEEL, AND IRON.
I WILL DO WHAT NEEDS TO BE DONE.

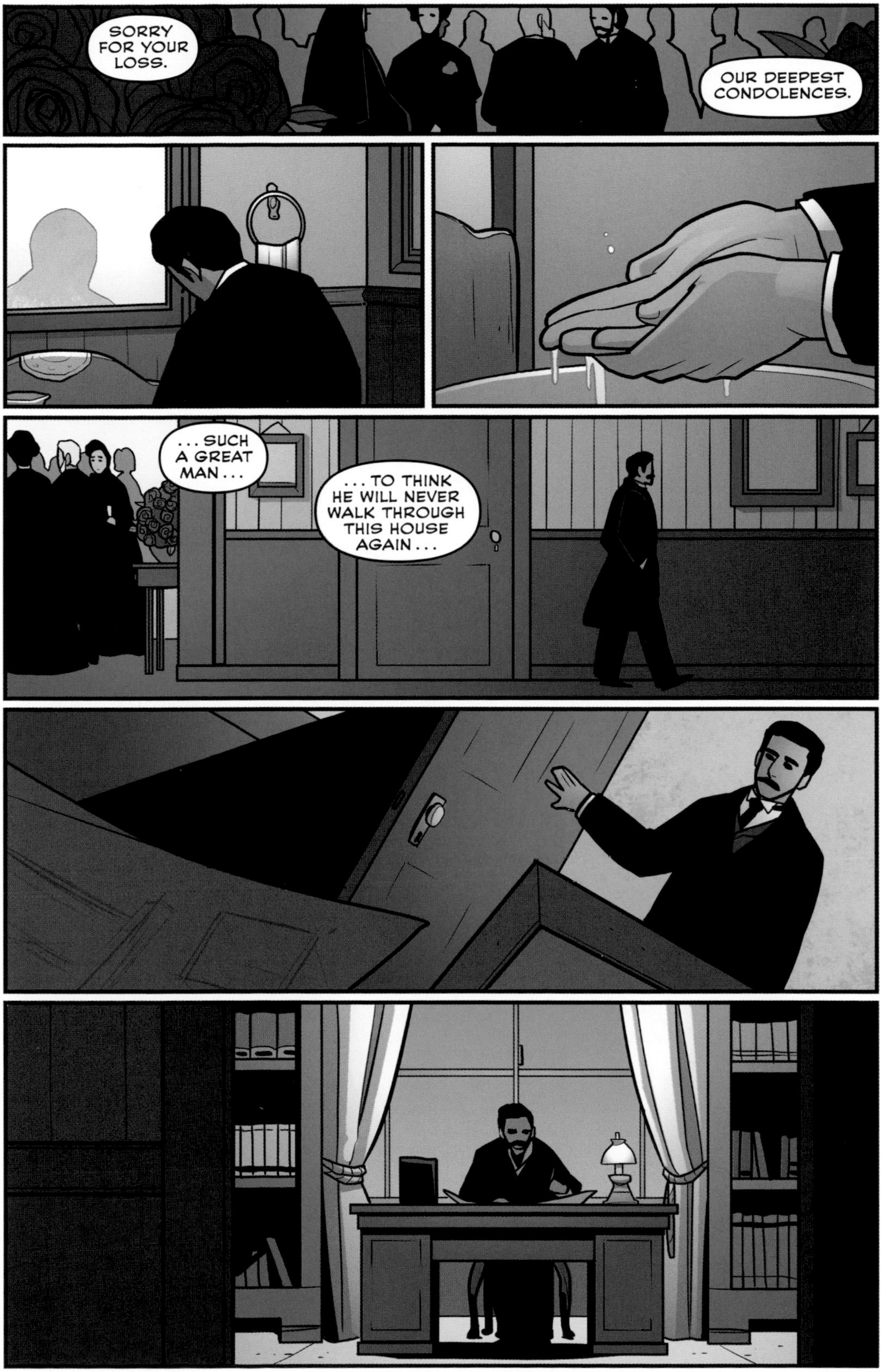
SORRY FOR YOUR LOSS.
OUR DEEPEST CONDOLENCES.
. . . SUCH A GREAT MAN . . .
. . . TO THINK HE WILL NEVER WALK THROUGH THIS HOUSE AGAIN . . .

BRIDGE COMPANY OFFICE, BROOKLYN

YOU CAN STOP PACING, WASH.

NEED I REMIND YOU THAT YOU FOUGHT IN THE WAR OF REBELLION?

BUILT BRIDGES UNDER FIRE.

WHAT'S BEHIND THOSE DOORS IS NOTHING MORE THAN A CHILDREN'S BIRTHDAY PARTY WAITING FOR THE GUEST OF HONOR.

EVENING, GENTLEMEN.

GOOD EVENING, COLONEL.

ONCE AGAIN, I SPEAK FOR EVERYONE— OUR SINCEREST CONDOLENCES.

THANK YOU, TRUSTEE MURPHY.

AND THANK YOU ALL FOR TAKING THE TIME FROM YOUR BUSY SCHEDULES TO ATTEND THE FUNERAL.

SO, LET ME START BY GOING OVER SOME MINOR ADJUSTMENTS IN THE ROADWAY THAT WILL RESULT IN A COST OVERAGE OF—

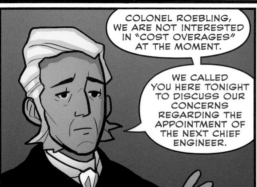

COLONEL ROEBLING, WE ARE NOT INTERESTED IN "COST OVERAGES" AT THE MOMENT.

WE CALLED YOU HERE TONIGHT TO DISCUSS OUR CONCERNS REGARDING THE APPOINTMENT OF THE NEXT CHIEF ENGINEER.

"CONCERNS"? I WAS UNDER THE IMPRESSION—

YOU'VE NEVER SUPERVISED ANYTHING OF THIS SCALE AND MAGNITUDE, MR. ROEBLING, ISN'T THAT RIGHT?

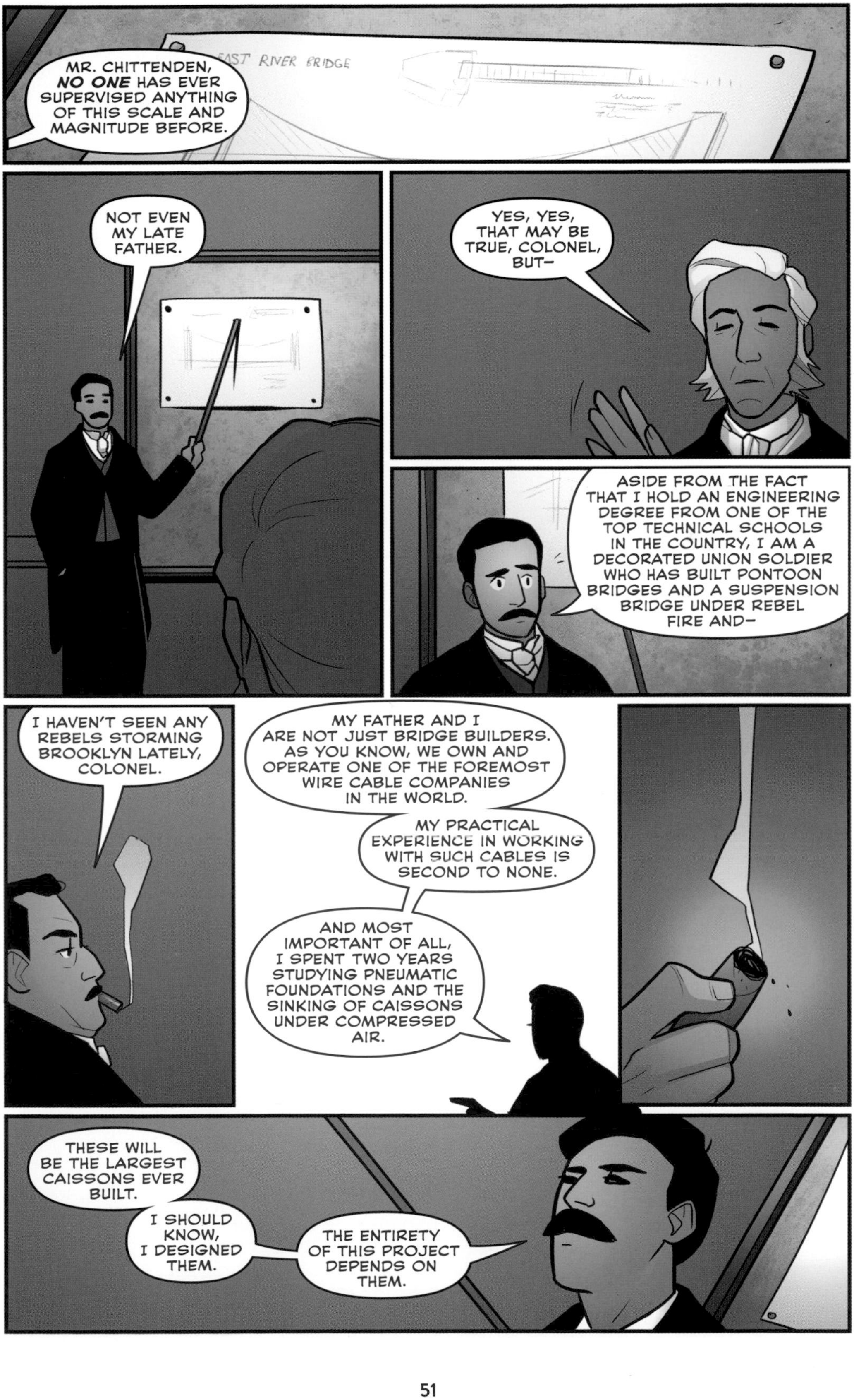
EAST RIVER BRIDGE
MR. CHITTENDEN, NO ONE HAS EVER SUPERVISED ANYTHING OF THIS SCALE AND MAGNITUDE BEFORE.
NOT EVEN MY LATE FATHER.
YES, YES, THAT MAY BE TRUE, COLONEL, BUT–
ASIDE FROM THE FACT THAT I HOLD AN ENGINEERING DEGREE FROM ONE OF THE TOP TECHNICAL SCHOOLS IN THE COUNTRY, I AM A DECORATED UNION SOLDIER WHO HAS BUILT PONTOON BRIDGES AND A SUSPENSION BRIDGE UNDER REBEL FIRE AND–
I HAVEN'T SEEN ANY REBELS STORMING BROOKLYN LATELY, COLONEL.
MY FATHER AND I ARE NOT JUST BRIDGE BUILDERS. AS YOU KNOW, WE OWN AND OPERATE ONE OF THE FOREMOST WIRE CABLE COMPANIES IN THE WORLD.
MY PRACTICAL EXPERIENCE IN WORKING WITH SUCH CABLES IS SECOND TO NONE.
AND MOST IMPORTANT OF ALL, I SPENT TWO YEARS STUDYING PNEUMATIC FOUNDATIONS AND THE SINKING OF CAISSONS UNDER COMPRESSED AIR.
THESE WILL BE THE LARGEST CAISSONS EVER BUILT.
I SHOULD KNOW, I DESIGNED THEM.
THE ENTIRETY OF THIS PROJECT DEPENDS ON THEM.

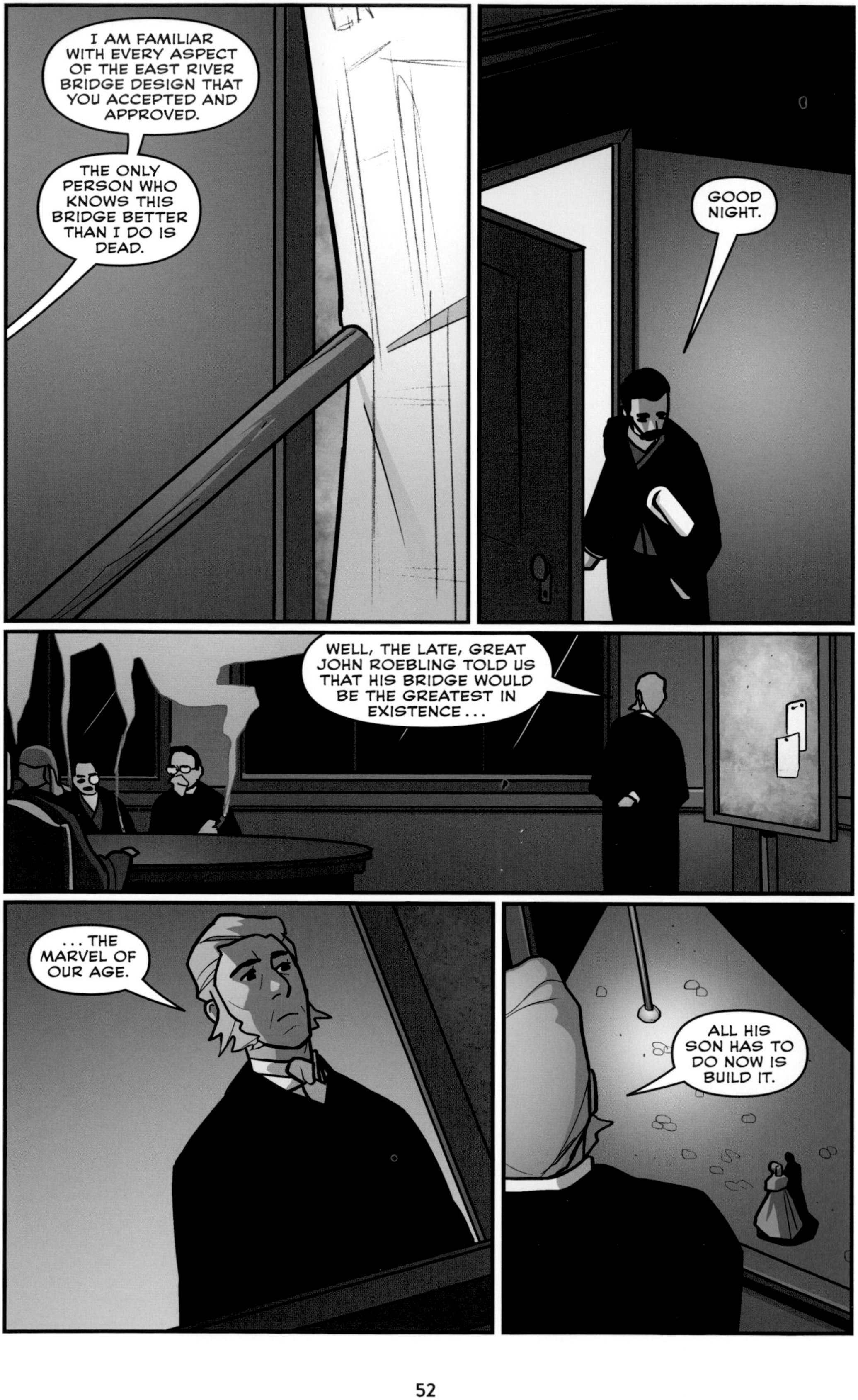
I AM FAMILIAR WITH EVERY ASPECT OF THE EAST RIVER BRIDGE DESIGN THAT YOU ACCEPTED AND APPROVED.
THE ONLY PERSON WHO KNOWS THIS BRIDGE BETTER THAN I DO IS DEAD.
GOOD NIGHT.
WELL, THE LATE, GREAT JOHN ROEBLING TOLD US THAT HIS BRIDGE WOULD BE THE GREATEST IN EXISTENCE . . .
. . . THE MARVEL OF OUR AGE.
ALL HIS SON HAS TO DO NOW IS BUILD IT.

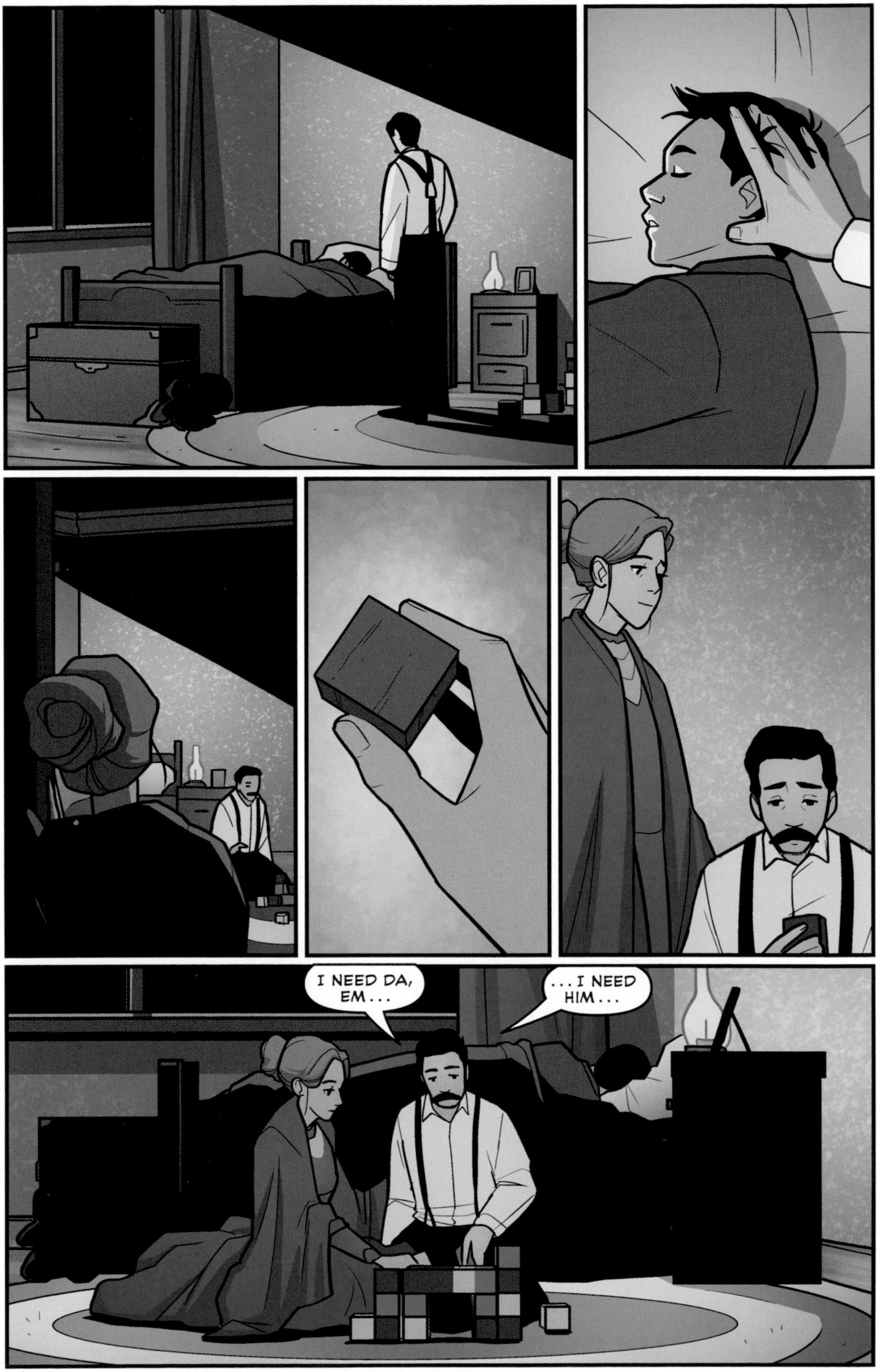
I NEED DA, EM . . .
. . . I NEED HIM . . .

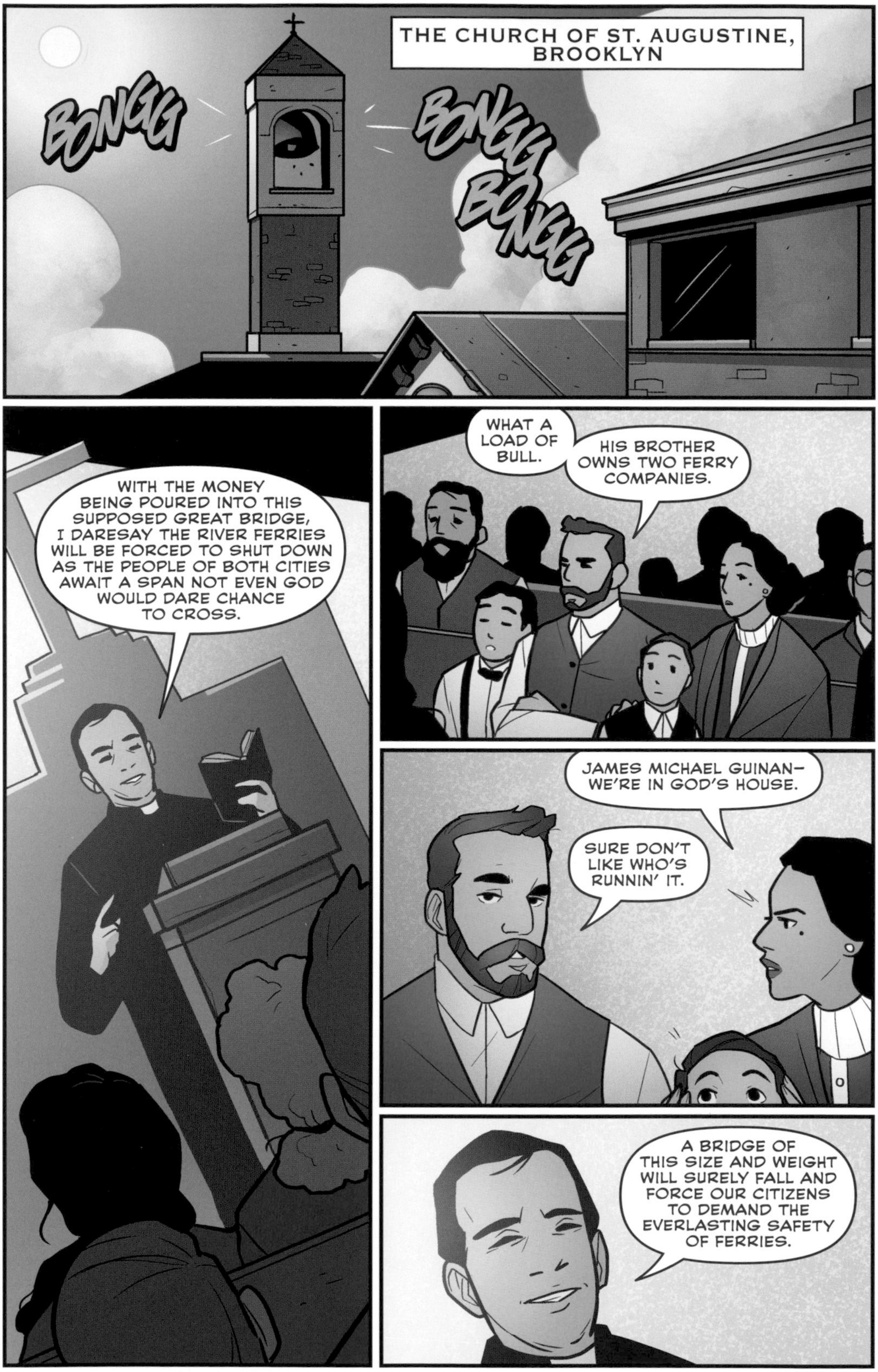
THE CHURCH OF ST. AUGUSTINE, BROOKLYN
BONGG
BONGG
BONGG
BONGG
WITH THE MONEY BEING POURED INTO THIS SUPPOSED GREAT BRIDGE, I DARESAY THE RIVER FERRIES WILL BE FORCED TO SHUT DOWN AS THE PEOPLE OF BOTH CITIES AWAIT A SPAN NOT EVEN GOD WOULD DARE CHANCE TO CROSS.
WHAT A LOAD OF BULL.
HIS BROTHER OWNS TWO FERRY COMPANIES.
JAMES MICHAEL GUINAN— WE'RE IN GOD'S HOUSE.
SURE DON'T LIKE WHO'S RUNNIN' IT.
A BRIDGE OF THIS SIZE AND WEIGHT WILL SURELY FALL AND FORCE OUR CITIZENS TO DEMAND THE EVERLASTING SAFETY OF FERRIES.

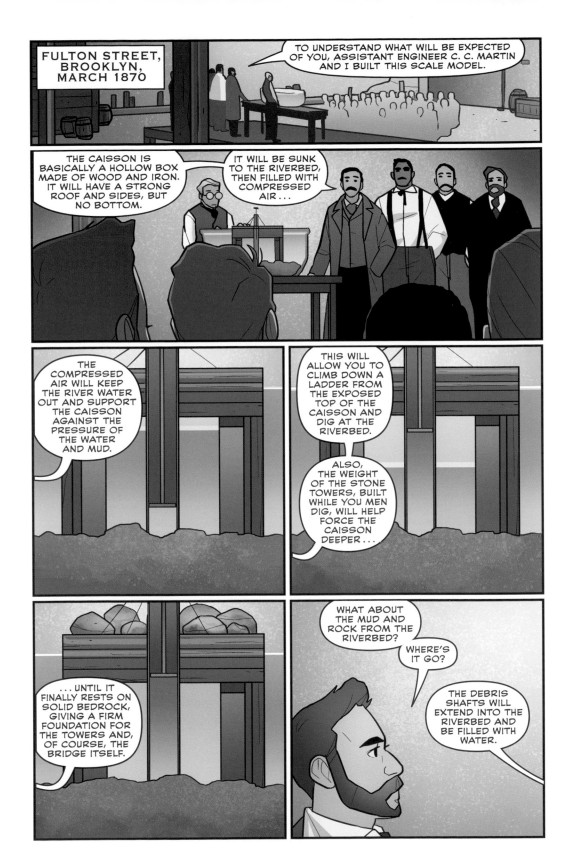

FULTON STREET, BROOKLYN, MARCH 1870

TO UNDERSTAND WHAT WILL BE EXPECTED OF YOU, ASSISTANT ENGINEER C. C. MARTIN AND I BUILT THIS SCALE MODEL.

THE CAISSON IS BASICALLY A HOLLOW BOX MADE OF WOOD AND IRON. IT WILL HAVE A STRONG ROOF AND SIDES, BUT NO BOTTOM.

IT WILL BE SUNK TO THE RIVERBED, THEN FILLED WITH COMPRESSED AIR . . .

THE COMPRESSED AIR WILL KEEP THE RIVER WATER OUT AND SUPPORT THE CAISSON AGAINST THE PRESSURE OF THE WATER AND MUD.

THIS WILL ALLOW YOU TO CLIMB DOWN A LADDER FROM THE EXPOSED TOP OF THE CAISSON AND DIG AT THE RIVERBED.

ALSO, THE WEIGHT OF THE STONE TOWERS, BUILT WHILE YOU MEN DIG, WILL HELP FORCE THE CAISSON DEEPER . . .

. . . UNTIL IT FINALLY RESTS ON SOLID BEDROCK, GIVING A FIRM FOUNDATION FOR THE TOWERS AND, OF COURSE, THE BRIDGE ITSELF.

WHAT ABOUT THE MUD AND ROCK FROM THE RIVERBED?

WHERE'S IT GO?

THE DEBRIS SHAFTS WILL EXTEND INTO THE RIVERBED AND BE FILLED WITH WATER.

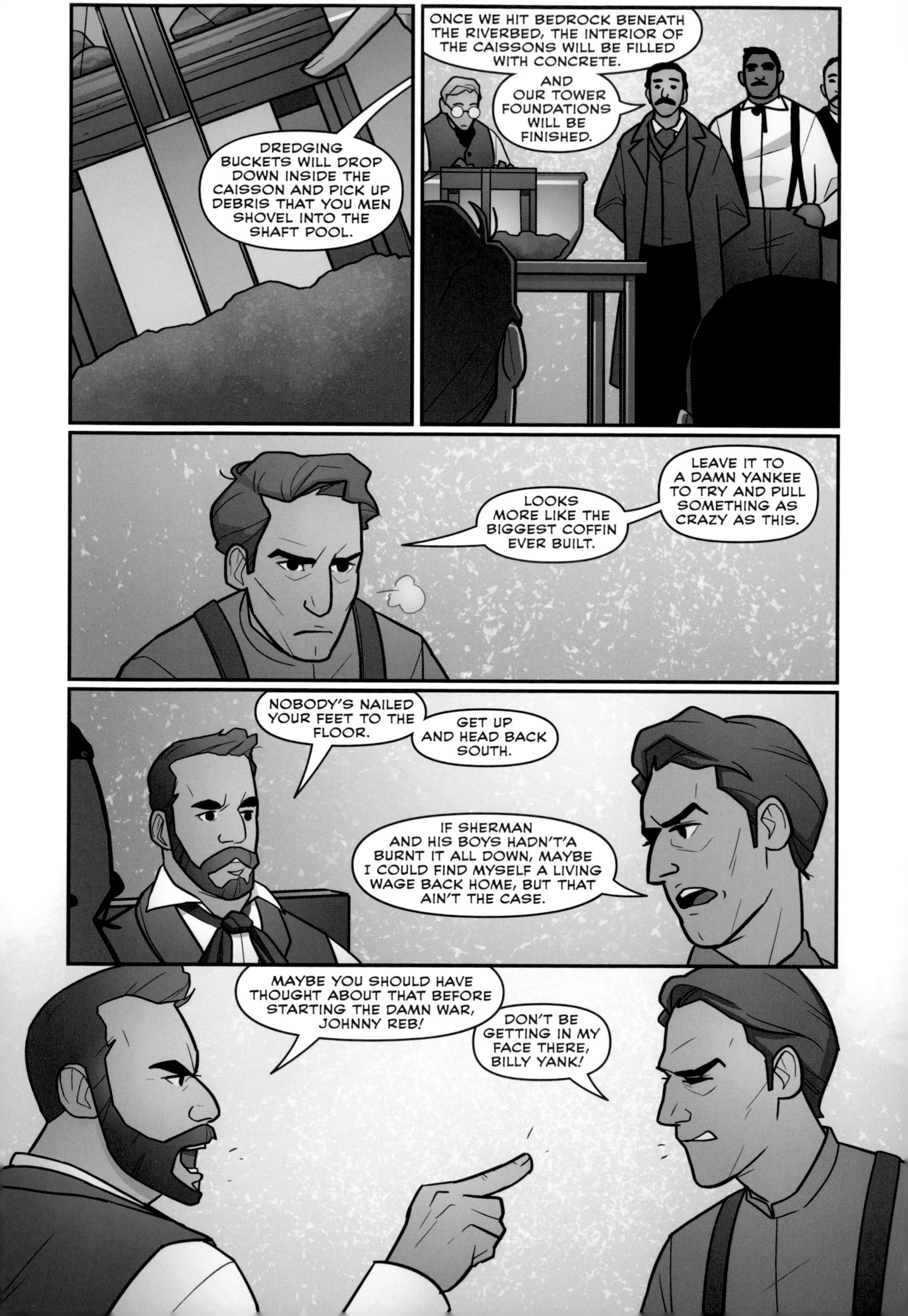
DREDGING BUCKETS WILL DROP DOWN INSIDE THE CAISSON AND PICK UP DEBRIS THAT YOU MEN SHOVEL INTO THE SHAFT POOL.
ONCE WE HIT BEDROCK BENEATH THE RIVERBED, THE INTERIOR OF THE CAISSONS WILL BE FILLED WITH CONCRETE.
AND OUR TOWER FOUNDATIONS WILL BE FINISHED.
LOOKS MORE LIKE THE BIGGEST COFFIN EVER BUILT.
LEAVE IT TO A DAMN YANKEE TO TRY AND PULL SOMETHING AS CRAZY AS THIS.
NOBODY'S NAILED YOUR FEET TO THE FLOOR.
GET UP AND HEAD BACK SOUTH.
IF SHERMAN AND HIS BOYS HADN'T'A BURNT IT ALL DOWN, MAYBE I COULD FIND MYSELF A LIVING WAGE BACK HOME, BUT THAT AIN'T THE CASE.
MAYBE YOU SHOULD HAVE THOUGHT ABOUT THAT BEFORE STARTING THE DAMN WAR, JOHNNY REB!
DON'T BE GETTING IN MY FACE THERE, BILLY YANK!

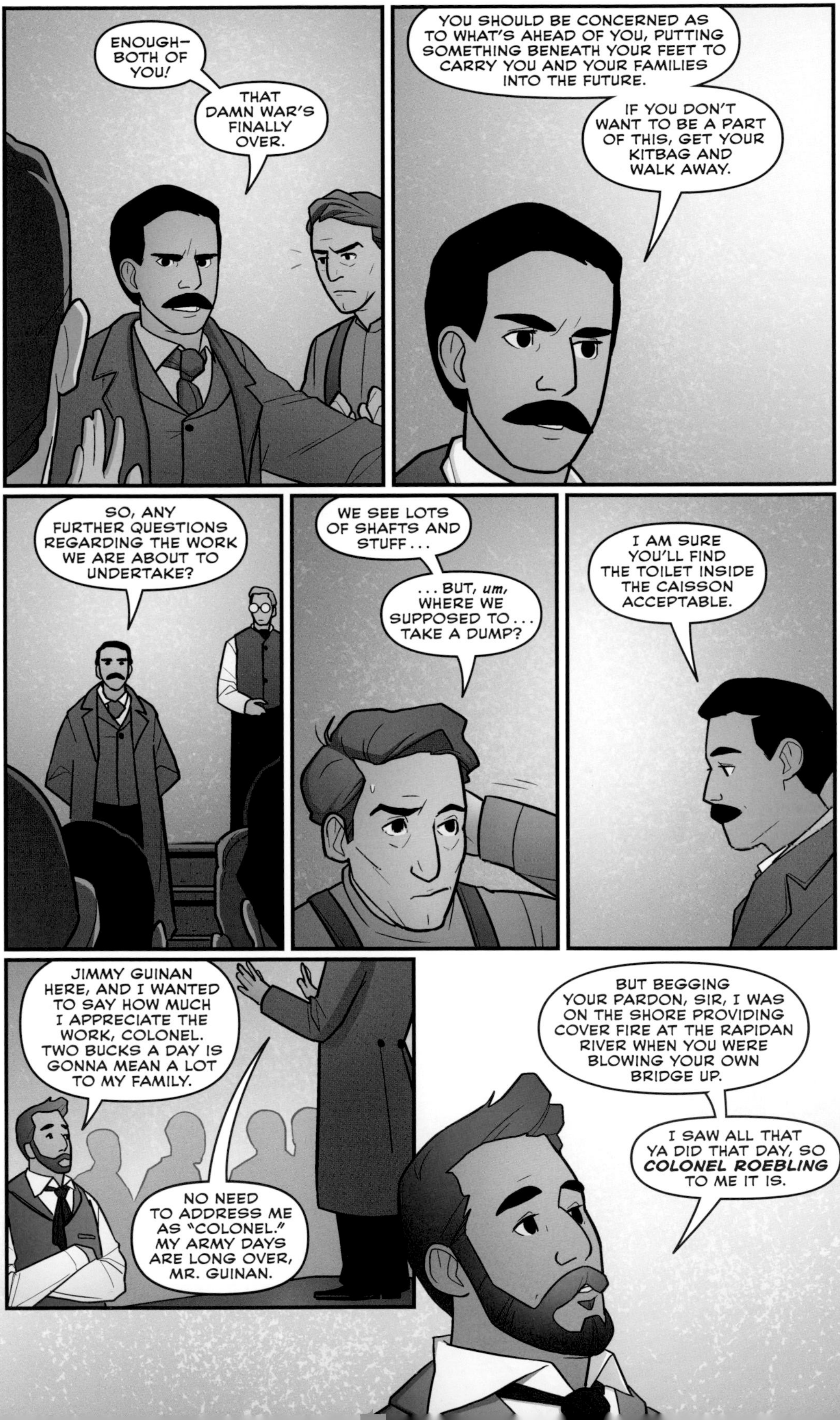
ENOUGH— BOTH OF YOU!
THAT DAMN WAR'S FINALLY OVER.
YOU SHOULD BE CONCERNED AS TO WHAT'S AHEAD OF YOU, PUTTING SOMETHING BENEATH YOUR FEET TO CARRY YOU AND YOUR FAMILIES INTO THE FUTURE.
IF YOU DON'T WANT TO BE A PART OF THIS, GET YOUR KITBAG AND WALK AWAY.
SO, ANY FURTHER QUESTIONS REGARDING THE WORK WE ARE ABOUT TO UNDERTAKE?
WE SEE LOTS OF SHAFTS AND STUFF . . .
. . . BUT, *um*, WHERE WE SUPPOSED TO . . . TAKE A DUMP?
I AM SURE YOU'LL FIND THE TOILET INSIDE THE CAISSON ACCEPTABLE.
JIMMY GUINAN HERE, AND I WANTED TO SAY HOW MUCH I APPRECIATE THE WORK, COLONEL. TWO BUCKS A DAY IS GONNA MEAN A LOT TO MY FAMILY.
NO NEED TO ADDRESS ME AS "COLONEL." MY ARMY DAYS ARE LONG OVER, MR. GUINAN.
BUT BEGGING YOUR PARDON, SIR, I WAS ON THE SHORE PROVIDING COVER FIRE AT THE RAPIDAN RIVER WHEN YOU WERE BLOWING YOUR OWN BRIDGE UP.
I SAW ALL THAT YA DID THAT DAY, SO ***COLONEL ROEBLING*** TO ME IT IS.

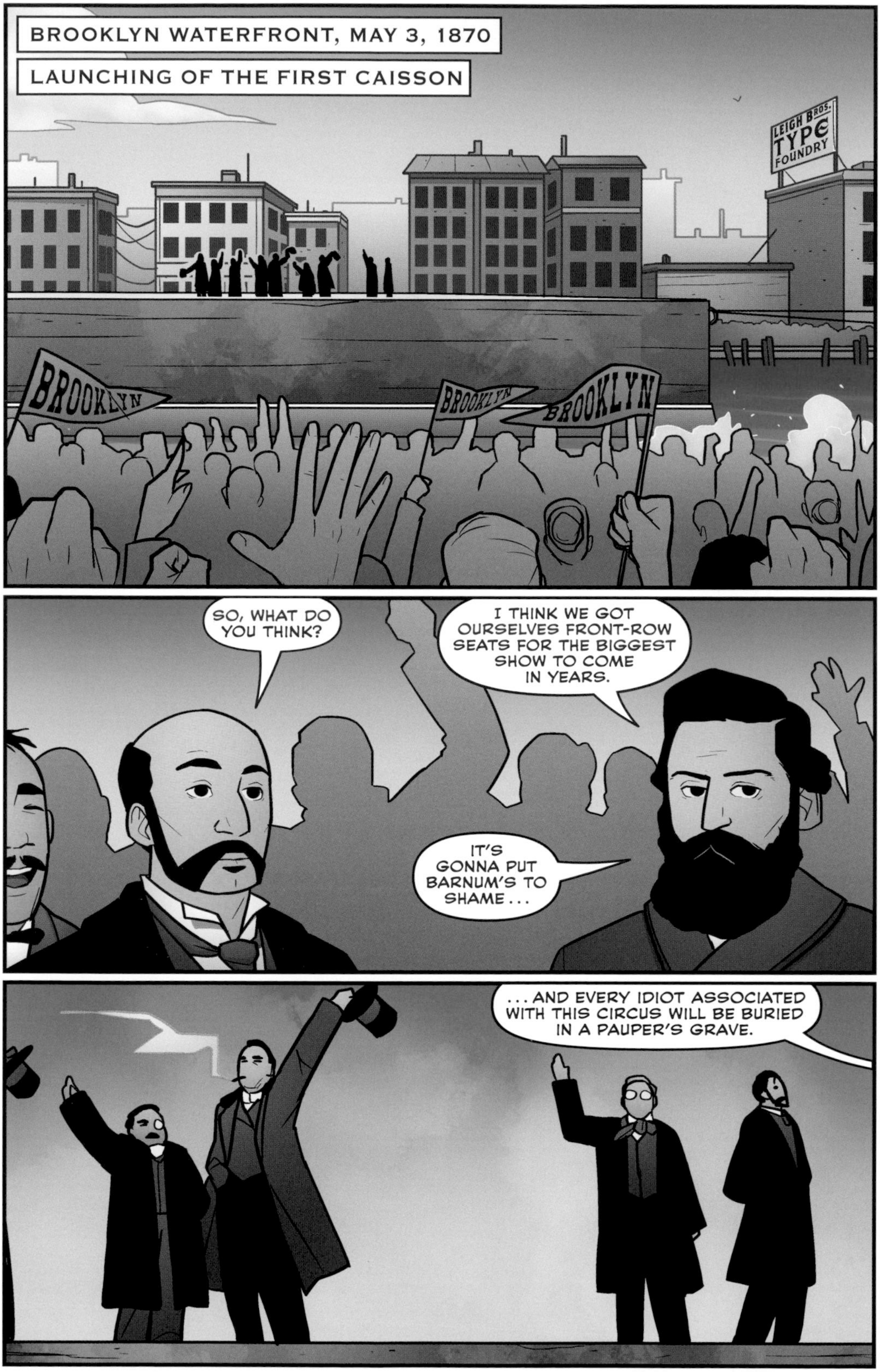
BROOKLYN WATERFRONT, MAY 3, 1870
LAUNCHING OF THE FIRST CAISSON
LEIGH BROS. TYPE FOUNDRY
BROOKLYN
BROOKLYN
BROOKLYN
SO, WHAT DO YOU THINK?
I THINK WE GOT OURSELVES FRONT-ROW SEATS FOR THE BIGGEST SHOW TO COME IN YEARS.
IT'S GONNA PUT BARNUM'S TO SHAME . . .
. . . AND EVERY IDIOT ASSOCIATED WITH THIS CIRCUS WILL BE BURIED IN A PAUPER'S GRAVE.

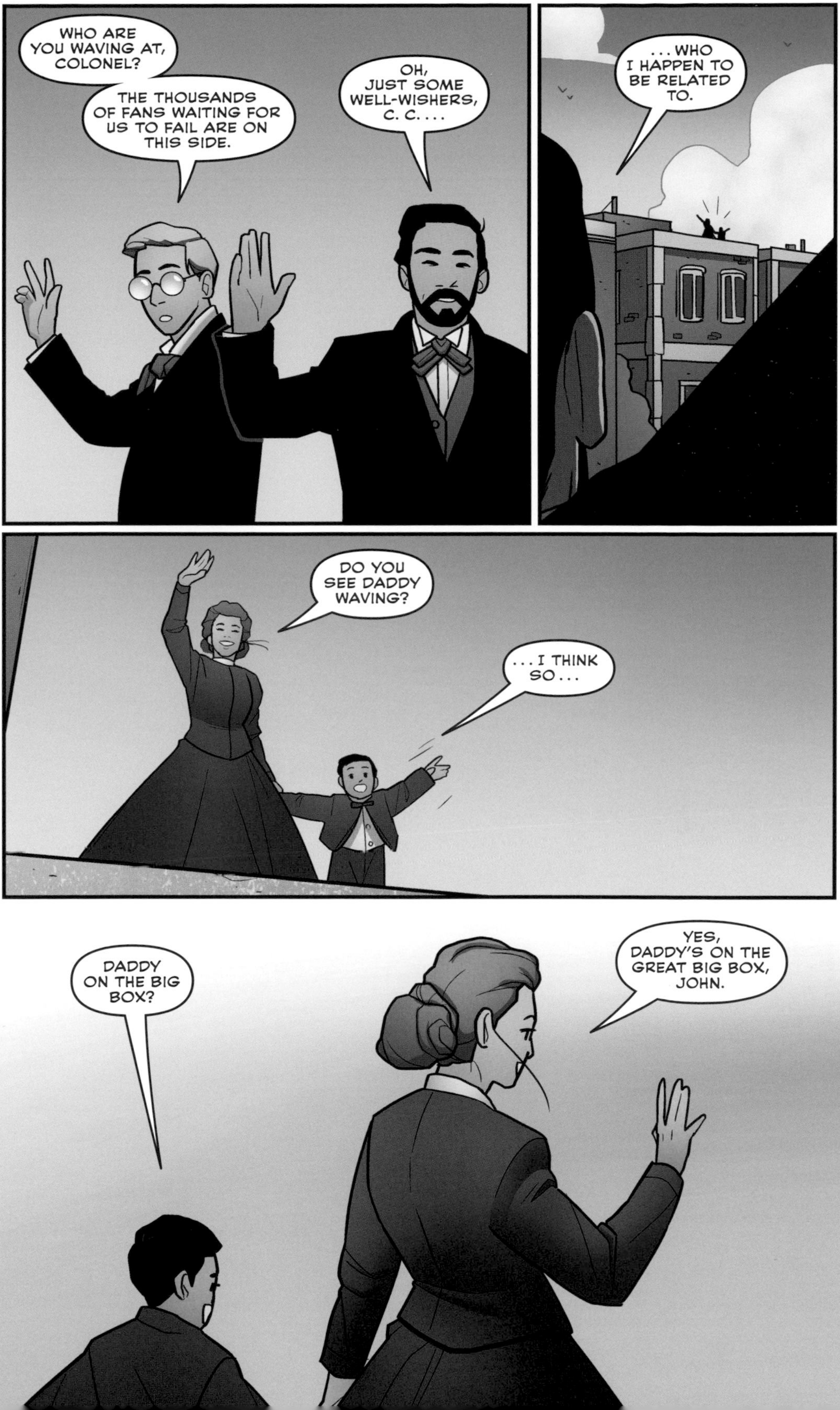
WHO ARE YOU WAVING AT, COLONEL?
THE THOUSANDS OF FANS WAITING FOR US TO FAIL ARE ON THIS SIDE.
OH, JUST SOME WELL-WISHERS, C. C. . . .
. . . WHO I HAPPEN TO BE RELATED TO.
DO YOU SEE DADDY WAVING?
. . . I THINK SO . . .
DADDY ON THE BIG BOX?
YES, DADDY'S ON THE GREAT BIG BOX, JOHN.

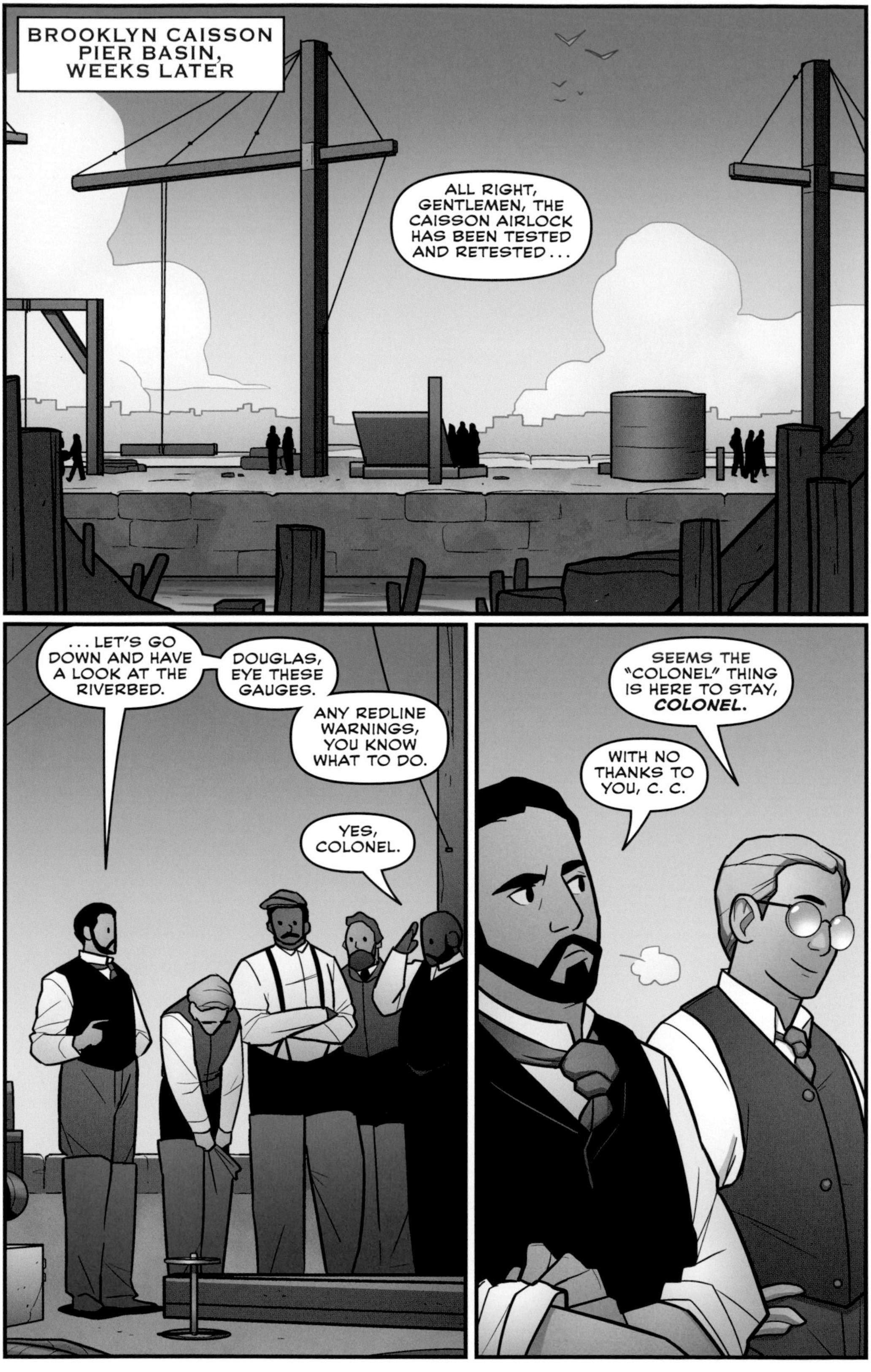
BROOKLYN CAISSON PIER BASIN, WEEKS LATER
ALL RIGHT, GENTLEMEN, THE CAISSON AIRLOCK HAS BEEN TESTED AND RETESTED . . .
. . . LET'S GO DOWN AND HAVE A LOOK AT THE RIVERBED.
DOUGLAS, EYE THESE GAUGES.
ANY REDLINE WARNINGS, YOU KNOW WHAT TO DO.
YES, COLONEL.
SEEMS THE "COLONEL" THING IS HERE TO STAY, **COLONEL.**
WITH NO THANKS TO YOU, C. C.

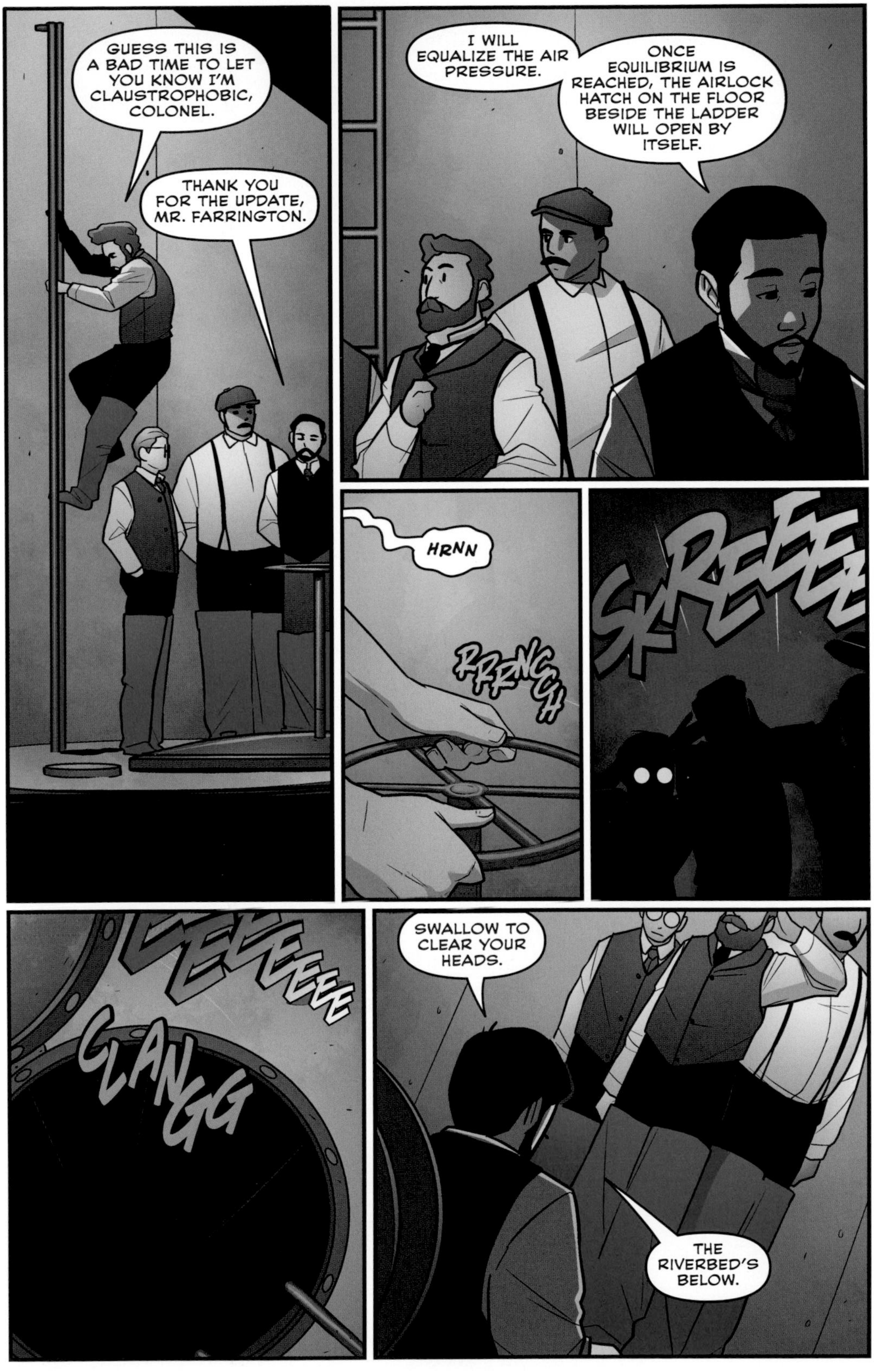
GUESS THIS IS A BAD TIME TO LET YOU KNOW I'M CLAUSTROPHOBIC, COLONEL.
THANK YOU FOR THE UPDATE, MR. FARRINGTON.
I WILL EQUALIZE THE AIR PRESSURE.
ONCE EQUILIBRIUM IS REACHED, THE AIRLOCK HATCH ON THE FLOOR BESIDE THE LADDER WILL OPEN BY ITSELF.
HRNN
RRRNGCH
SKREEEE
EEEEEEE
CLANGG
SWALLOW TO CLEAR YOUR HEADS.
THE RIVERBED'S BELOW.

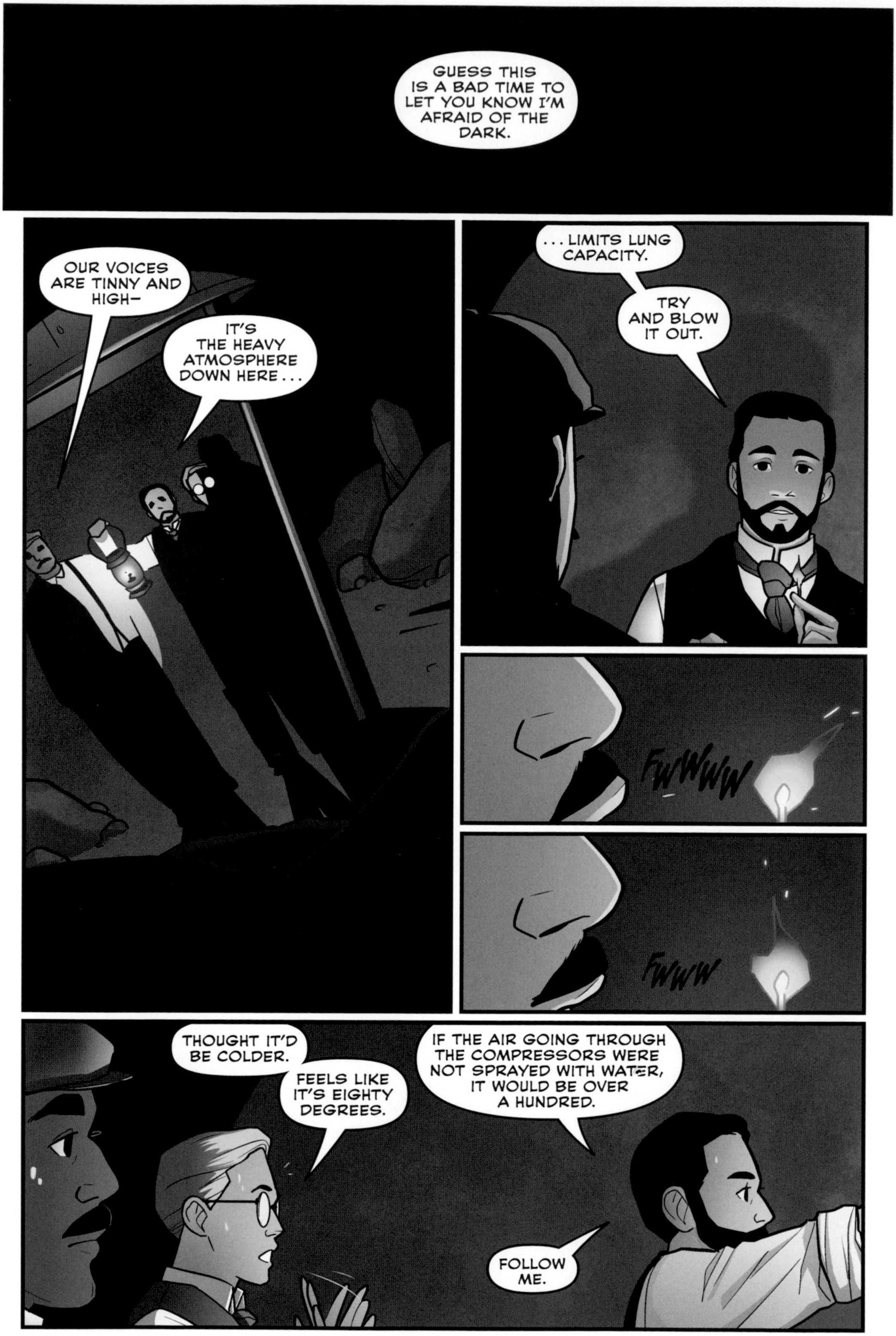
GUESS THIS IS A BAD TIME TO LET YOU KNOW I'M AFRAID OF THE DARK.
OUR VOICES ARE TINNY AND HIGH—
IT'S THE HEAVY ATMOSPHERE DOWN HERE . . .
. . . LIMITS LUNG CAPACITY.
TRY AND BLOW IT OUT.
FWWWW
FWWW
THOUGHT IT'D BE COLDER.
FEELS LIKE IT'S EIGHTY DEGREES.
IF THE AIR GOING THROUGH THE COMPRESSORS WERE NOT SPRAYED WITH WATER, IT WOULD BE OVER A HUNDRED.
FOLLOW ME.

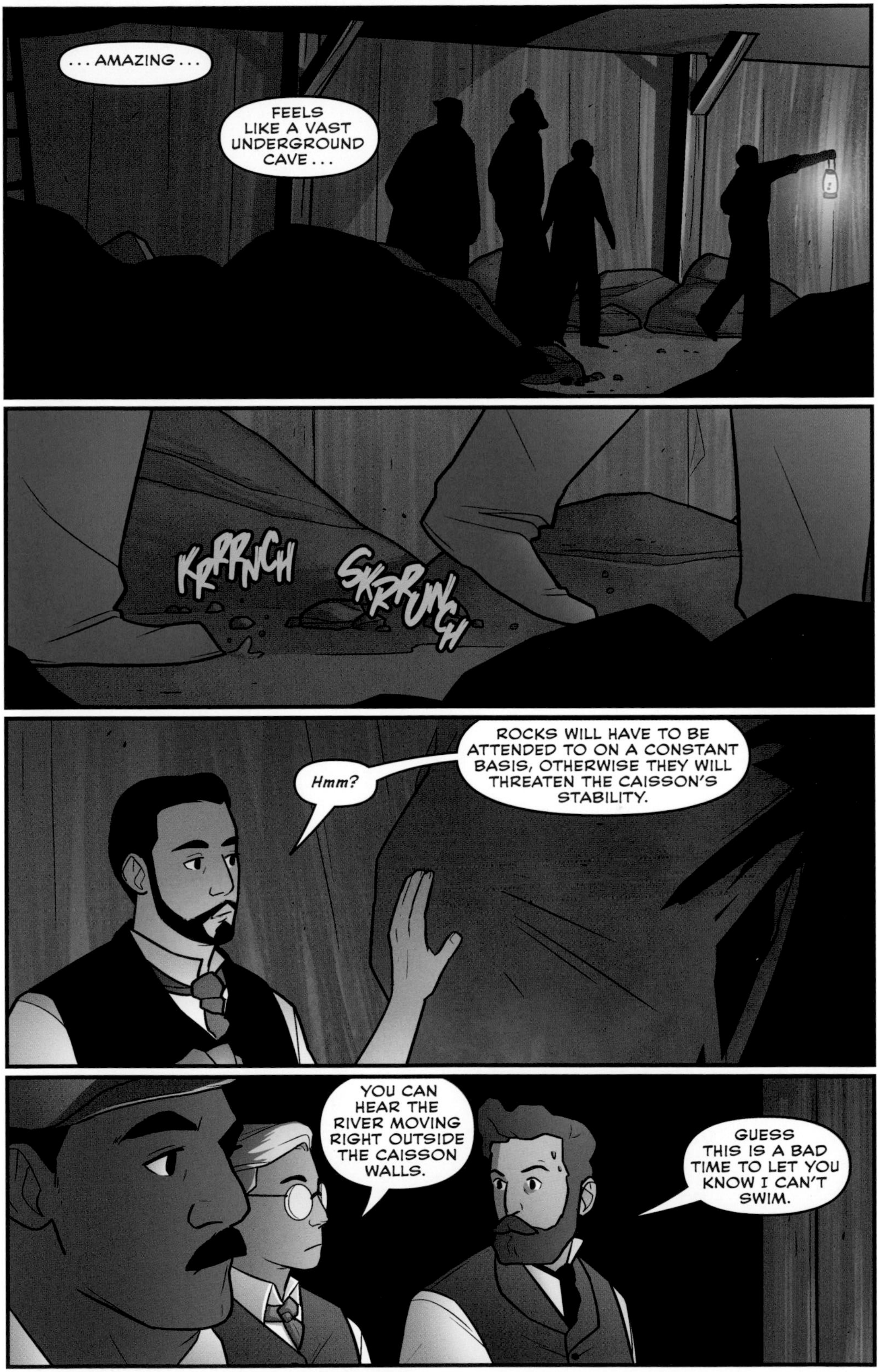
. . . AMAZING . . .
FEELS LIKE A VAST UNDERGROUND CAVE . . .
KRRRNCH
SKRRUNCH
ROCKS WILL HAVE TO BE ATTENDED TO ON A CONSTANT BASIS, OTHERWISE THEY WILL THREATEN THE CAISSON'S STABILITY.
Hmm?
YOU CAN HEAR THE RIVER MOVING RIGHT OUTSIDE THE CAISSON WALLS.
GUESS THIS IS A BAD TIME TO LET YOU KNOW I CAN'T SWIM.

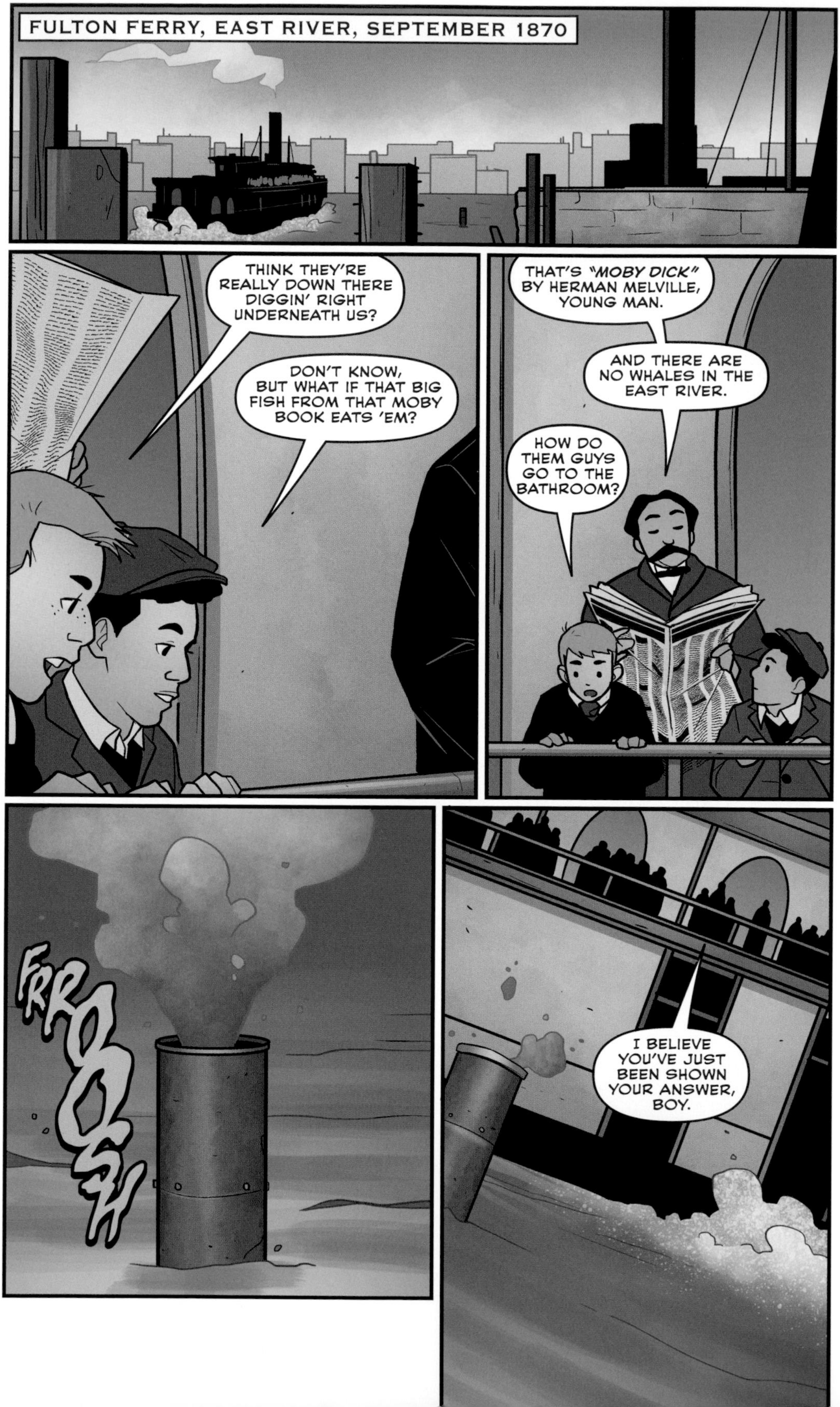
FULTON FERRY, EAST RIVER, SEPTEMBER 1870
THINK THEY'RE REALLY DOWN THERE DIGGIN' RIGHT UNDERNEATH US?
DON'T KNOW, BUT WHAT IF THAT BIG FISH FROM THAT MOBY BOOK EATS 'EM?
THAT'S "MOBY DICK" BY HERMAN MELVILLE, YOUNG MAN.
AND THERE ARE NO WHALES IN THE EAST RIVER.
HOW DO THEM GUYS GO TO THE BATHROOM?
FRROOSH
I BELIEVE YOU'VE JUST BEEN SHOWN YOUR ANSWER, BOY.

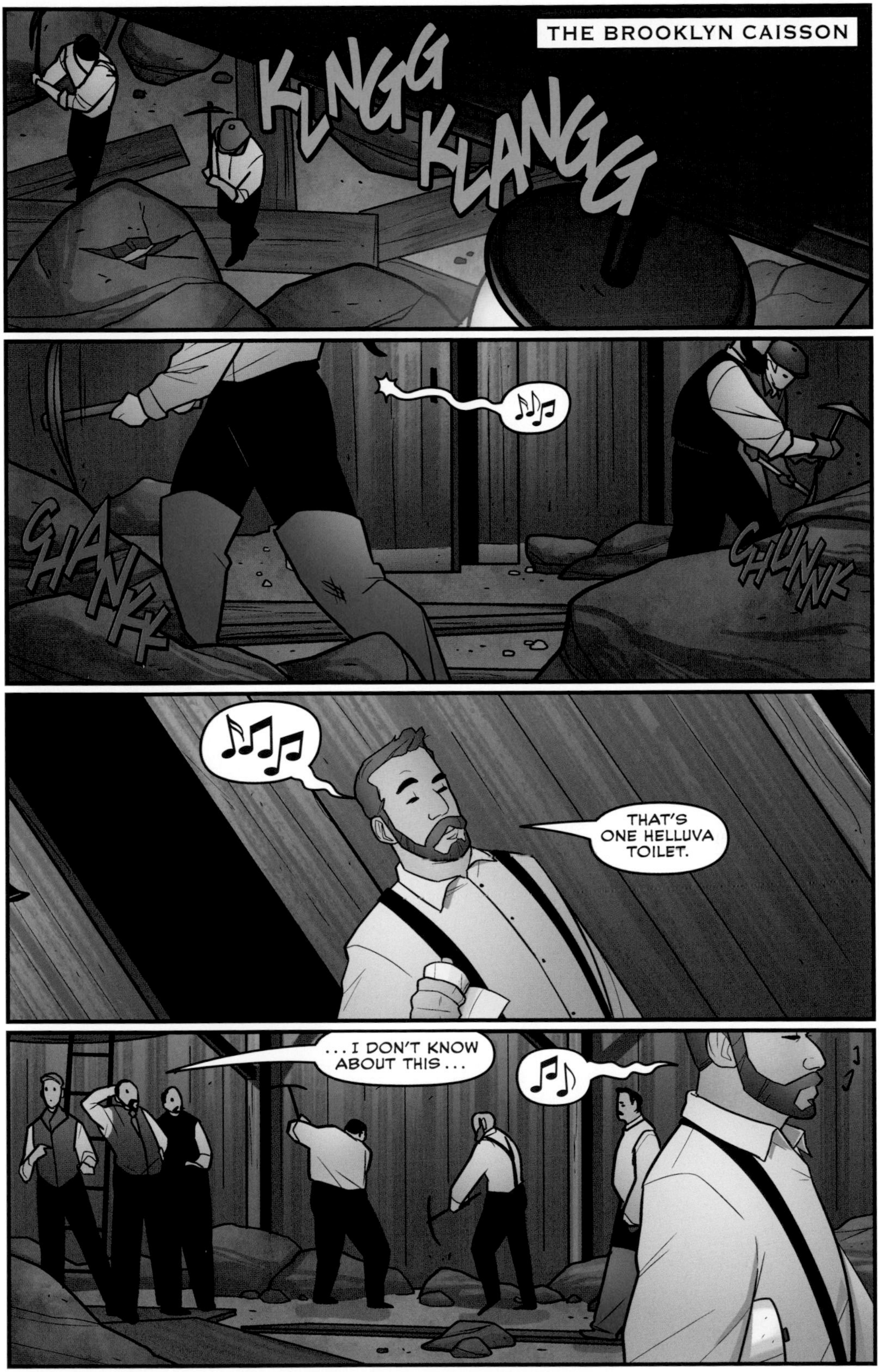
THE BROOKLYN CAISSON
KLNGG KLANGG
CHANKK
CHUNNK
THAT'S ONE HELLUVA TOILET.
. . . I DON'T KNOW ABOUT THIS . . .

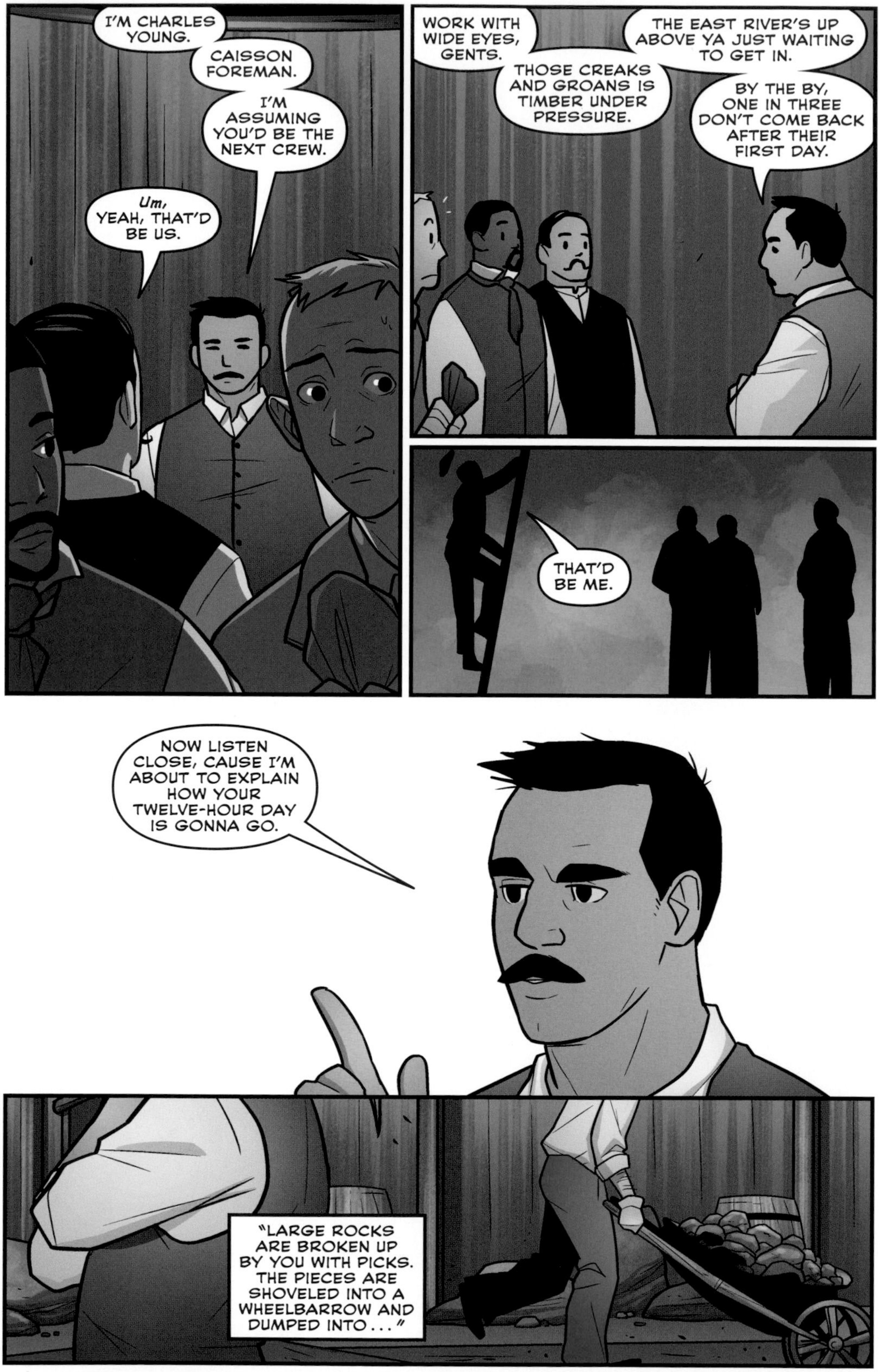
I'M CHARLES YOUNG.
CAISSON FOREMAN.
I'M ASSUMING YOU'D BE THE NEXT CREW.
Um, YEAH, THAT'D BE US.
WORK WITH WIDE EYES, GENTS.
THE EAST RIVER'S UP ABOVE YA JUST WAITING TO GET IN.
THOSE CREAKS AND GROANS IS TIMBER UNDER PRESSURE.
BY THE BY, ONE IN THREE DON'T COME BACK AFTER THEIR FIRST DAY.
THAT'D BE ME.
NOW LISTEN CLOSE, CAUSE I'M ABOUT TO EXPLAIN HOW YOUR TWELVE-HOUR DAY IS GONNA GO.
"LARGE ROCKS ARE BROKEN UP BY YOU WITH PICKS. THE PIECES ARE SHOVELED INTO A WHEELBARROW AND DUMPED INTO . . ."

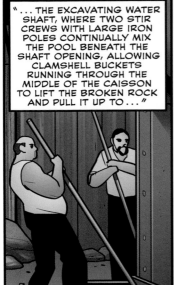

"... THE EXCAVATING WATER SHAFT, WHERE TWO STIR CREWS WITH LARGE IRON POLES CONTINUALLY MIX THE POOL BENEATH THE SHAFT OPENING, ALLOWING CLAMSHELL BUCKETS RUNNING THROUGH THE MIDDLE OF THE CAISSON TO LIFT THE BROKEN ROCK AND PULL IT UP TO ..."

"... THE CAISSON SURFACE, WHERE THE ROCKS ARE LOADED BY TOPSIDE CREWS INTO WHEELBARROWS AND CARTED AWAY."

YOU HOGS UNDERSTAND?

YES, SIR!

KRAK

GOT US ANOTHER BOULDER, C. C.!

YOU GOT IT, C. C.

GET THREE OTHER HOGS AND SPLIT IT UP, GUINAN.

CHANK

KRAK

GOT ANOTHER SPLIT BOULDER TO GET UP.

GIMME A SECOND ...

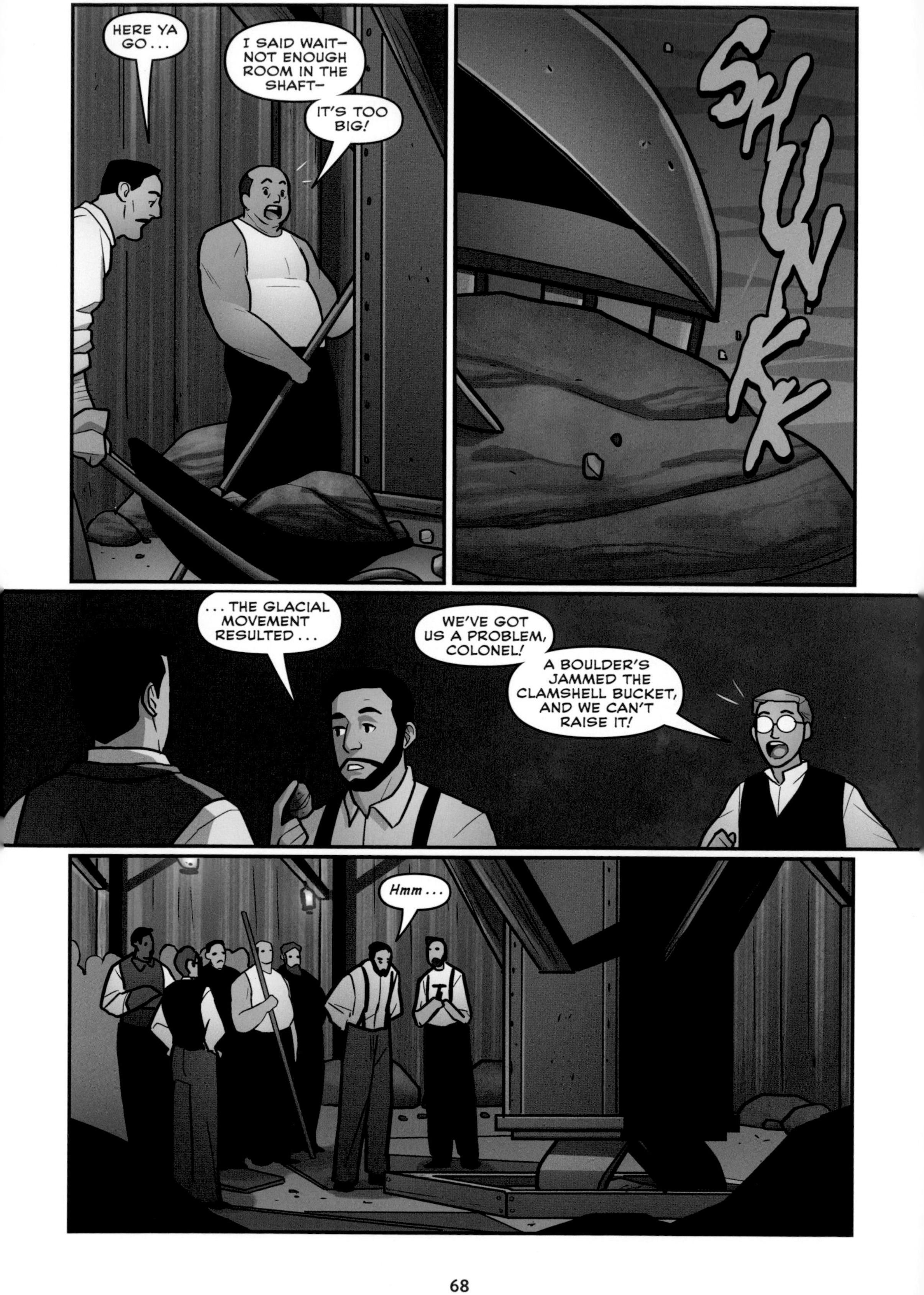
HERE YA GO . . .
I SAID WAIT— NOT ENOUGH ROOM IN THE SHAFT—
IT'S TOO BIG!
SHUNKK
. . . THE GLACIAL MOVEMENT RESULTED . . .
WE'VE GOT US A PROBLEM, COLONEL!
A BOULDER'S JAMMED THE CLAMSHELL BUCKET, AND WE CAN'T RAISE IT!
Hmm . . .

HAMMER AND CHISEL, C. C.

TIME ME. I'D LIKE TO TEST A THEORY.

THIS ISN'T SOMETHING YOU SHOULD BE DOING, COLONEL. I CAN GET—

ACTUALLY, IT IS, C. C.

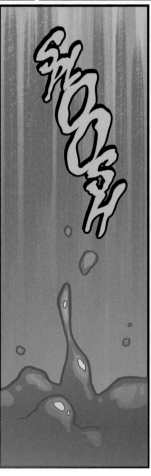

SWOOSH

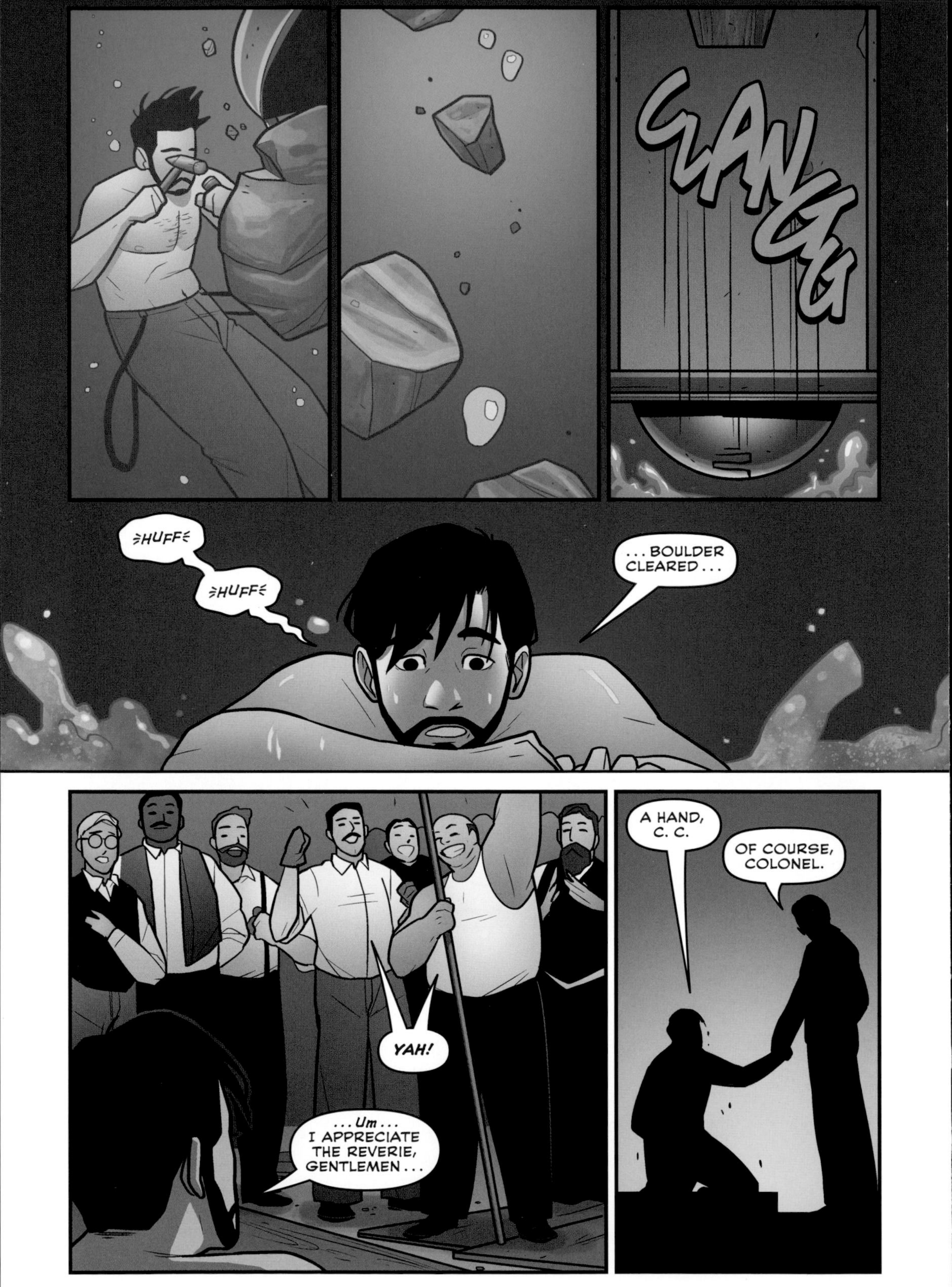

CLANGG
≶HUFF≶
≶HUFF≶
... BOULDER CLEARED ...
A HAND, C. C.
OF COURSE, COLONEL.
YAH!
... Um ... I APPRECIATE THE REVERIE, GENTLEMEN ...

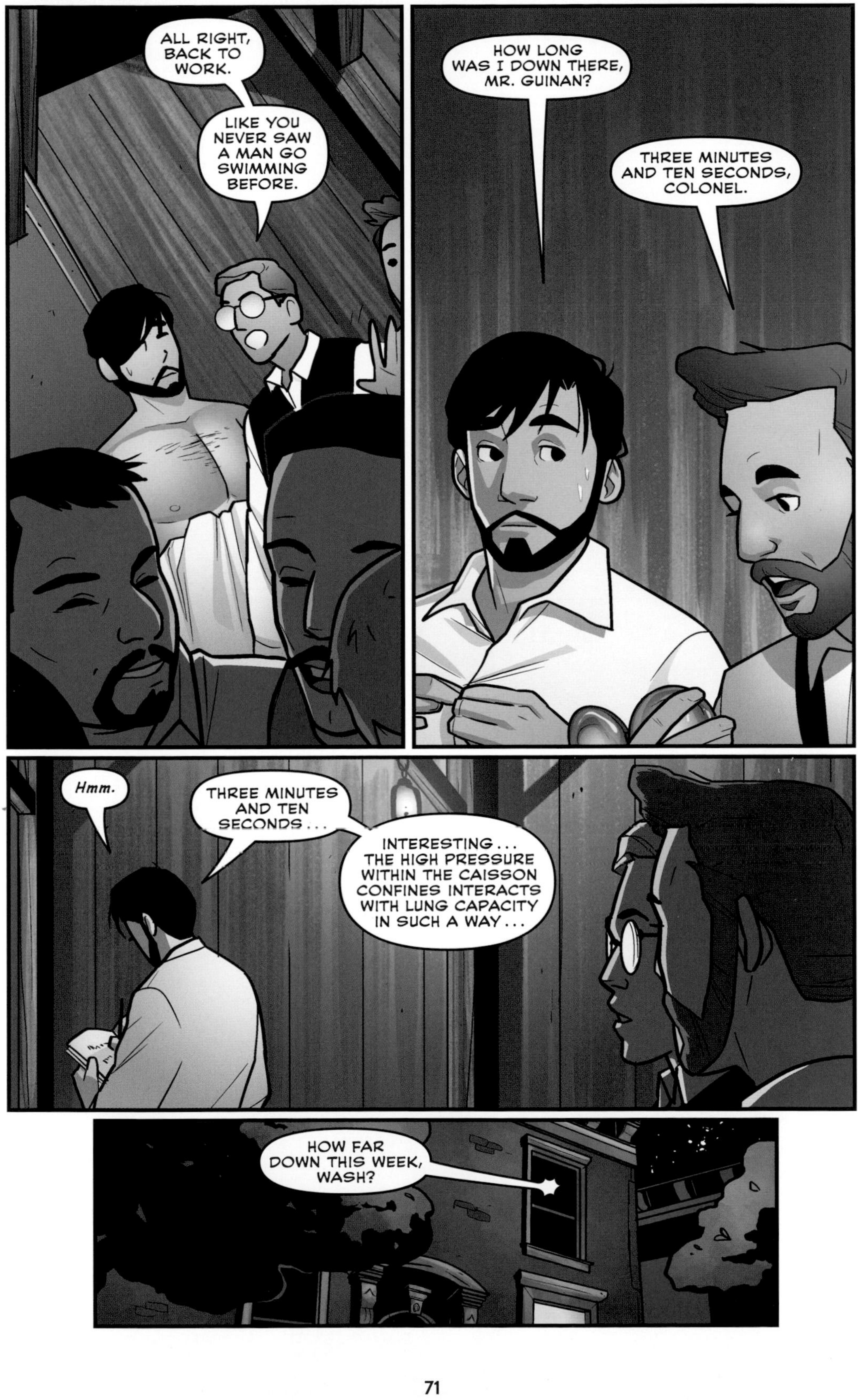
ALL RIGHT, BACK TO WORK.
LIKE YOU NEVER SAW A MAN GO SWIMMING BEFORE.
HOW LONG WAS I DOWN THERE, MR. GUINAN?
THREE MINUTES AND TEN SECONDS, COLONEL.
Hmm.
THREE MINUTES AND TEN SECONDS . . .
INTERESTING . . . THE HIGH PRESSURE WITHIN THE CAISSON CONFINES INTERACTS WITH LUNG CAPACITY IN SUCH A WAY . . .
HOW FAR DOWN THIS WEEK, WASH?

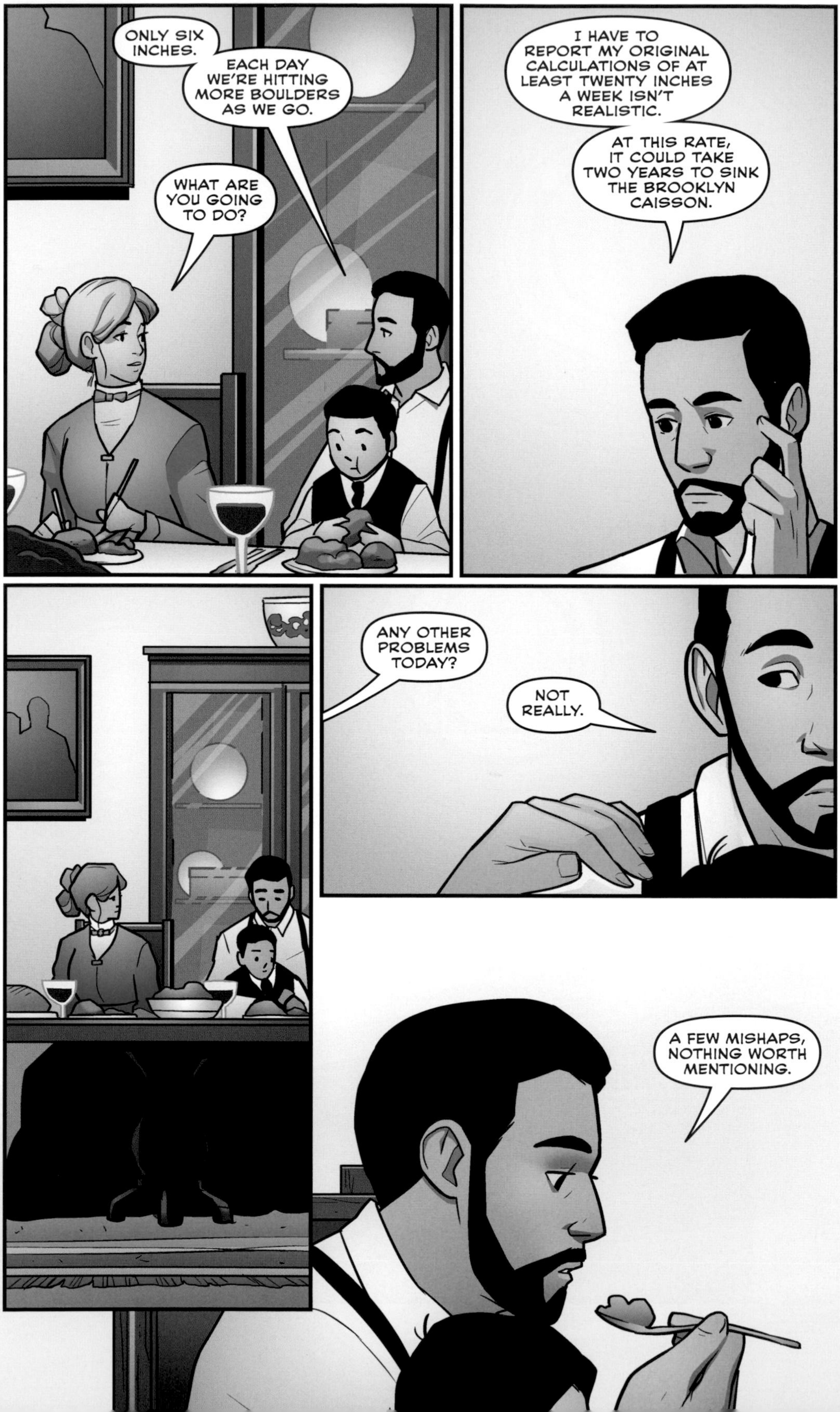
ONLY SIX INCHES.
EACH DAY WE'RE HITTING MORE BOULDERS AS WE GO.
WHAT ARE YOU GOING TO DO?
I HAVE TO REPORT MY ORIGINAL CALCULATIONS OF AT LEAST TWENTY INCHES A WEEK ISN'T REALISTIC.
AT THIS RATE, IT COULD TAKE TWO YEARS TO SINK THE BROOKLYN CAISSON.
ANY OTHER PROBLEMS TODAY?
NOT REALLY.
A FEW MISHAPS, NOTHING WORTH MENTIONING.

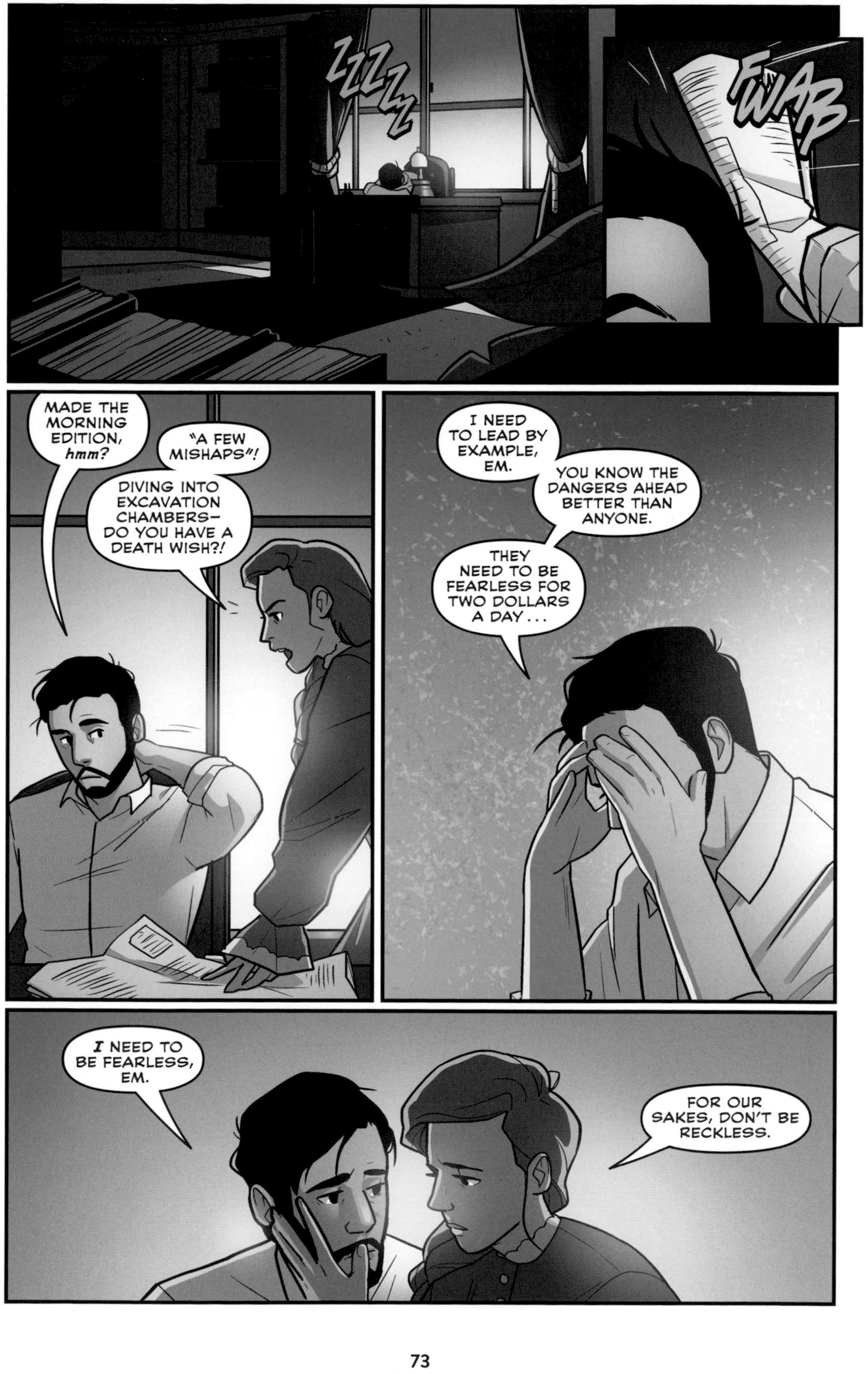
ZZZZZ
FWAP
MADE THE MORNING EDITION, *hmm?*
"A FEW MISHAPS"!
DIVING INTO EXCAVATION CHAMBERS— DO YOU HAVE A DEATH WISH?!
I NEED TO LEAD BY EXAMPLE, EM.
YOU KNOW THE DANGERS AHEAD BETTER THAN ANYONE.
THEY NEED TO BE FEARLESS FOR TWO DOLLARS A DAY . . .
I NEED TO BE FEARLESS, EM.
FOR OUR SAKES, DON'T BE RECKLESS.

THE BROOKLYN CAISSON

THE THOUGHT OF BEING UNDER THE RIVER WHILE DAILY LIFE CONTINUES ABOVE IS QUITE IMPRESSIVE, MR. MARTIN . . .

OUR SCHEDULED PUBLICITY TIME HAS ARRIVED, COLONEL.

FINE.

HAVE ANOTHER IRON SUPPORT BEAM PLACED AT THIS JUNCTURE, C. C.

HELLO. THOMAS KINSELLA, *BROOKLYN EAGLE*. HONOR TO MEET YOU.

EVERY BROOKLYNITE IS INTERESTED IN BRIDGING THE EAST RIVER, AND WE'RE SURE THAT NOT ONLY WILL IT BE SAFE, BUT BEAUTIFUL TO BOOT.

THANKS FOR YOUR KIND WORDS. I ENJOYED YOUR ARTICLE ON THE CAISSON LAUNCHING.

THE MORE PEOPLE KNOW ABOUT THE IMMENSITY AND TENACITY BEHIND THIS GREAT PUBLIC WORK, THE EASIER IT WILL BE TO QUIET THE PEOPLE OF LIMITED VISION, COLONEL ROEBLING.

"COLONEL"? I THOUGHT YOU HAD YOUR FOOT CRUSHED AND DIED BACK IN '69?

OBVIOUSLY NOT. THAT WAS MY FATHER, JOHN ROEBLING.

BUT YOU'RE BUILDING HIS BRIDGE. HE DID DESIGN IT, YES?

MAYBE A FEATURE ARTICLE IN MY PAPER CAN HELP CLEAR UP WHICH ROEBLING IS—

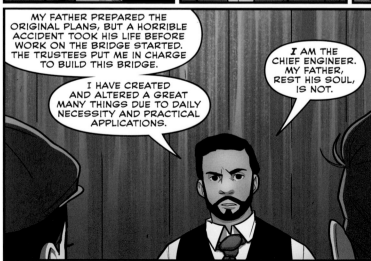

MY FATHER PREPARED THE ORIGINAL PLANS, BUT A HORRIBLE ACCIDENT TOOK HIS LIFE BEFORE WORK ON THE BRIDGE STARTED. THE TRUSTEES PUT ME IN CHARGE TO BUILD THIS BRIDGE.

I HAVE CREATED AND ALTERED A GREAT MANY THINGS DUE TO DAILY NECESSITY AND PRACTICAL APPLICATIONS.

I AM THE CHIEF ENGINEER. MY FATHER, REST HIS SOUL, IS NOT.

RRRRNGGH

Hmm?

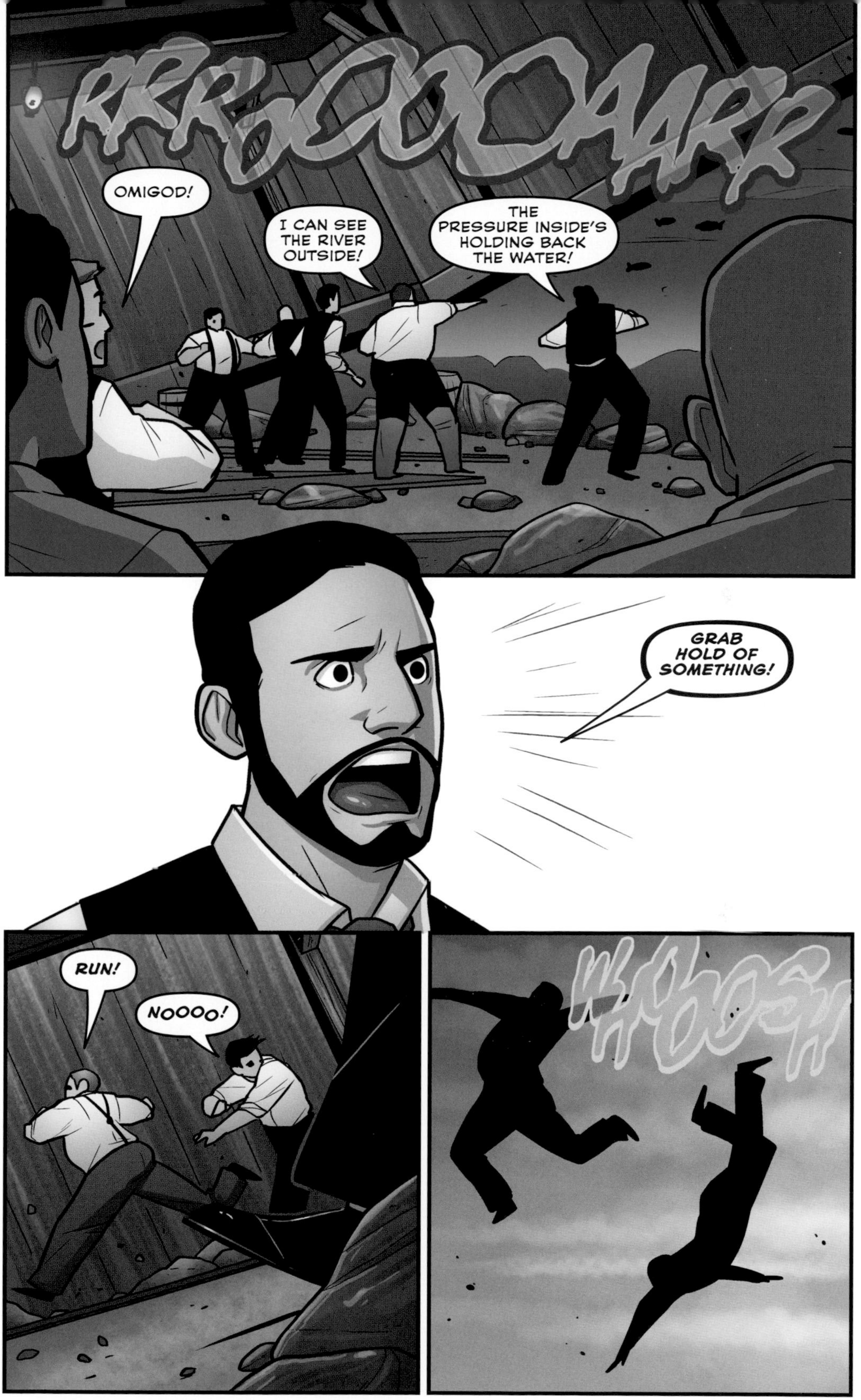
OMIGOD!
I CAN SEE THE RIVER OUTSIDE!
THE PRESSURE INSIDE'S HOLDING BACK THE WATER!
GRAB HOLD OF SOMETHING!
RUN!
NOOOO!
WHOOSH

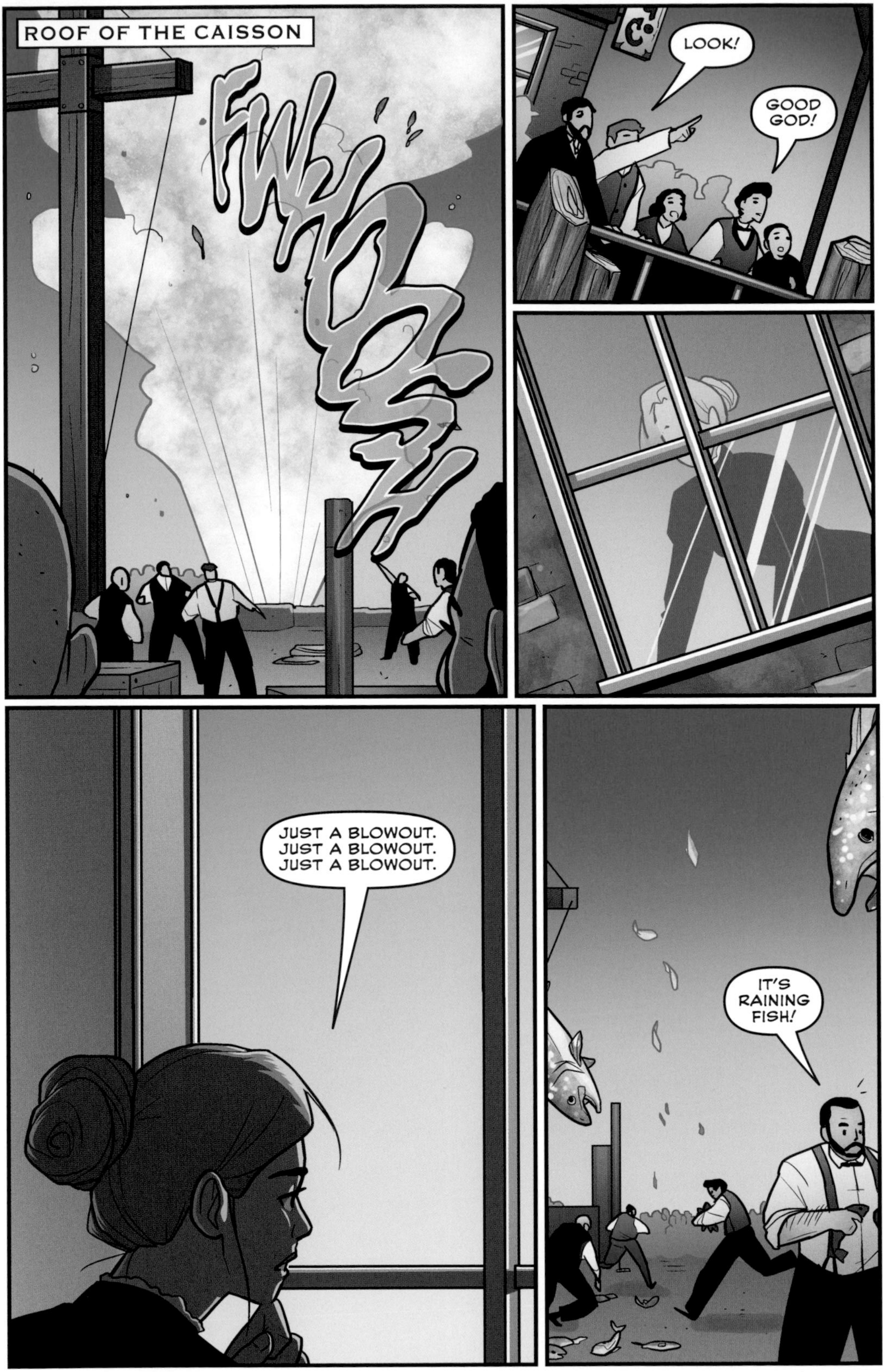
ROOF OF THE CAISSON
FWHOOSH
LOOK!
GOOD GOD!
JUST A BLOWOUT. JUST A BLOWOUT. JUST A BLOWOUT.
IT'S RAINING FISH!

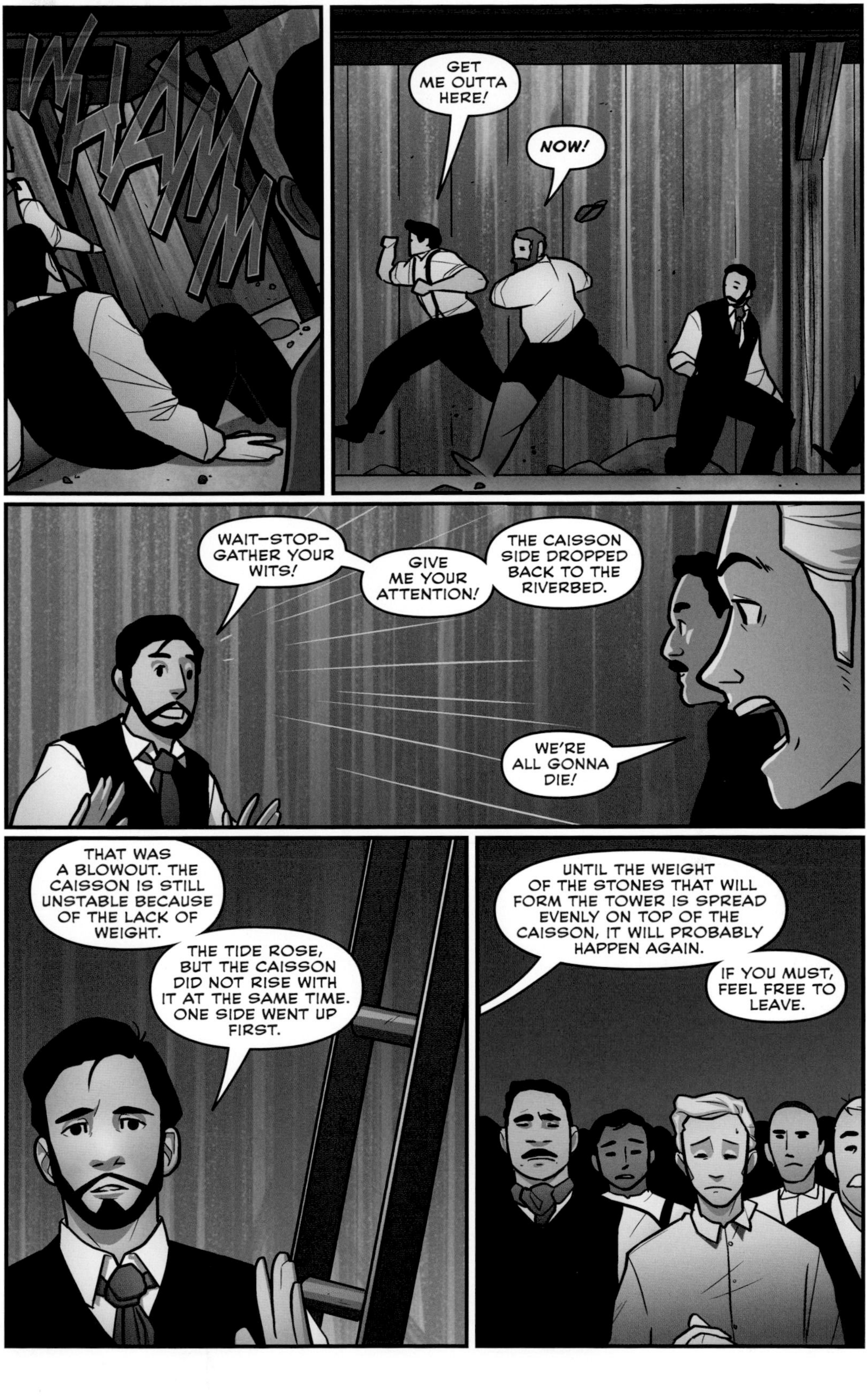
WHAM
GET ME OUTTA HERE!
NOW!
WAIT—STOP—GATHER YOUR WITS!
GIVE ME YOUR ATTENTION!
THE CAISSON SIDE DROPPED BACK TO THE RIVERBED.
WE'RE ALL GONNA DIE!
THAT WAS A BLOWOUT. THE CAISSON IS STILL UNSTABLE BECAUSE OF THE LACK OF WEIGHT.
THE TIDE ROSE, BUT THE CAISSON DID NOT RISE WITH IT AT THE SAME TIME. ONE SIDE WENT UP FIRST.
UNTIL THE WEIGHT OF THE STONES THAT WILL FORM THE TOWER IS SPREAD EVENLY ON TOP OF THE CAISSON, IT WILL PROBABLY HAPPEN AGAIN.
IF YOU MUST, FEEL FREE TO LEAVE.

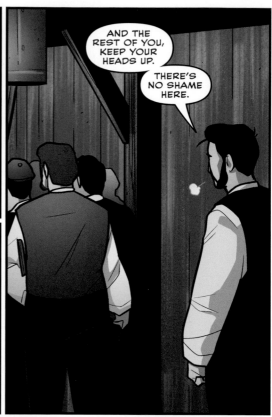

AND THE REST OF YOU, KEEP YOUR HEADS UP.

THERE'S NO SHAME HERE.

MY NERVES, COLONEL... I CAN'T TAKE IT...

NO SHAME, BOY. I UNDERSTAND.

MR. ROEBLING...

...I'M READY TO FINISH THE TOUR.

IT SEEMS THE *BROOKLYN EAGLE* IS GOING TO HAVE AN EXCLUSIVE, MR. KINSELLA.

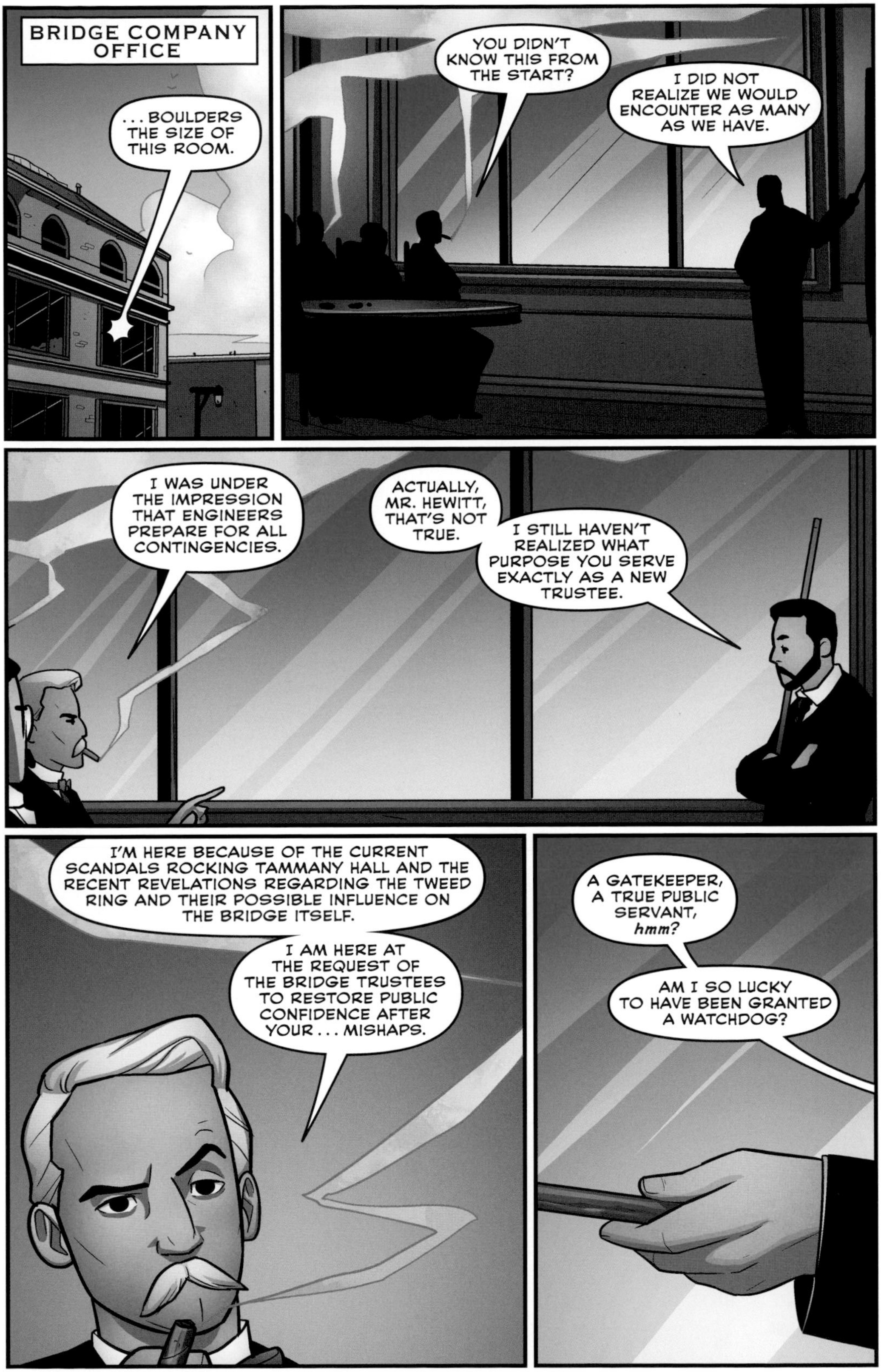
BRIDGE COMPANY OFFICE
. . . BOULDERS THE SIZE OF THIS ROOM.
YOU DIDN'T KNOW THIS FROM THE START?
I DID NOT REALIZE WE WOULD ENCOUNTER AS MANY AS WE HAVE.
I WAS UNDER THE IMPRESSION THAT ENGINEERS PREPARE FOR ALL CONTINGENCIES.
ACTUALLY, MR. HEWITT, THAT'S NOT TRUE.
I STILL HAVEN'T REALIZED WHAT PURPOSE YOU SERVE EXACTLY AS A NEW TRUSTEE.
I'M HERE BECAUSE OF THE CURRENT SCANDALS ROCKING TAMMANY HALL AND THE RECENT REVELATIONS REGARDING THE TWEED RING AND THEIR POSSIBLE INFLUENCE ON THE BRIDGE ITSELF.
I AM HERE AT THE REQUEST OF THE BRIDGE TRUSTEES TO RESTORE PUBLIC CONFIDENCE AFTER YOUR . . . MISHAPS.
A GATEKEEPER, A TRUE PUBLIC SERVANT, *hmm?*
AM I SO LUCKY TO HAVE BEEN GRANTED A WATCHDOG?

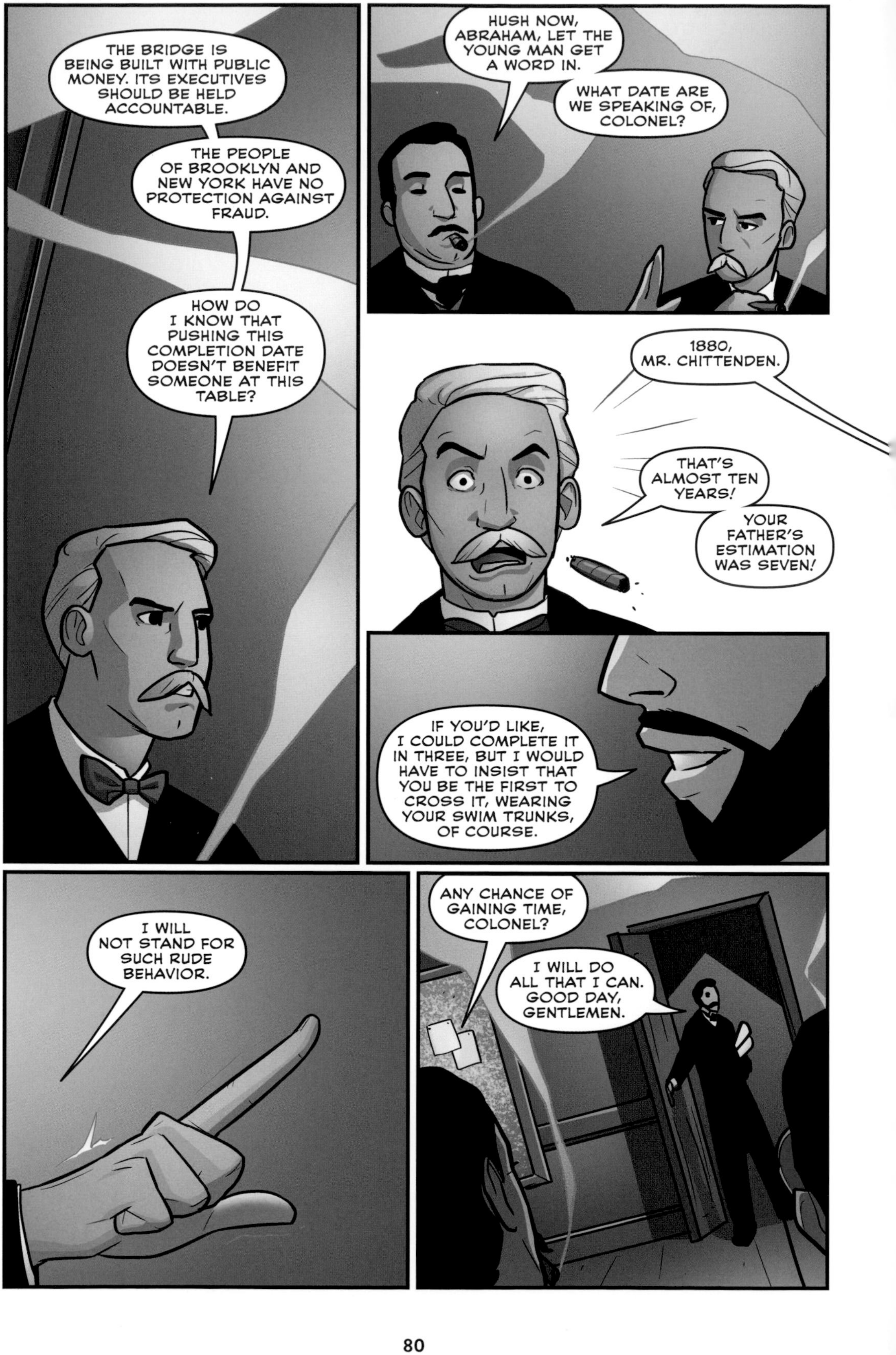
THE BRIDGE IS BEING BUILT WITH PUBLIC MONEY. ITS EXECUTIVES SHOULD BE HELD ACCOUNTABLE.
THE PEOPLE OF BROOKLYN AND NEW YORK HAVE NO PROTECTION AGAINST FRAUD.
HOW DO I KNOW THAT PUSHING THIS COMPLETION DATE DOESN'T BENEFIT SOMEONE AT THIS TABLE?
HUSH NOW, ABRAHAM, LET THE YOUNG MAN GET A WORD IN.
WHAT DATE ARE WE SPEAKING OF, COLONEL?
1880, MR. CHITTENDEN.
THAT'S ALMOST TEN YEARS!
YOUR FATHER'S ESTIMATION WAS SEVEN!
IF YOU'D LIKE, I COULD COMPLETE IT IN THREE, BUT I WOULD HAVE TO INSIST THAT YOU BE THE FIRST TO CROSS IT, WEARING YOUR SWIM TRUNKS, OF COURSE.
I WILL NOT STAND FOR SUCH RUDE BEHAVIOR.
ANY CHANCE OF GAINING TIME, COLONEL?
I WILL DO ALL THAT I CAN. GOOD DAY, GENTLEMEN.

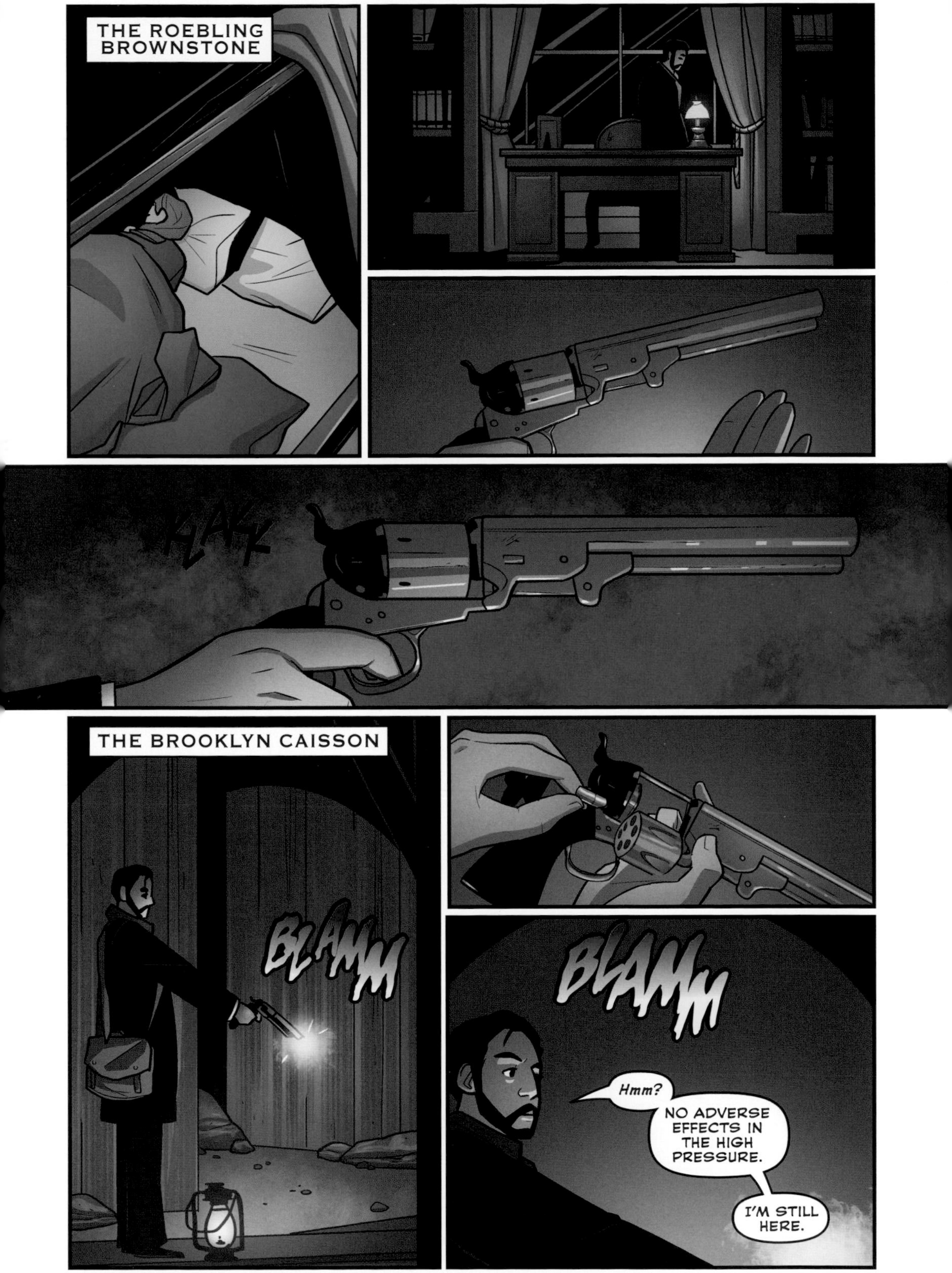
THE ROEBLING BROWNSTONE
KLAK
THE BROOKLYN CAISSON
BLAMM
BLAMM
Hmm?
NO ADVERSE EFFECTS IN THE HIGH PRESSURE.
I'M STILL HERE.

...IT'S GOING TO TAKE SOMETHING A LITTLE STRONGER...

...TO DESTROY THESE BOULDERS...

KABOOM

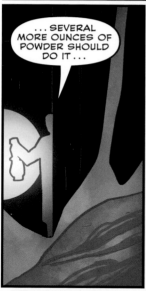

...SEVERAL MORE OUNCES OF POWDER SHOULD DO IT...

Fssss

KABOOM

BROADWAY, NEW YORK CITY

DECEMBER 1, 1870

EXTRA! EXTRA! GET YER PAPER HERE!

BROOKLYN CAISSON DOWN ANOTHER EIGHTEEN INCHES THIS WEEK!

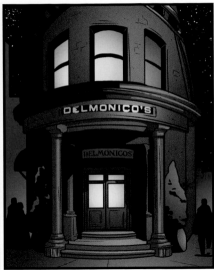

THANK YOU FOR FORCING THIS SPLENDID ISOLATION, EM.

THE PLEASURE IS ALL MINE.

YOUR TURN ON THE PUZZLE, COLONEL ROEBLING.

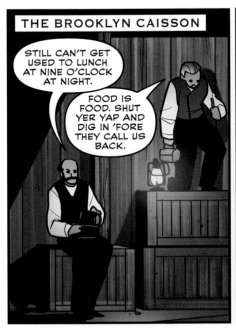

THE BROOKLYN CAISSON

STILL CAN'T GET USED TO LUNCH AT NINE O'CLOCK AT NIGHT.

FOOD IS FOOD. SHUT YER YAP AND DIG IN 'FORE THEY CALL US BACK.

DAMMIT.

MUD ON MY APPLES AGAIN.

I GOTTA GET A NEW FOOD BOX.

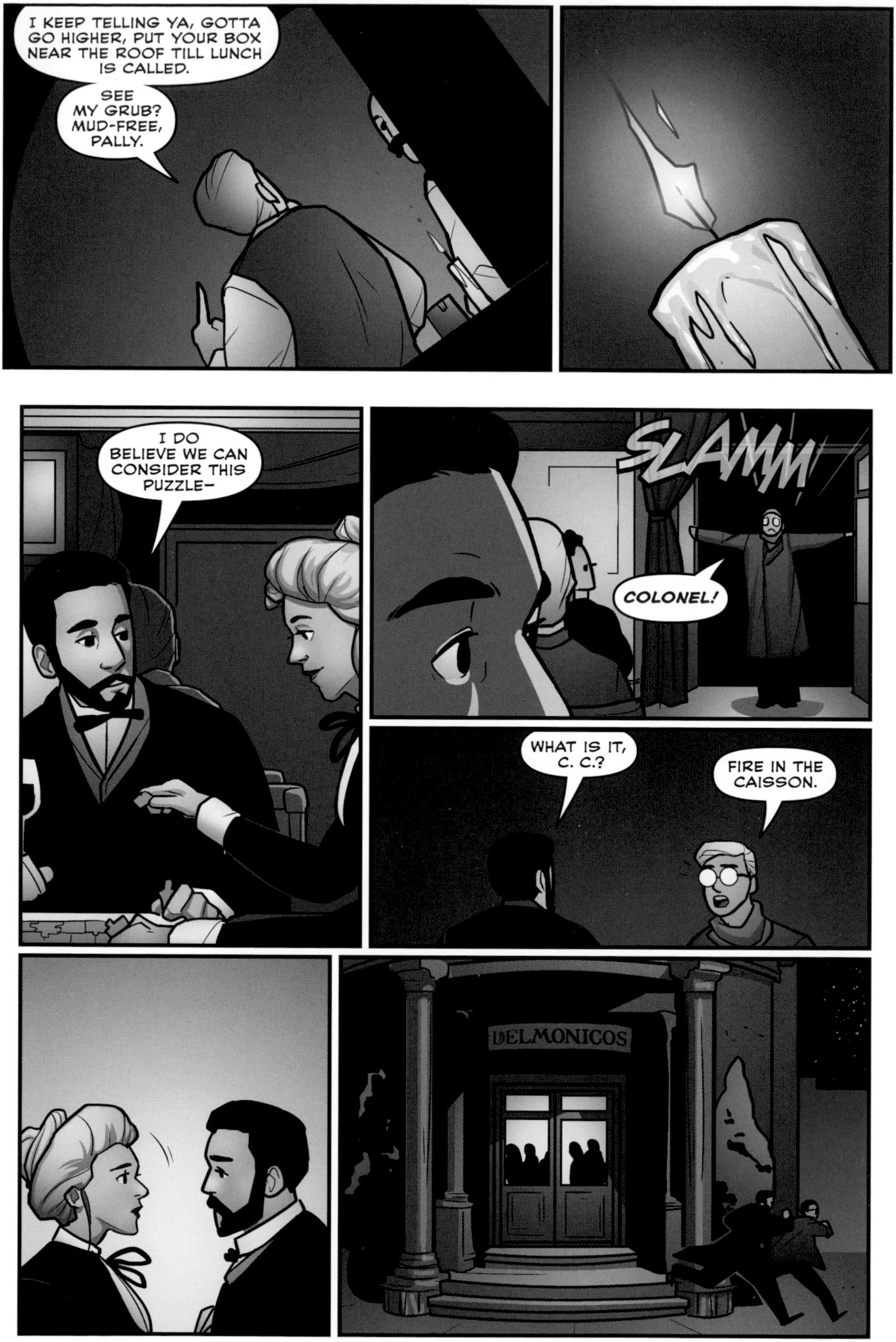
I KEEP TELLING YA, GOTTA GO HIGHER, PUT YOUR BOX NEAR THE ROOF TILL LUNCH IS CALLED.
SEE MY GRUB? MUD-FREE, PALLY.
I DO BELIEVE WE CAN CONSIDER THIS PUZZLE–
SLAMM
COLONEL!
WHAT IS IT, C. C.?
FIRE IN THE CAISSON.
DELMONICOS

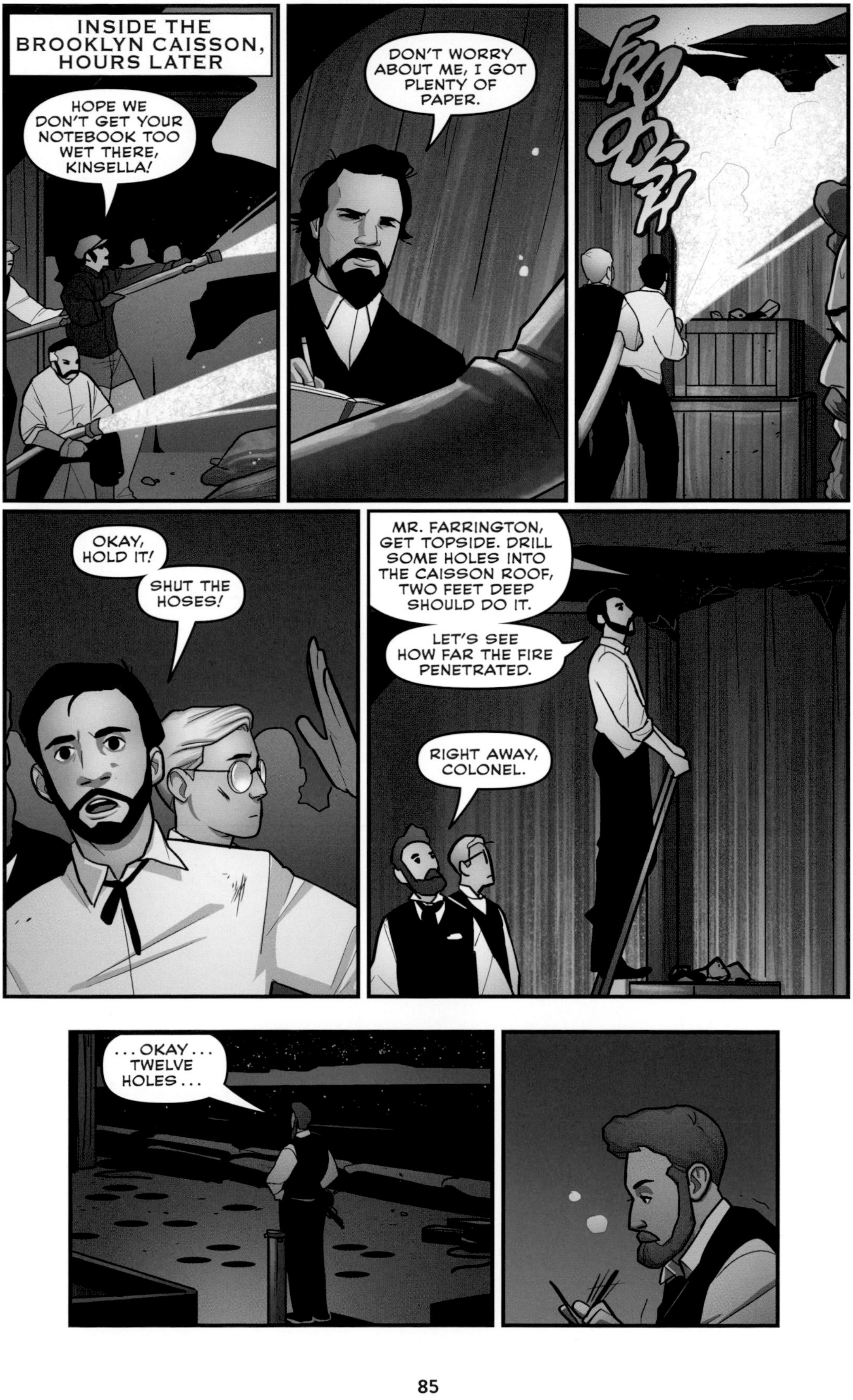
INSIDE THE BROOKLYN CAISSON, HOURS LATER
HOPE WE DON'T GET YOUR NOTEBOOK TOO WET THERE, KINSELLA!
DON'T WORRY ABOUT ME, I GOT PLENTY OF PAPER.
OKAY, HOLD IT!
SHUT THE HOSES!
MR. FARRINGTON, GET TOPSIDE. DRILL SOME HOLES INTO THE CAISSON ROOF, TWO FEET DEEP SHOULD DO IT.
LET'S SEE HOW FAR THE FIRE PENETRATED.
RIGHT AWAY, COLONEL.
. . . OKAY . . . TWELVE HOLES . . .

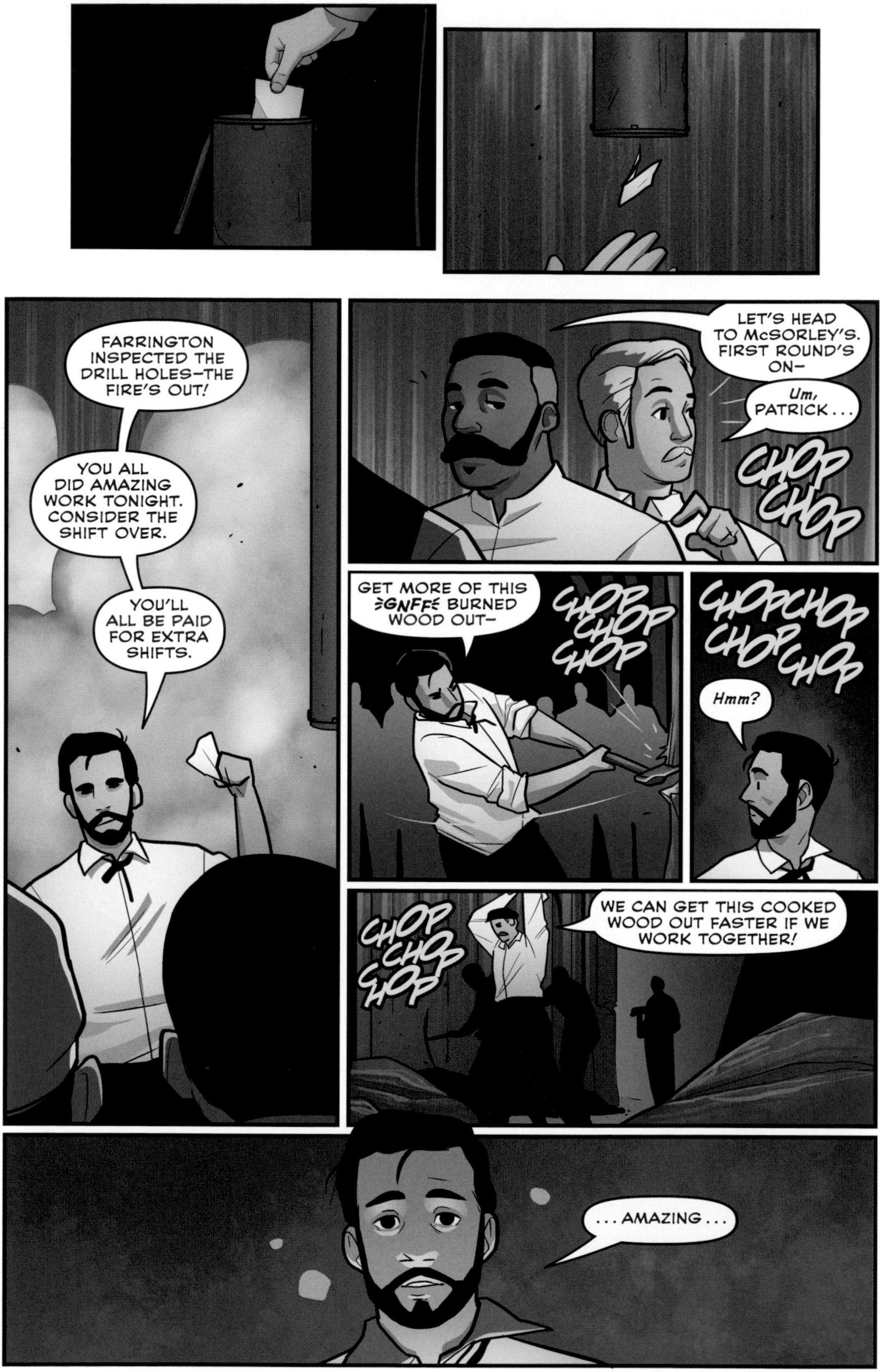
FARRINGTON INSPECTED THE DRILL HOLES—THE FIRE'S OUT!
YOU ALL DID AMAZING WORK TONIGHT. CONSIDER THE SHIFT OVER.
YOU'LL ALL BE PAID FOR EXTRA SHIFTS.
LET'S HEAD TO McSORLEY'S. FIRST ROUND'S ON—
Um, PATRICK...
CHOP CHOP
GET MORE OF THIS *GNFF* BURNED WOOD OUT—
CHOP CHOP CHOP
CHOPCHOP CHOP CHOP
Hmm?
CHOP CHOP CHOP
WE CAN GET THIS COOKED WOOD OUT FASTER IF WE WORK TOGETHER!
...AMAZING...

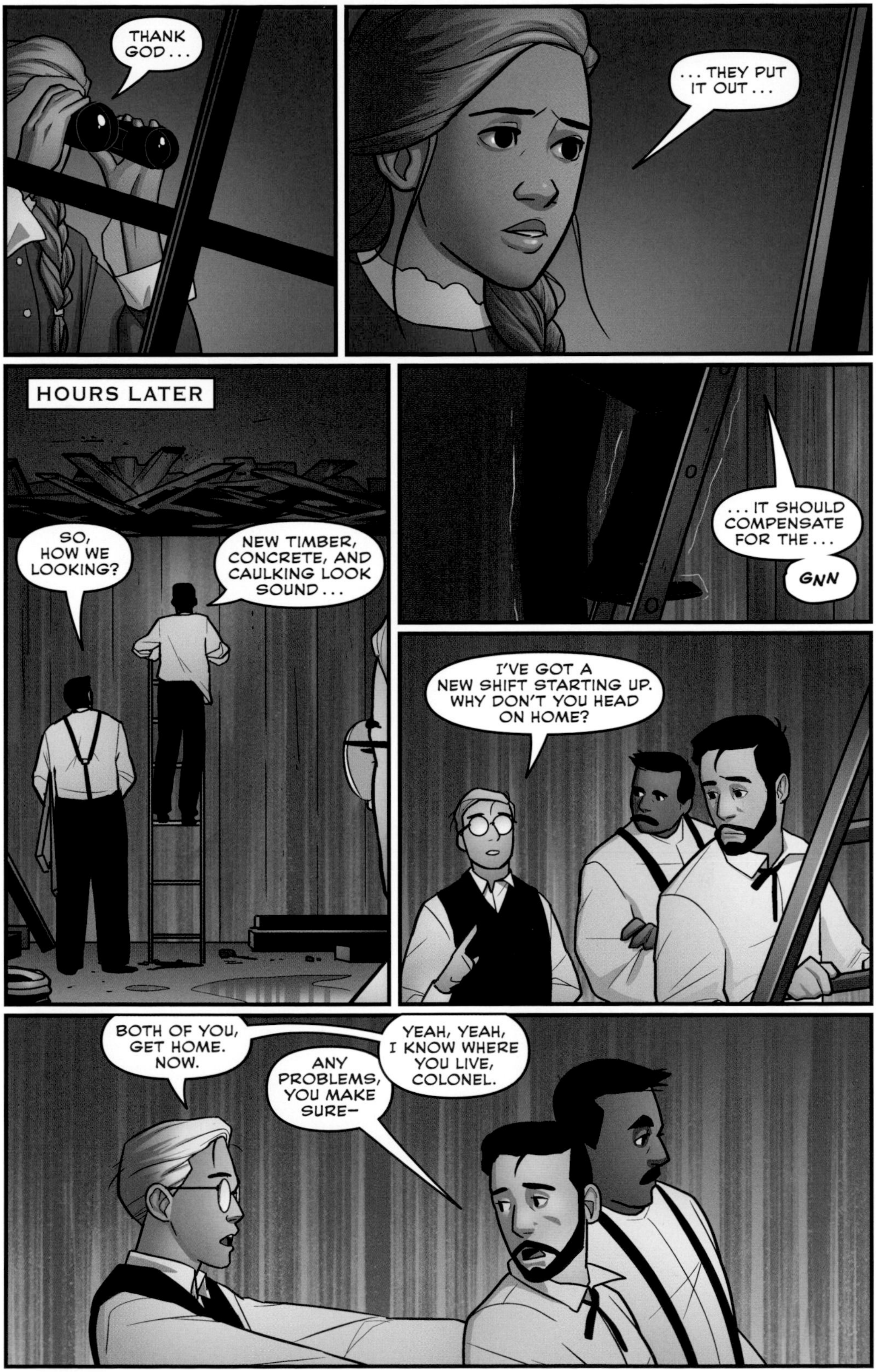

THANK GOD . . .
. . . THEY PUT IT OUT . . .
HOURS LATER
SO, HOW WE LOOKING?
NEW TIMBER, CONCRETE, AND CAULKING LOOK SOUND . . .
. . . IT SHOULD COMPENSATE FOR THE . . .
GNN
I'VE GOT A NEW SHIFT STARTING UP. WHY DON'T YOU HEAD ON HOME?
BOTH OF YOU, GET HOME. NOW.
ANY PROBLEMS, YOU MAKE SURE–
YEAH, YEAH, I KNOW WHERE YOU LIVE, COLONEL.

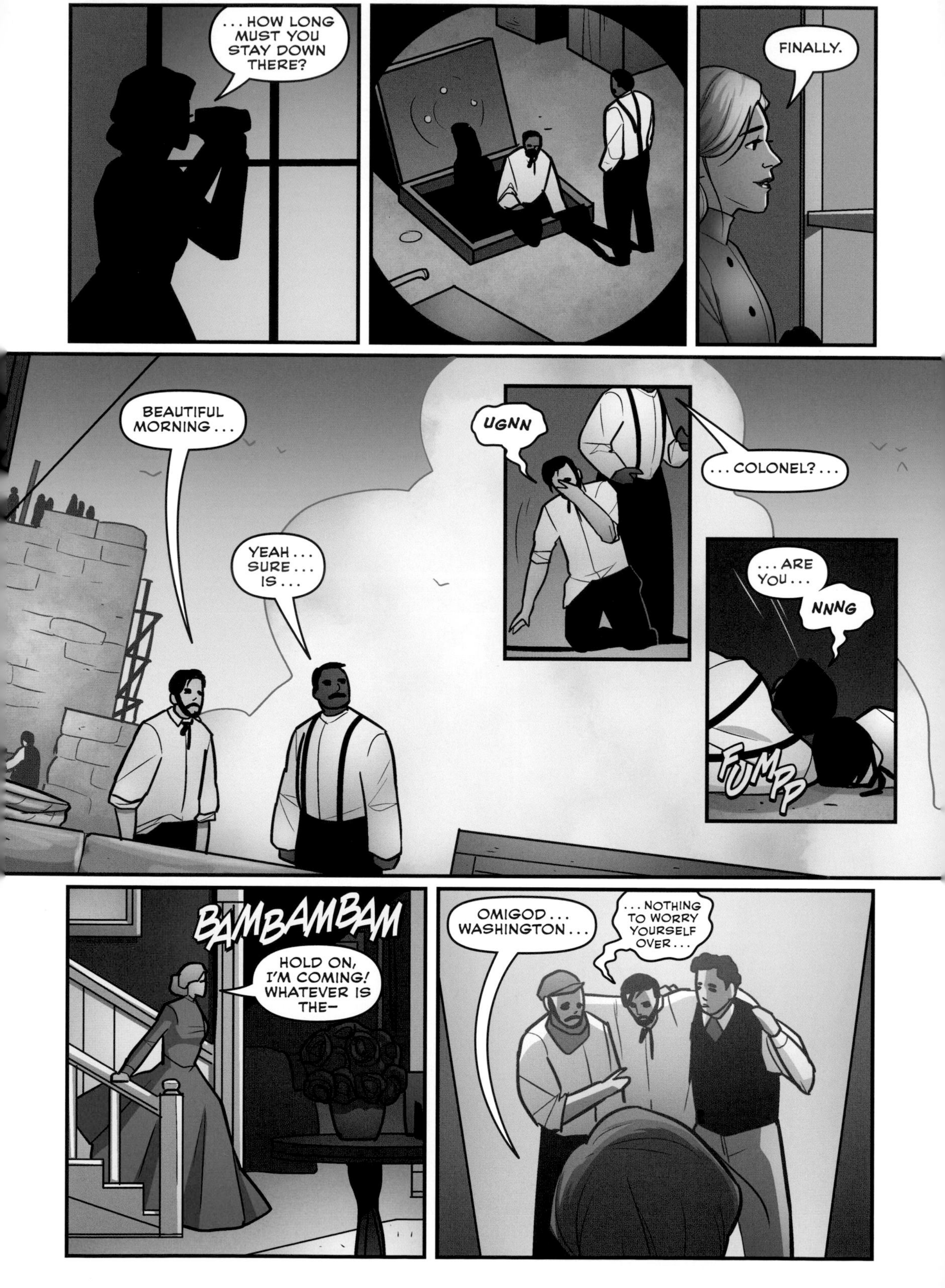
...HOW LONG MUST YOU STAY DOWN THERE?
FINALLY.
BEAUTIFUL MORNING...
YEAH... SURE... IS...
UGNN
...COLONEL?...
...ARE YOU...
NNNG
FUMPP
BAMBAMBAM
HOLD ON, I'M COMING! WHATEVER IS THE–
OMIGOD... WASHINGTON...
...NOTHING TO WORRY YOURSELF OVER...

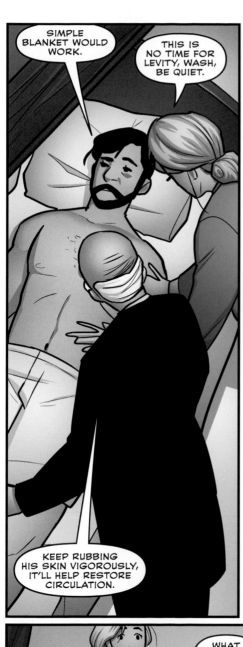

SIMPLE BLANKET WOULD WORK.

THIS IS NO TIME FOR LEVITY, WASH, BE QUIET.

KEEP RUBBING HIS SKIN VIGOROUSLY, IT'LL HELP RESTORE CIRCULATION.

NOW THAT'S A PRESCRIPTION I CAN AGREE WITH.

SHUSH, YOU!

KNOK KNOK

Um, SORRY TO BOTHER YOU, BUT . . .

WHAT IS IT, C. C.?

WE DIDN'T GET THE FIRE, DID WE?

NO, COLONEL.

WE DIDN'T.

WHAT ARE YOU DOING?

TIME TO SEPARATE THE BROTH FROM THE NOODLES, EM.

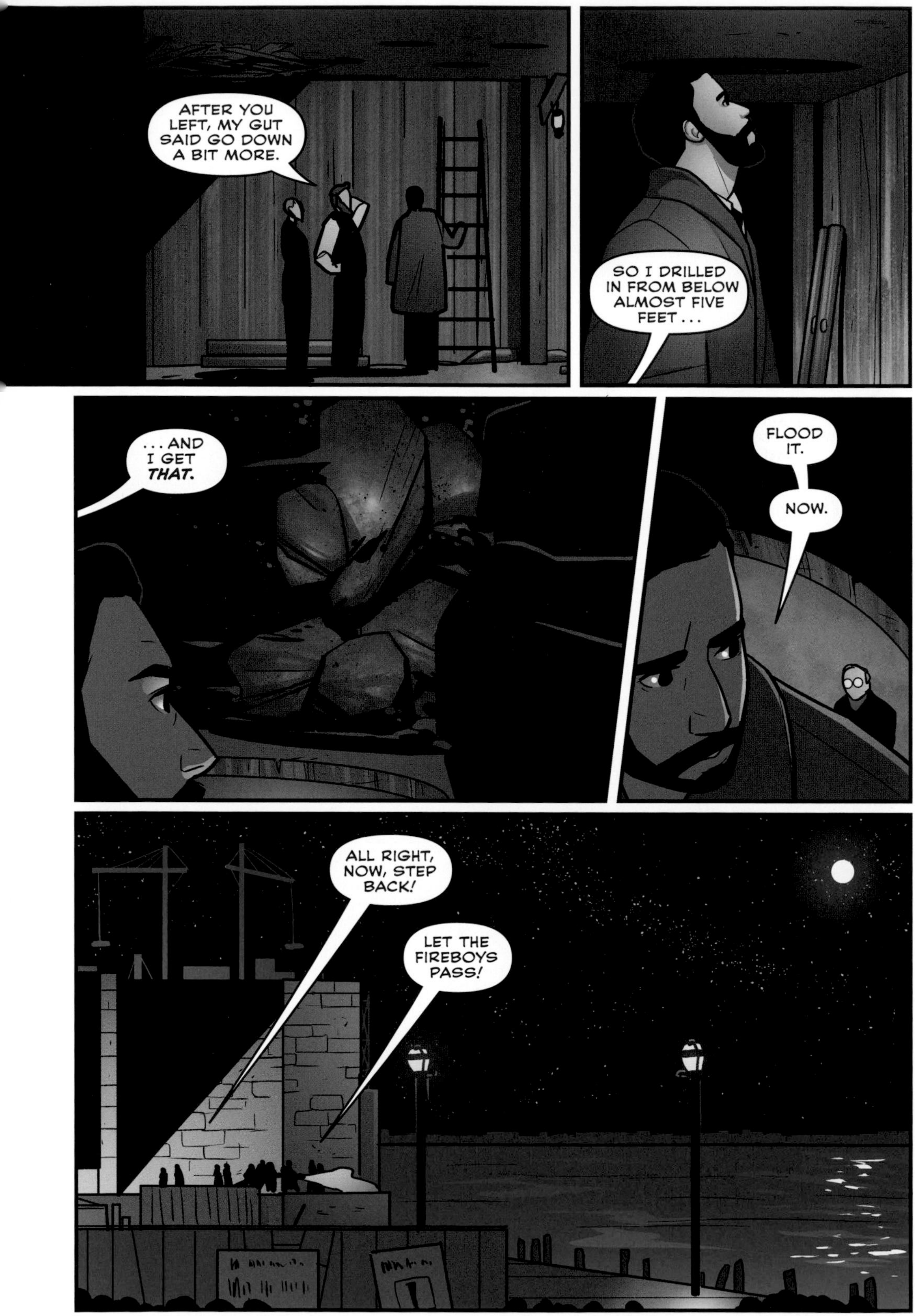

AFTER YOU LEFT, MY GUT SAID GO DOWN A BIT MORE.
SO I DRILLED IN FROM BELOW ALMOST FIVE FEET . . .
. . . AND I GET *THAT.*
FLOOD IT.
NOW.
ALL RIGHT, NOW, STEP BACK!
LET THE FIREBOYS PASS!

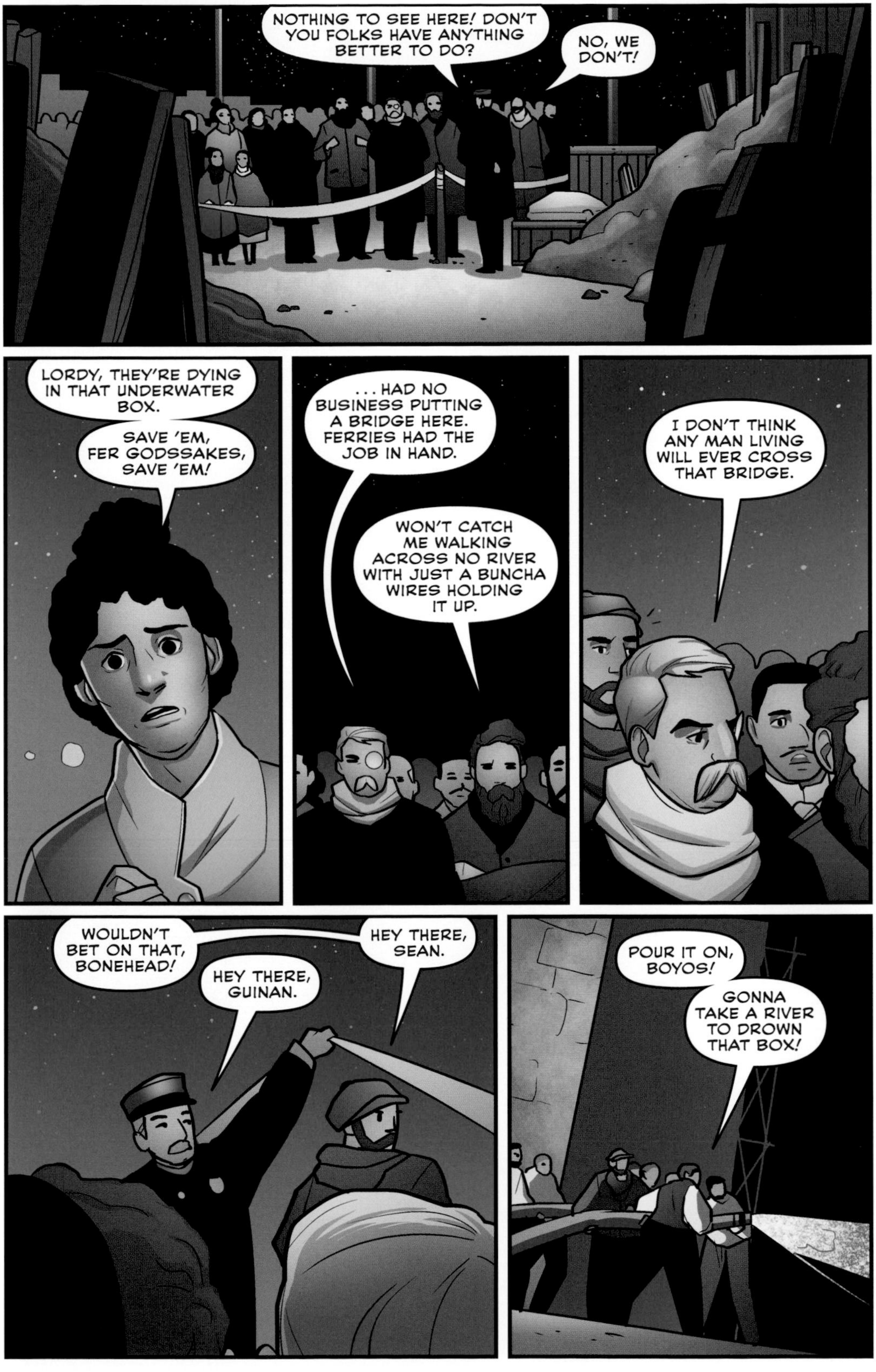
NOTHING TO SEE HERE! DON'T YOU FOLKS HAVE ANYTHING BETTER TO DO?
NO, WE DON'T!
LORDY, THEY'RE DYING IN THAT UNDERWATER BOX.
SAVE 'EM, FER GODSSAKES, SAVE 'EM!
. . . HAD NO BUSINESS PUTTING A BRIDGE HERE. FERRIES HAD THE JOB IN HAND.
WON'T CATCH ME WALKING ACROSS NO RIVER WITH JUST A BUNCHA WIRES HOLDING IT UP.
I DON'T THINK ANY MAN LIVING WILL EVER CROSS THAT BRIDGE.
WOULDN'T BET ON THAT, BONEHEAD!
HEY THERE, SEAN.
HEY THERE, GUINAN.
POUR IT ON, BOYOS!
GONNA TAKE A RIVER TO DROWN THAT BOX!

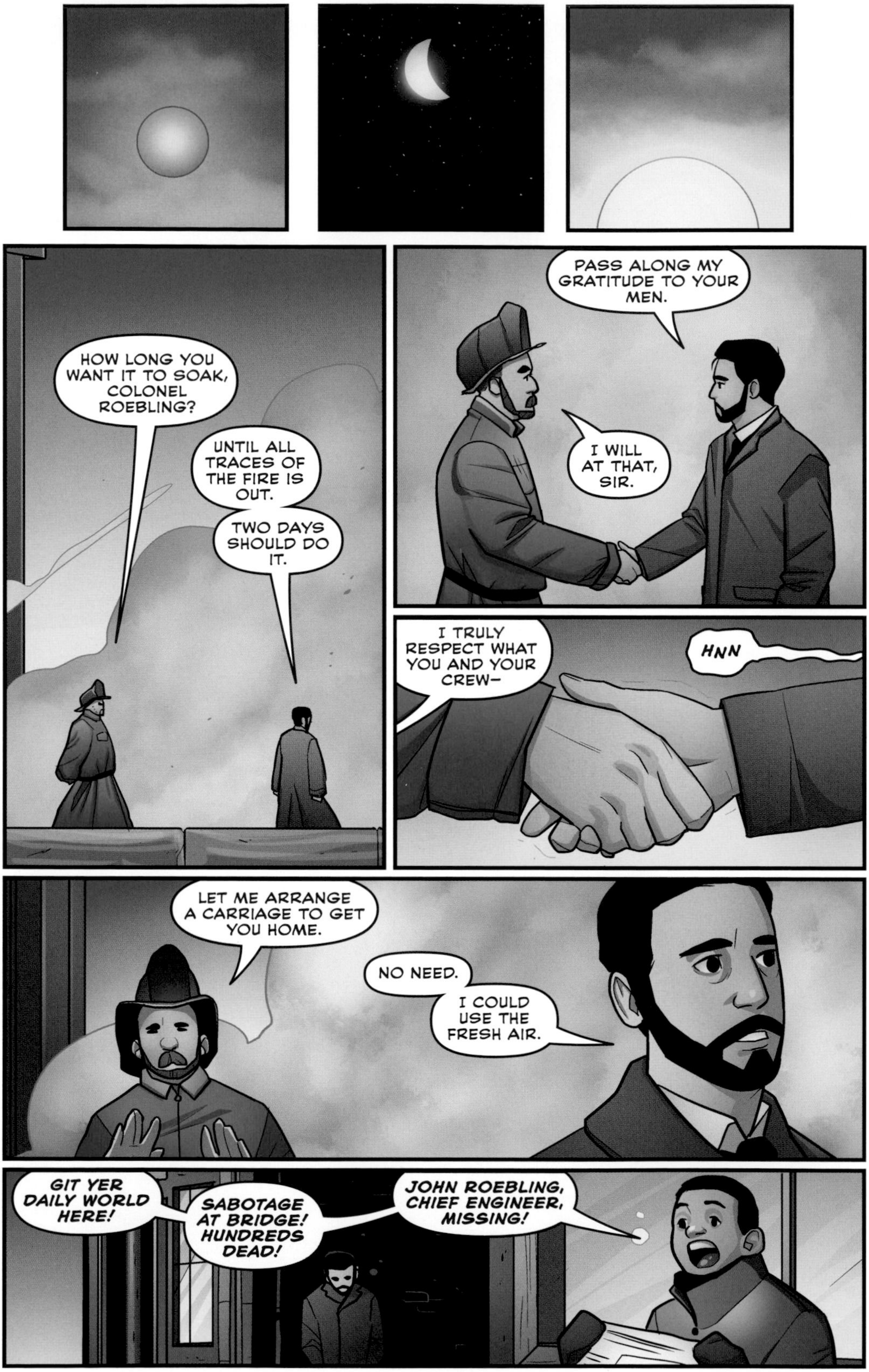
HOW LONG YOU WANT IT TO SOAK, COLONEL ROEBLING?
UNTIL ALL TRACES OF THE FIRE IS OUT.
TWO DAYS SHOULD DO IT.
PASS ALONG MY GRATITUDE TO YOUR MEN.
I WILL AT THAT, SIR.
I TRULY RESPECT WHAT YOU AND YOUR CREW—
HNN
LET ME ARRANGE A CARRIAGE TO GET YOU HOME.
NO NEED.
I COULD USE THE FRESH AIR.
GIT YER DAILY WORLD HERE!
SABOTAGE AT BRIDGE! HUNDREDS DEAD!
JOHN ROEBLING, CHIEF ENGINEER, MISSING!

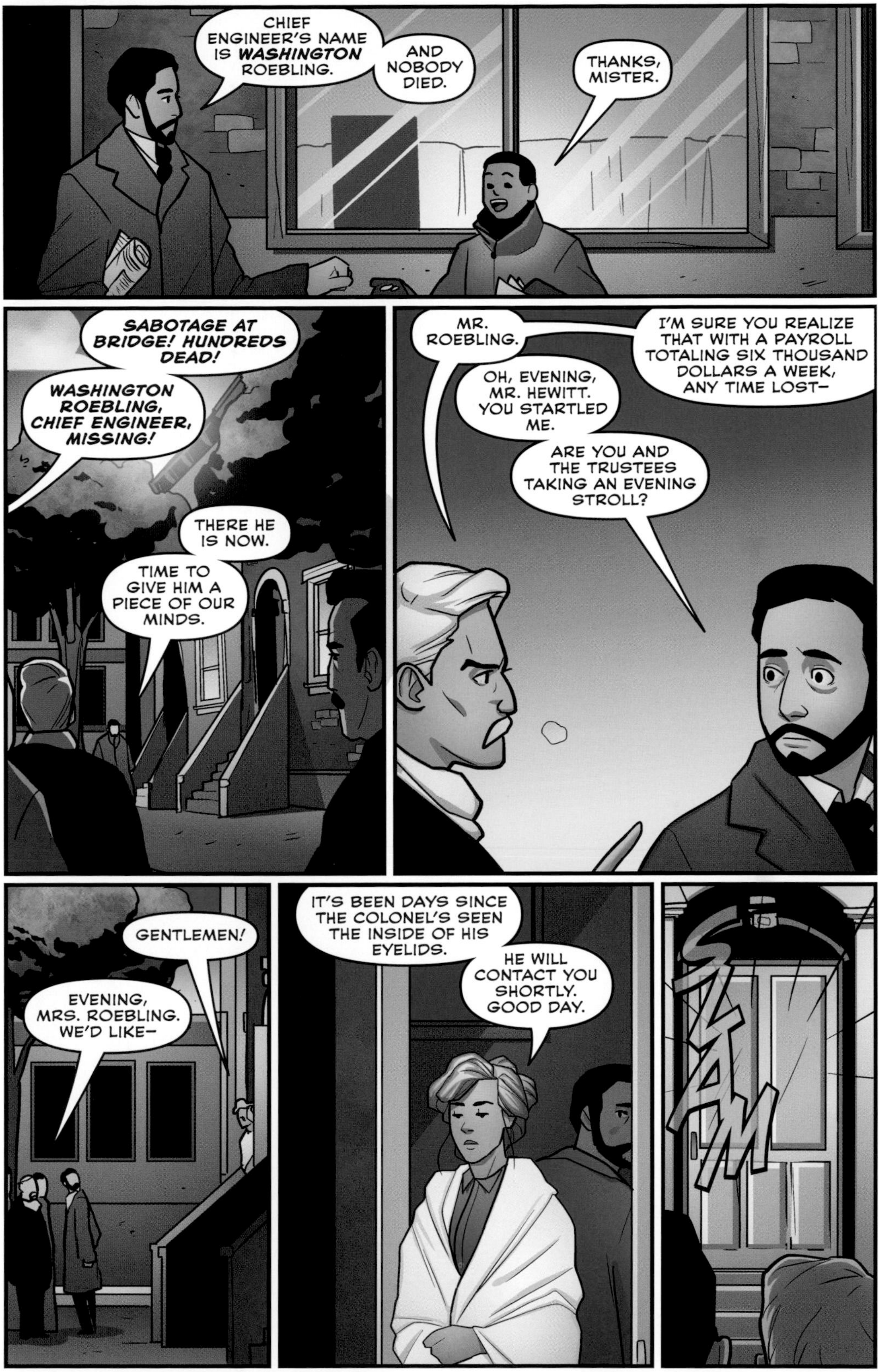
CHIEF ENGINEER'S NAME IS **WASHINGTON** ROEBLING.
AND NOBODY DIED.
THANKS, MISTER.
SABOTAGE AT BRIDGE! HUNDREDS DEAD!
WASHINGTON ROEBLING, CHIEF ENGINEER, MISSING!
THERE HE IS NOW.
TIME TO GIVE HIM A PIECE OF OUR MINDS.
MR. ROEBLING.
I'M SURE YOU REALIZE THAT WITH A PAYROLL TOTALING SIX THOUSAND DOLLARS A WEEK, ANY TIME LOST—
OH, EVENING, MR. HEWITT. YOU STARTLED ME.
ARE YOU AND THE TRUSTEES TAKING AN EVENING STROLL?
GENTLEMEN!
EVENING, MRS. ROEBLING. WE'D LIKE—
IT'S BEEN DAYS SINCE THE COLONEL'S SEEN THE INSIDE OF HIS EYELIDS.
HE WILL CONTACT YOU SHORTLY. GOOD DAY.
SLAM

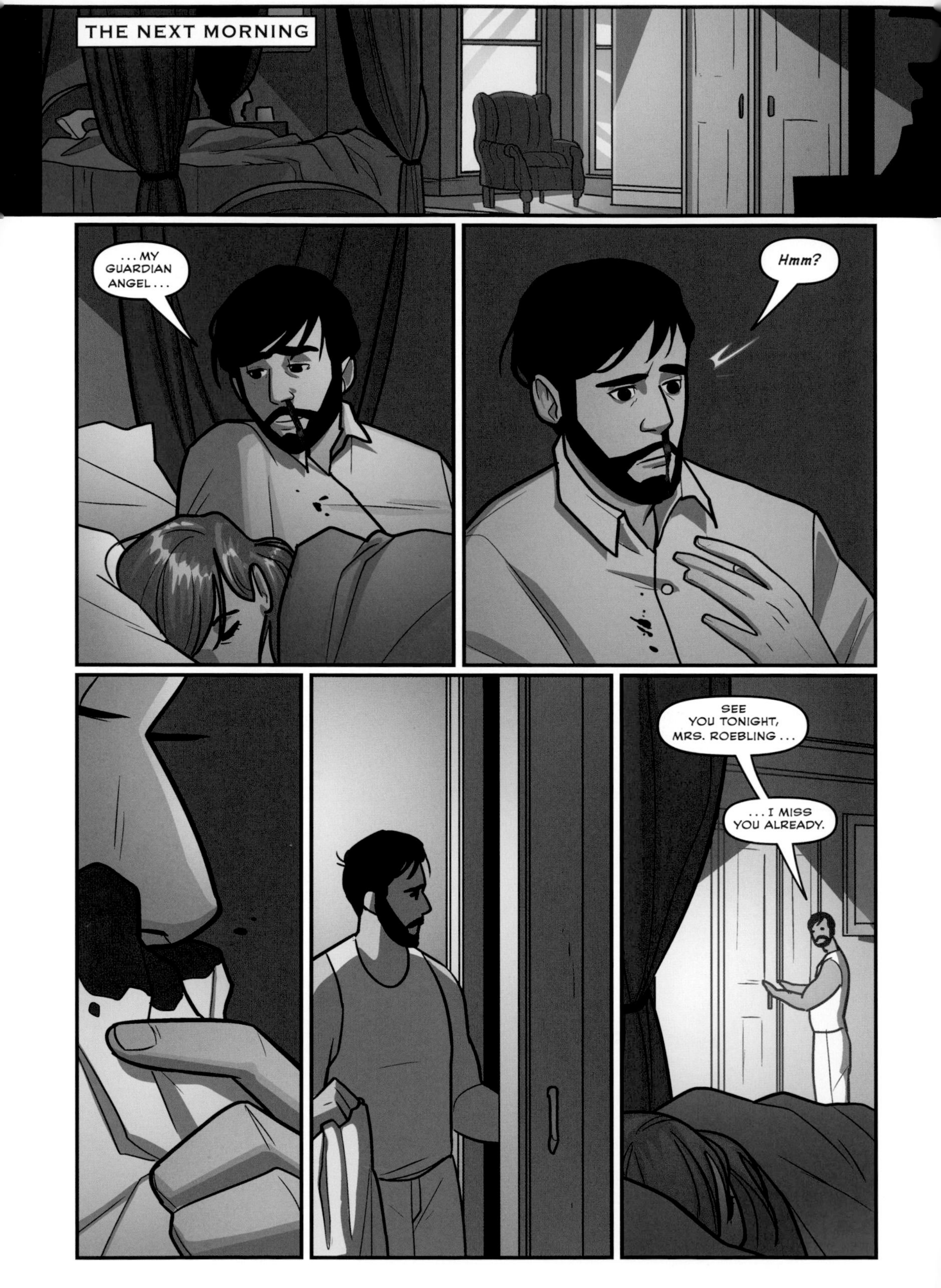
THE NEXT MORNING
. . . MY GUARDIAN ANGEL . . .
Hmm?
SEE YOU TONIGHT, MRS. ROEBLING . . .
. . . I MISS YOU ALREADY.

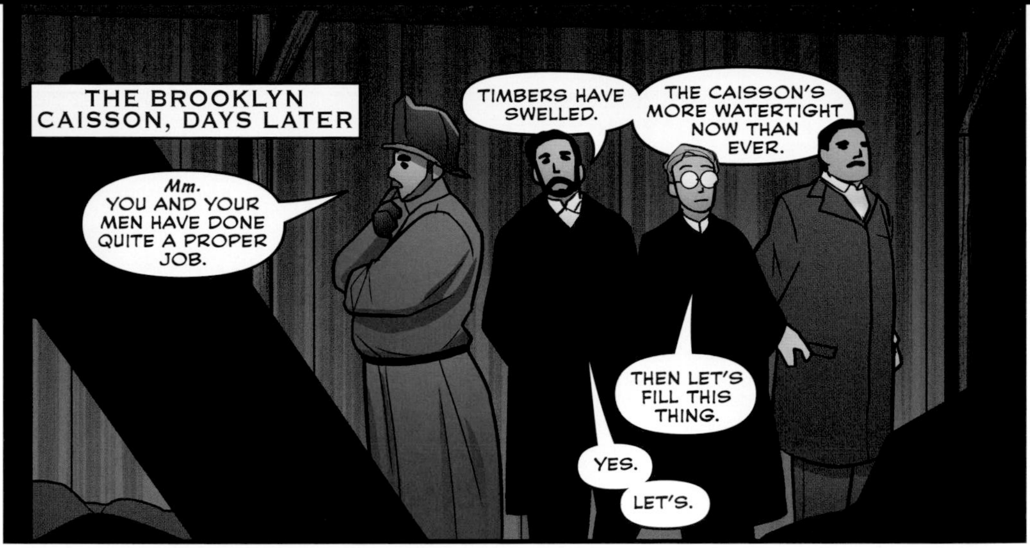
THE BROOKLYN CAISSON, DAYS LATER
Mm. YOU AND YOUR MEN HAVE DONE QUITE A PROPER JOB.
TIMBERS HAVE SWELLED.
THE CAISSON'S MORE WATERTIGHT NOW THAN EVER.
THEN LET'S FILL THIS THING.
YES.
LET'S.

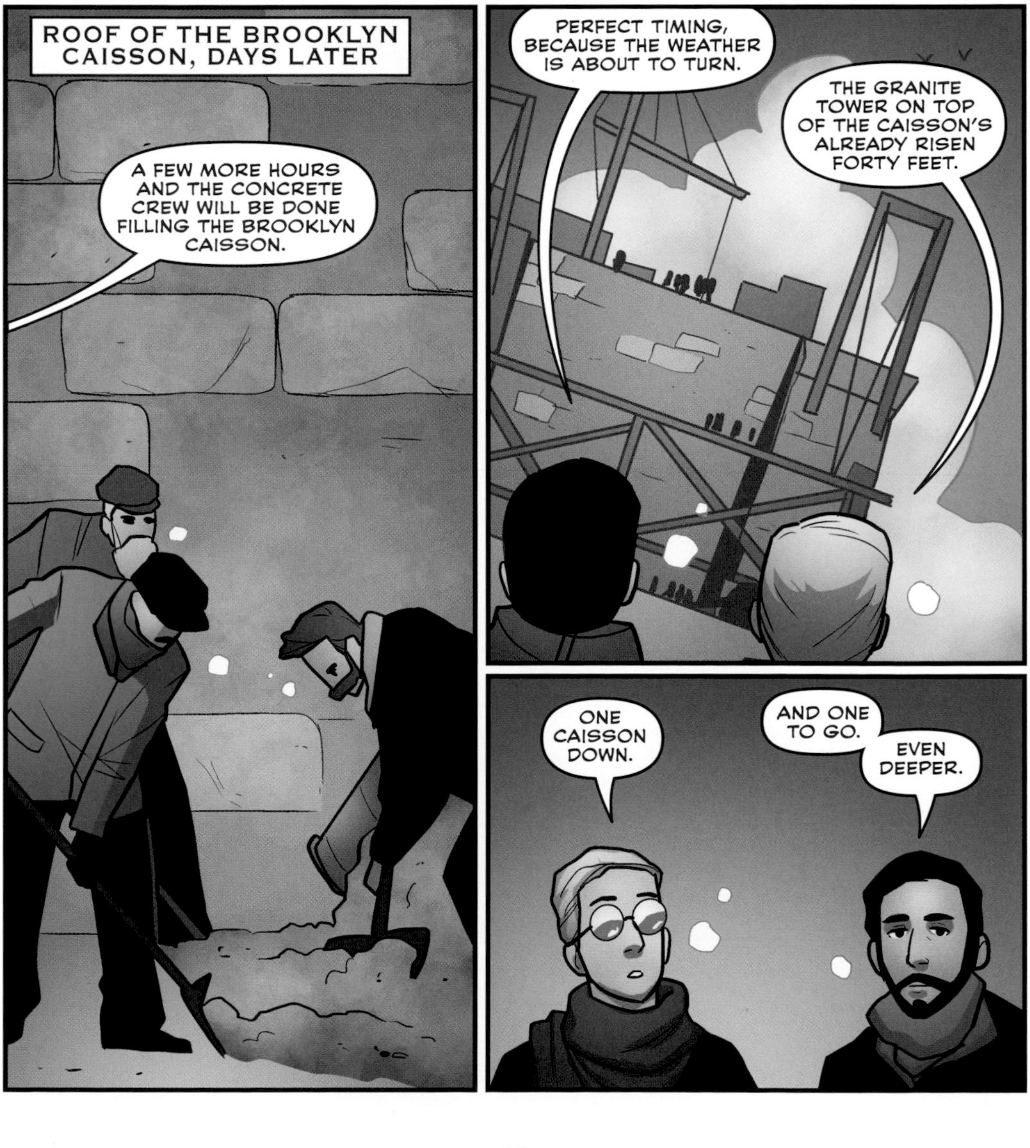
ROOF OF THE BROOKLYN CAISSON, DAYS LATER
A FEW MORE HOURS AND THE CONCRETE CREW WILL BE DONE FILLING THE BROOKLYN CAISSON.
PERFECT TIMING, BECAUSE THE WEATHER IS ABOUT TO TURN.
THE GRANITE TOWER ON TOP OF THE CAISSON'S ALREADY RISEN FORTY FEET.
ONE CAISSON DOWN.
AND ONE TO GO.
EVEN DEEPER.

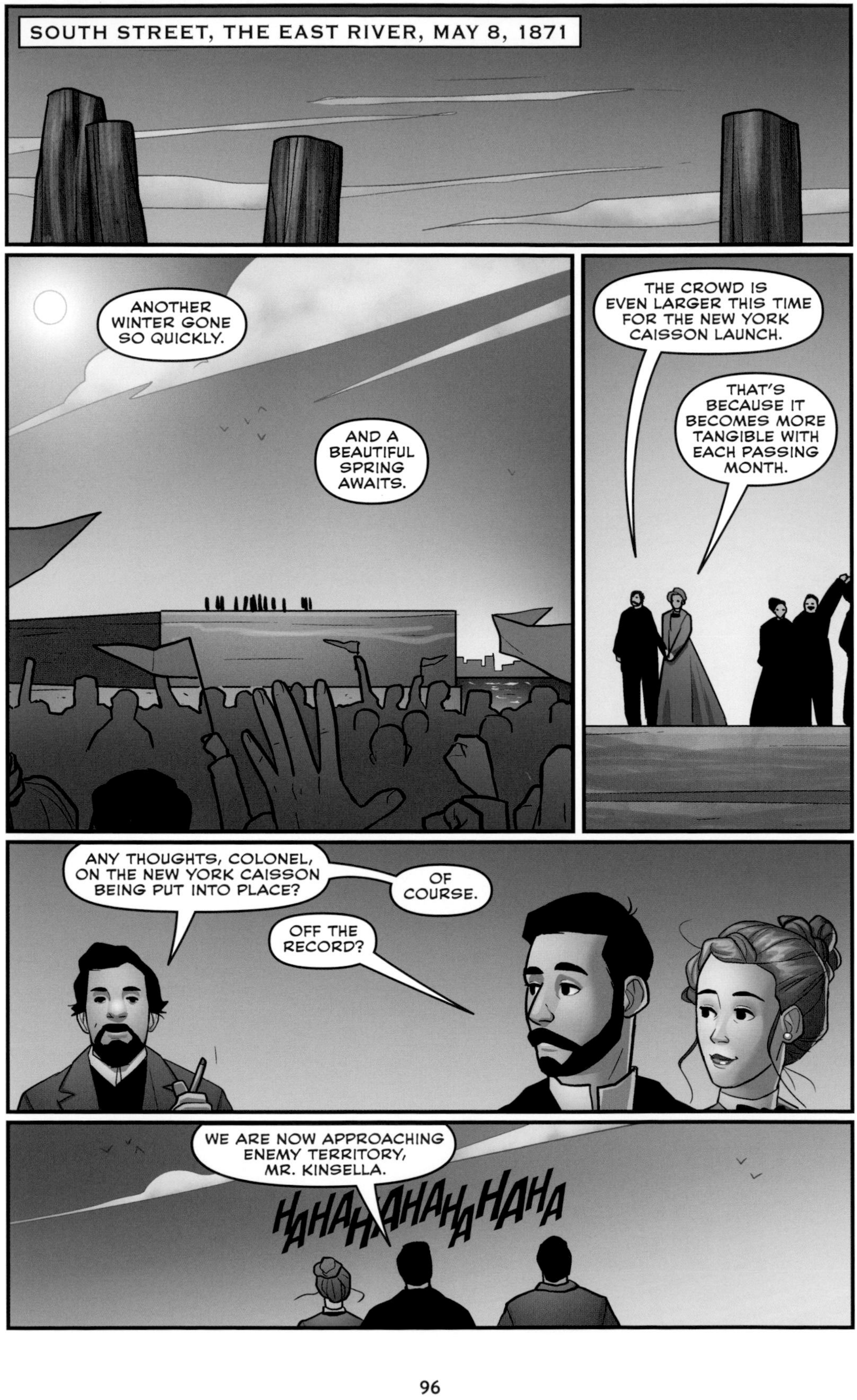
SOUTH STREET, THE EAST RIVER, MAY 8, 1871
ANOTHER WINTER GONE SO QUICKLY.
AND A BEAUTIFUL SPRING AWAITS.
THE CROWD IS EVEN LARGER THIS TIME FOR THE NEW YORK CAISSON LAUNCH.
THAT'S BECAUSE IT BECOMES MORE TANGIBLE WITH EACH PASSING MONTH.
ANY THOUGHTS, COLONEL, ON THE NEW YORK CAISSON BEING PUT INTO PLACE?
OF COURSE.
OFF THE RECORD?
WE ARE NOW APPROACHING ENEMY TERRITORY, MR. KINSELLA.
HAHAHAHAHAHAHAHA

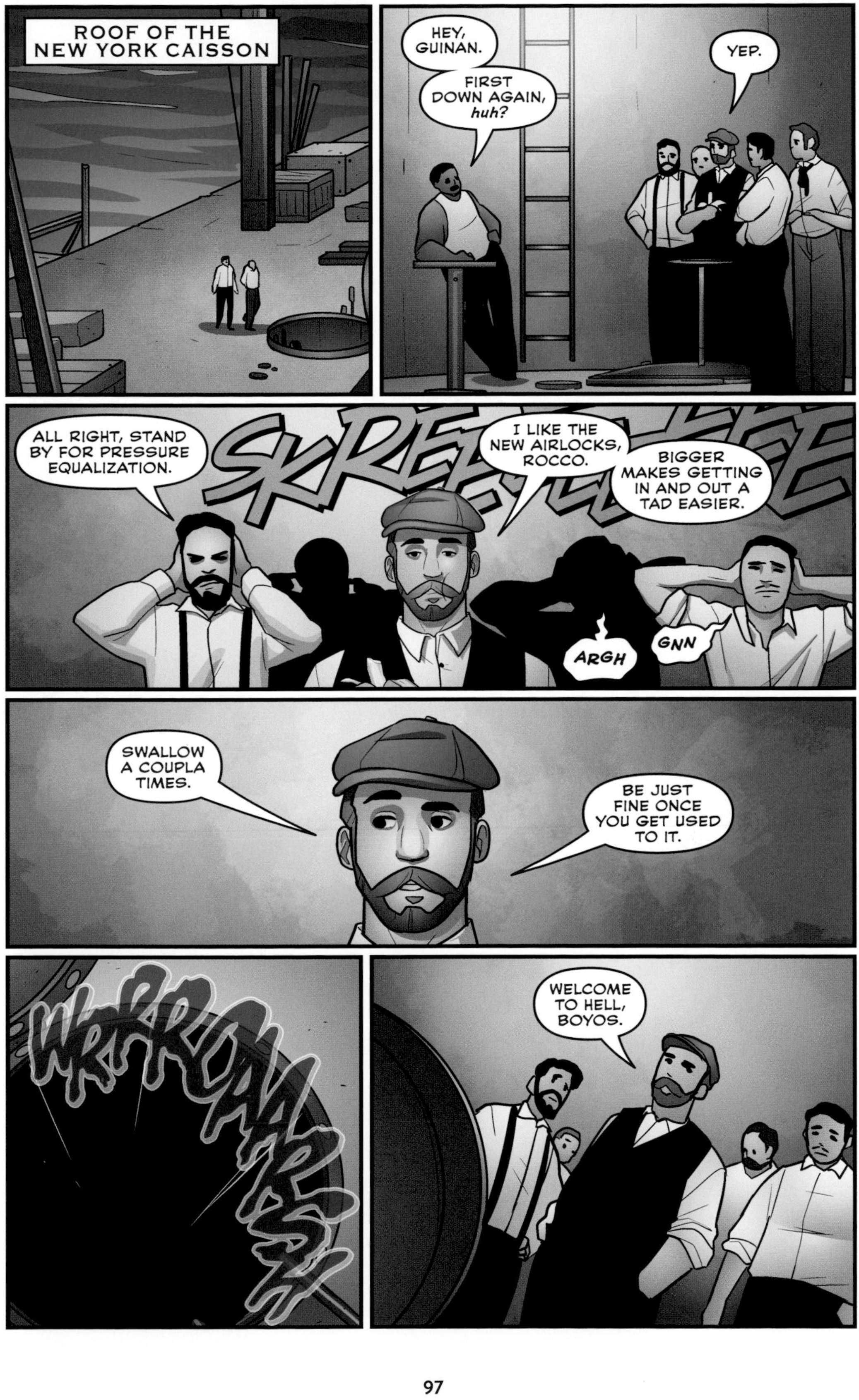
ROOF OF THE NEW YORK CAISSON
HEY, GUINAN.
FIRST DOWN AGAIN, *huh?*
YEP.
ALL RIGHT, STAND BY FOR PRESSURE EQUALIZATION.
I LIKE THE NEW AIRLOCKS, ROCCO.
BIGGER MAKES GETTING IN AND OUT A TAD EASIER.
ARGH
GNN
SWALLOW A COUPLA TIMES.
BE JUST FINE ONCE YOU GET USED TO IT.
WELCOME TO HELL, BOYOS.

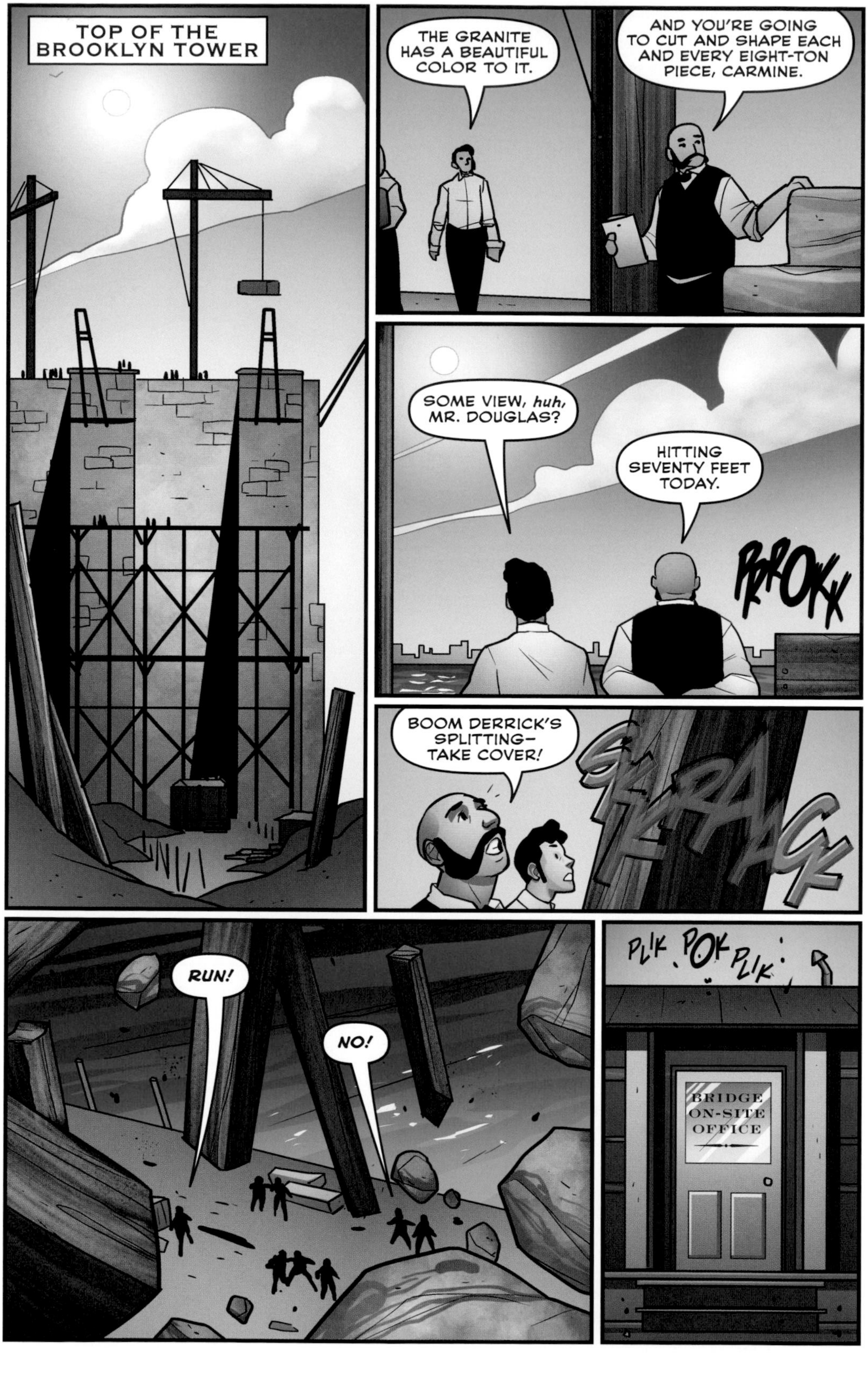
TOP OF THE BROOKLYN TOWER
THE GRANITE HAS A BEAUTIFUL COLOR TO IT.
AND YOU'RE GOING TO CUT AND SHAPE EACH AND EVERY EIGHT-TON PIECE, CARMINE.
SOME VIEW, *huh,* MR. DOUGLAS?
HITTING SEVENTY FEET TODAY.
PRROKK
BOOM DERRICK'S SPLITTING– TAKE COVER!
RUN!
NO!
PLIK POK PLIK
BRIDGE ON-SITE OFFICE

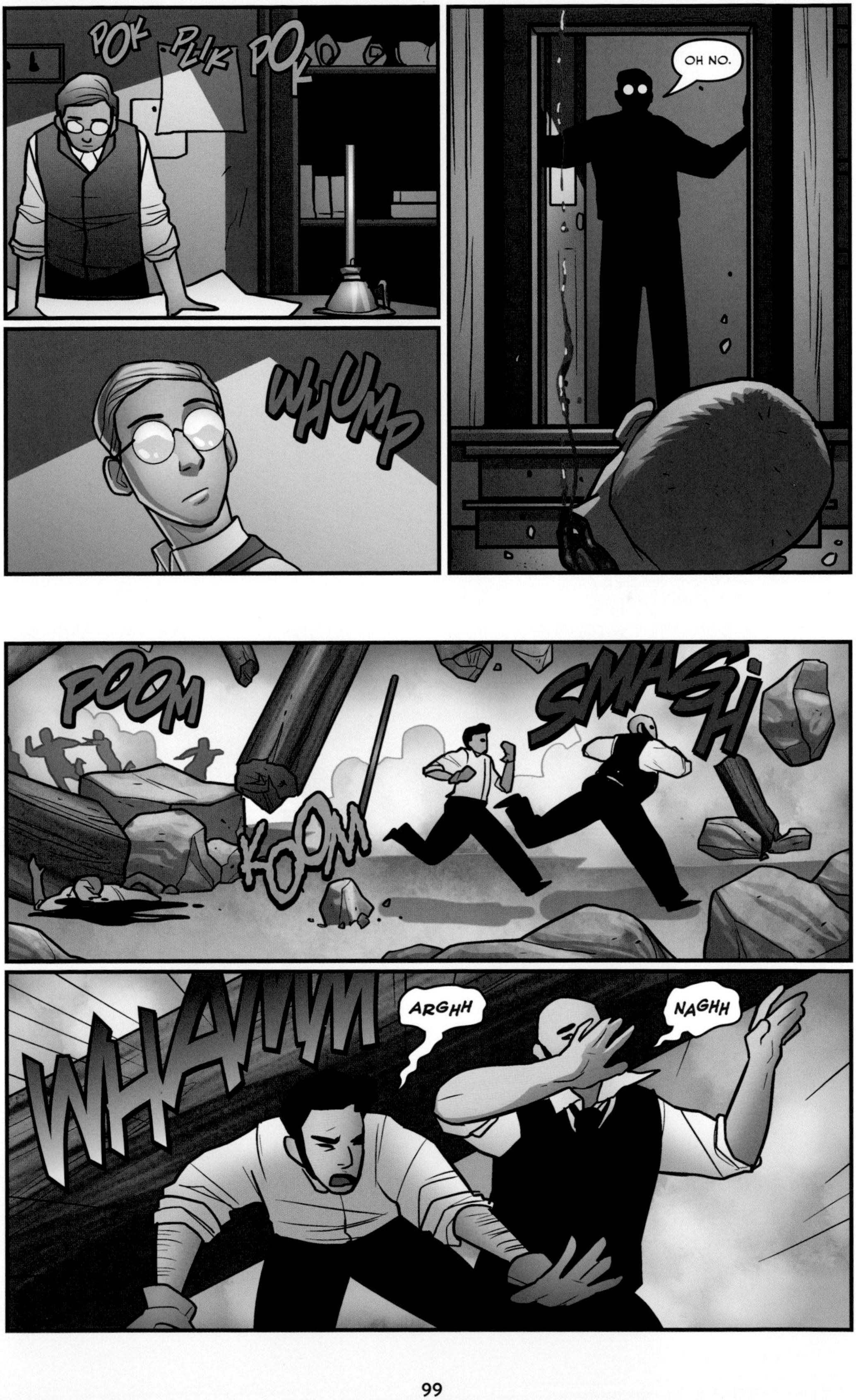
POK PLIK POK
OH NO.
WHUMP
POOM
KOOM
SMASH
WHAMM
ARGHH
NAGHH

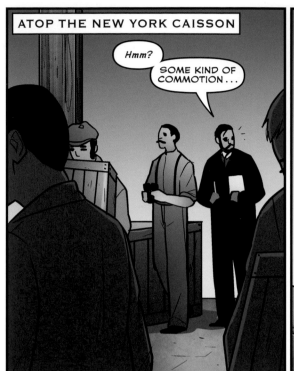

ATOP THE NEW YORK CAISSON

Hmm?

SOME KIND OF COMMOTION . . .

GLASSES!

GOOD GOD.

ALL HANDS WITH ME TO THE BOAT!

TO THE BROOKLYN TOWER!

HURRY!

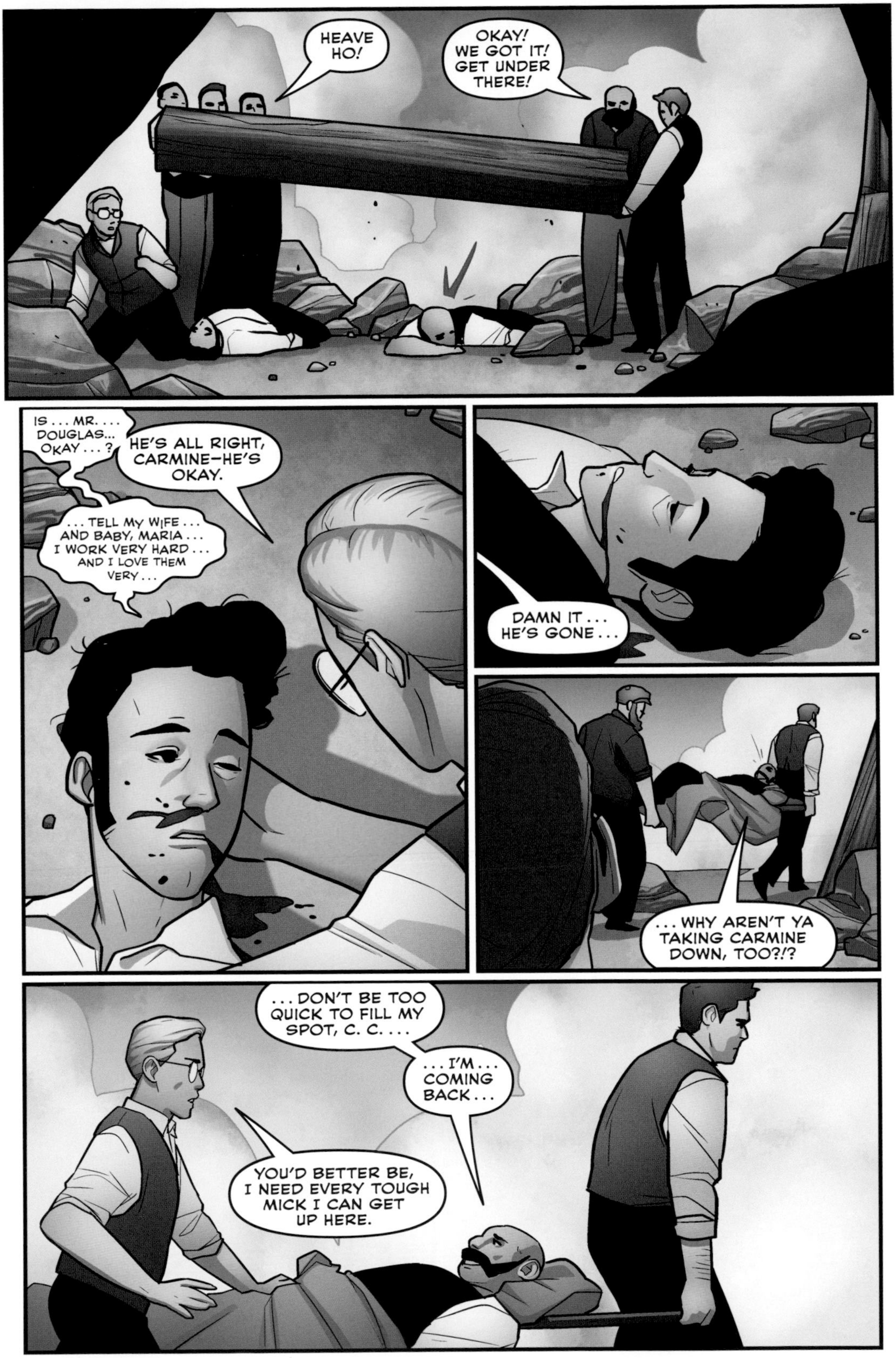
HEAVE HO!
OKAY! WE GOT IT! GET UNDER THERE!
IS . . . MR. . . . DOUGLAS... OKAY . . . ?
HE'S ALL RIGHT, CARMINE—HE'S OKAY.
. . . TELL MY WIFE . . . AND BABY, MARIA . . . I WORK VERY HARD . . . AND I LOVE THEM VERY . . .
DAMN IT . . . HE'S GONE . . .
. . . WHY AREN'T YA TAKING CARMINE DOWN, TOO?!?
. . . DON'T BE TOO QUICK TO FILL MY SPOT, C. C. . . .
. . . I'M . . . COMING BACK . . .
YOU'D BETTER BE, I NEED EVERY TOUGH MICK I CAN GET UP HERE.

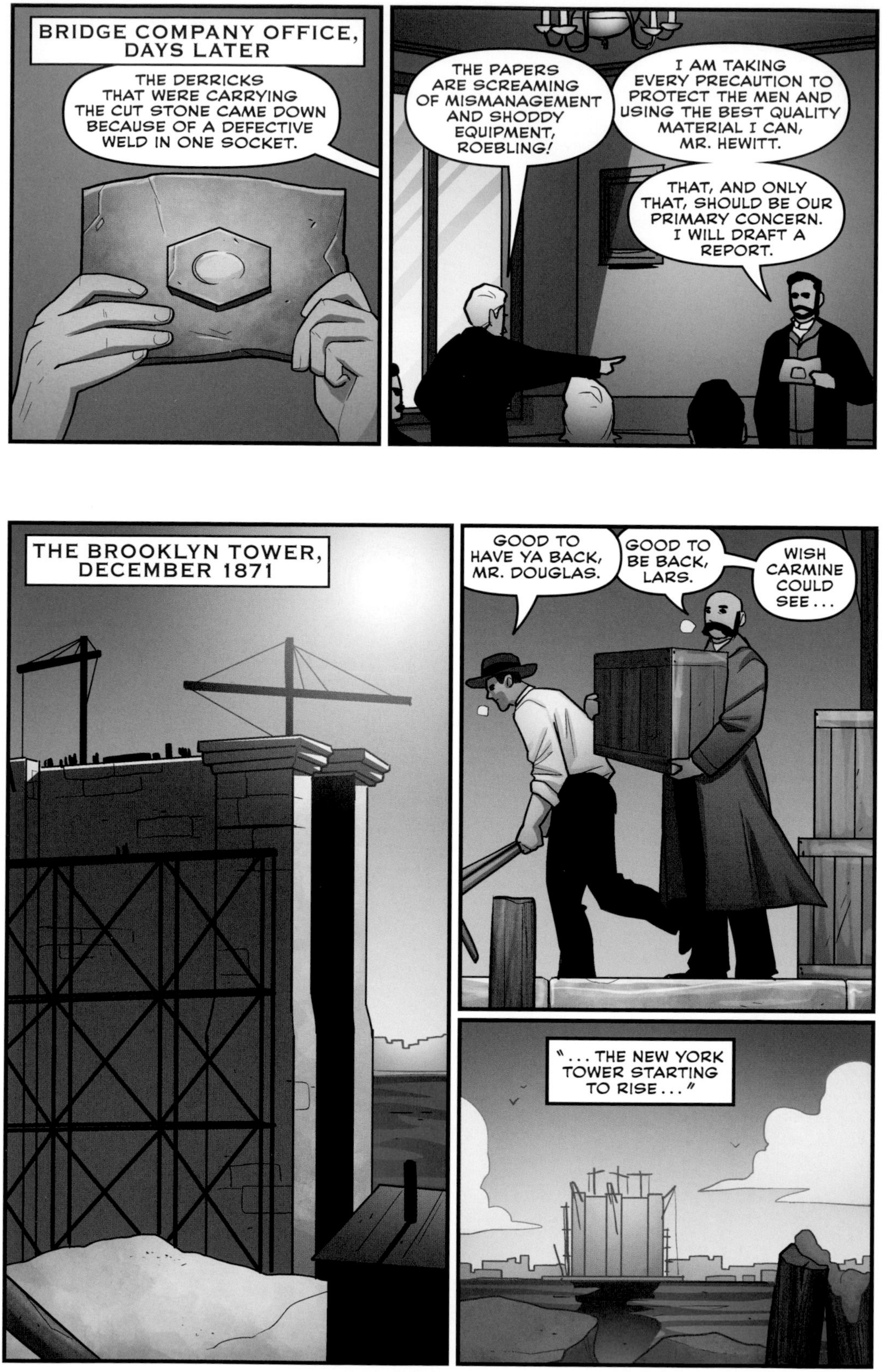

BRIDGE COMPANY OFFICE, DAYS LATER
THE DERRICKS THAT WERE CARRYING THE CUT STONE CAME DOWN BECAUSE OF A DEFECTIVE WELD IN ONE SOCKET.
THE PAPERS ARE SCREAMING OF MISMANAGEMENT AND SHODDY EQUIPMENT, ROEBLING!
I AM TAKING EVERY PRECAUTION TO PROTECT THE MEN AND USING THE BEST QUALITY MATERIAL I CAN, MR. HEWITT.
THAT, AND ONLY THAT, SHOULD BE OUR PRIMARY CONCERN. I WILL DRAFT A REPORT.
THE BROOKLYN TOWER, DECEMBER 1871
GOOD TO HAVE YA BACK, MR. DOUGLAS.
GOOD TO BE BACK, LARS.
WISH CARMINE COULD SEE . . .
". . . THE NEW YORK TOWER STARTING TO RISE . . ."

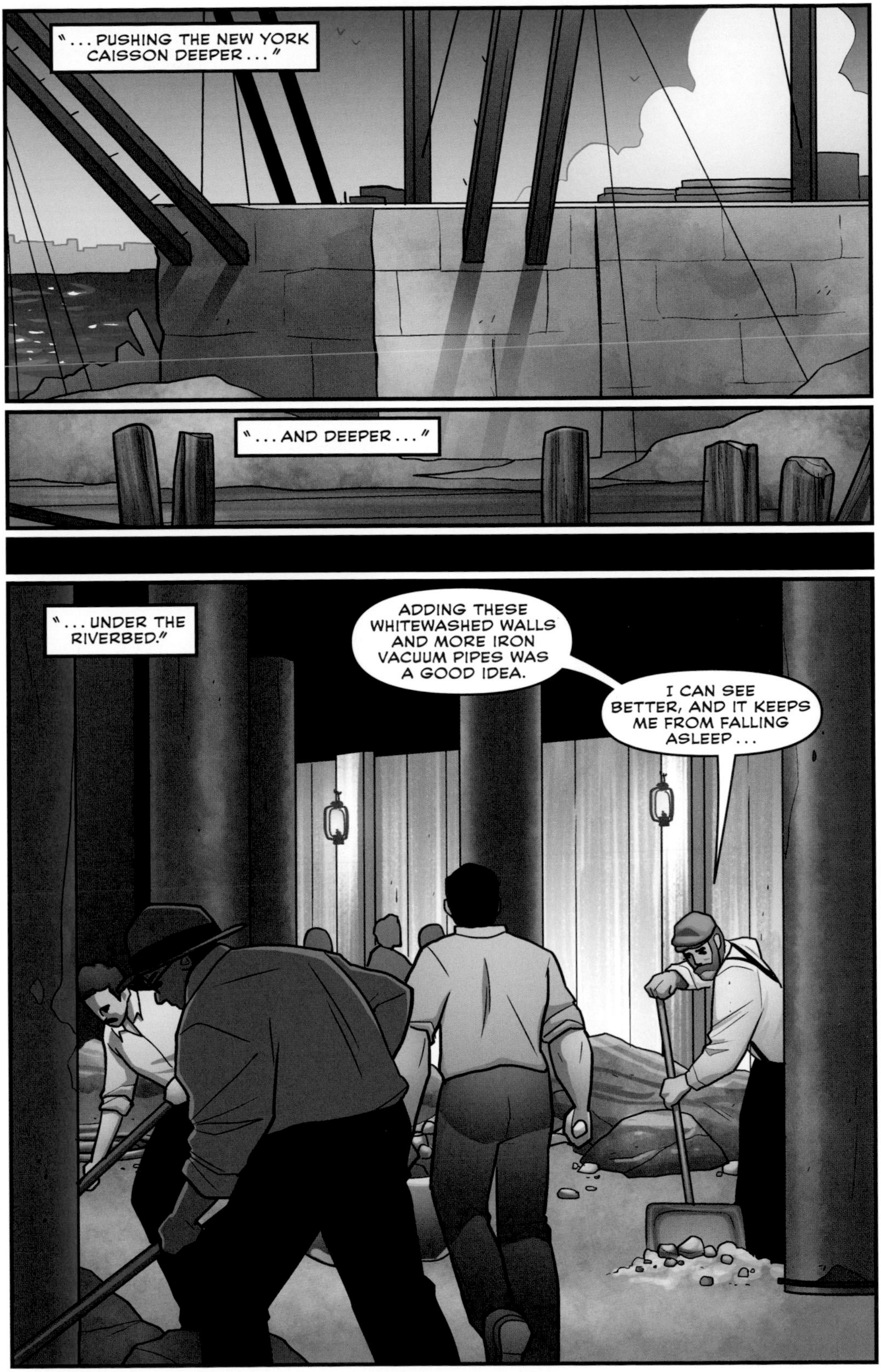
"... PUSHING THE NEW YORK CAISSON DEEPER ..."
"... AND DEEPER ..."
"... UNDER THE RIVERBED."
ADDING THESE WHITEWASHED WALLS AND MORE IRON VACUUM PIPES WAS A GOOD IDEA.
I CAN SEE BETTER, AND IT KEEPS ME FROM FALLING ASLEEP ...

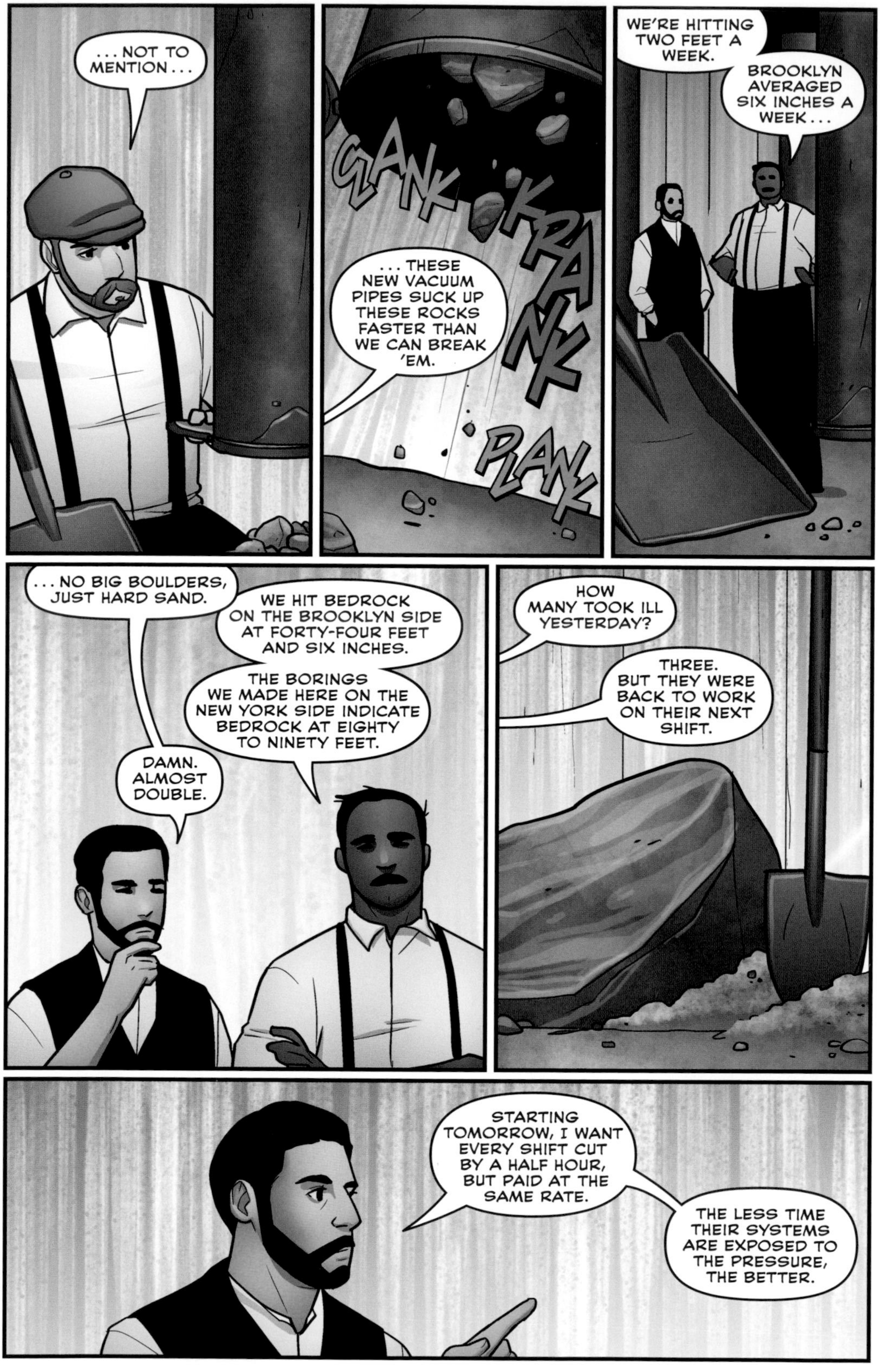
. . . NOT TO MENTION . . .
CLANK
KRANK
. . . THESE NEW VACUUM PIPES SUCK UP THESE ROCKS FASTER THAN WE CAN BREAK 'EM.
PLANK
WE'RE HITTING TWO FEET A WEEK.
BROOKLYN AVERAGED SIX INCHES A WEEK . . .
. . . NO BIG BOULDERS, JUST HARD SAND.
WE HIT BEDROCK ON THE BROOKLYN SIDE AT FORTY-FOUR FEET AND SIX INCHES.
THE BORINGS WE MADE HERE ON THE NEW YORK SIDE INDICATE BEDROCK AT EIGHTY TO NINETY FEET.
DAMN. ALMOST DOUBLE.
HOW MANY TOOK ILL YESTERDAY?
THREE. BUT THEY WERE BACK TO WORK ON THEIR NEXT SHIFT.
STARTING TOMORROW, I WANT EVERY SHIFT CUT BY A HALF HOUR, BUT PAID AT THE SAME RATE.
THE LESS TIME THEIR SYSTEMS ARE EXPOSED TO THE PRESSURE, THE BETTER.

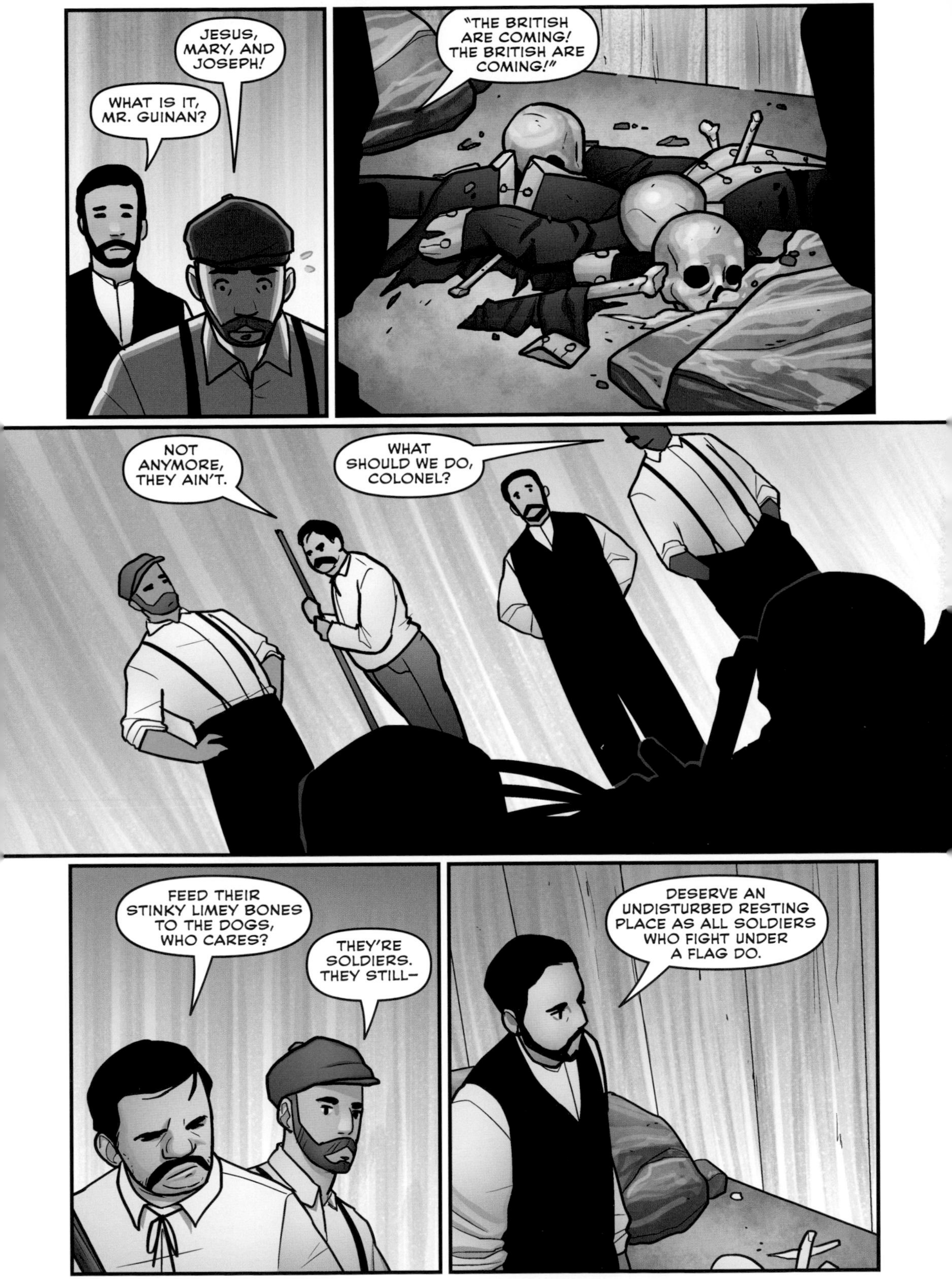

WHAT IS IT, MR. GUINAN?
JESUS, MARY, AND JOSEPH!
"THE BRITISH ARE COMING! THE BRITISH ARE COMING!"
NOT ANYMORE, THEY AIN'T.
WHAT SHOULD WE DO, COLONEL?
FEED THEIR STINKY LIMEY BONES TO THE DOGS, WHO CARES?
THEY'RE SOLDIERS. THEY STILL–
DESERVE AN UNDISTURBED RESTING PLACE AS ALL SOLDIERS WHO FIGHT UNDER A FLAG DO.

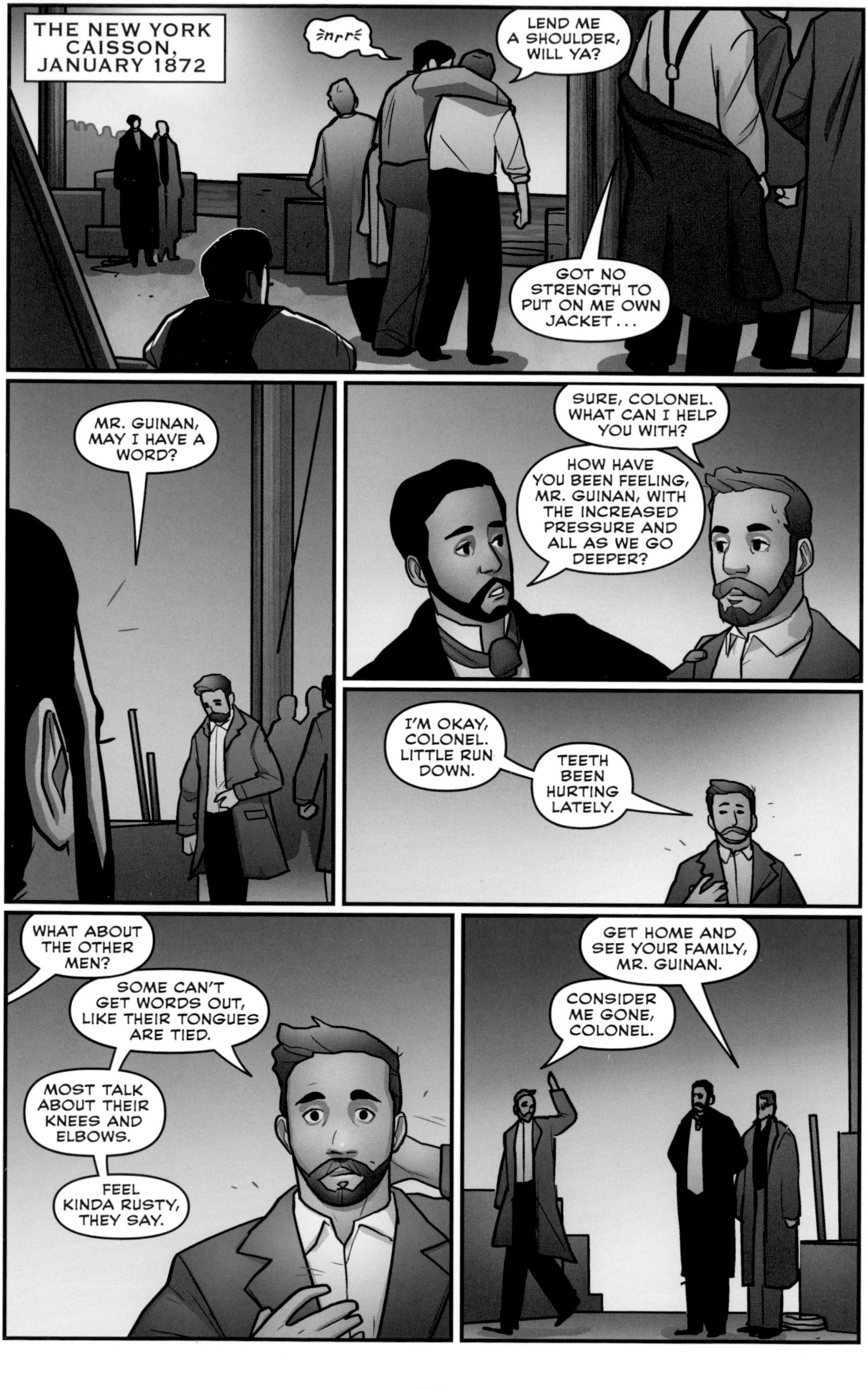
THE NEW YORK CAISSON, JANUARY 1872
LEND ME A SHOULDER, WILL YA?
GOT NO STRENGTH TO PUT ON ME OWN JACKET . . .
MR. GUINAN, MAY I HAVE A WORD?
SURE, COLONEL. WHAT CAN I HELP YOU WITH?
HOW HAVE YOU BEEN FEELING, MR. GUINAN, WITH THE INCREASED PRESSURE AND ALL AS WE GO DEEPER?
I'M OKAY, COLONEL. LITTLE RUN DOWN.
TEETH BEEN HURTING LATELY.
WHAT ABOUT THE OTHER MEN?
SOME CAN'T GET WORDS OUT, LIKE THEIR TONGUES ARE TIED.
MOST TALK ABOUT THEIR KNEES AND ELBOWS.
FEEL KINDA RUSTY, THEY SAY.
GET HOME AND SEE YOUR FAMILY, MR. GUINAN.
CONSIDER ME GONE, COLONEL.

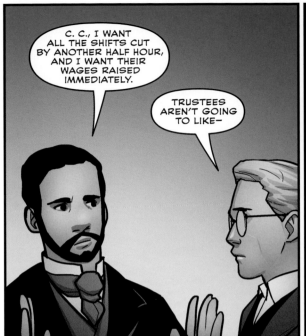

C. C., I WANT ALL THE SHIFTS CUT BY ANOTHER HALF HOUR, AND I WANT THEIR WAGES RAISED IMMEDIATELY.

TRUSTEES AREN'T GOING TO LIKE—

BLAARGH

...LEAVE ME BE... DAMN IT... I'M ALL RIGHT...

GET BLANKETS AROUND THAT MAN!

WE'RE GETTING HIM TO A HOSPITAL!

A BAD NIGHT, EM.

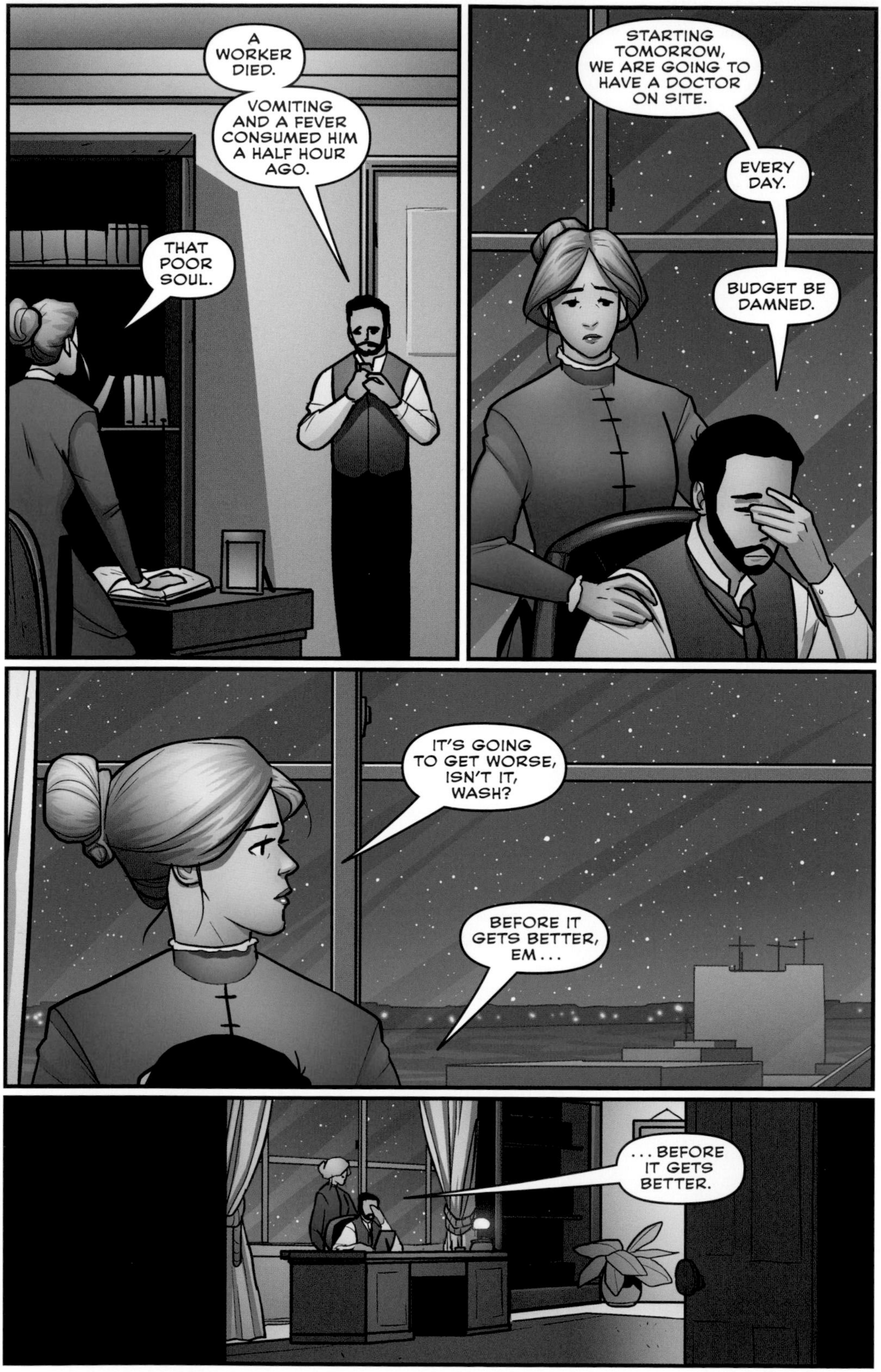
A WORKER DIED.
VOMITING AND A FEVER CONSUMED HIM A HALF HOUR AGO.
THAT POOR SOUL.
STARTING TOMORROW, WE ARE GOING TO HAVE A DOCTOR ON SITE.
EVERY DAY.
BUDGET BE DAMNED.
IT'S GOING TO GET WORSE, ISN'T IT, WASH?
BEFORE IT GETS BETTER, EM . . .
. . . BEFORE IT GETS BETTER.

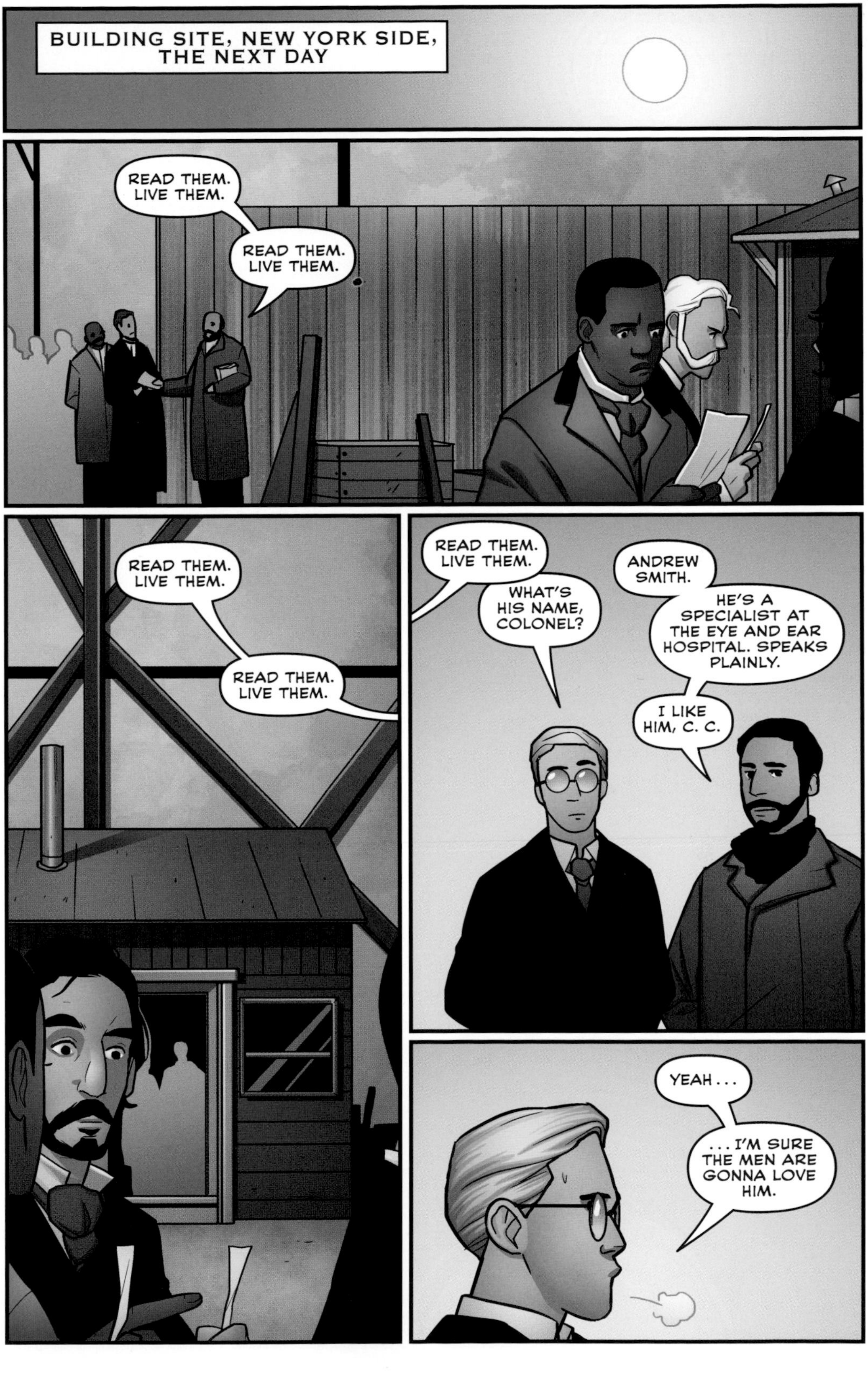
BUILDING SITE, NEW YORK SIDE, THE NEXT DAY
READ THEM. LIVE THEM.
READ THEM. LIVE THEM.
READ THEM. LIVE THEM.
READ THEM. LIVE THEM.
READ THEM. LIVE THEM.
WHAT'S HIS NAME, COLONEL?
ANDREW SMITH.
HE'S A SPECIALIST AT THE EYE AND EAR HOSPITAL. SPEAKS PLAINLY.
I LIKE HIM, C. C.
YEAH . . .
. . . I'M SURE THE MEN ARE GONNA LOVE HIM.

INSIDE THE NEW YORK CAISSON

"ONE: NEVER ENTER THE CAISSON WITH AN EMPTY STOMACH."

BETTER STOP PUKING WHEN I GET DOWN HERE.

"TWO: DO NOT OVEREXERT YOURSELF THE FIRST HOUR OUT OF AIRLOCK, AND LIE DOWN IF POSSIBLE."

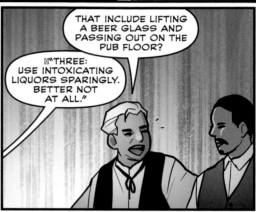

THAT INCLUDE LIFTING A BEER GLASS AND PASSING OUT ON THE PUB FLOOR?

"THREE: USE INTOXICATING LIQUORS SPARINGLY. BETTER NOT AT ALL."

BWHAHAHAHAHAHA

"FOUR: SEE THAT THE BOWELS ARE OPEN AT LEAST ONCE EVERY DAY."

WETTING MY PANTS COMING DOWN HERE COUNT?

"FIVE: REPORT ILLNESS TO THE BRIDGE OFFICE."

YEAH, BYE-BYE WAGE CHECK.

READ THEM. LIVE THEM.

MAKES GREAT TOILET PAPER.

SHRIP SHRIP

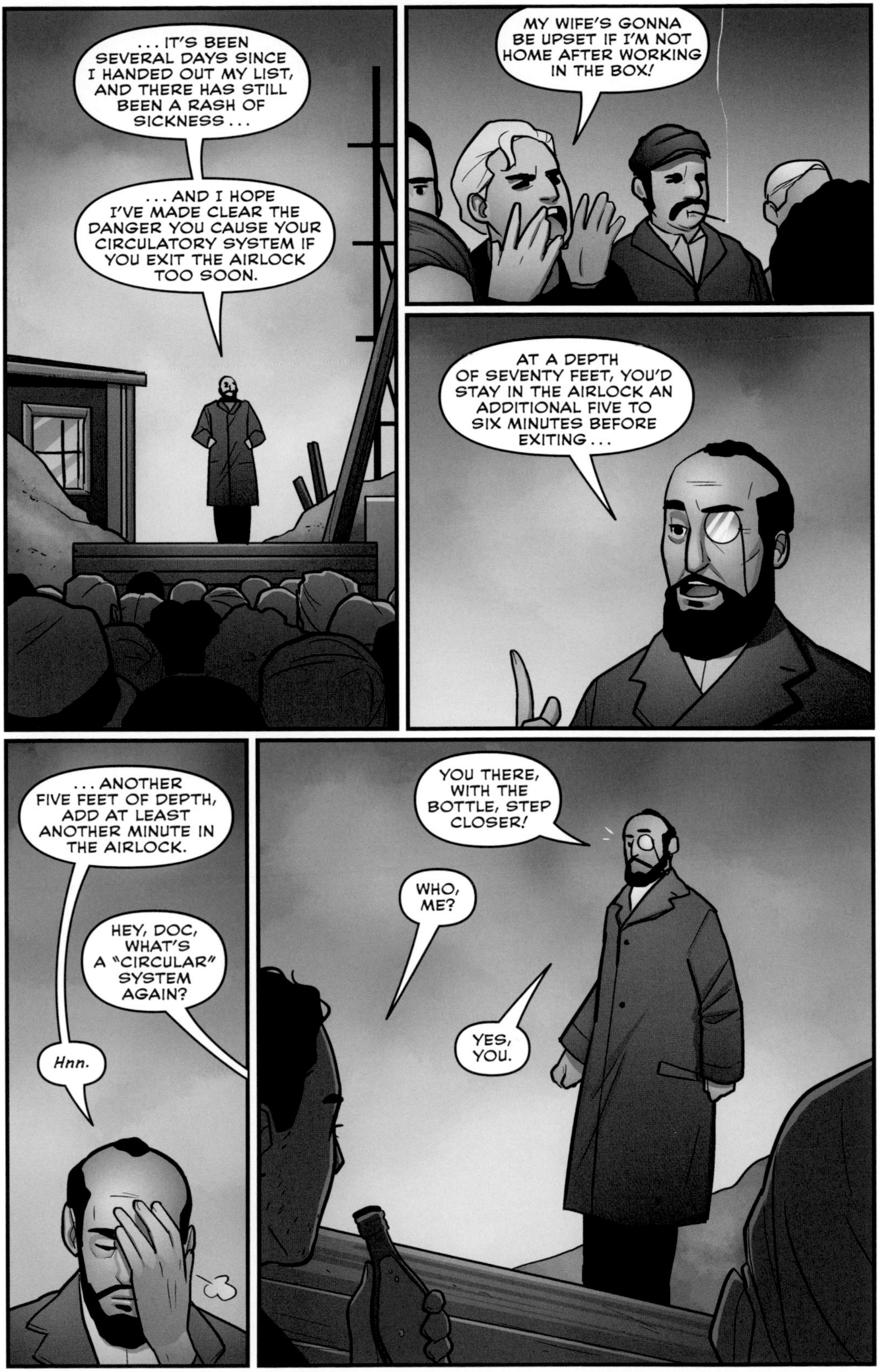

... IT'S BEEN SEVERAL DAYS SINCE I HANDED OUT MY LIST, AND THERE HAS STILL BEEN A RASH OF SICKNESS ...
... AND I HOPE I'VE MADE CLEAR THE DANGER YOU CAUSE YOUR CIRCULATORY SYSTEM IF YOU EXIT THE AIRLOCK TOO SOON.
MY WIFE'S GONNA BE UPSET IF I'M NOT HOME AFTER WORKING IN THE BOX!
AT A DEPTH OF SEVENTY FEET, YOU'D STAY IN THE AIRLOCK AN ADDITIONAL FIVE TO SIX MINUTES BEFORE EXITING ...
... ANOTHER FIVE FEET OF DEPTH, ADD AT LEAST ANOTHER MINUTE IN THE AIRLOCK.
HEY, DOC, WHAT'S A "CIRCULAR" SYSTEM AGAIN?
Hnn.
YOU THERE, WITH THE BOTTLE, STEP CLOSER!
WHO, ME?
YES, YOU.

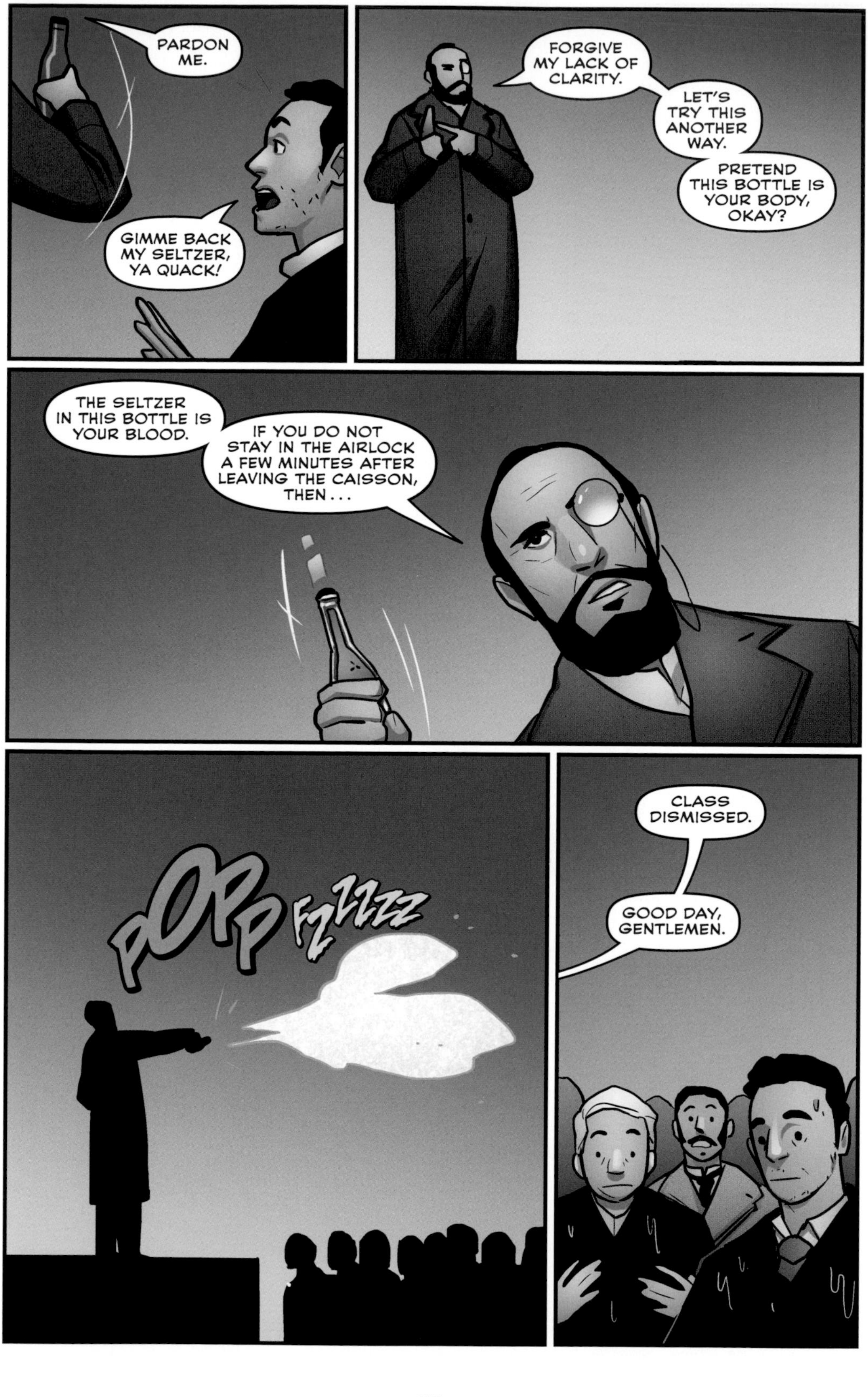

PARDON ME.
GIMME BACK MY SELTZER, YA QUACK!
FORGIVE MY LACK OF CLARITY.
LET'S TRY THIS ANOTHER WAY.
PRETEND THIS BOTTLE IS YOUR BODY, OKAY?
THE SELTZER IN THIS BOTTLE IS YOUR BLOOD.
IF YOU DO NOT STAY IN THE AIRLOCK A FEW MINUTES AFTER LEAVING THE CAISSON, THEN . . .
POPP
FZZZZZ
CLASS DISMISSED.
GOOD DAY, GENTLEMEN.

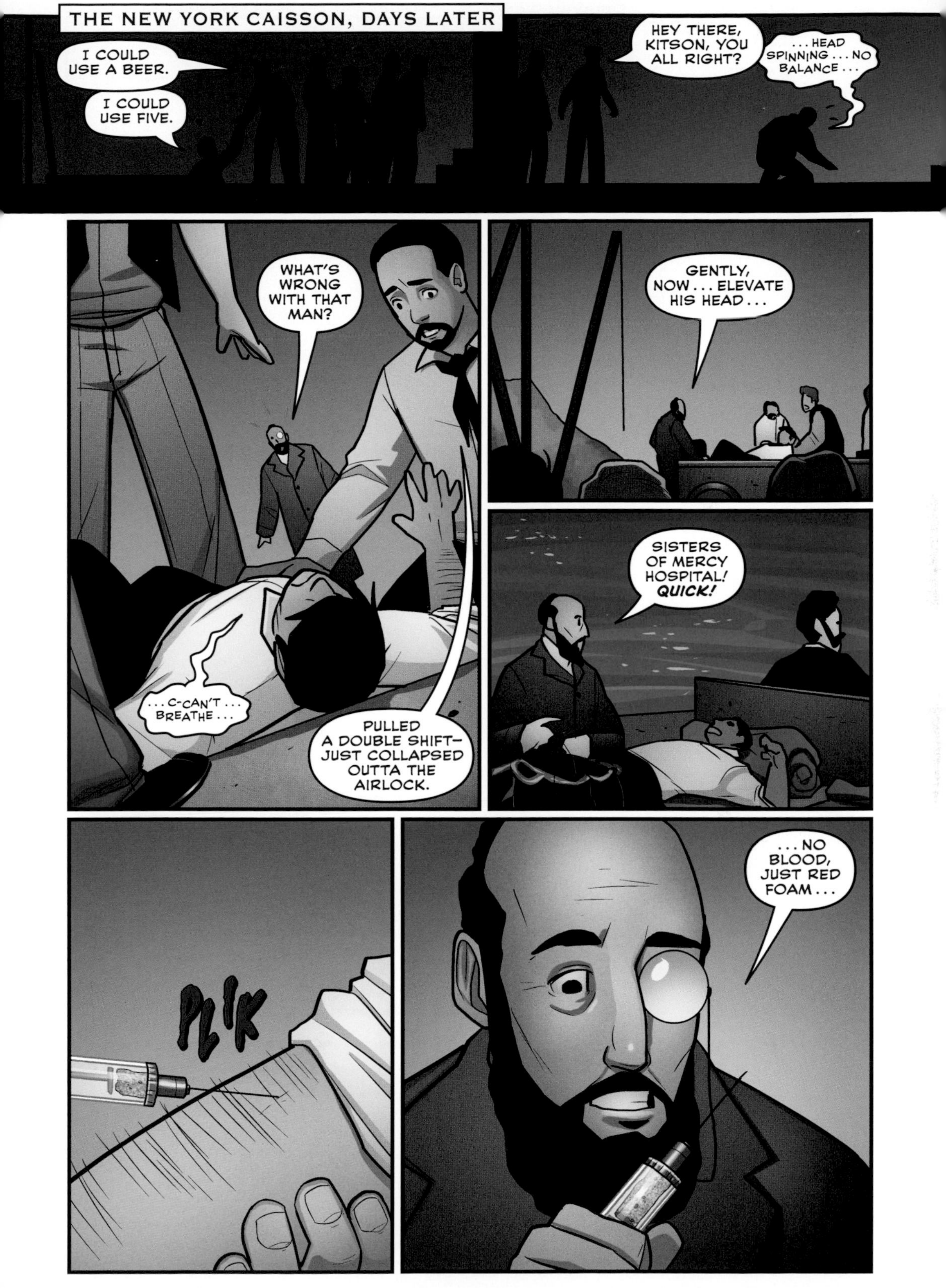
THE NEW YORK CAISSON, DAYS LATER
I COULD USE A BEER.
I COULD USE FIVE.
HEY THERE, KITSON, YOU ALL RIGHT?
. . . HEAD SPINNING . . . NO BALANCE . . .
WHAT'S WRONG WITH THAT MAN?
. . . C-CAN'T . . . BREATHE . . .
PULLED A DOUBLE SHIFT— JUST COLLAPSED OUTTA THE AIRLOCK.
GENTLY, NOW . . . ELEVATE HIS HEAD . . .
SISTERS OF MERCY HOSPITAL! ***QUICK!***
PLIK
. . . NO BLOOD, JUST RED FOAM . . .

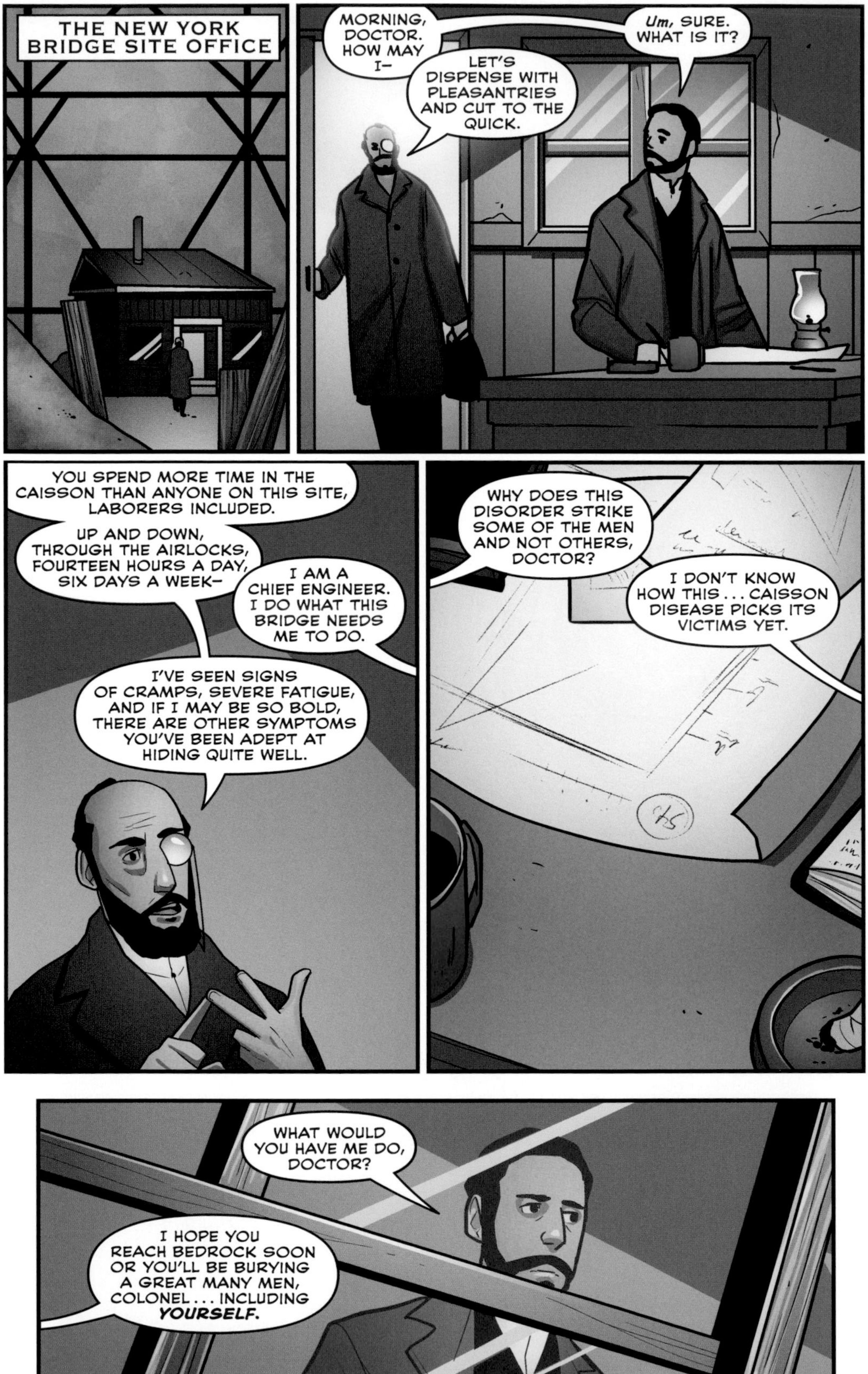
THE NEW YORK BRIDGE SITE OFFICE
MORNING, DOCTOR. HOW MAY I–
LET'S DISPENSE WITH PLEASANTRIES AND CUT TO THE QUICK.
Um, SURE. WHAT IS IT?
YOU SPEND MORE TIME IN THE CAISSON THAN ANYONE ON THIS SITE, LABORERS INCLUDED.
UP AND DOWN, THROUGH THE AIRLOCKS, FOURTEEN HOURS A DAY, SIX DAYS A WEEK–
I AM A CHIEF ENGINEER. I DO WHAT THIS BRIDGE NEEDS ME TO DO.
I'VE SEEN SIGNS OF CRAMPS, SEVERE FATIGUE, AND IF I MAY BE SO BOLD, THERE ARE OTHER SYMPTOMS YOU'VE BEEN ADEPT AT HIDING QUITE WELL.
WHY DOES THIS DISORDER STRIKE SOME OF THE MEN AND NOT OTHERS, DOCTOR?
I DON'T KNOW HOW THIS . . . CAISSON DISEASE PICKS ITS VICTIMS YET.
WHAT WOULD YOU HAVE ME DO, DOCTOR?
I HOPE YOU REACH BEDROCK SOON OR YOU'LL BE BURYING A GREAT MANY MEN, COLONEL . . . INCLUDING ***YOURSELF***.

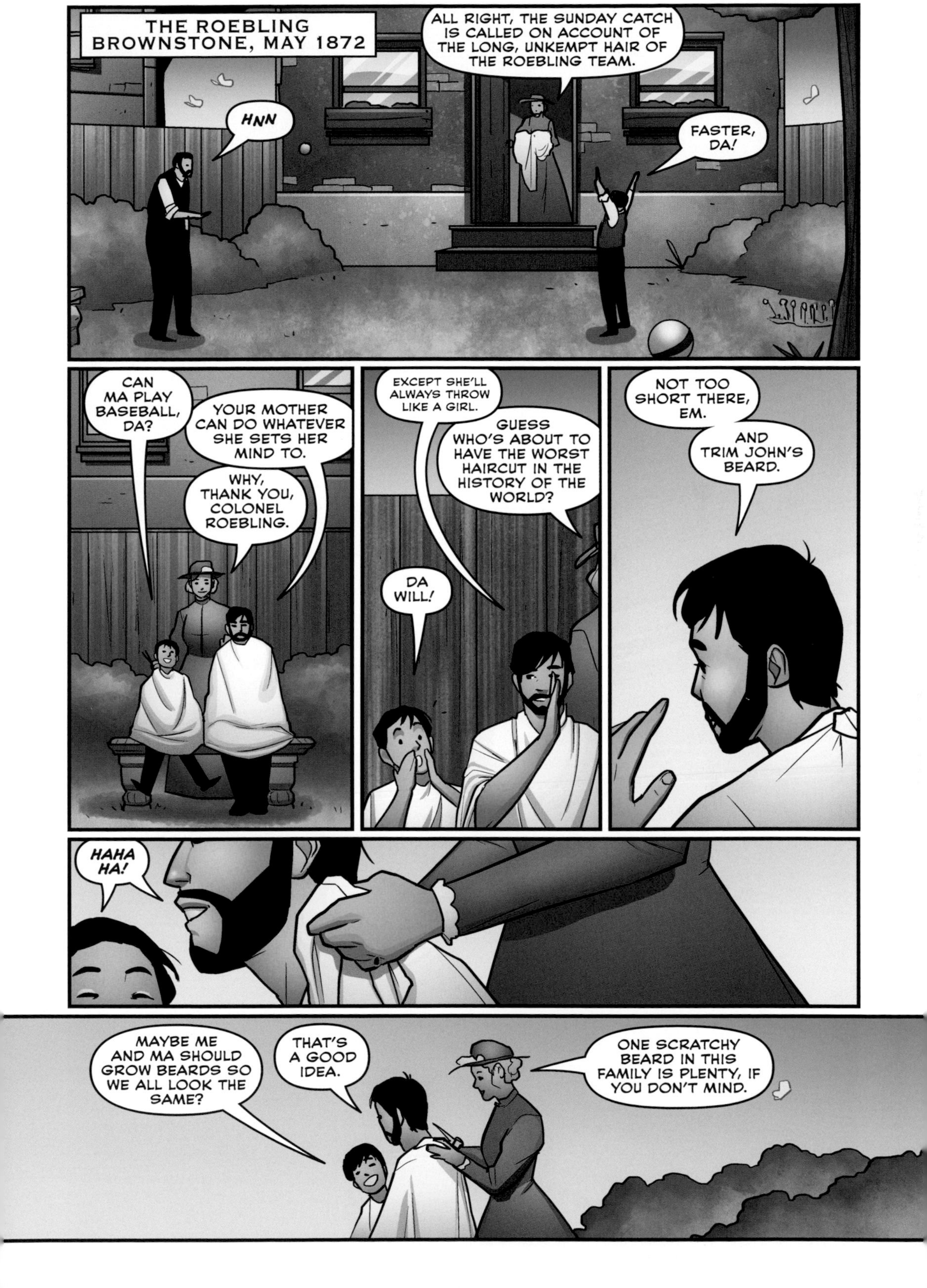
THE ROEBLING BROWNSTONE, MAY 1872
ALL RIGHT, THE SUNDAY CATCH IS CALLED ON ACCOUNT OF THE LONG, UNKEMPT HAIR OF THE ROEBLING TEAM.
HNN
FASTER, DA!
CAN MA PLAY BASEBALL, DA?
YOUR MOTHER CAN DO WHATEVER SHE SETS HER MIND TO.
WHY, THANK YOU, COLONEL ROEBLING.
EXCEPT SHE'LL ALWAYS THROW LIKE A GIRL.
GUESS WHO'S ABOUT TO HAVE THE WORST HAIRCUT IN THE HISTORY OF THE WORLD?
DA WILL!
NOT TOO SHORT THERE, EM.
AND TRIM JOHN'S BEARD.
HAHA HA!
MAYBE ME AND MA SHOULD GROW BEARDS SO WE ALL LOOK THE SAME?
THAT'S A GOOD IDEA.
ONE SCRATCHY BEARD IN THIS FAMILY IS PLENTY, IF YOU DON'T MIND.

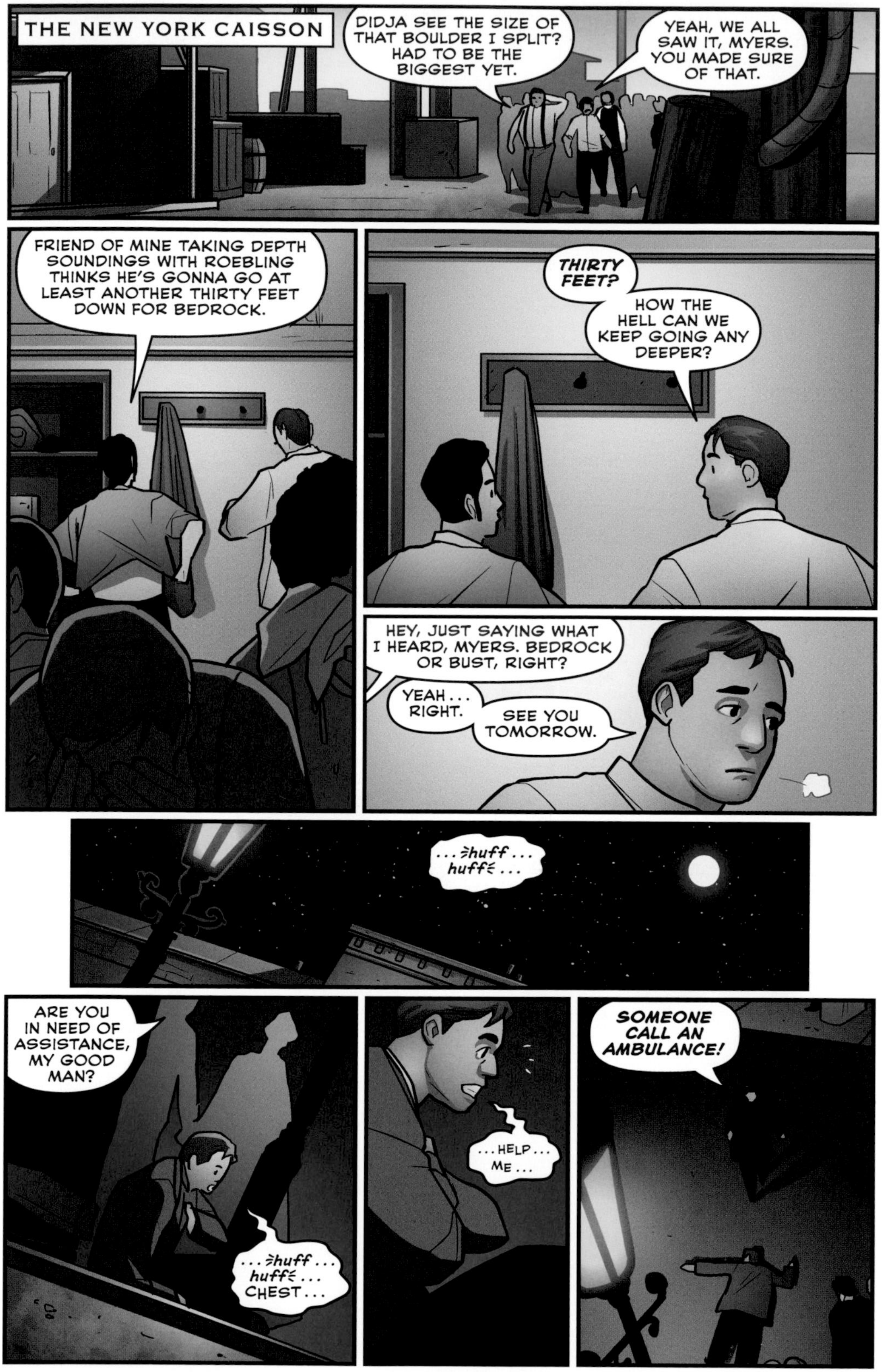
THE NEW YORK CAISSON
DIDJA SEE THE SIZE OF THAT BOULDER I SPLIT? HAD TO BE THE BIGGEST YET.
YEAH, WE ALL SAW IT, MYERS. YOU MADE SURE OF THAT.
FRIEND OF MINE TAKING DEPTH SOUNDINGS WITH ROEBLING THINKS HE'S GONNA GO AT LEAST ANOTHER THIRTY FEET DOWN FOR BEDROCK.
THIRTY FEET?
HOW THE HELL CAN WE KEEP GOING ANY DEEPER?
HEY, JUST SAYING WHAT I HEARD, MYERS. BEDROCK OR BUST, RIGHT?
YEAH... RIGHT.
SEE YOU TOMORROW.
...huff... huff...
ARE YOU IN NEED OF ASSISTANCE, MY GOOD MAN?
...huff... huff... CHEST...
...HELP... ME...
SOMEONE CALL AN AMBULANCE!

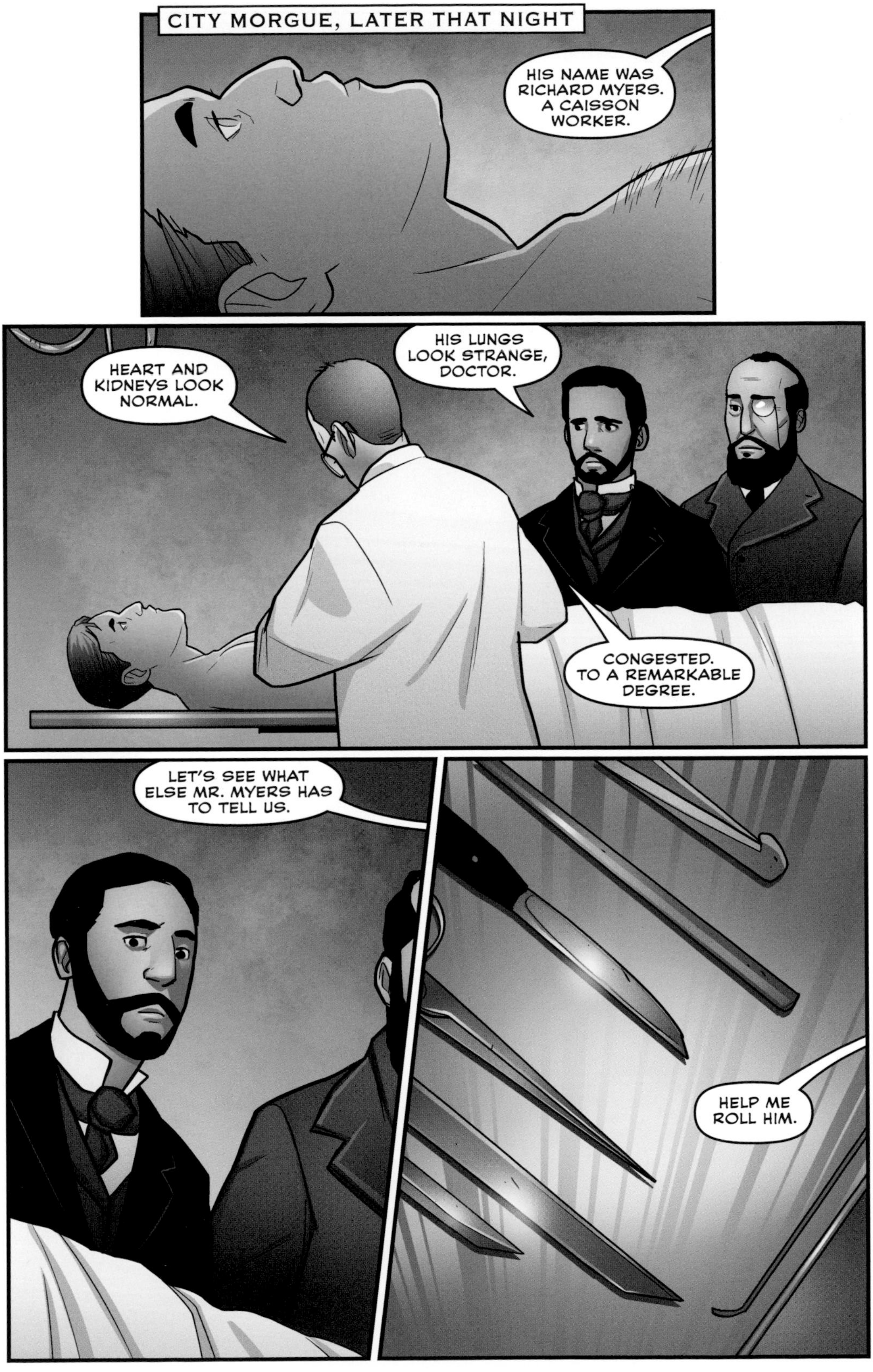
CITY MORGUE, LATER THAT NIGHT
HIS NAME WAS RICHARD MYERS. A CAISSON WORKER.
HEART AND KIDNEYS LOOK NORMAL.
HIS LUNGS LOOK STRANGE, DOCTOR.
CONGESTED. TO A REMARKABLE DEGREE.
LET'S SEE WHAT ELSE MR. MYERS HAS TO TELL US.
HELP ME ROLL HIM.

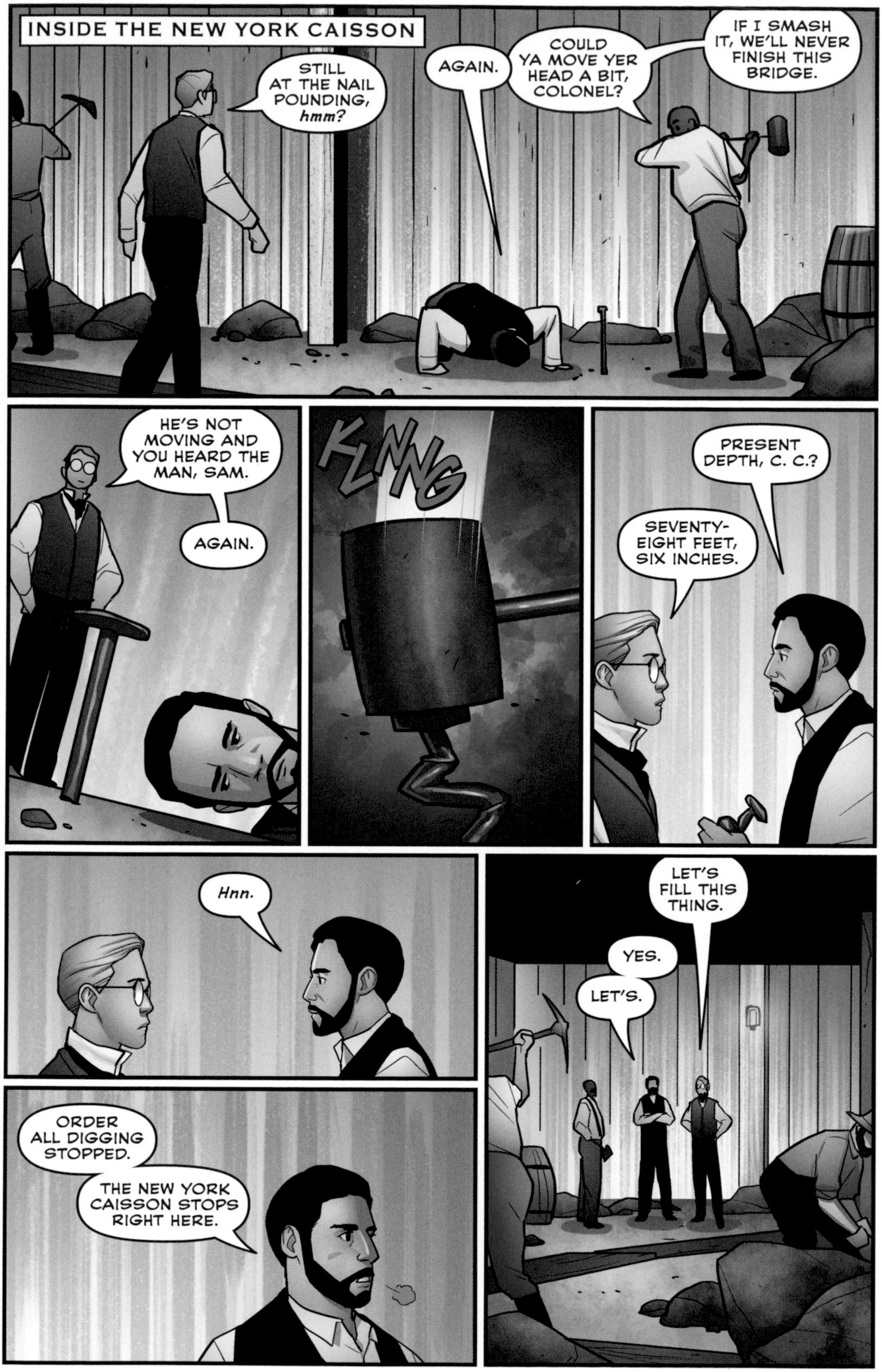
INSIDE THE NEW YORK CAISSON
STILL AT THE NAIL POUNDING, *hmm?*
AGAIN.
COULD YA MOVE YER HEAD A BIT, COLONEL?
IF I SMASH IT, WE'LL NEVER FINISH THIS BRIDGE.
HE'S NOT MOVING AND YOU HEARD THE MAN, SAM.
AGAIN.
KLNNG
PRESENT DEPTH, C. C.?
SEVENTY-EIGHT FEET, SIX INCHES.
Hnn.
ORDER ALL DIGGING STOPPED.
THE NEW YORK CAISSON STOPS RIGHT HERE.
LET'S FILL THIS THING.
YES.
LET'S.

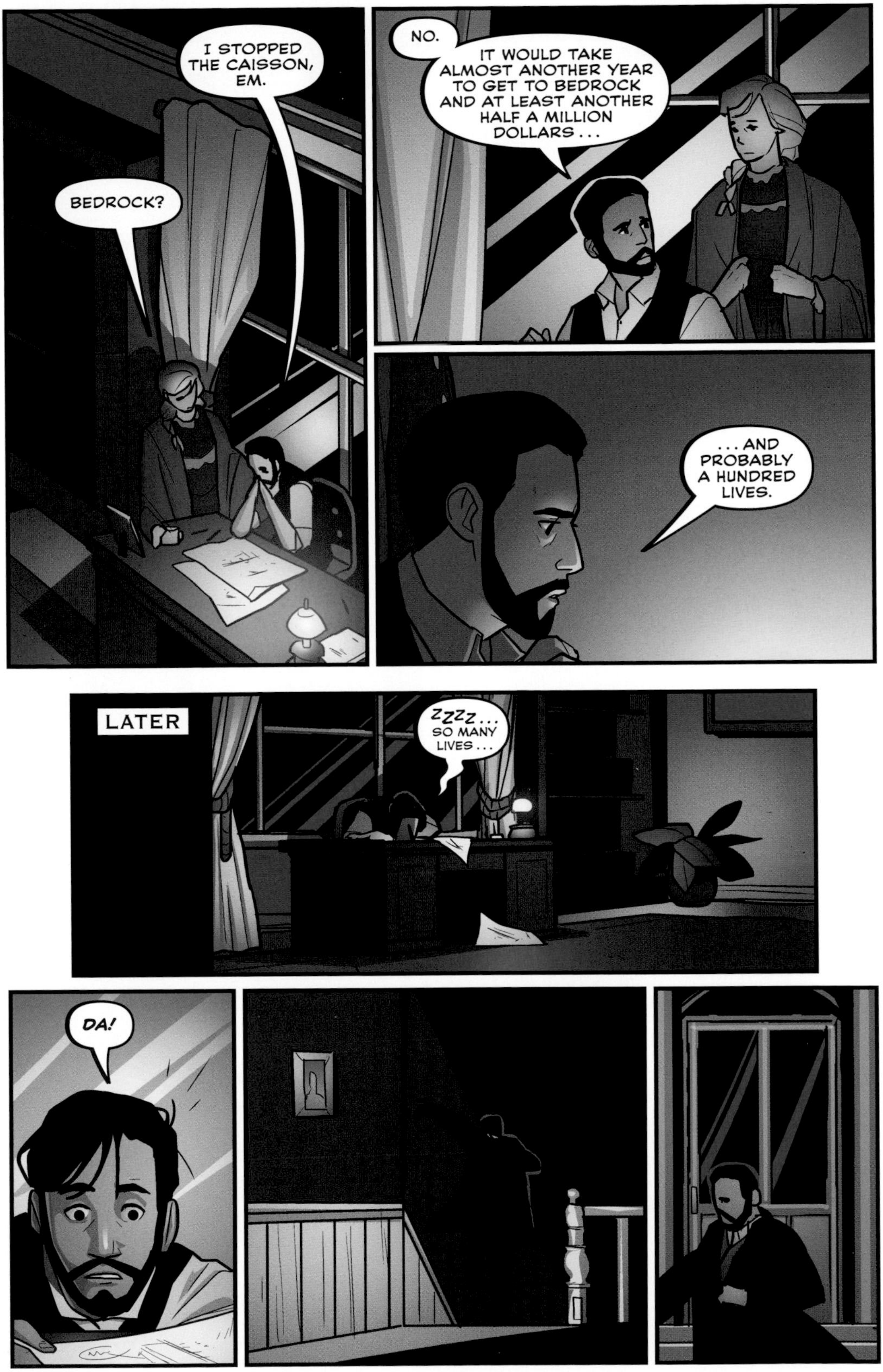
I STOPPED THE CAISSON, EM.
BEDROCK?
NO.
IT WOULD TAKE ALMOST ANOTHER YEAR TO GET TO BEDROCK AND AT LEAST ANOTHER HALF A MILLION DOLLARS . . .
. . . AND PROBABLY A HUNDRED LIVES.
LATER
ZZZZ . . . SO MANY LIVES . . .
DA!

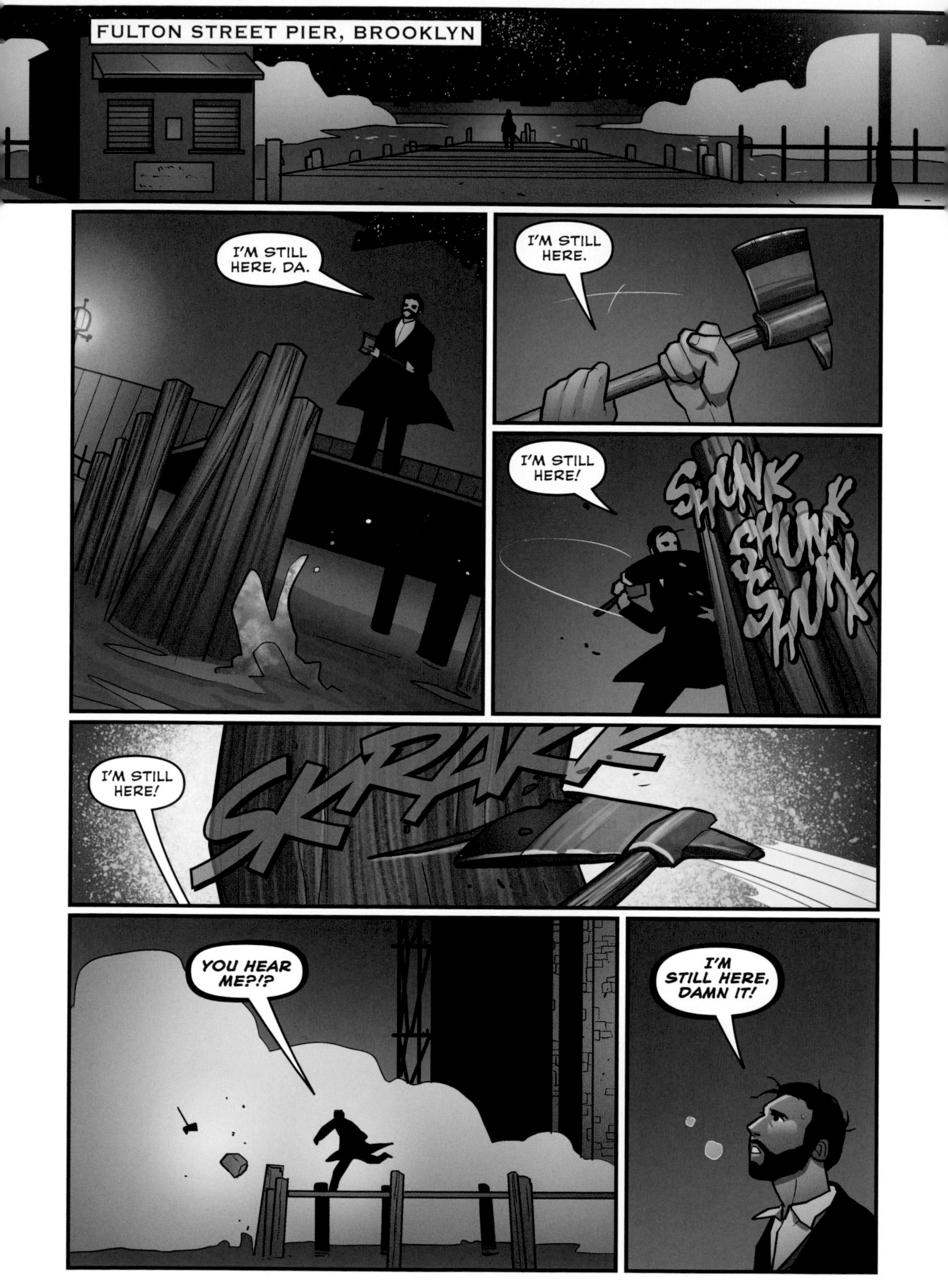
FULTON STREET PIER, BROOKLYN
I'M STILL HERE, DA.
I'M STILL HERE.
I'M STILL HERE!
SHUNK SHUNK SHUNK
I'M STILL HERE!
SKRAKK
YOU HEAR ME?!?
I'M STILL HERE, DAMN IT!

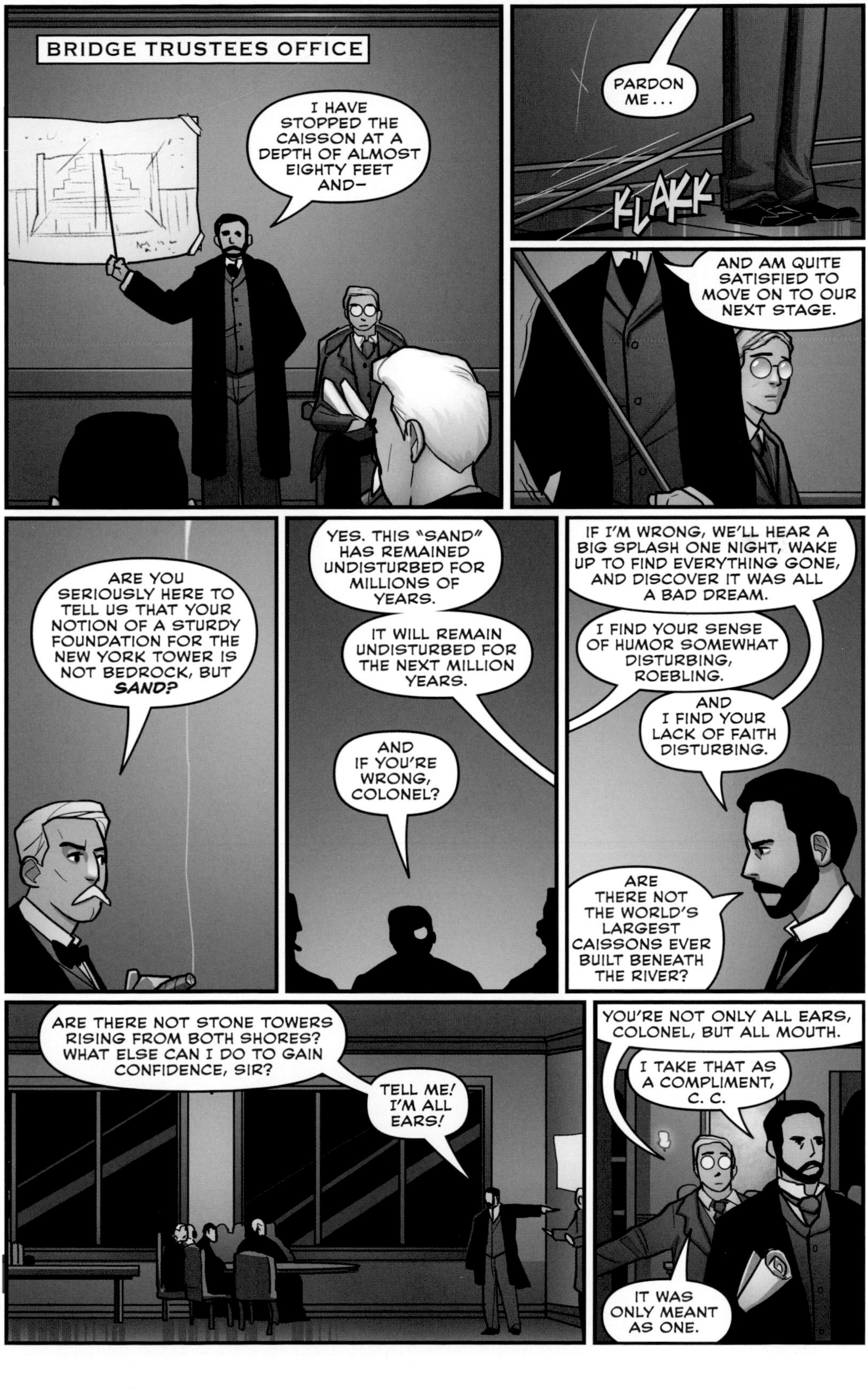
BRIDGE TRUSTEES OFFICE
I HAVE STOPPED THE CAISSON AT A DEPTH OF ALMOST EIGHTY FEET AND—
PARDON ME . . .
KLAKK
AND AM QUITE SATISFIED TO MOVE ON TO OUR NEXT STAGE.
ARE YOU SERIOUSLY HERE TO TELL US THAT YOUR NOTION OF A STURDY FOUNDATION FOR THE NEW YORK TOWER IS NOT BEDROCK, BUT *SAND?*
YES. THIS "SAND" HAS REMAINED UNDISTURBED FOR MILLIONS OF YEARS.
IT WILL REMAIN UNDISTURBED FOR THE NEXT MILLION YEARS.
AND IF YOU'RE WRONG, COLONEL?
IF I'M WRONG, WE'LL HEAR A BIG SPLASH ONE NIGHT, WAKE UP TO FIND EVERYTHING GONE, AND DISCOVER IT WAS ALL A BAD DREAM.
I FIND YOUR SENSE OF HUMOR SOMEWHAT DISTURBING, ROEBLING.
AND I FIND YOUR LACK OF FAITH DISTURBING.
ARE THERE NOT THE WORLD'S LARGEST CAISSONS EVER BUILT BENEATH THE RIVER?
ARE THERE NOT STONE TOWERS RISING FROM BOTH SHORES? WHAT ELSE CAN I DO TO GAIN CONFIDENCE, SIR?
TELL ME! I'M ALL EARS!
YOU'RE NOT ONLY ALL EARS, COLONEL, BUT ALL MOUTH.
I TAKE THAT AS A COMPLIMENT, C. C.
IT WAS ONLY MEANT AS ONE.

THE BROOKLYN TOWER, DECEMBER 1872

WHAT DO YOU WANT TO DO, COLONEL?

WEATHER'S TOO TREACHEROUS, AND IT'S ONLY EXPECTED TO GET WORSE, DOUGLAS.

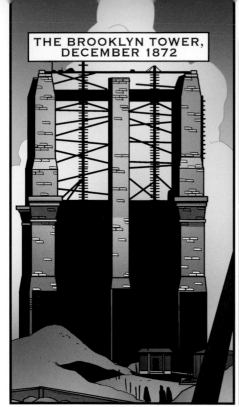

WE'LL START UP AGAIN IN MARCH.

C. C., PLEASE SCHEDULE THE NEXT WEEKLY MEETING FOR TUESDAY.

ALL ASSISTANTS MANDATORY.

YOU GOT IT, COLONEL. GET SOME REST.

COLONEL!

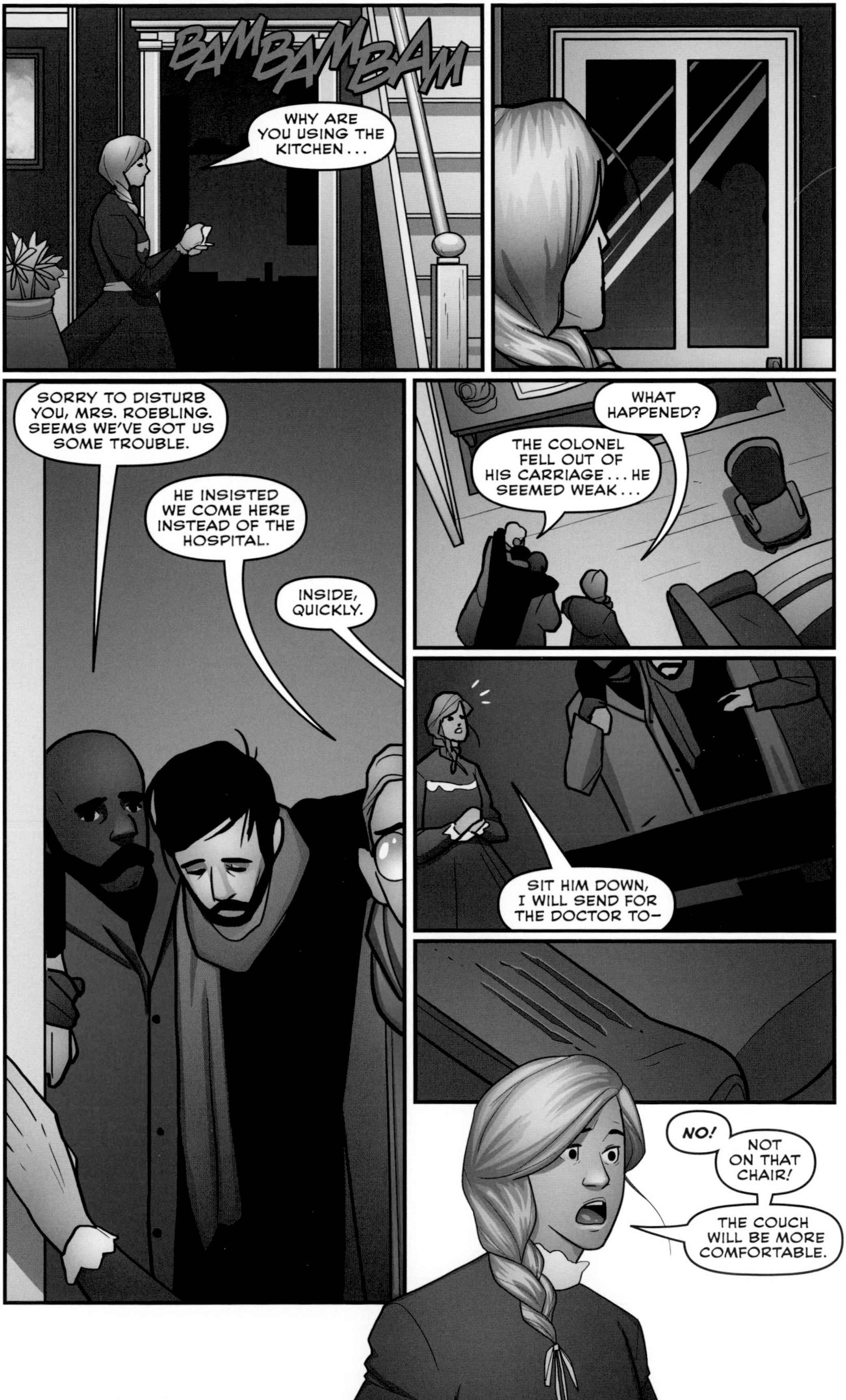
BAM BAM BAM
WHY ARE YOU USING THE KITCHEN . . .
SORRY TO DISTURB YOU, MRS. ROEBLING. SEEMS WE'VE GOT US SOME TROUBLE.
HE INSISTED WE COME HERE INSTEAD OF THE HOSPITAL.
INSIDE, QUICKLY.
WHAT HAPPENED?
THE COLONEL FELL OUT OF HIS CARRIAGE . . . HE SEEMED WEAK . . .
SIT HIM DOWN, I WILL SEND FOR THE DOCTOR TO–
NO!
NOT ON THAT CHAIR!
THE COUCH WILL BE MORE COMFORTABLE.

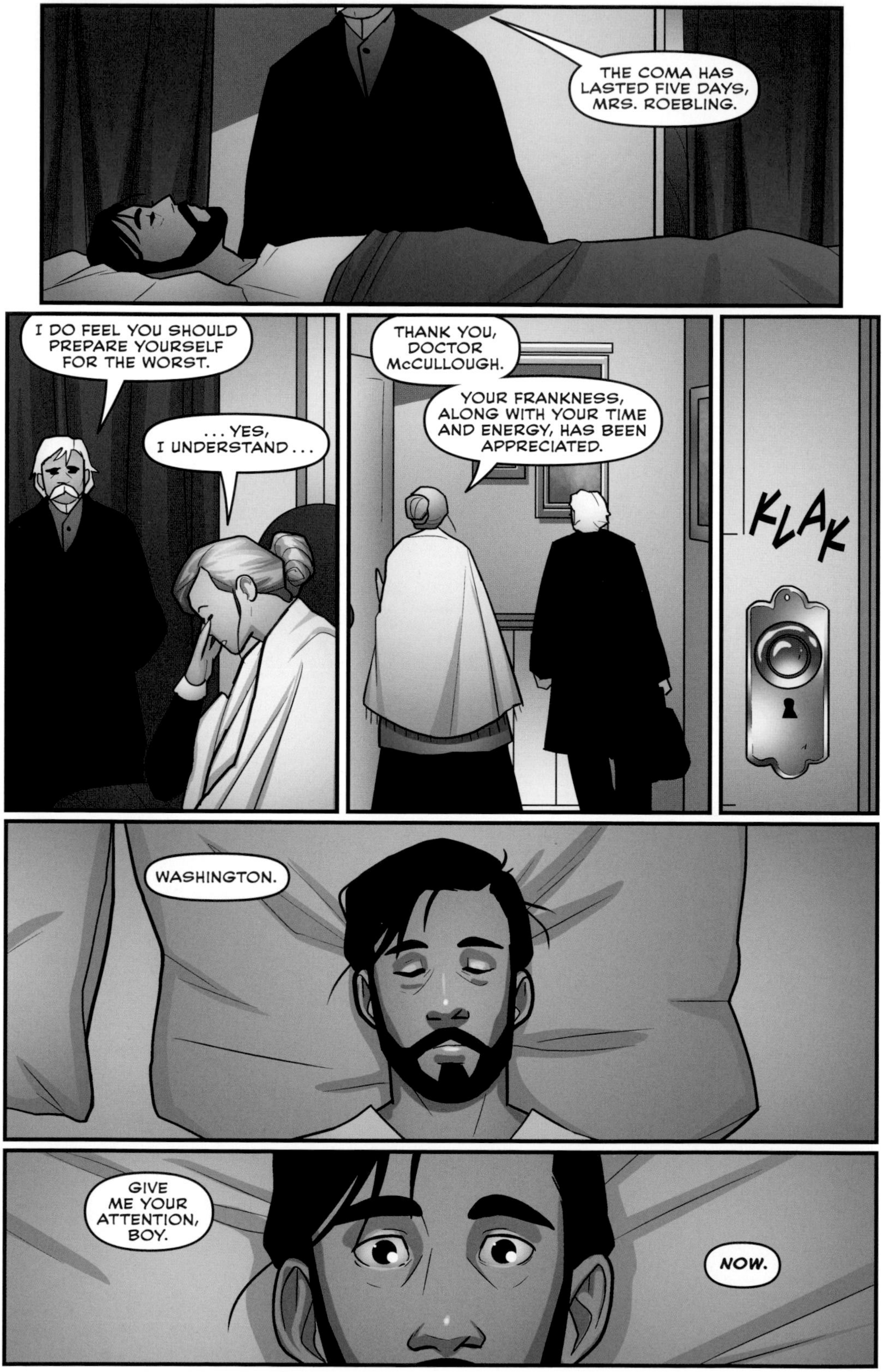
THE COMA HAS LASTED FIVE DAYS, MRS. ROEBLING.
I DO FEEL YOU SHOULD PREPARE YOURSELF FOR THE WORST.
...YES, I UNDERSTAND...
THANK YOU, DOCTOR McCULLOUGH.
YOUR FRANKNESS, ALONG WITH YOUR TIME AND ENERGY, HAS BEEN APPRECIATED.
KLAK
WASHINGTON.
GIVE ME YOUR ATTENTION, BOY.
NOW.

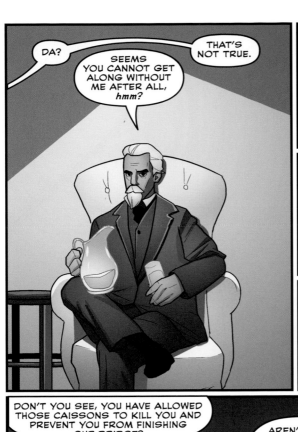

DA?

SEEMS YOU CANNOT GET ALONG WITHOUT ME AFTER ALL, *hmm?*

THAT'S NOT TRUE.

WHAT WORDS DO YOU NOT UNDERSTAND?

"LITTLE CHANCE OF RECOVERY"...

...OR "PREPARE YOURSELF FOR THE WORST"?

DON'T YOU SEE, YOU HAVE ALLOWED THOSE CAISSONS TO KILL YOU AND PREVENT YOU FROM FINISHING OUR BRIDGE.

"OUR BRIDGE"? HOW THE HELL IS IT *"OUR BRIDGE"?!*

AREN'T *YOU* THE ONE WHO DECIDED TO DIE BEFORE A LICK OF WORK GOT DONE?

I'M NOT THE ONE WHO ALLOWED MY FOOT TO BE CRUSHED LIKE A ROTTEN APPLE! THAT WAS YOU, DA! THAT WAS *YOU!*

UP ON THE BROOKLYN TOWER—YOU CAN TASTE IT NOW, YES. FEEL OUR BRIDGE LEAPING OVER THAT RIVER—CLEARER THAN THAT DAY WE WERE STUCK ON THE FERRY?

STOP SAYING *"OUR"* BRIDGE.

IT'S ANYTHING BUT.

THEN WHOSE BRIDGE IS IT, WASHINGTON?

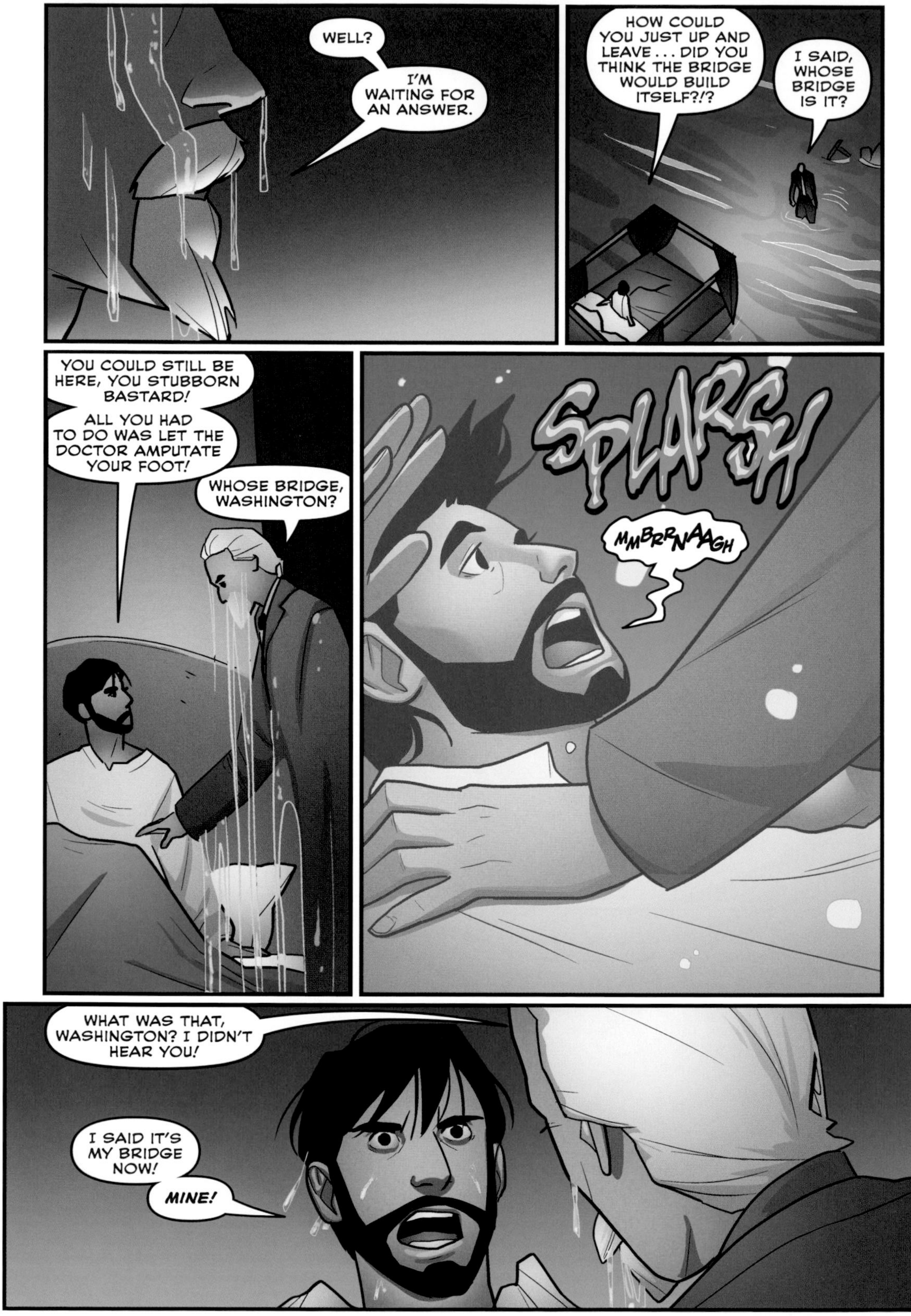
WELL?
I'M WAITING FOR AN ANSWER.
HOW COULD YOU JUST UP AND LEAVE . . . DID YOU THINK THE BRIDGE WOULD BUILD ITSELF?!?
I SAID, WHOSE BRIDGE IS IT?
YOU COULD STILL BE HERE, YOU STUBBORN BASTARD!
ALL YOU HAD TO DO WAS LET THE DOCTOR AMPUTATE YOUR FOOT!
WHOSE BRIDGE, WASHINGTON?
SPLARSH
MMBRRNAAGH
WHAT WAS THAT, WASHINGTON? I DIDN'T HEAR YOU!
I SAID IT'S MY BRIDGE NOW!
MINE!

IT'S *MY* DAMN BRIDGE NOW, DA!

UNFF

GNNR

AGHH

WASH... YOU'RE UP... HOW...?

THE MAIN CABLES—THE DIAGONAL STAYS—THE ROADWAY...

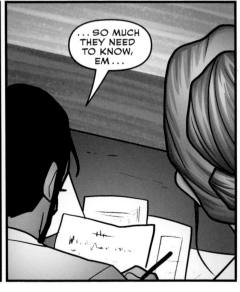

...SO MUCH THEY NEED TO KNOW, EM...

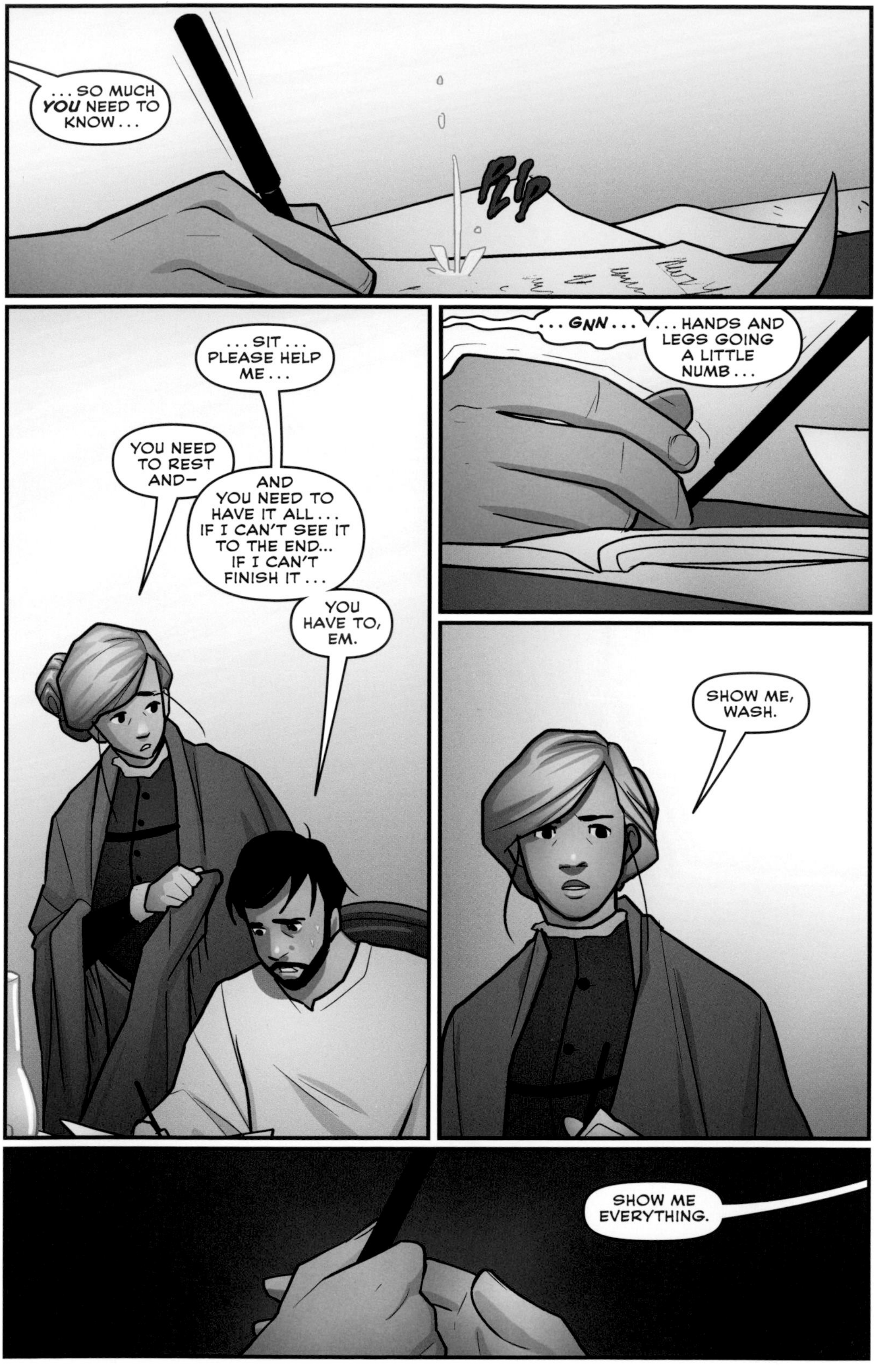

...SO MUCH YOU NEED TO KNOW...
PLIP
...SIT... PLEASE HELP ME...
YOU NEED TO REST AND–
AND YOU NEED TO HAVE IT ALL... IF I CAN'T SEE IT TO THE END... IF I CAN'T FINISH IT...
YOU HAVE TO, EM.
...GNN...
...HANDS AND LEGS GOING A LITTLE NUMB...
SHOW ME, WASH.
SHOW ME EVERYTHING.

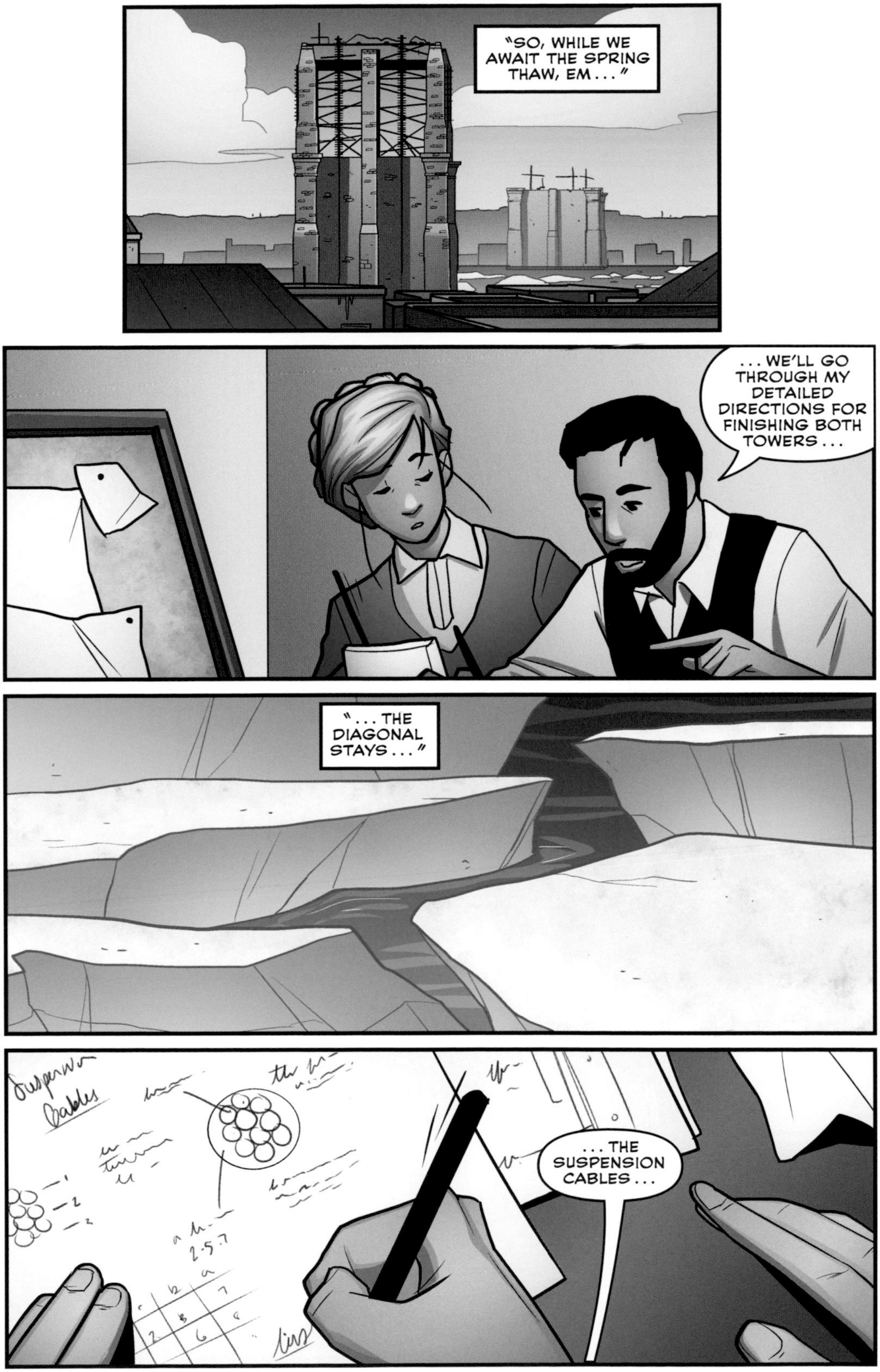
"SO, WHILE WE AWAIT THE SPRING THAW, EM . . ."
. . . WE'LL GO THROUGH MY DETAILED DIRECTIONS FOR FINISHING BOTH TOWERS . . .
". . . THE DIAGONAL STAYS . . ."
. . . THE SUSPENSION CABLES . . .

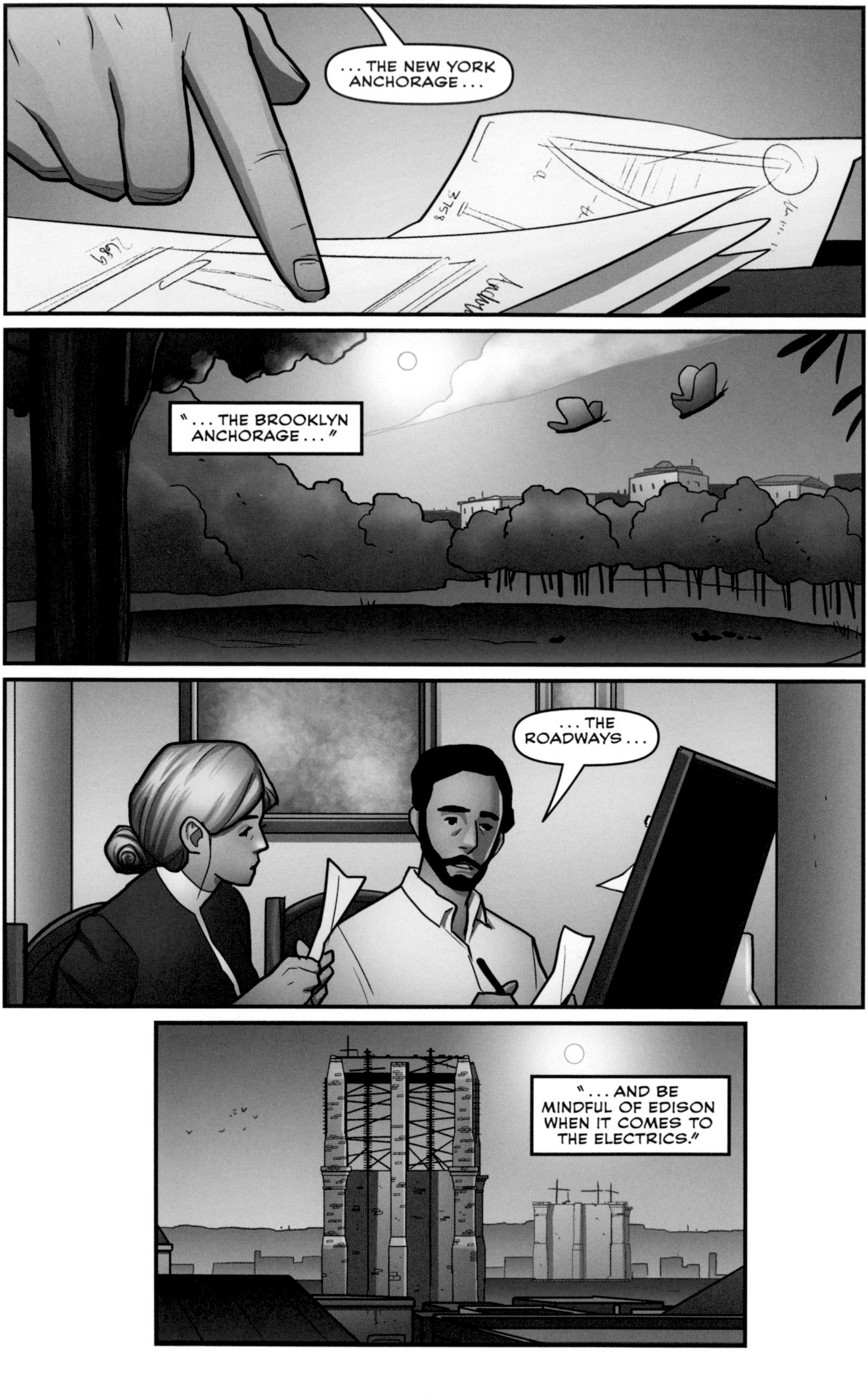
. . . THE NEW YORK ANCHORAGE . . .
" . . . THE BROOKLYN ANCHORAGE . . ."
. . . THE ROADWAYS . . .
" . . . AND BE MINDFUL OF EDISON WHEN IT COMES TO THE ELECTRICS."

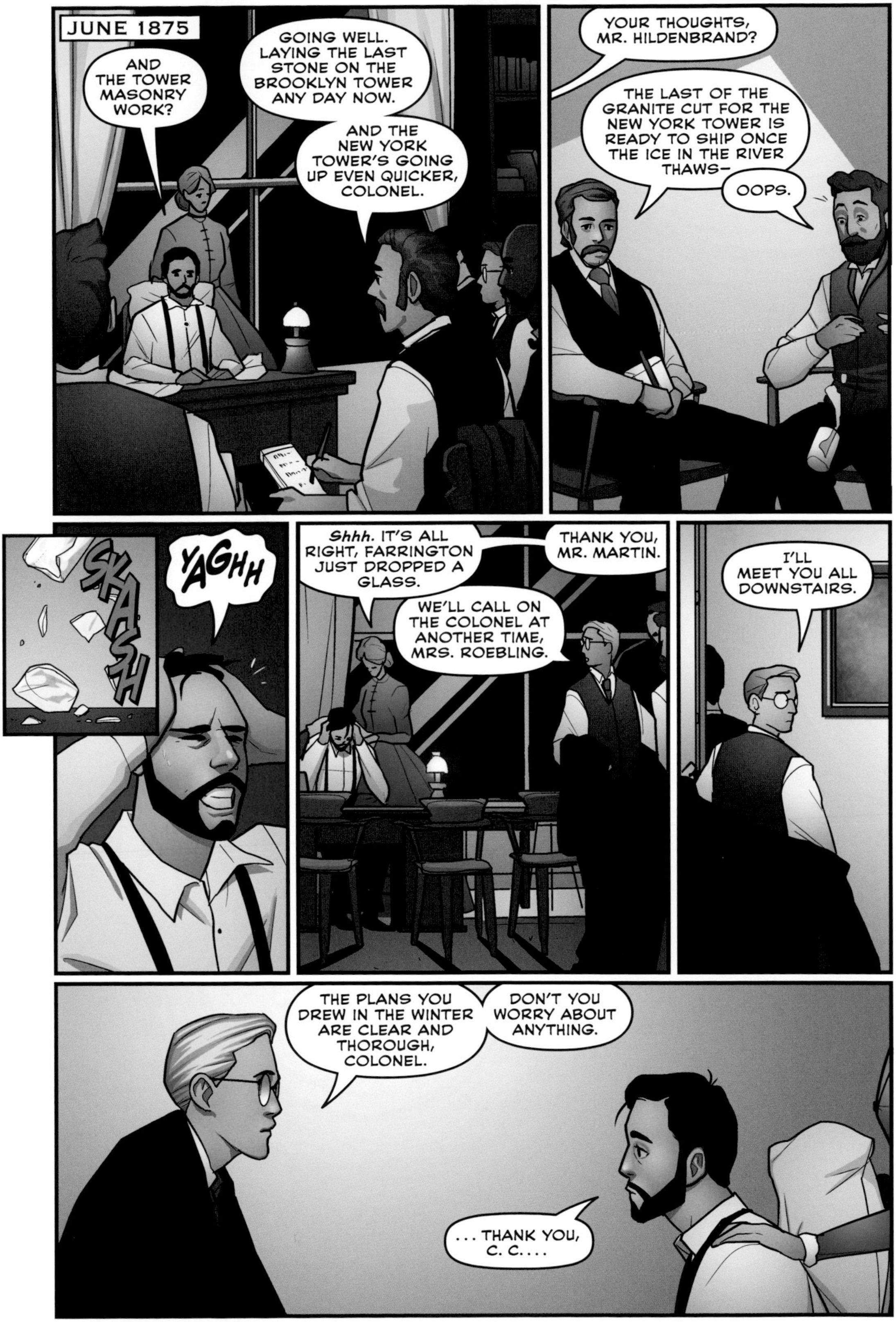
JUNE 1875
AND THE TOWER MASONRY WORK?
GOING WELL. LAYING THE LAST STONE ON THE BROOKLYN TOWER ANY DAY NOW.
AND THE NEW YORK TOWER'S GOING UP EVEN QUICKER, COLONEL.
YOUR THOUGHTS, MR. HILDENBRAND?
THE LAST OF THE GRANITE CUT FOR THE NEW YORK TOWER IS READY TO SHIP ONCE THE ICE IN THE RIVER THAWS—
OOPS.
SKASH
YAGHH
Shhh. IT'S ALL RIGHT, FARRINGTON JUST DROPPED A GLASS.
THANK YOU, MR. MARTIN.
WE'LL CALL ON THE COLONEL AT ANOTHER TIME, MRS. ROEBLING.
I'LL MEET YOU ALL DOWNSTAIRS.
THE PLANS YOU DREW IN THE WINTER ARE CLEAR AND THOROUGH, COLONEL.
DON'T YOU WORRY ABOUT ANYTHING.
... THANK YOU, C. C. ...

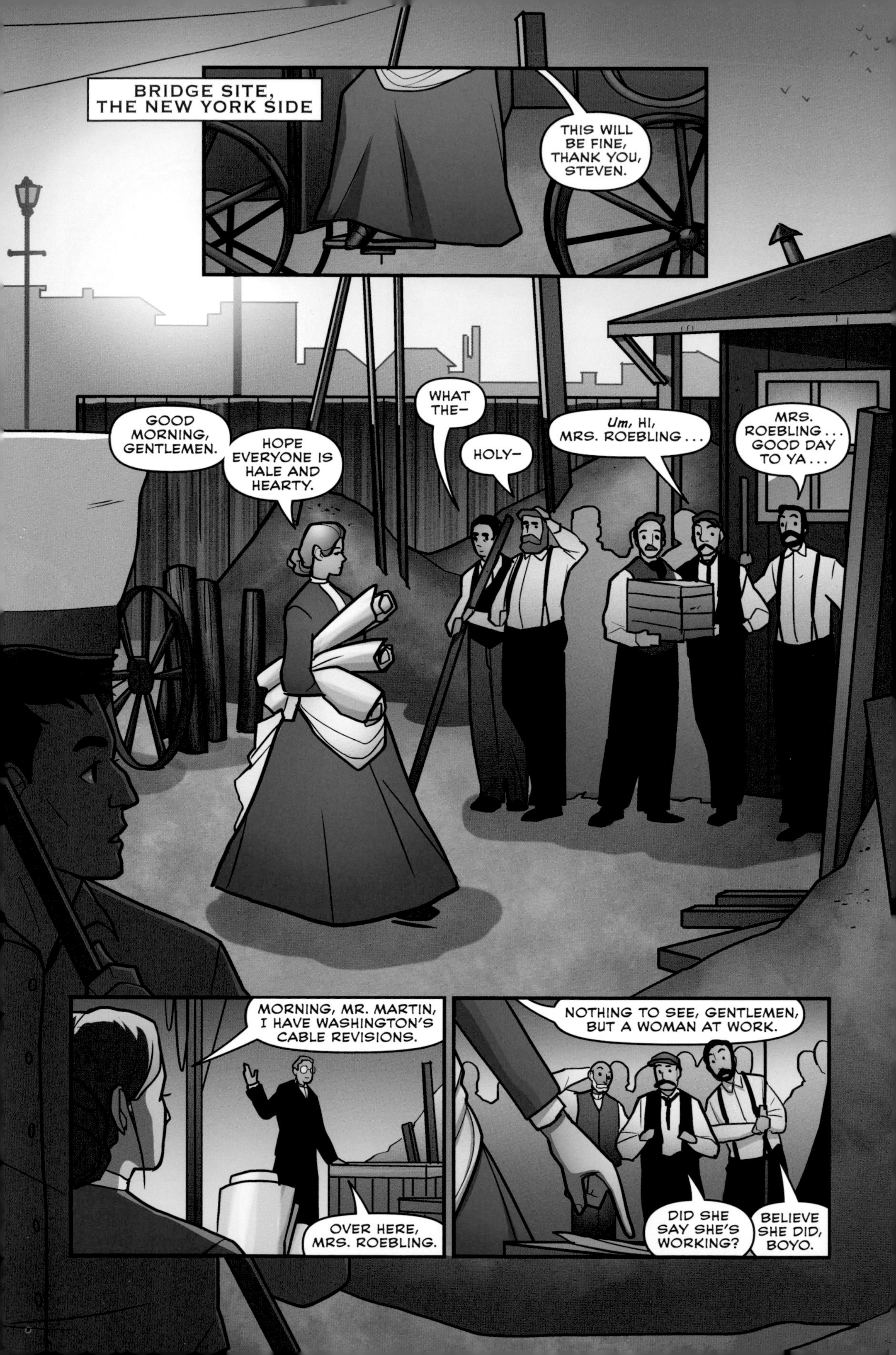
BRIDGE SITE, THE NEW YORK SIDE
THIS WILL BE FINE, THANK YOU, STEVEN.
GOOD MORNING, GENTLEMEN.
HOPE EVERYONE IS HALE AND HEARTY.
WHAT THE–
HOLY–
Um, HI, MRS. ROEBLING . . .
MRS. ROEBLING . . . GOOD DAY TO YA . . .
MORNING, MR. MARTIN, I HAVE WASHINGTON'S CABLE REVISIONS.
OVER HERE, MRS. ROEBLING.
NOTHING TO SEE, GENTLEMEN, BUT A WOMAN AT WORK.
DID SHE SAY SHE'S WORKING?
BELIEVE SHE DID, BOYO.

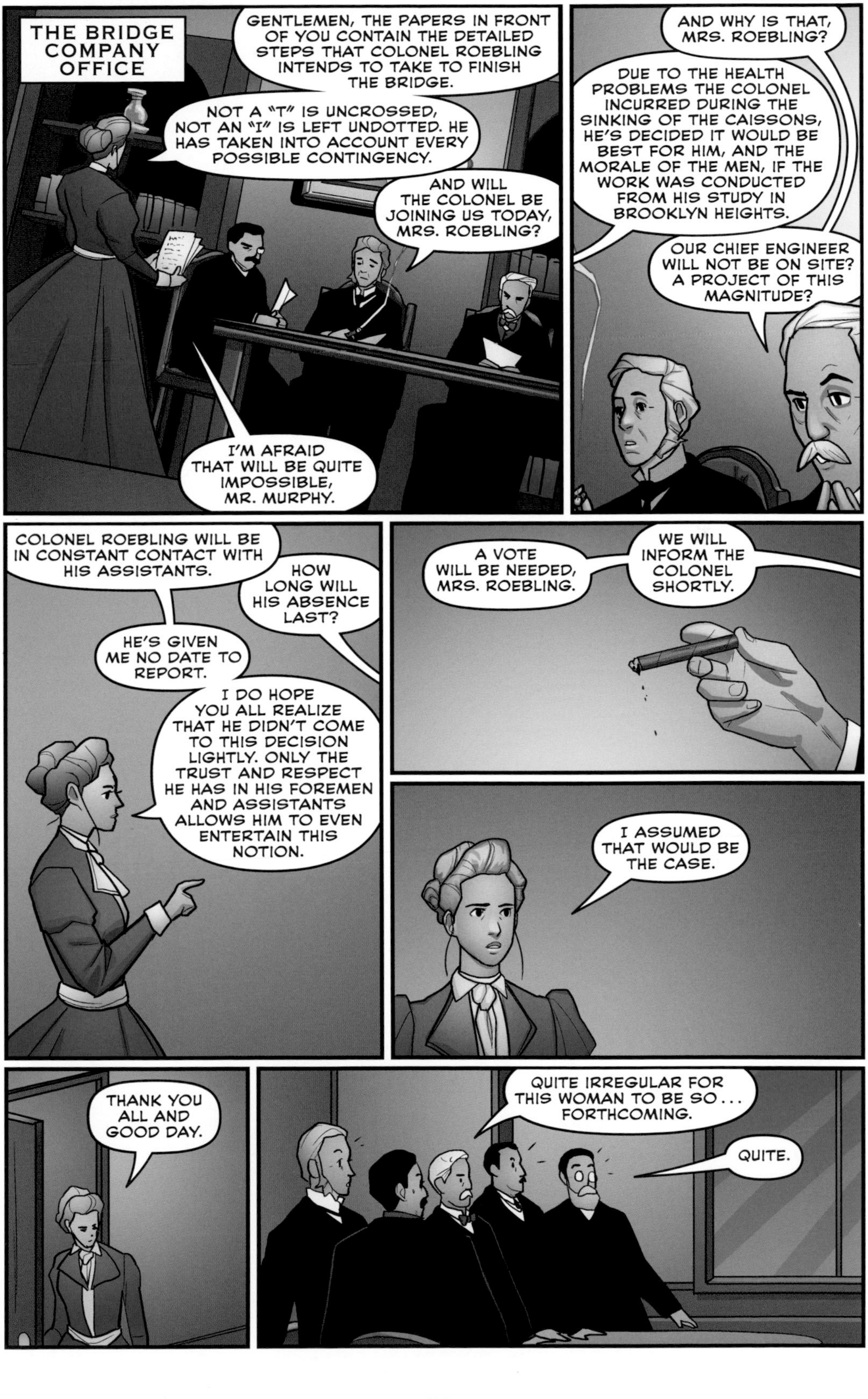
THE BRIDGE COMPANY OFFICE
GENTLEMEN, THE PAPERS IN FRONT OF YOU CONTAIN THE DETAILED STEPS THAT COLONEL ROEBLING INTENDS TO TAKE TO FINISH THE BRIDGE.
NOT A "T" IS UNCROSSED, NOT AN "I" IS LEFT UNDOTTED. HE HAS TAKEN INTO ACCOUNT EVERY POSSIBLE CONTINGENCY.
AND WILL THE COLONEL BE JOINING US TODAY, MRS. ROEBLING?
I'M AFRAID THAT WILL BE QUITE IMPOSSIBLE, MR. MURPHY.
AND WHY IS THAT, MRS. ROEBLING?
DUE TO THE HEALTH PROBLEMS THE COLONEL INCURRED DURING THE SINKING OF THE CAISSONS, HE'S DECIDED IT WOULD BE BEST FOR HIM, AND THE MORALE OF THE MEN, IF THE WORK WAS CONDUCTED FROM HIS STUDY IN BROOKLYN HEIGHTS.
OUR CHIEF ENGINEER WILL NOT BE ON SITE? A PROJECT OF THIS MAGNITUDE?
COLONEL ROEBLING WILL BE IN CONSTANT CONTACT WITH HIS ASSISTANTS.
HOW LONG WILL HIS ABSENCE LAST?
HE'S GIVEN ME NO DATE TO REPORT.
I DO HOPE YOU ALL REALIZE THAT HE DIDN'T COME TO THIS DECISION LIGHTLY. ONLY THE TRUST AND RESPECT HE HAS IN HIS FOREMEN AND ASSISTANTS ALLOWS HIM TO EVEN ENTERTAIN THIS NOTION.
A VOTE WILL BE NEEDED, MRS. ROEBLING.
WE WILL INFORM THE COLONEL SHORTLY.
I ASSUMED THAT WOULD BE THE CASE.
THANK YOU ALL AND GOOD DAY.
QUITE IRREGULAR FOR THIS WOMAN TO BE SO . . . FORTHCOMING.
QUITE.

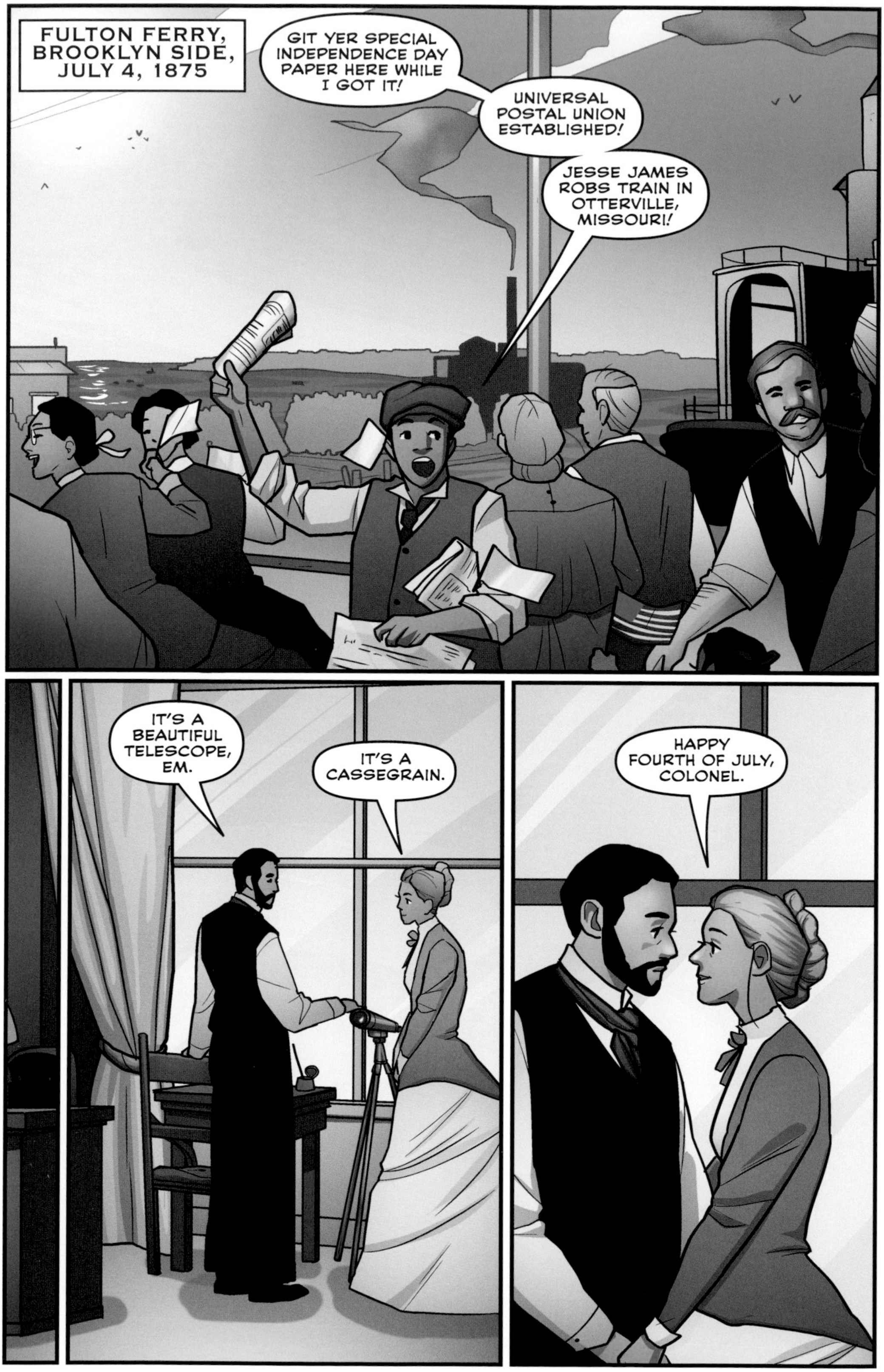
FULTON FERRY, BROOKLYN SIDE, JULY 4, 1875
GIT YER SPECIAL INDEPENDENCE DAY PAPER HERE WHILE I GOT IT!
UNIVERSAL POSTAL UNION ESTABLISHED!
JESSE JAMES ROBS TRAIN IN OTTERVILLE, MISSOURI!
IT'S A BEAUTIFUL TELESCOPE, EM.
IT'S A CASSEGRAIN.
HAPPY FOURTH OF JULY, COLONEL.

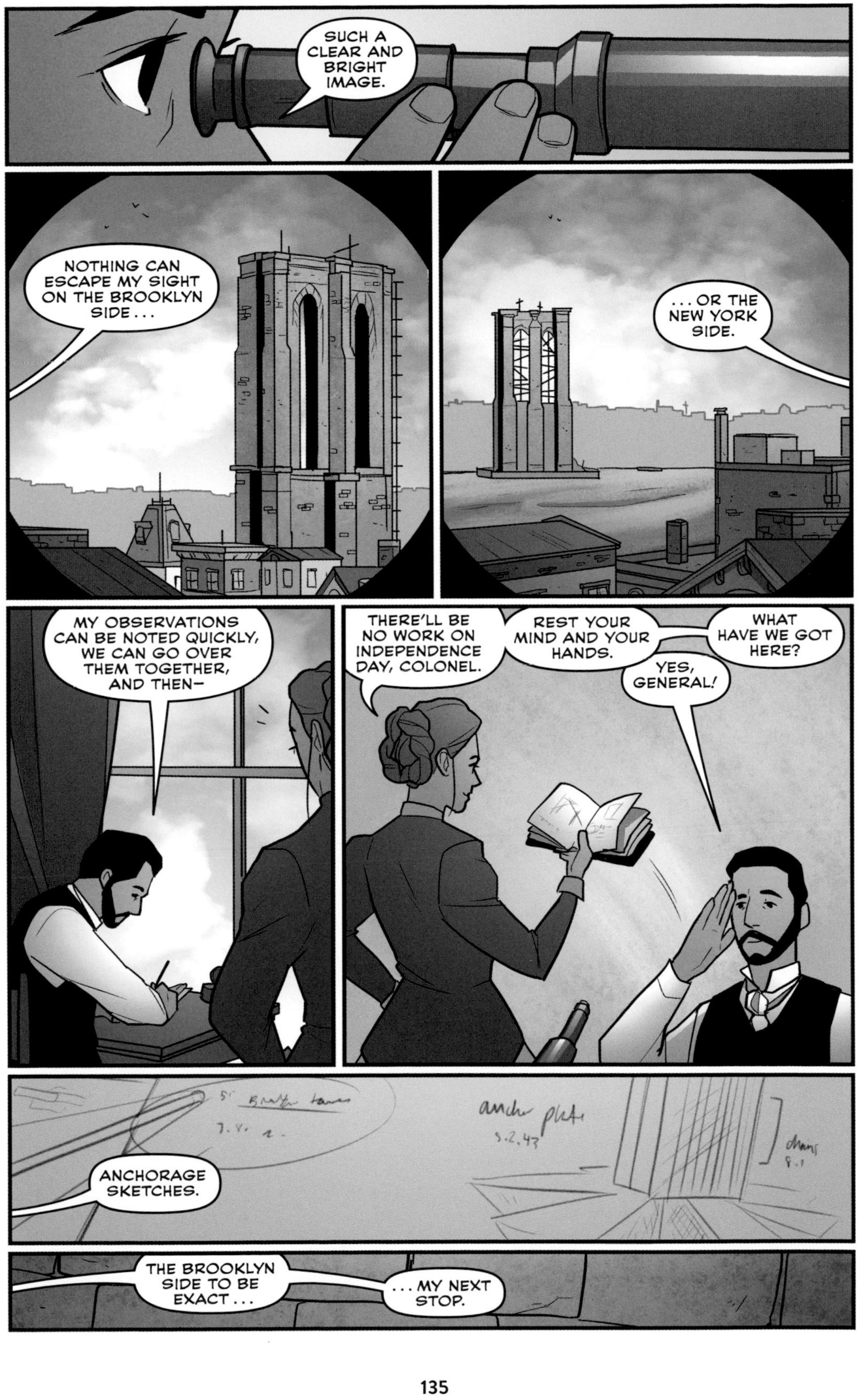
SUCH A CLEAR AND BRIGHT IMAGE.
NOTHING CAN ESCAPE MY SIGHT ON THE BROOKLYN SIDE . . .
. . . OR THE NEW YORK SIDE.
MY OBSERVATIONS CAN BE NOTED QUICKLY, WE CAN GO OVER THEM TOGETHER, AND THEN–
THERE'LL BE NO WORK ON INDEPENDENCE DAY, COLONEL.
REST YOUR MIND AND YOUR HANDS.
WHAT HAVE WE GOT HERE?
YES, GENERAL!
ANCHORAGE SKETCHES.
THE BROOKLYN SIDE TO BE EXACT . . .
. . . MY NEXT STOP.

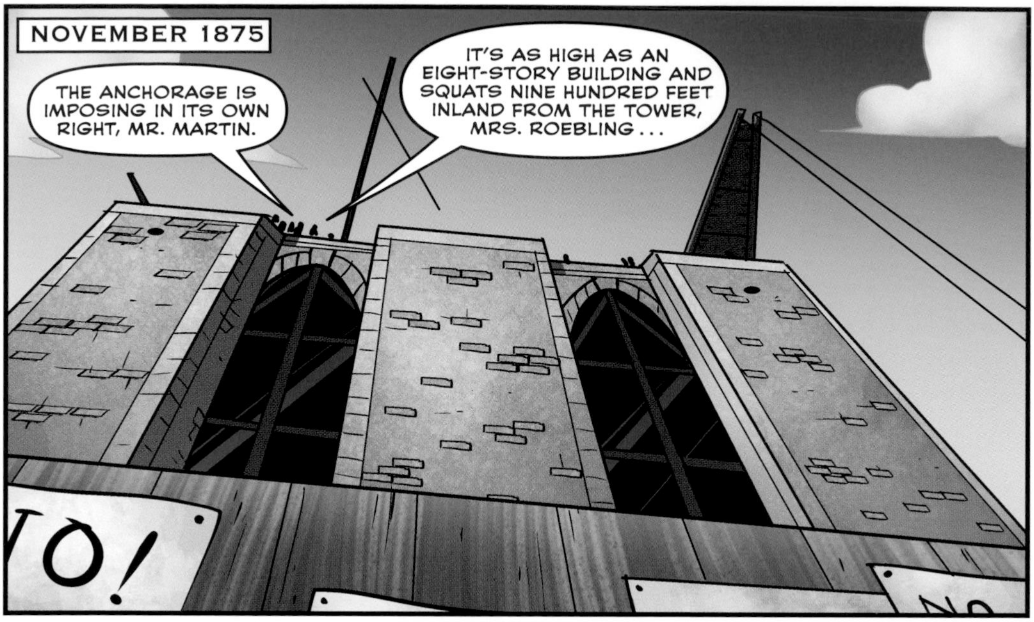
NOVEMBER 1875
THE ANCHORAGE IS IMPOSING IN ITS OWN RIGHT, MR. MARTIN.
IT'S AS HIGH AS AN EIGHT-STORY BUILDING AND SQUATS NINE HUNDRED FEET INLAND FROM THE TOWER, MRS. ROEBLING . . .

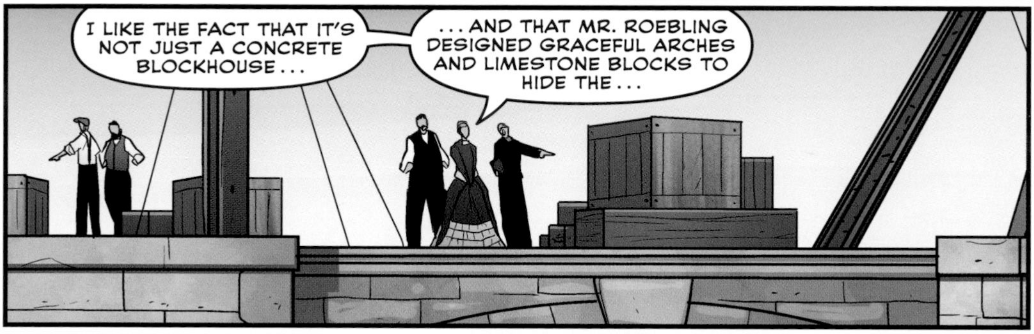
I LIKE THE FACT THAT IT'S NOT JUST A CONCRETE BLOCKHOUSE . . .
. . . AND THAT MR. ROEBLING DESIGNED GRACEFUL ARCHES AND LIMESTONE BLOCKS TO HIDE THE . . .

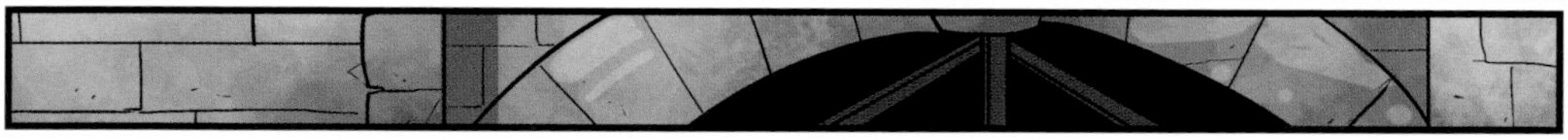

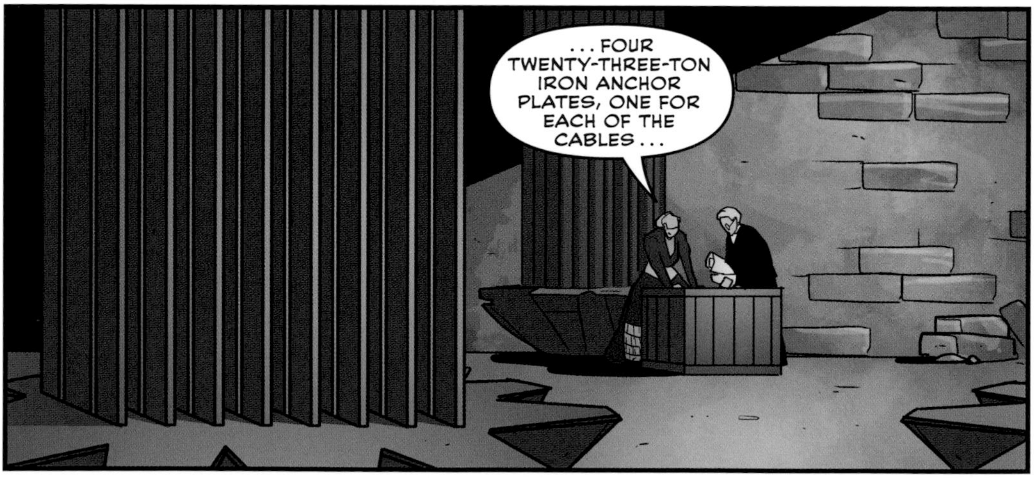
. . . FOUR TWENTY-THREE-TON IRON ANCHOR PLATES, ONE FOR EACH OF THE CABLES . . .

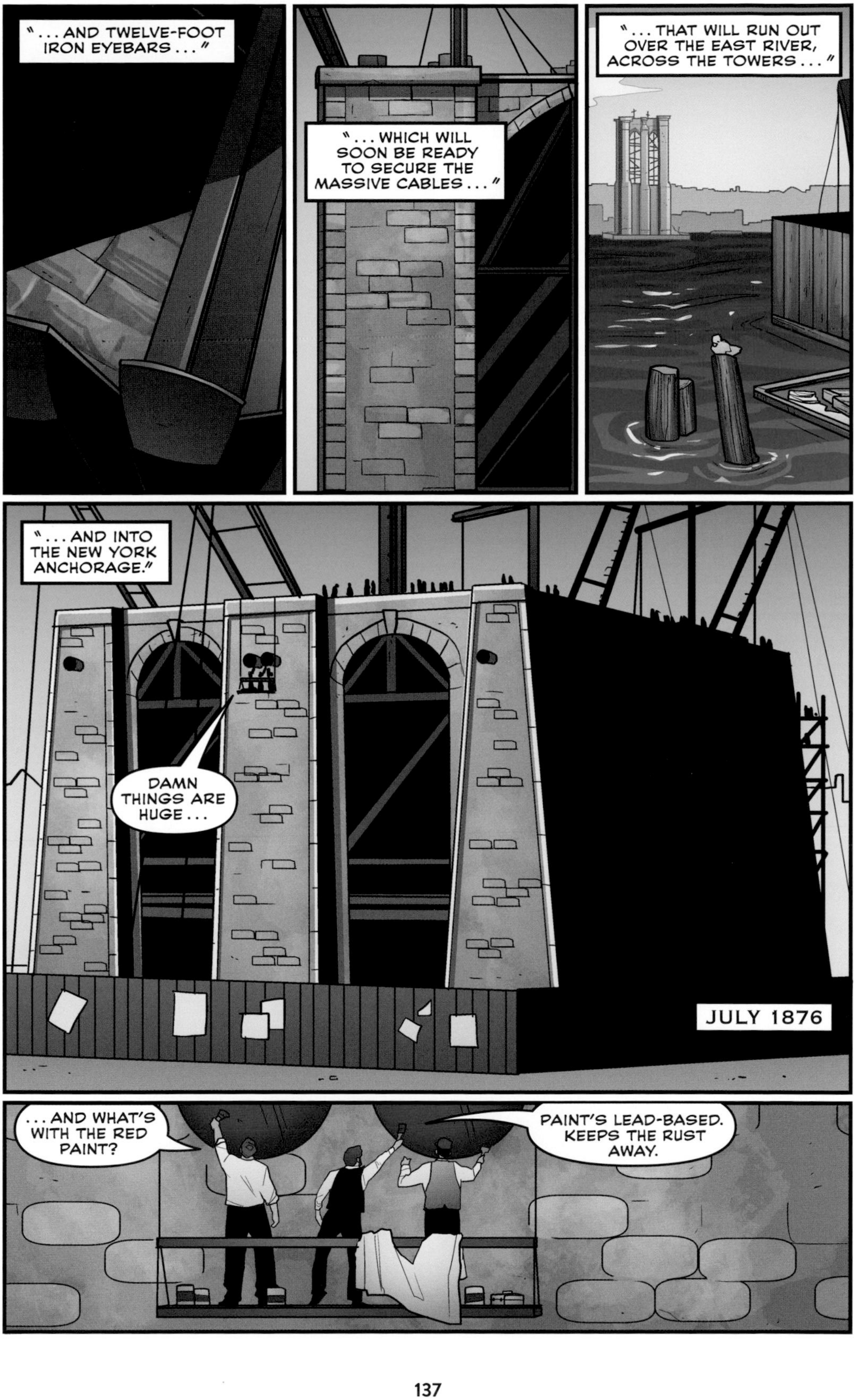
"... AND TWELVE-FOOT IRON EYEBARS ..."
"... WHICH WILL SOON BE READY TO SECURE THE MASSIVE CABLES ..."
"... THAT WILL RUN OUT OVER THE EAST RIVER, ACROSS THE TOWERS ..."
"... AND INTO THE NEW YORK ANCHORAGE."
DAMN THINGS ARE HUGE ...
JULY 1876
... AND WHAT'S WITH THE RED PAINT?
PAINT'S LEAD-BASED. KEEPS THE RUST AWAY.

WORD IS, SHE'S HELPIN' BUILD THE BRIDGE WITH HIM LAID UP, GUINAN.

THAT THE WORD, huh?

WHAT THE HELL'S HE THINKING HAVING A WOMAN PUTTING UP A BRIDGE?

THE COLONEL KNOWS WHAT HE'S DOING. THINGS ARE GETTING DONE.

IT'S THE KINDA THINKING GETS A LOTTA MEN KILLED, I TELL YA.

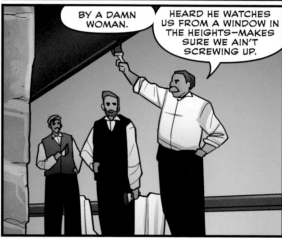

BY A DAMN WOMAN.

HEARD HE WATCHES US FROM A WINDOW IN THE HEIGHTS—MAKES SURE WE AIN'T SCREWING UP.

I'D BE GIVING US THE ONCE-OVER EVERY SO OFTEN, TOO, IF I WERE HIM.

NICE EVEN STROKES, GENTLEMEN.

FULL COVERAGE.

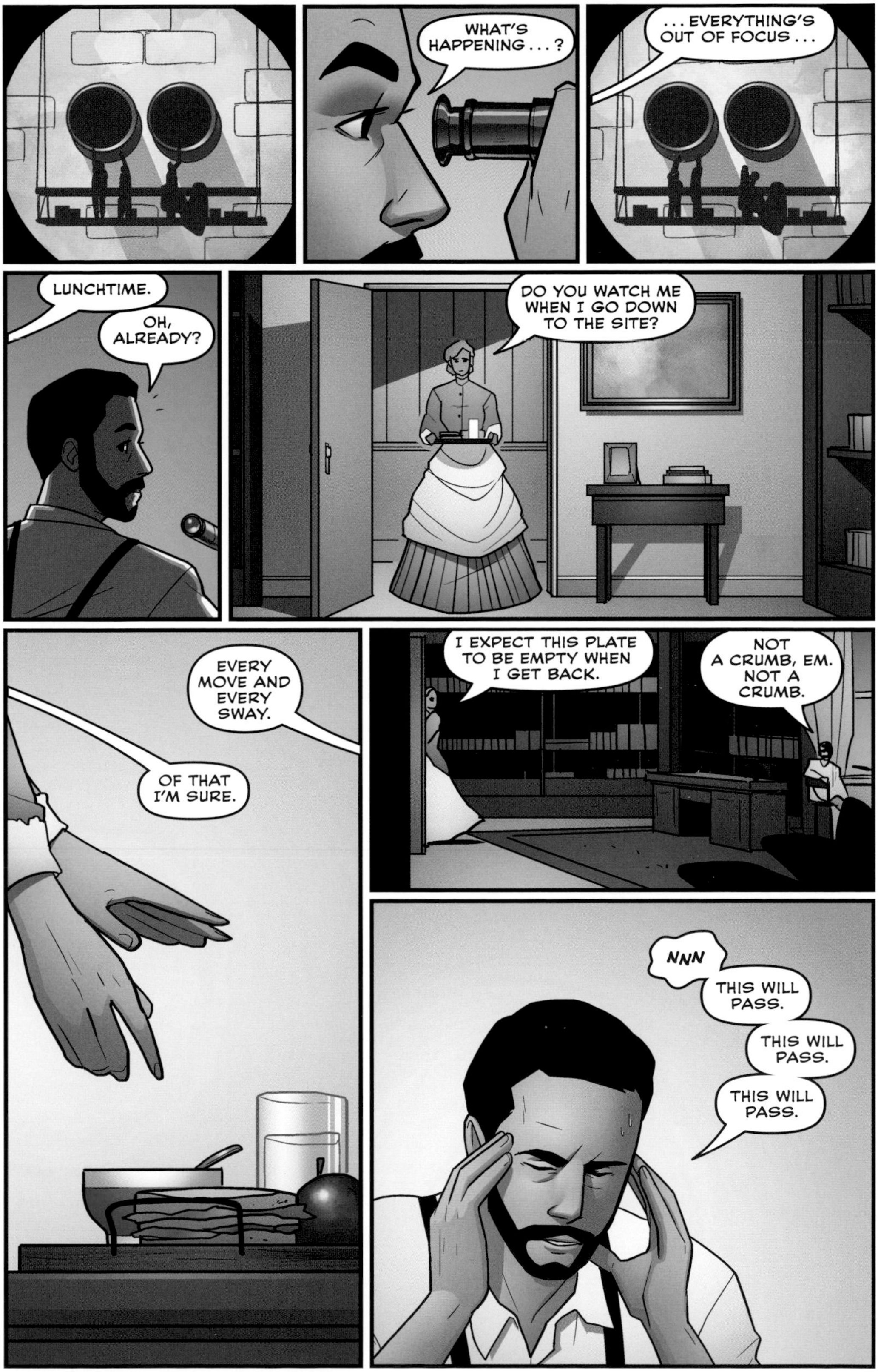
WHAT'S HAPPENING . . . ?
. . . EVERYTHING'S OUT OF FOCUS . . .
LUNCHTIME.
OH, ALREADY?
DO YOU WATCH ME WHEN I GO DOWN TO THE SITE?
EVERY MOVE AND EVERY SWAY.
OF THAT I'M SURE.
I EXPECT THIS PLATE TO BE EMPTY WHEN I GET BACK.
NOT A CRUMB, EM. NOT A CRUMB.
NNN
THIS WILL PASS.
THIS WILL PASS.
THIS WILL PASS.

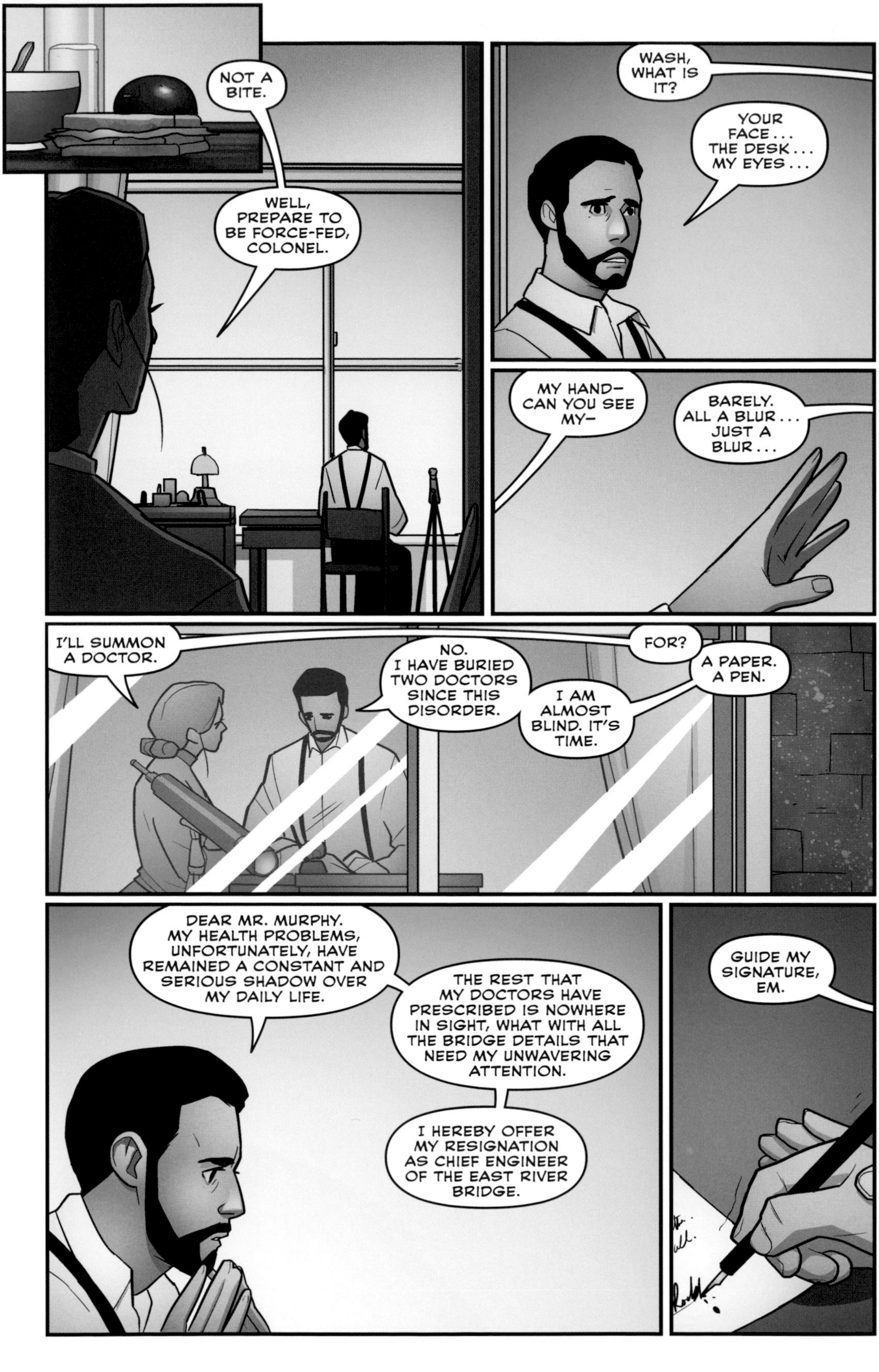
NOT A BITE.
WELL, PREPARE TO BE FORCE-FED, COLONEL.
WASH, WHAT IS IT?
YOUR FACE . . . THE DESK . . . MY EYES . . .
MY HAND– CAN YOU SEE MY–
BARELY. ALL A BLUR . . . JUST A BLUR . . .
I'LL SUMMON A DOCTOR.
NO. I HAVE BURIED TWO DOCTORS SINCE THIS DISORDER.
FOR?
I AM ALMOST BLIND. IT'S TIME.
A PAPER. A PEN.
DEAR MR. MURPHY. MY HEALTH PROBLEMS, UNFORTUNATELY, HAVE REMAINED A CONSTANT AND SERIOUS SHADOW OVER MY DAILY LIFE.
THE REST THAT MY DOCTORS HAVE PRESCRIBED IS NOWHERE IN SIGHT, WHAT WITH ALL THE BRIDGE DETAILS THAT NEED MY UNWAVERING ATTENTION.
I HEREBY OFFER MY RESIGNATION AS CHIEF ENGINEER OF THE EAST RIVER BRIDGE.
GUIDE MY SIGNATURE, EM.

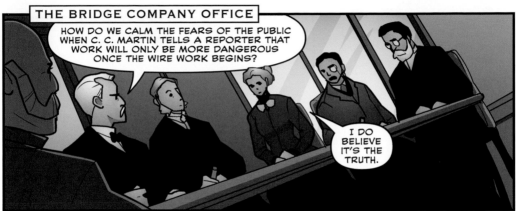

THE BRIDGE COMPANY OFFICE
HOW DO WE CALM THE FEARS OF THE PUBLIC WHEN C. C. MARTIN TELLS A REPORTER THAT WORK WILL ONLY BE MORE DANGEROUS ONCE THE WIRE WORK BEGINS?
I DO BELIEVE IT'S THE TRUTH.
IT'S THESE KIND OF "TRUTHS" THAT MAKE PEOPLE TURN THEIR ATTENTION ONCE AGAIN TO PLANS FOR A TUNNEL UNDER THE EAST RIVER.
YES, BUILDING A TUNNEL POSES NO PHYSICAL DANGERS WHATSOEVER TO THE PUBLIC AT LARGE, MR. HEWITT.
HMPH.
I DO HAVE ANOTHER ENGAGEMENT, BUT I'VE COME TODAY ON MY HUSBAND'S BEHALF TO GIVE YOU THIS.
A GOOD DAY TO YOU ALL.
WELL THEN, LET'S HEAR FROM ROEBLING . . . "GENTLEMEN, I AM PLEASED TO INFORM YOU . . ."

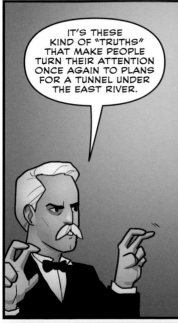

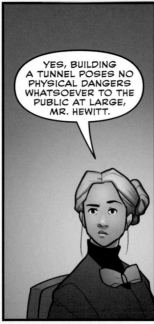

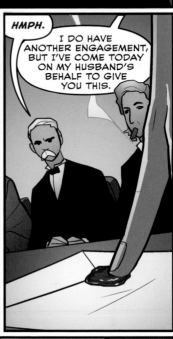

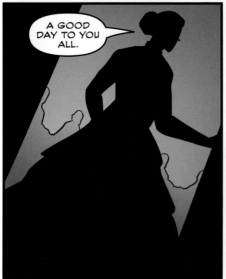

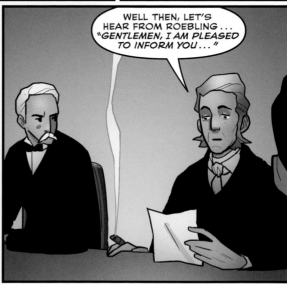

"...THAT THE FIRST CABLE WILL SOON BE TAKEN ACROSS THE TOWERS, THEREBY SIGNALING THE BEGINNING OF THE END OF OUR GREAT MISSION..."

SHRIP SHRIP SHRIP

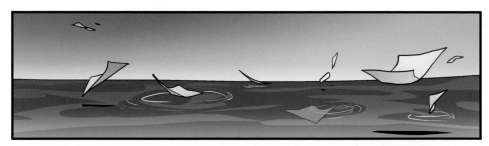

IT'S BEEN TWO DAYS SINCE MY RESIGNATION. NOT A WORD IN THE PAPERS.

WHY HAVEN'T THEY PUT YOU FORMALLY IN CHARGE, C. C.?

Um, JUST LUCKY, I GUESS.

YES, QUITE LUCKY.

THEY'RE TAKING ADVANTAGE OF MY GOODWILL.

THEY'RE TAKING ADVANTAGE OF YOUR GERMAN WORK ETHIC.

MY *AMERICAN* WORK ETHIC.

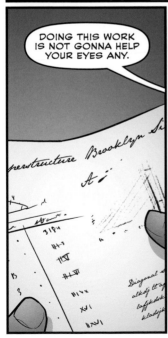

DOING THIS WORK IS NOT GONNA HELP YOUR EYES ANY.

BUT I'LL RUN IT BY WHOEVER THEY NAME TO TAKE YOUR PLACE.

THANK YOU, MR. MARTIN.

NO NEED TO THANK ME, MRS. ROEBLING. WE'RE ALL PART OF THE SAME TEAM.

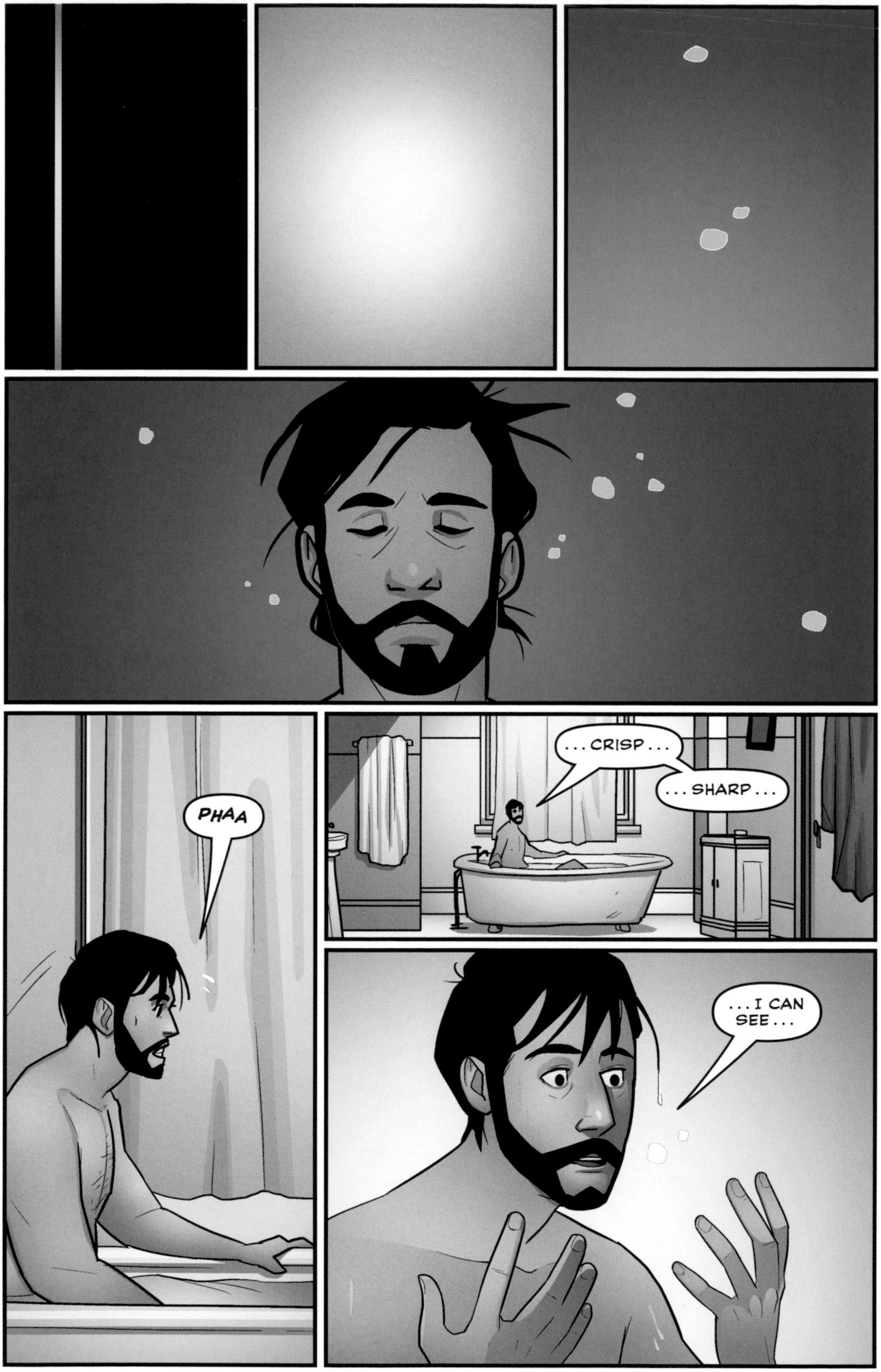
PHAA
. . . CRISP . . .
. . . SHARP . . .
. . . I CAN SEE . . .

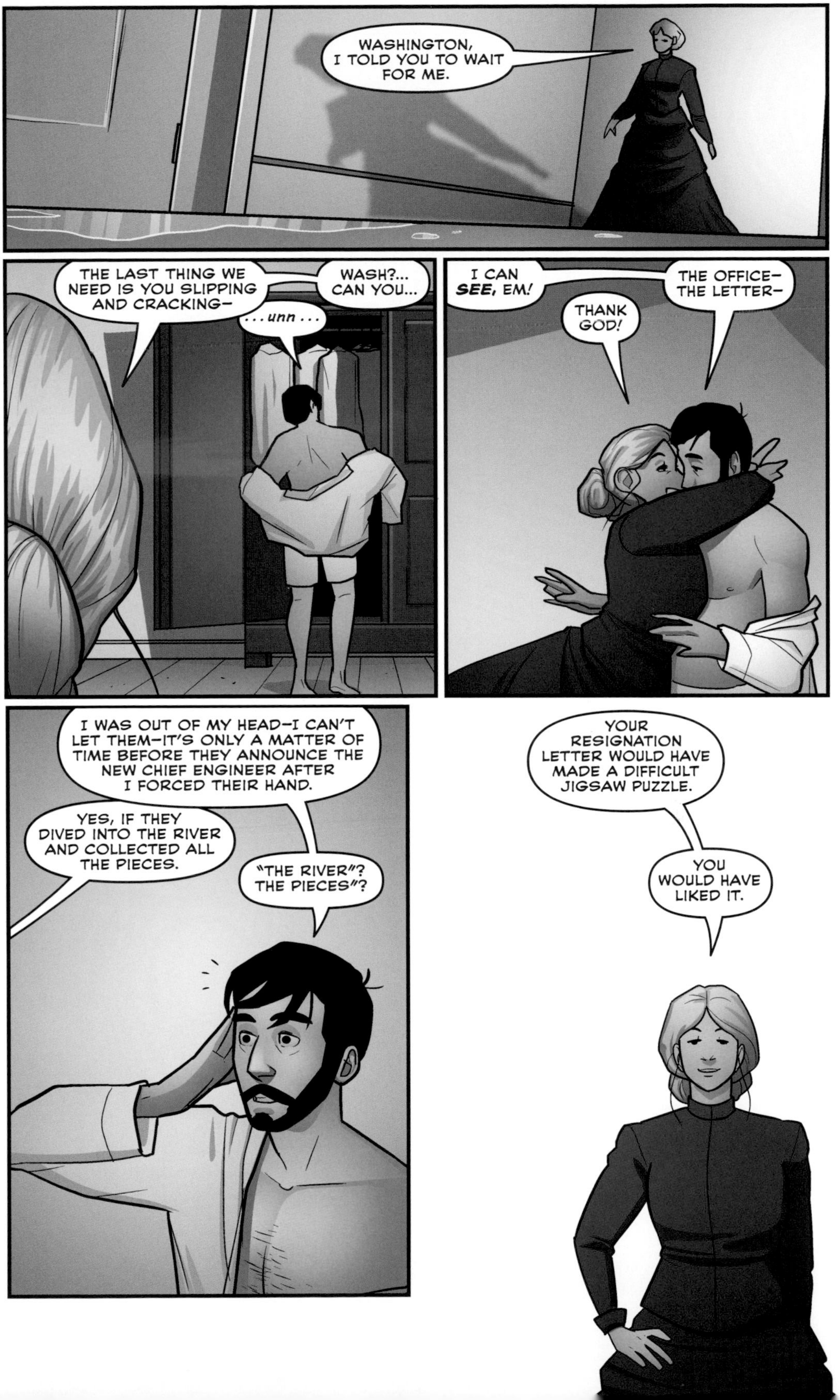
WASHINGTON, I TOLD YOU TO WAIT FOR ME.
THE LAST THING WE NEED IS YOU SLIPPING AND CRACKING—
WASH?... CAN YOU...
...unn...
I CAN SEE, EM!
THE OFFICE— THE LETTER—
THANK GOD!
I WAS OUT OF MY HEAD—I CAN'T LET THEM—IT'S ONLY A MATTER OF TIME BEFORE THEY ANNOUNCE THE NEW CHIEF ENGINEER AFTER I FORCED THEIR HAND.
YES, IF THEY DIVED INTO THE RIVER AND COLLECTED ALL THE PIECES.
"THE RIVER"? THE PIECES"?
YOUR RESIGNATION LETTER WOULD HAVE MADE A DIFFICULT JIGSAW PUZZLE.
YOU WOULD HAVE LIKED IT.

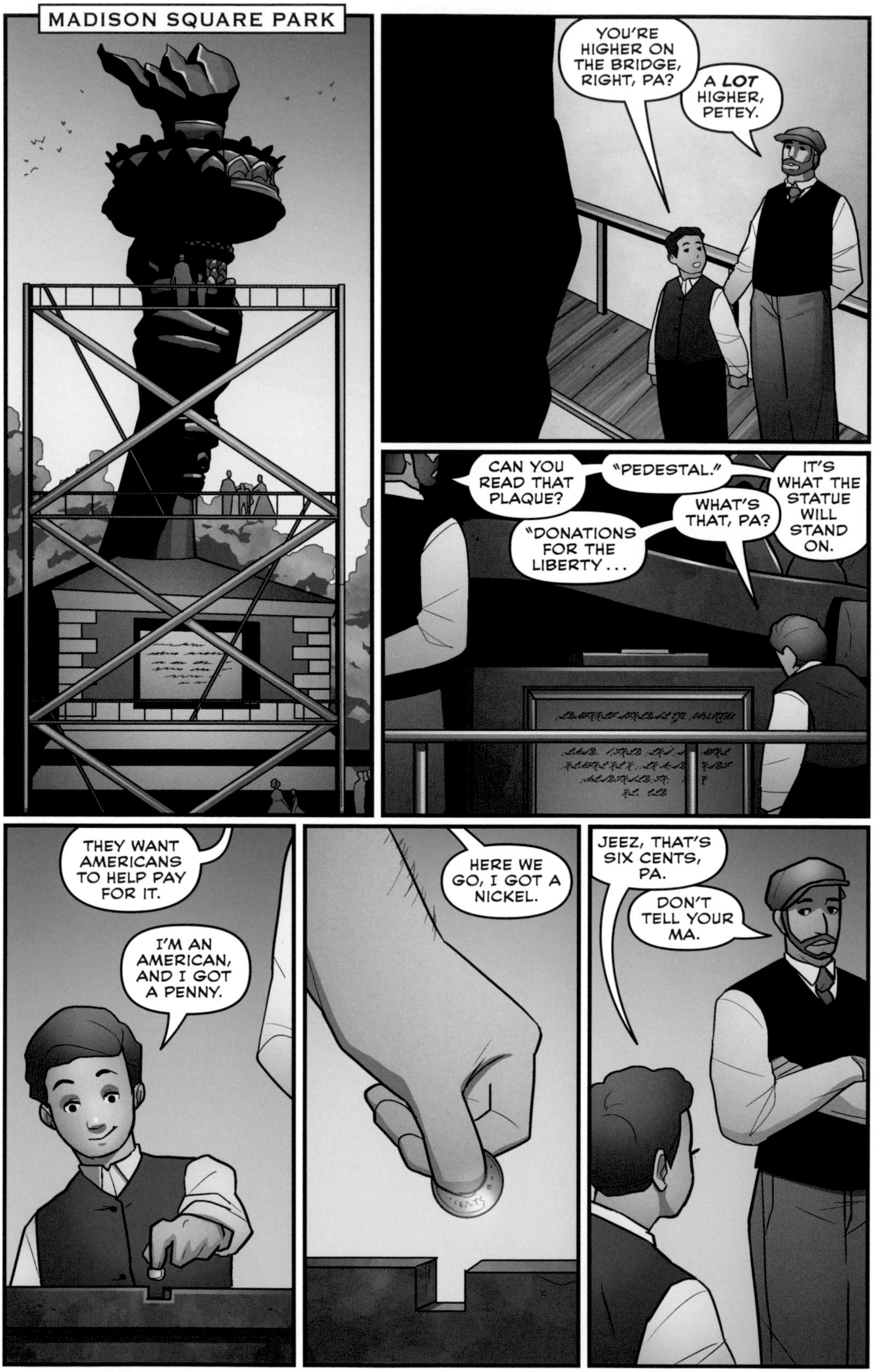
MADISON SQUARE PARK
YOU'RE HIGHER ON THE BRIDGE, RIGHT, PA?
A LOT HIGHER, PETEY.
CAN YOU READ THAT PLAQUE?
"DONATIONS FOR THE LIBERTY . . .
"PEDESTAL."
WHAT'S THAT, PA?
IT'S WHAT THE STATUE WILL STAND ON.
THEY WANT AMERICANS TO HELP PAY FOR IT.
I'M AN AMERICAN, AND I GOT A PENNY.
HERE WE GO, I GOT A NICKEL.
JEEZ, THAT'S SIX CENTS, PA.
DON'T TELL YOUR MA.

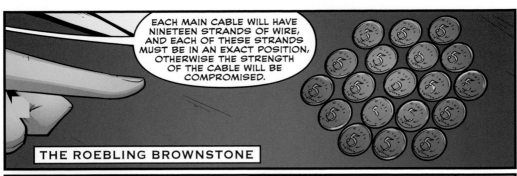

EACH MAIN CABLE WILL HAVE NINETEEN STRANDS OF WIRE, AND EACH OF THESE STRANDS MUST BE IN AN EXACT POSITION, OTHERWISE THE STRENGTH OF THE CABLE WILL BE COMPROMISED.

THE ROEBLING BROWNSTONE

WILL YOUR FAMILY MILL BE READY FOR PRODUCTION?

MY BROTHERS IN TRENTON HAVE ASSURED ME THAT THEY WILL BE PREPARED ONCE WE ARE AWARDED THE CONTRACT.

COLONEL, WE'LL NEED TO SPLICE AND TEST THE TRAVELER ROPE SOON SO WE CAN START TRANSPORTING THE MEN AND WIRE OVER.

SOMEONE TO CROSS THE RIVER, *hmm?*

I'VE HAD A DOZEN MEN OFFER UP A WEEK'S WAGES TO BE THE FIRST ONE.

YES, I IMAGINED YOU WOULD.

IT IS A ONCE-IN-A-LIFETIME OPPORTUNITY.

READY TO TAKE A RIDE, MR. FARRINGTON?

WHAT? *ME?*

GUESS THIS IS A BAD TIME TO LET YOU KNOW...

BROOKLYN TOWER, AUGUST 25, 1876

...I'M AFRAID OF HEIGHTS.

READY?

HELL YES, I'M READY.

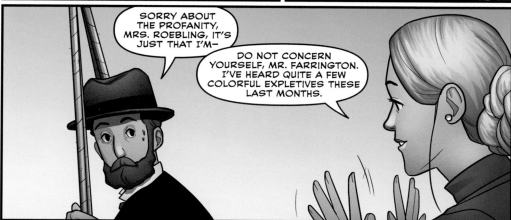

SORRY ABOUT THE PROFANITY, MRS. ROEBLING, IT'S JUST THAT I'M—

DO NOT CONCERN YOURSELF, MR. FARRINGTON. I'VE HEARD QUITE A FEW COLORFUL EXPLETIVES THESE LAST MONTHS.

OKAY THEN, LET'S DO THIS THING!

WAVE IT, C. C.!

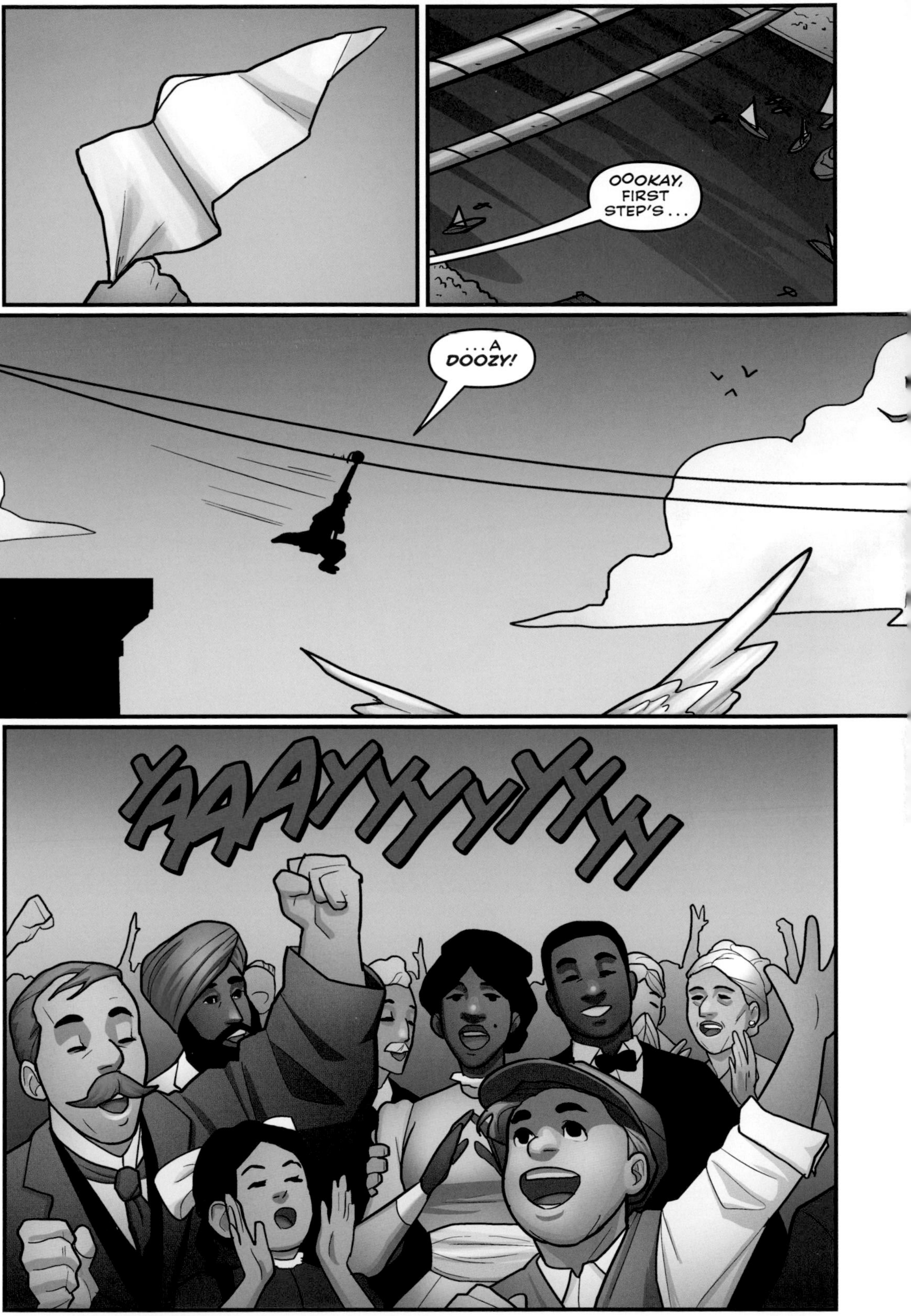
OOOKAY, FIRST STEP'S...
...A DOOZY!
YAAAYYYYYYH

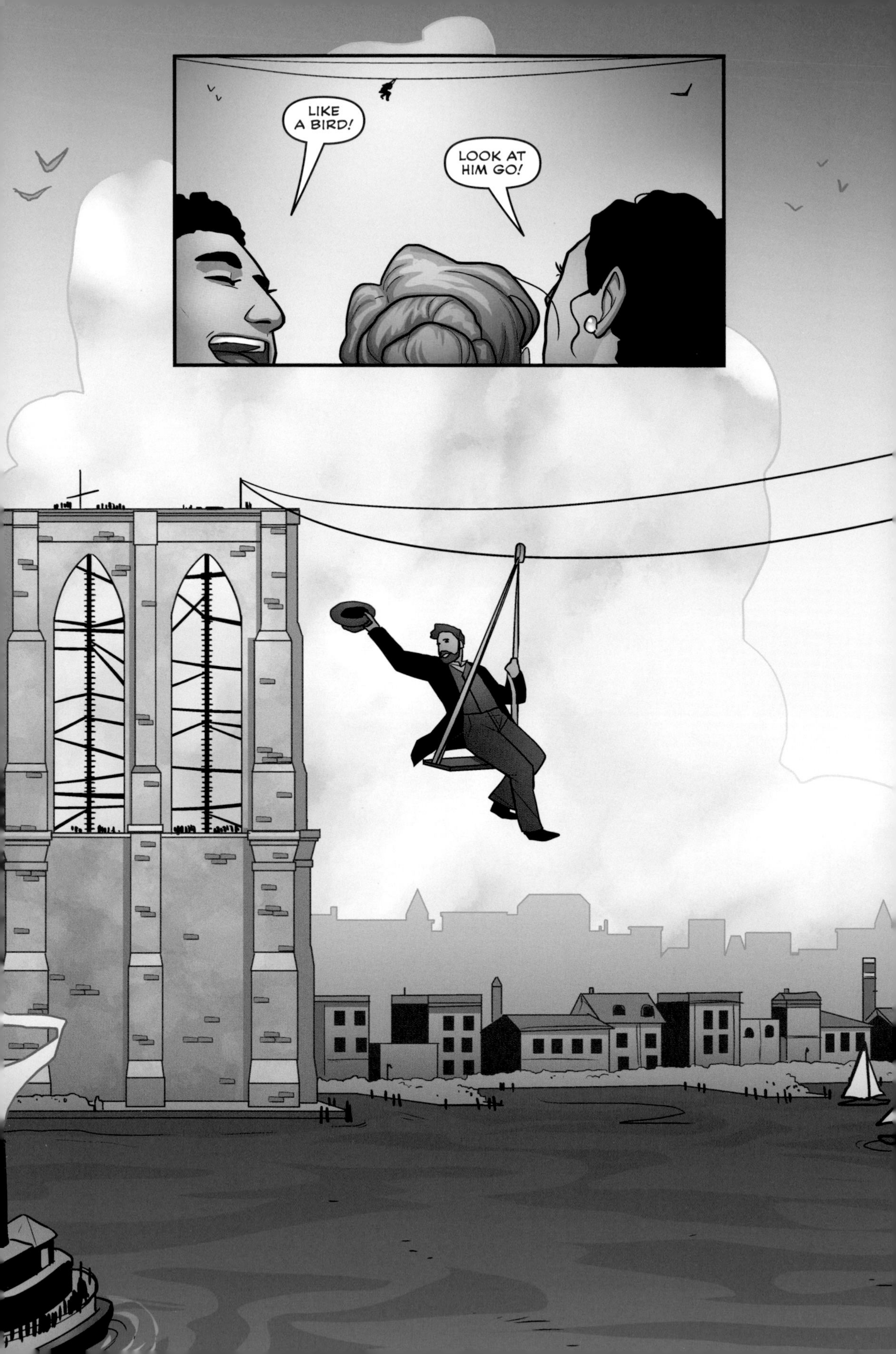
LIKE A BIRD!
LOOK AT HIM GO!

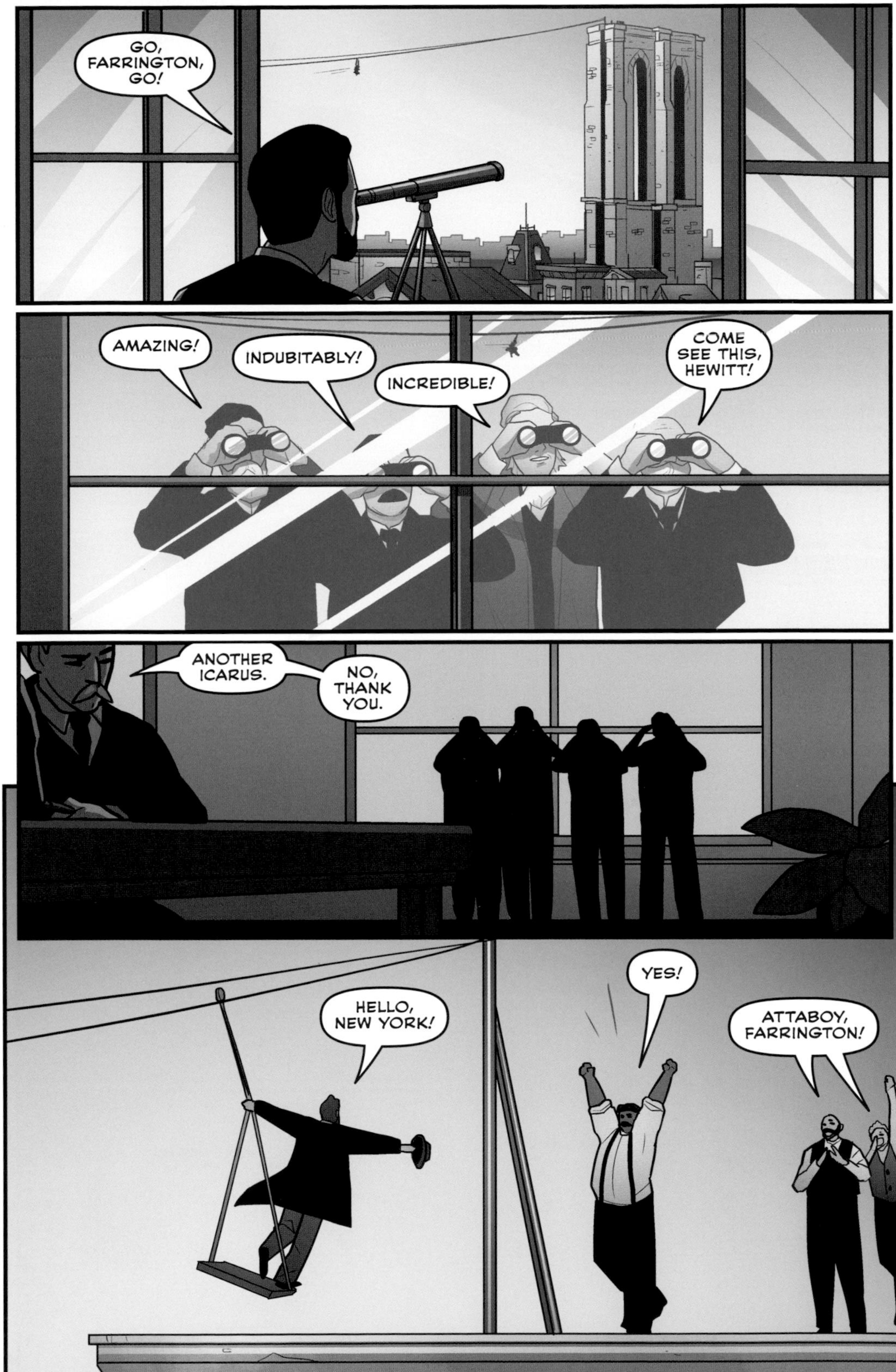
GO, FARRINGTON, GO!
AMAZING!
INDUBITABLY!
INCREDIBLE!
COME SEE THIS, HEWITT!
ANOTHER ICARUS.
NO, THANK YOU.
HELLO, NEW YORK!
YES!
ATTABOY, FARRINGTON!

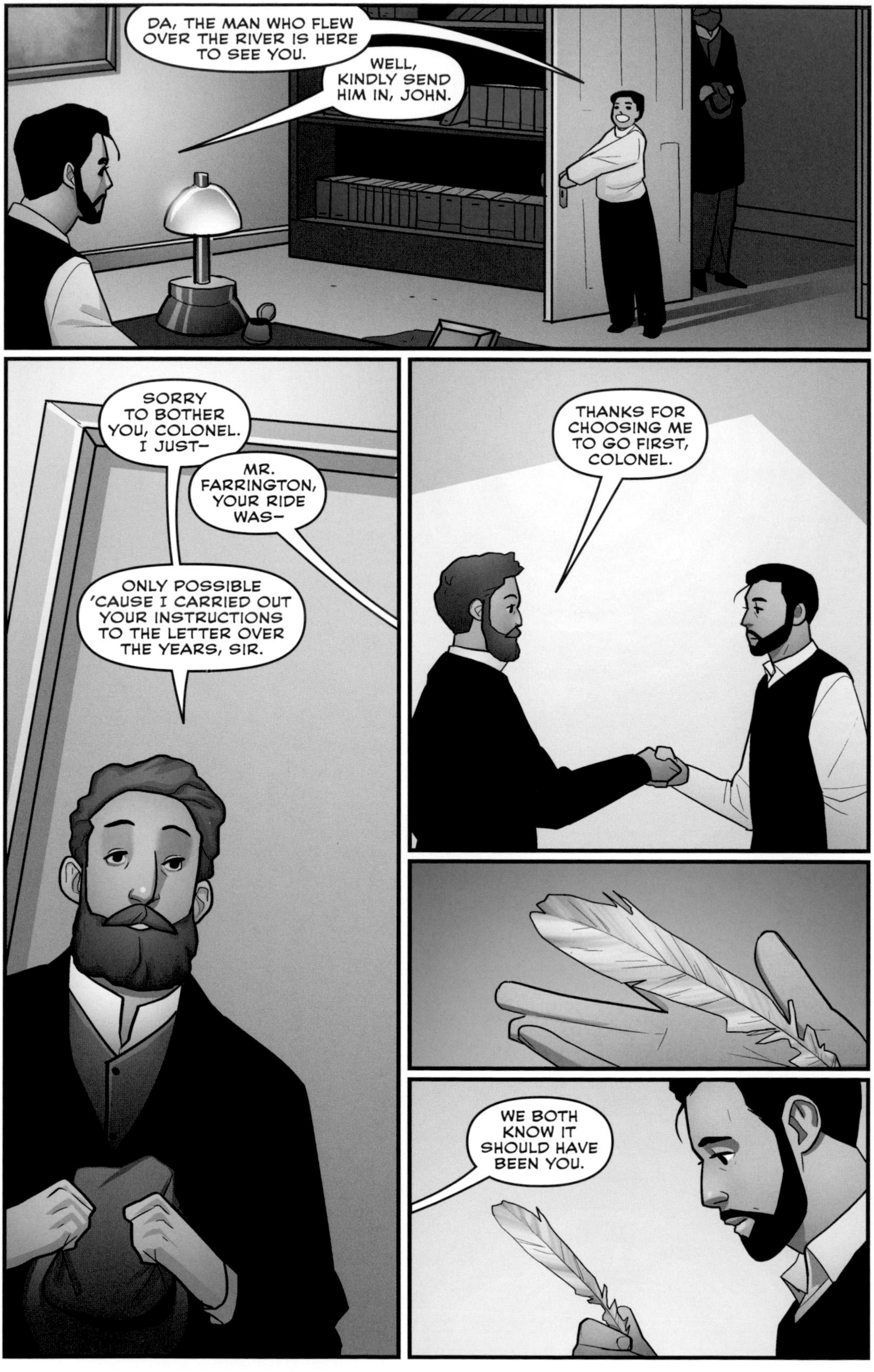
DA, THE MAN WHO FLEW OVER THE RIVER IS HERE TO SEE YOU.
WELL, KINDLY SEND HIM IN, JOHN.
SORRY TO BOTHER YOU, COLONEL. I JUST—
MR. FARRINGTON, YOUR RIDE WAS—
ONLY POSSIBLE 'CAUSE I CARRIED OUT YOUR INSTRUCTIONS TO THE LETTER OVER THE YEARS, SIR.
THANKS FOR CHOOSING ME TO GO FIRST, COLONEL.
WE BOTH KNOW IT SHOULD HAVE BEEN YOU.

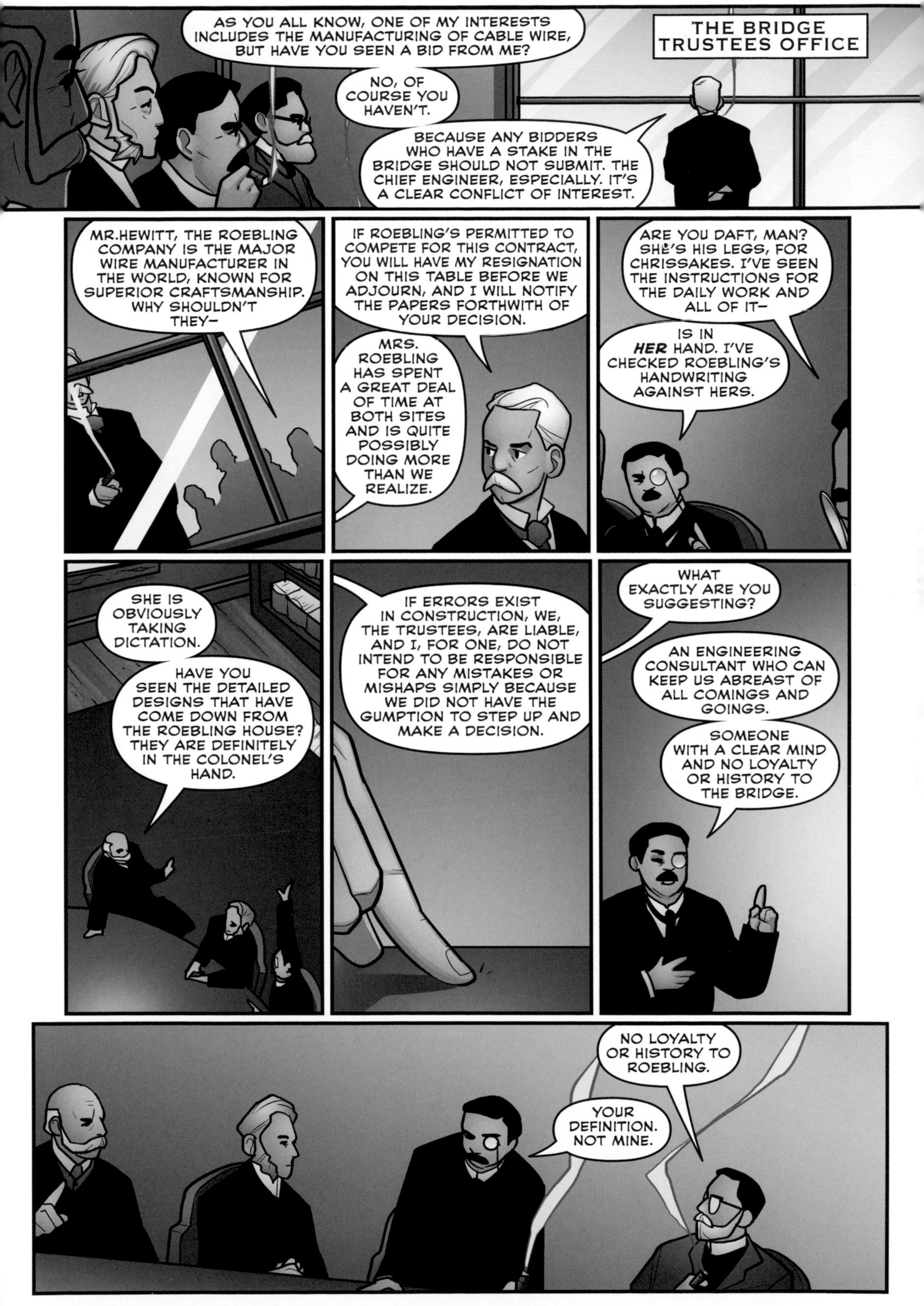
THE BRIDGE TRUSTEES OFFICE
AS YOU ALL KNOW, ONE OF MY INTERESTS INCLUDES THE MANUFACTURING OF CABLE WIRE, BUT HAVE YOU SEEN A BID FROM ME?
NO, OF COURSE YOU HAVEN'T.
BECAUSE ANY BIDDERS WHO HAVE A STAKE IN THE BRIDGE SHOULD NOT SUBMIT. THE CHIEF ENGINEER, ESPECIALLY. IT'S A CLEAR CONFLICT OF INTEREST.
MR.HEWITT, THE ROEBLING COMPANY IS THE MAJOR WIRE MANUFACTURER IN THE WORLD, KNOWN FOR SUPERIOR CRAFTSMANSHIP. WHY SHOULDN'T THEY—
IF ROEBLING'S PERMITTED TO COMPETE FOR THIS CONTRACT, YOU WILL HAVE MY RESIGNATION ON THIS TABLE BEFORE WE ADJOURN, AND I WILL NOTIFY THE PAPERS FORTHWITH OF YOUR DECISION.
MRS. ROEBLING HAS SPENT A GREAT DEAL OF TIME AT BOTH SITES AND IS QUITE POSSIBLY DOING MORE THAN WE REALIZE.
ARE YOU DAFT, MAN? SHE'S HIS LEGS, FOR CHRISSAKES. I'VE SEEN THE INSTRUCTIONS FOR THE DAILY WORK AND ALL OF IT—
IS IN ***HER*** HAND. I'VE CHECKED ROEBLING'S HANDWRITING AGAINST HERS.
SHE IS OBVIOUSLY TAKING DICTATION.
HAVE YOU SEEN THE DETAILED DESIGNS THAT HAVE COME DOWN FROM THE ROEBLING HOUSE? THEY ARE DEFINITELY IN THE COLONEL'S HAND.
IF ERRORS EXIST IN CONSTRUCTION, WE, THE TRUSTEES, ARE LIABLE, AND I, FOR ONE, DO NOT INTEND TO BE RESPONSIBLE FOR ANY MISTAKES OR MISHAPS SIMPLY BECAUSE WE DID NOT HAVE THE GUMPTION TO STEP UP AND MAKE A DECISION.
WHAT EXACTLY ARE YOU SUGGESTING?
AN ENGINEERING CONSULTANT WHO CAN KEEP US ABREAST OF ALL COMINGS AND GOINGS.
SOMEONE WITH A CLEAR MIND AND NO LOYALTY OR HISTORY TO THE BRIDGE.
NO LOYALTY OR HISTORY TO ROEBLING.
YOUR DEFINITION. NOT MINE.

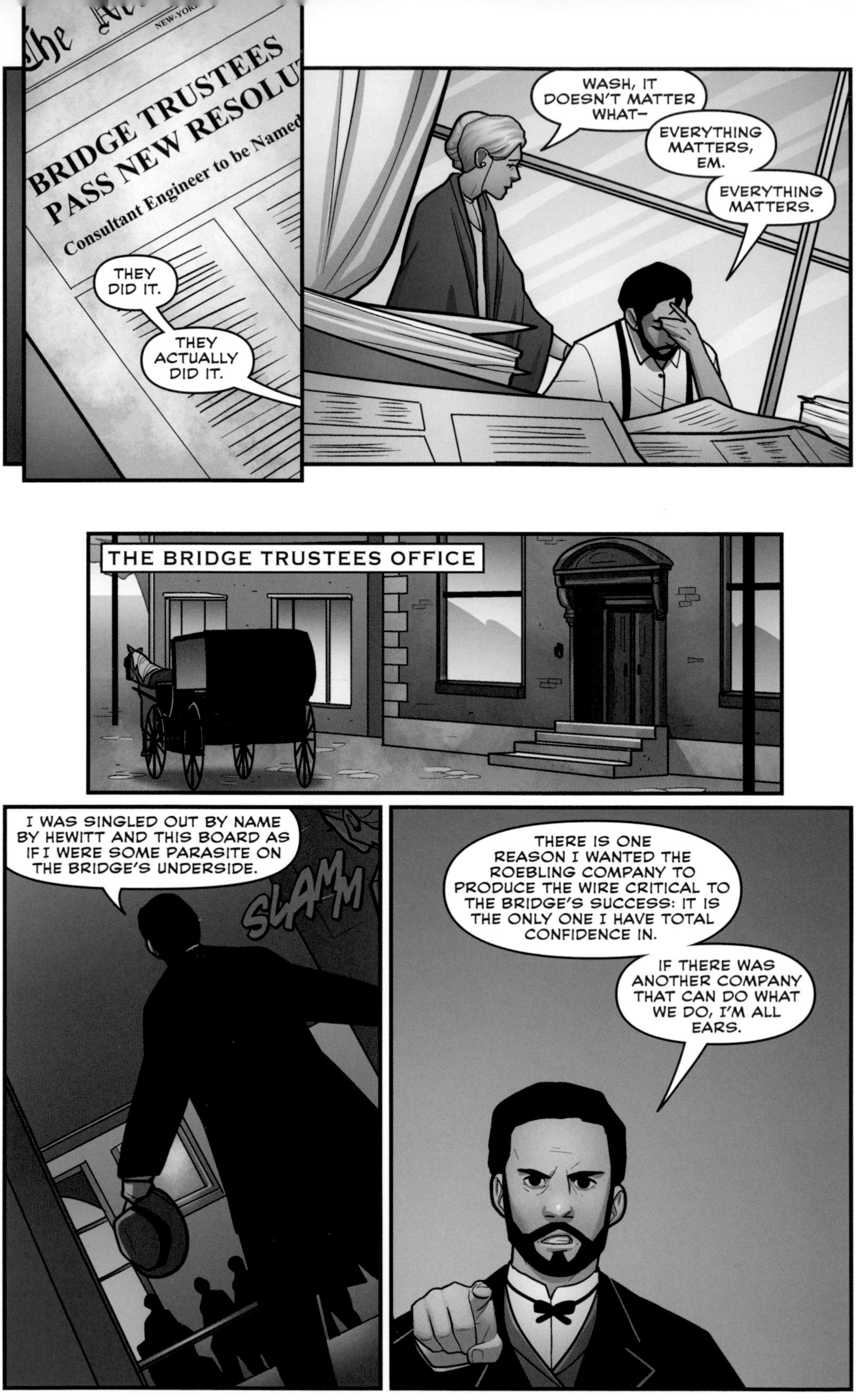
BRIDGE TRUSTEES PASS NEW RESOLU
Consultant Engineer to be Named
THEY DID IT.
THEY ACTUALLY DID IT.
WASH, IT DOESN'T MATTER WHAT–
EVERYTHING MATTERS, EM.
EVERYTHING MATTERS.
THE BRIDGE TRUSTEES OFFICE
I WAS SINGLED OUT BY NAME BY HEWITT AND THIS BOARD AS IF I WERE SOME PARASITE ON THE BRIDGE'S UNDERSIDE.
SLAMM
THERE IS ONE REASON I WANTED THE ROEBLING COMPANY TO PRODUCE THE WIRE CRITICAL TO THE BRIDGE'S SUCCESS: IT IS THE ONLY ONE I HAVE TOTAL CONFIDENCE IN.
IF THERE WAS ANOTHER COMPANY THAT CAN DO WHAT WE DO, I'M ALL EARS.

NOW, NOW, COLONEL, WE CAN RECTIFY—

SINCE MR. HEWITT'S BID WITHDRAWAL HAS LEFT YOU ALL WEAK IN THE KNEES, LET ME TELL YOU THAT HIS CABLE WIRE COMPANY HAS NO FACILITIES WHATSOEVER TO MAKE THE STEEL WIRE, AND IT WOULD BE IN YOUR BEST INTERESTS TO LOOK INTO THE BACKGROUND OF EVERY BID THAT CROSSES YOUR TABLE.

HOW DARE YOU SLANDER ME IN FRONT OF THIS BOARD, ROEBLING!

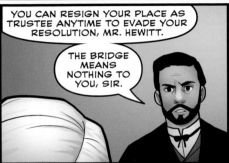

YOU CAN RESIGN YOUR PLACE AS TRUSTEE ANYTIME TO EVADE YOUR RESOLUTION, MR. HEWITT.

THE BRIDGE MEANS NOTHING TO YOU, SIR.

CONTINUING TO WORK ON THIS BRIDGE HAS BEEN A MATTER OF PRIDE AND HONOR. THE MOMENT I AM UNABLE TO FULFILL MY DUTIES AS CHIEF ENGINEER, I WILL GIVE YOU AMPLE WARNING.

ALSO, AS A POINT OF INFORMATION, I HAVE SOLD ALL MY STOCK IN ROEBLING AND SONS WIRE COMPANY, ELIMINATING ANY POSSIBLE CONFLICT OF INTEREST.

FOR US TO SIT HERE AND BE SCOLDED LIKE WE ARE CHILDREN IS UNCONSCIONABLE!

UNDERESTIMATION CAN BE QUITE THE BOONDOGGLE, ROEBLING.

AND DON'T WORRY, GENTLEMEN, I WILL GIVE YOU AMPLE WARNING IN CASE I PLAN ON DYING.

155

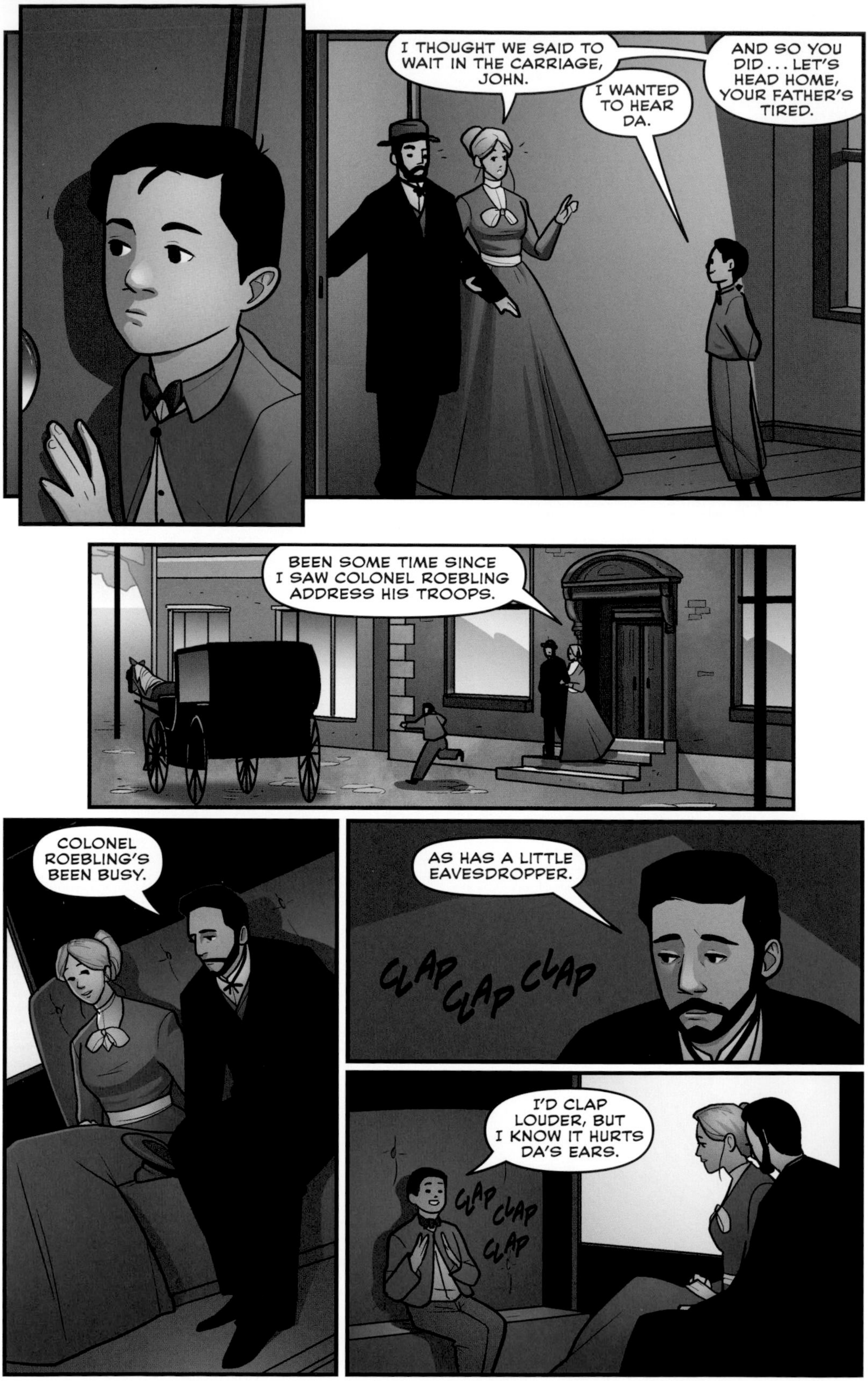
I THOUGHT WE SAID TO WAIT IN THE CARRIAGE, JOHN.
I WANTED TO HEAR DA.
AND SO YOU DID . . . LET'S HEAD HOME, YOUR FATHER'S TIRED.
BEEN SOME TIME SINCE I SAW COLONEL ROEBLING ADDRESS HIS TROOPS.
COLONEL ROEBLING'S BEEN BUSY.
AS HAS A LITTLE EAVESDROPPER.
CLAP CLAP CLAP
I'D CLAP LOUDER, BUT I KNOW IT HURTS DA'S EARS.
CLAP CLAP CLAP

THE BRIDGE TRUSTEES OFFICE

BEFORE US ARE THE BIDS FROM SIX COMPANIES. CHROME STEEL INC., WAGNER STEEL WORKS, AND J. LLOYD HAIGH WIRE. ALL HAVE SUBMITTED BIDS FOR CRUCIBLE STEEL.

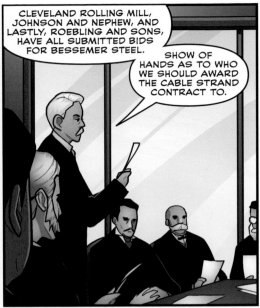

CLEVELAND ROLLING MILL, JOHNSON AND NEPHEW, AND LASTLY, ROEBLING AND SONS, HAVE ALL SUBMITTED BIDS FOR BESSEMER STEEL.

SHOW OF HANDS AS TO WHO WE SHOULD AWARD THE CABLE STRAND CONTRACT TO.

THE NEXT DAY

J. LLOYD H

ARE YOU SURPRISED THE BRIDGE TRUSTEES AWARDED THE CONTRACT TO YOU, MR. HAIGH?

YES AND NO.

THE ROEBLINGS PRODUCE SOME WONDERFUL WIRE, AND THE COLONEL BEING THE CHIEF ENGINEER, WELL, LET'S JUST SAY I THOUGHT THE ODDS WOULD BE IN HIS FAVOR.

AND THE "NO"?

THE TRUSTEES SAW FIT TO AWARD MY COMPANY THE WIRE CONTRACT FOR ONE REASON: I MAKE A DAMN GOOD WIRE.

AND I WANT BOTH CITIES TO KNOW THAT ONLY THE BEST, THAT'S CRUCIBLE STEEL, IS GOING INTO THE WIRE I PRODUCE.

WHY? BECAUSE THIS BRIDGE AND THE PEOPLE OF THESE TWO GREAT CITIES DESERVE THE BEST.

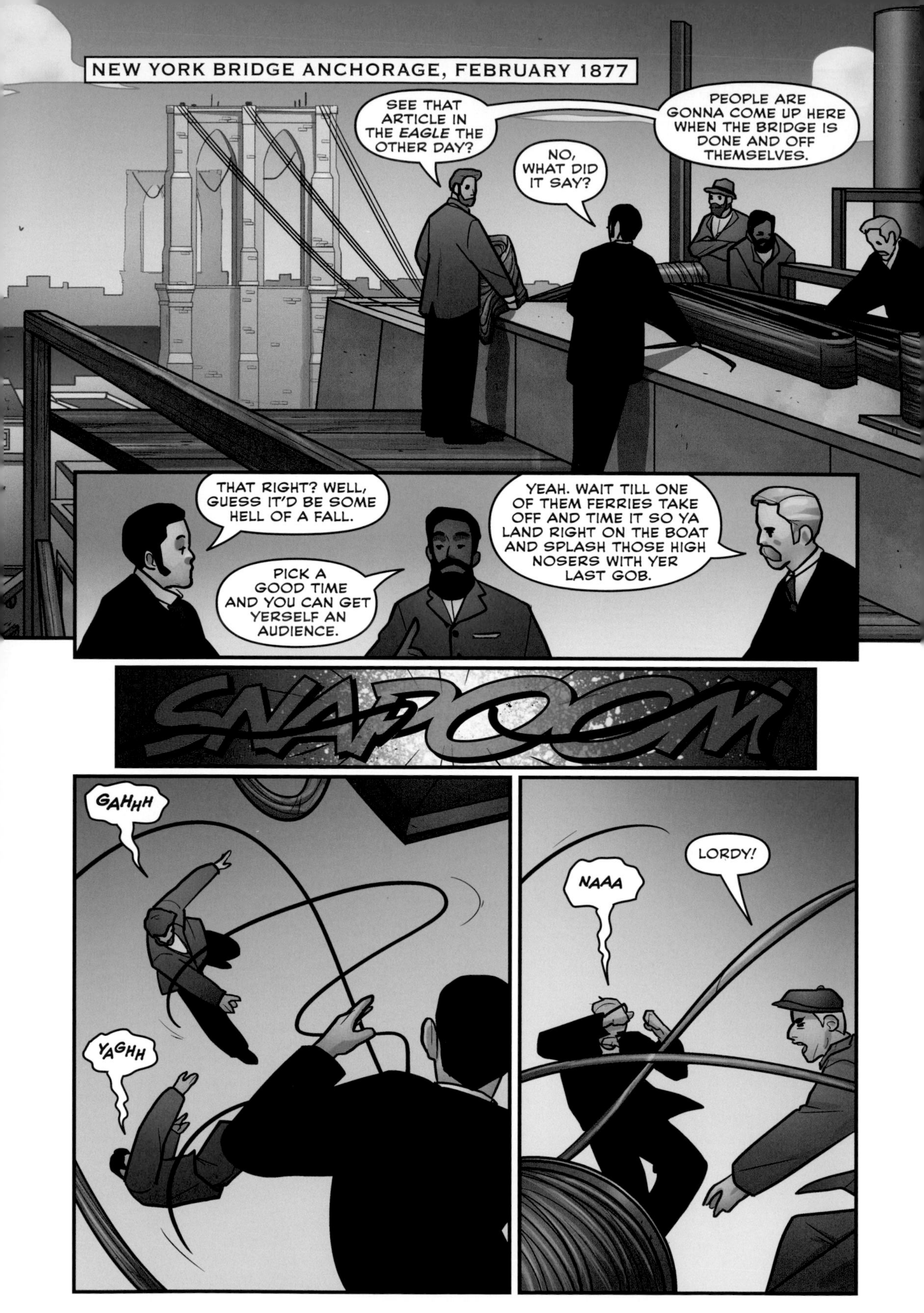

NEW YORK BRIDGE ANCHORAGE, FEBRUARY 1877
SEE THAT ARTICLE IN THE *EAGLE* THE OTHER DAY?
PEOPLE ARE GONNA COME UP HERE WHEN THE BRIDGE IS DONE AND OFF THEMSELVES.
NO, WHAT DID IT SAY?
THAT RIGHT? WELL, GUESS IT'D BE SOME HELL OF A FALL.
PICK A GOOD TIME AND YOU CAN GET YERSELF AN AUDIENCE.
YEAH. WAIT TILL ONE OF THEM FERRIES TAKE OFF AND TIME IT SO YA LAND RIGHT ON THE BOAT AND SPLASH THOSE HIGH NOSERS WITH YER LAST GOB.
SNAPOOM
GAHHH
YAGHH
NAAA
LORDY!

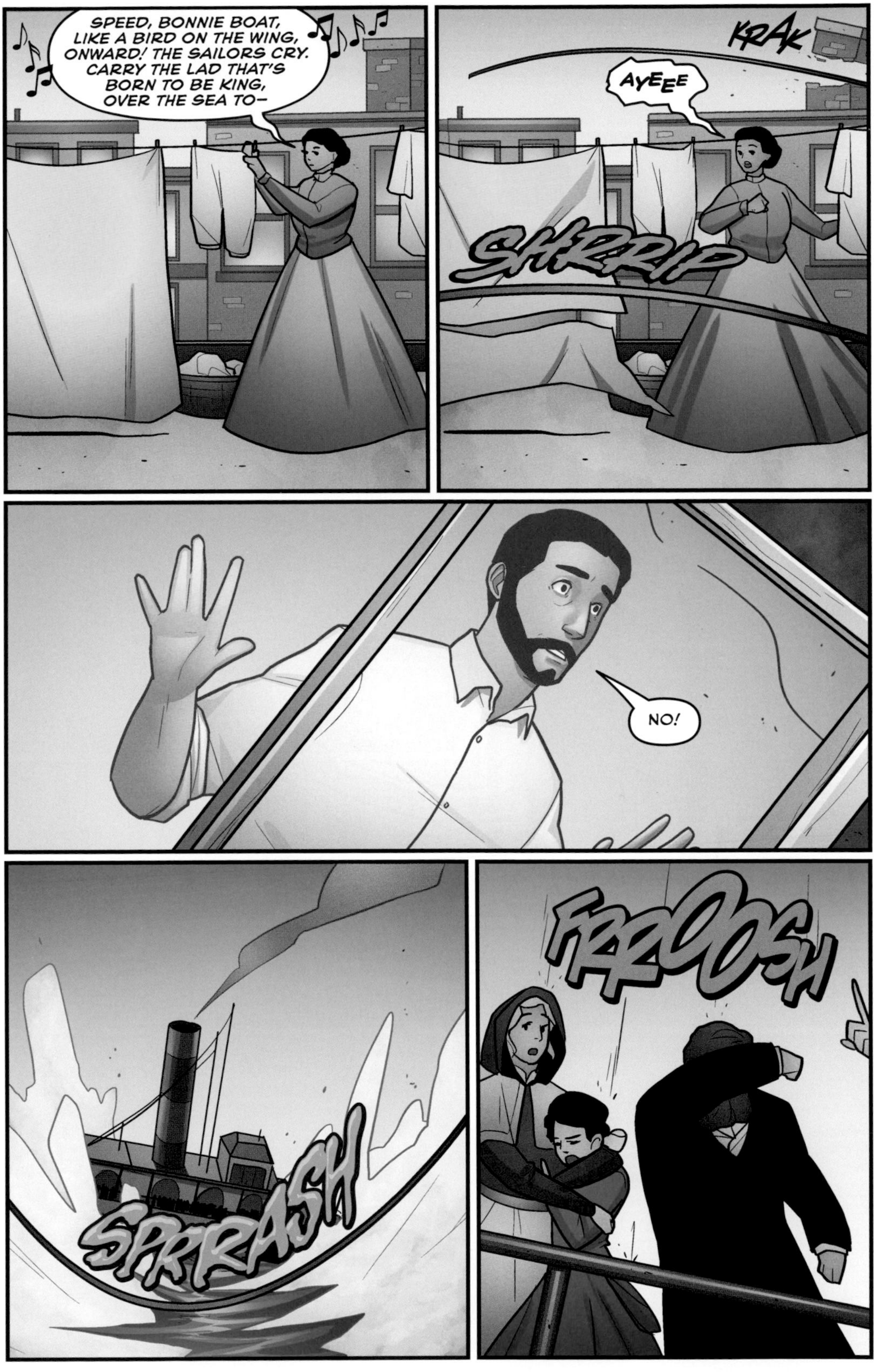
SPEED, BONNIE BOAT, LIKE A BIRD ON THE WING, ONWARD! THE SAILORS CRY. CARRY THE LAD THAT'S BORN TO BE KING, OVER THE SEA TO—
KRAK
AYEEE
SHRRIP
NO!
SPRRASH
FRROOSH

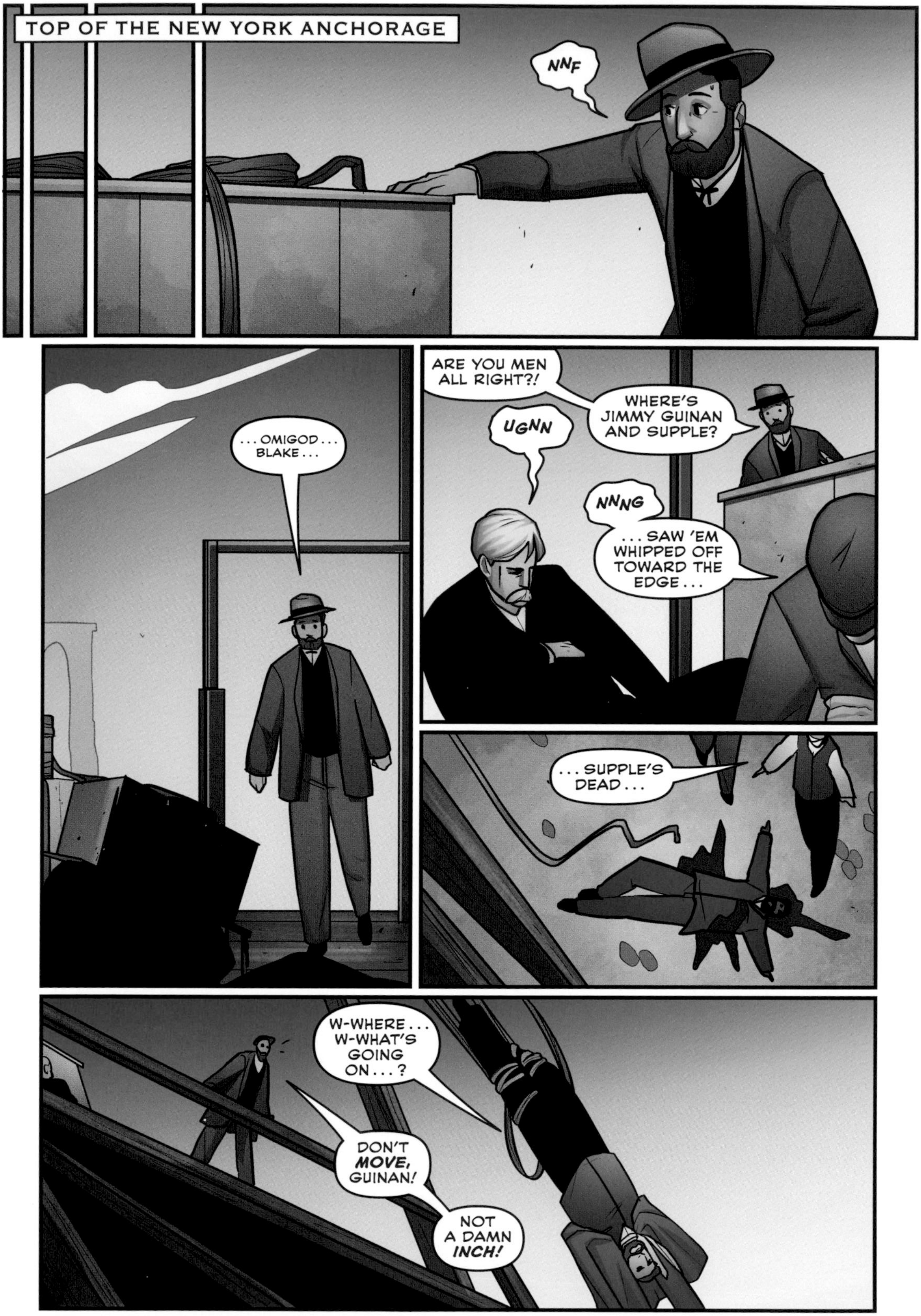
TOP OF THE NEW YORK ANCHORAGE
NNF
...OMIGOD... BLAKE...
ARE YOU MEN ALL RIGHT?!
WHERE'S JIMMY GUINAN AND SUPPLE?
UGNN
NNNG
...SAW 'EM WHIPPED OFF TOWARD THE EDGE...
...SUPPLE'S DEAD...
W-WHERE... W-WHAT'S GOING ON...?
DON'T *MOVE,* GUINAN!
NOT A DAMN *INCH!*

GENTLY... GENTLY...

THE ROEBLING BROWNSTONE

IT'S AS BRITTLE AS GLASS.

THAT BASTARD HAIGH IS PUTTING REJECTED WIRE INTO THE CABLES!

THE TRUSTEES, SHOULD WE—

NO.

NOT UNTIL WE HAVE SOLID AND IRREFUTABLE PROOF.

AND THE CABLE SPINNING?

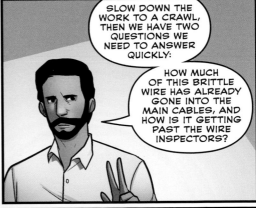

SLOW DOWN THE WORK TO A CRAWL, THEN WE HAVE TWO QUESTIONS WE NEED TO ANSWER QUICKLY:

HOW MUCH OF THIS BRITTLE WIRE HAS ALREADY GONE INTO THE MAIN CABLES, AND HOW IS IT GETTING PAST THE WIRE INSPECTORS?

I SUGGEST WE FOLLOW THE WIRE...

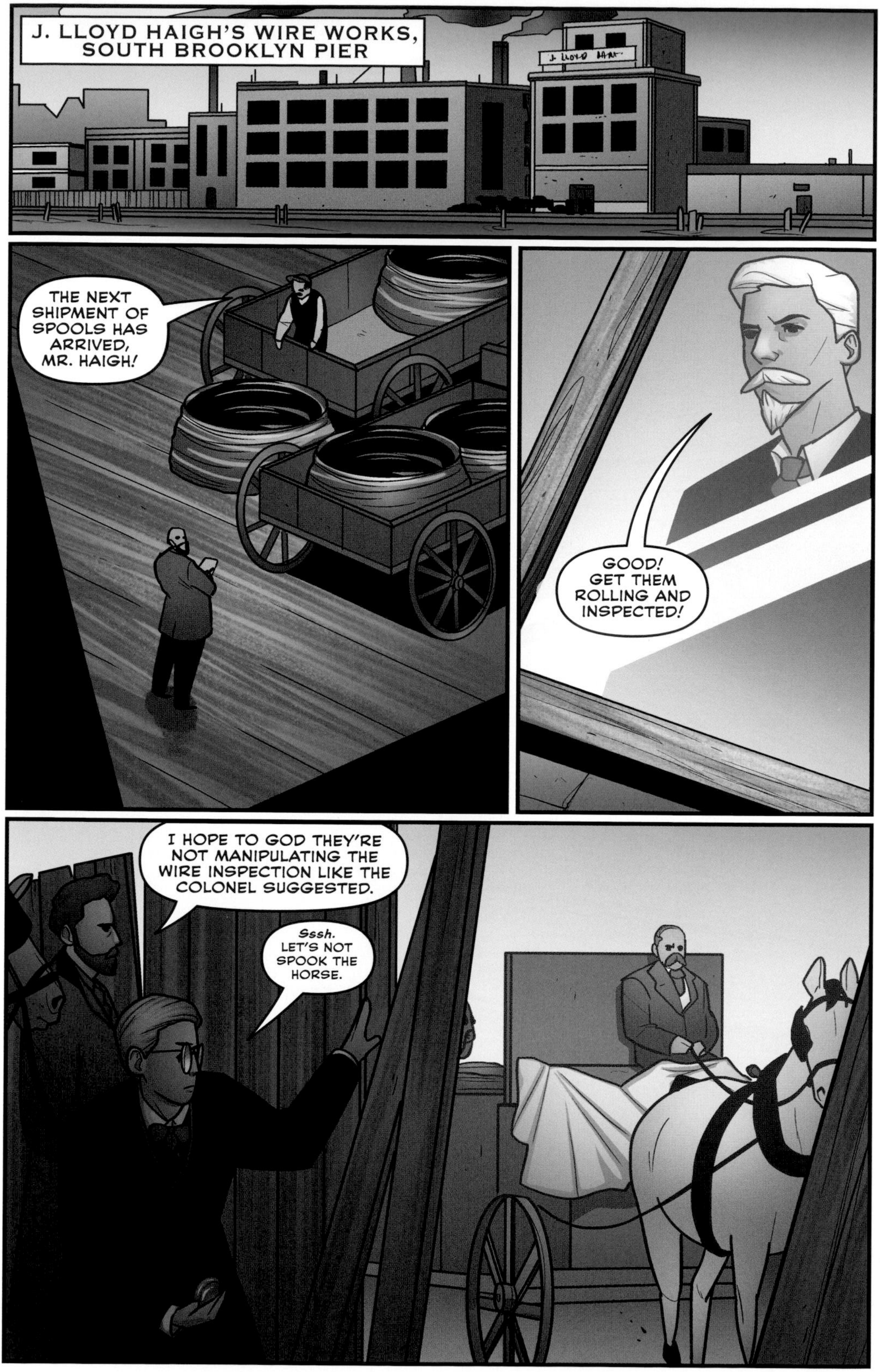
J. LLOYD HAIGH'S WIRE WORKS, SOUTH BROOKLYN PIER
THE NEXT SHIPMENT OF SPOOLS HAS ARRIVED, MR. HAIGH!
GOOD! GET THEM ROLLING AND INSPECTED!
I HOPE TO GOD THEY'RE NOT MANIPULATING THE WIRE INSPECTION LIKE THE COLONEL SUGGESTED.
Sssh. LET'S NOT SPOOK THE HORSE.

AND THE FIRST WAGON IS ENTERING THE STATION AT 7:42 A.M.

EAST RIVER BRIDGE WIRE INSPECTION STATION

DID YOU NOTATE THAT?

YEP.

WHAT?

THEY'RE NEVER GONNA LOOK THE SAME.

NEW YORK. BROOKLYN. BEGINNING OF THE END, YA MIGHT SAY.

BRIDGE WON'T BE THE BIGGEST THING FOREVER.

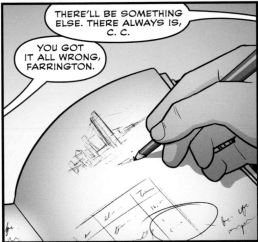

THERE'LL BE SOMETHING ELSE. THERE ALWAYS IS, C. C.

YOU GOT IT ALL WRONG, FARRINGTON.

I DO, huh? ENLIGHTEN ME.

IT'S THE BEGINNING OF THE BEGINNING. AND WE'RE HERE FOR IT. RIGHT OUT OF THE GATE.

NEW YORK NEVER STAYS THE SAME.

NEVER HAS. NEVER WILL.

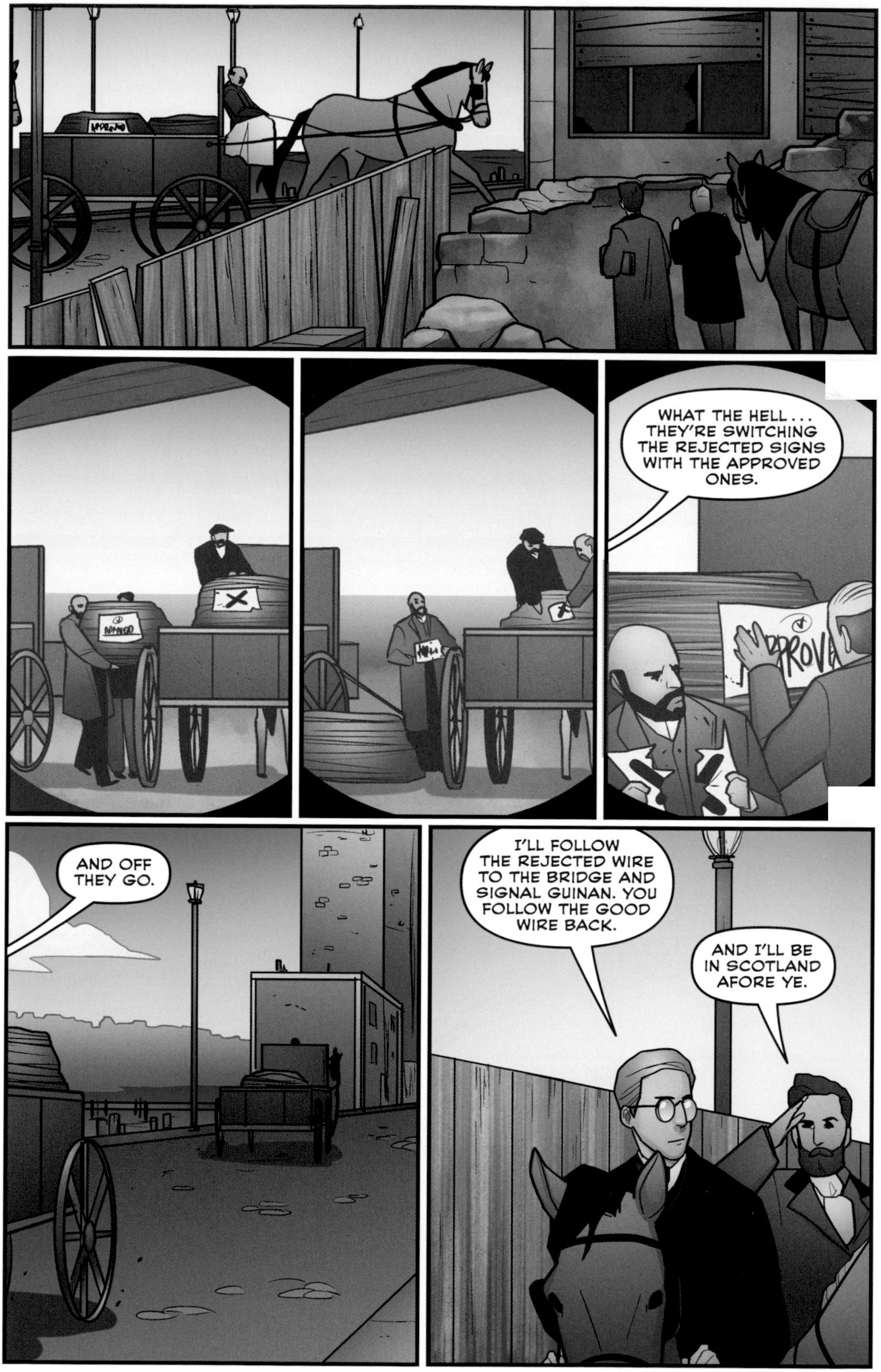
WHAT THE HELL . . . THEY'RE SWITCHING THE REJECTED SIGNS WITH THE APPROVED ONES.
AND OFF THEY GO.
I'LL FOLLOW THE REJECTED WIRE TO THE BRIDGE AND SIGNAL GUINAN. YOU FOLLOW THE GOOD WIRE BACK.
AND I'LL BE IN SCOTLAND AFORE YE.

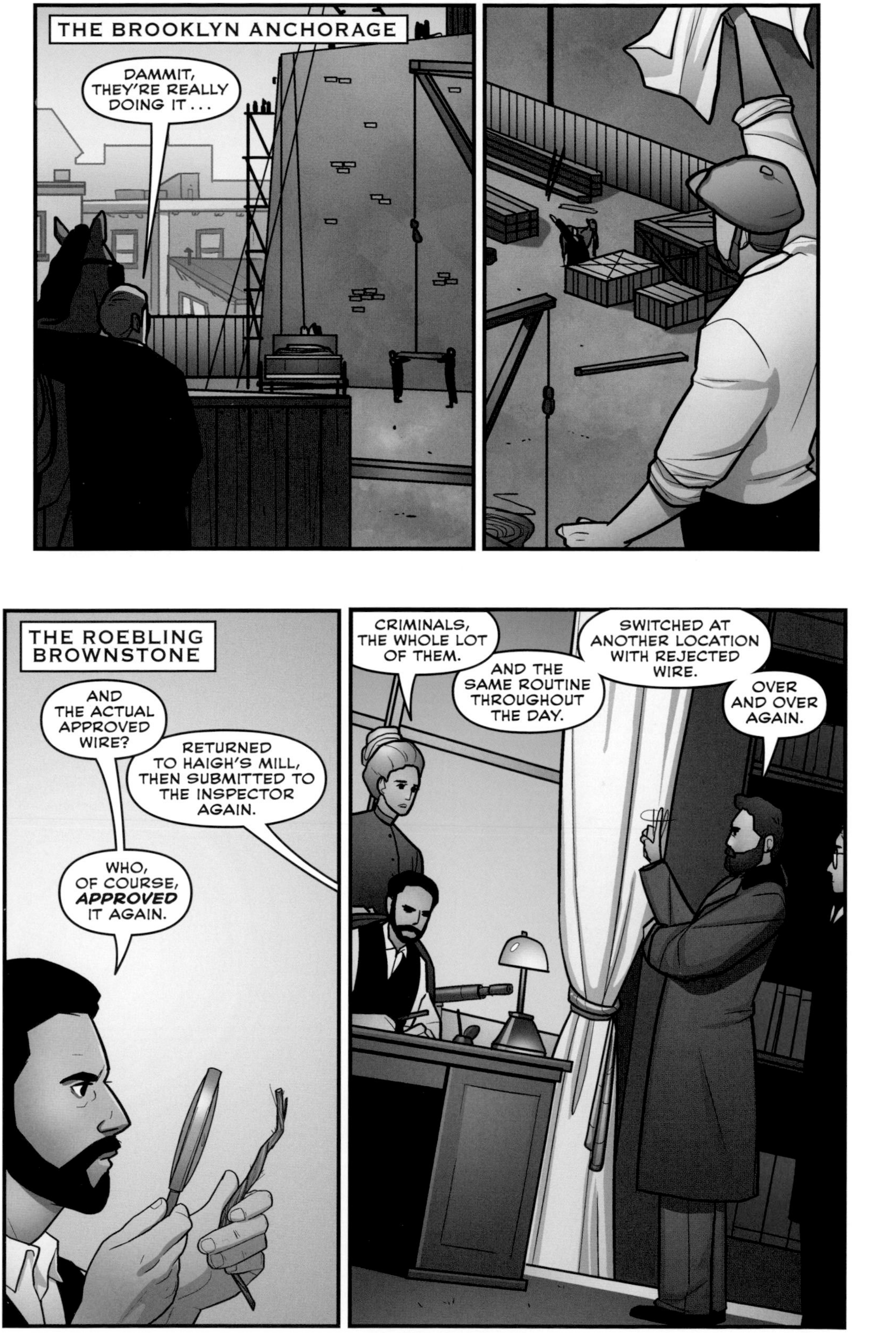
THE BROOKLYN ANCHORAGE
DAMMIT, THEY'RE REALLY DOING IT . . .
THE ROEBLING BROWNSTONE
AND THE ACTUAL APPROVED WIRE?
RETURNED TO HAIGH'S MILL, THEN SUBMITTED TO THE INSPECTOR AGAIN.
WHO, OF COURSE, ***APPROVED*** IT AGAIN.
CRIMINALS, THE WHOLE LOT OF THEM.
AND THE SAME ROUTINE THROUGHOUT THE DAY.
SWITCHED AT ANOTHER LOCATION WITH REJECTED WIRE.
OVER AND OVER AGAIN.

THANK YOU ALL FOR AGREEING TO COME TO MY HOME TONIGHT AND SAVING ME THE ENERGY OF TRAVELING.

MY MEN HAVE FOUND SEVERAL TONS OF REJECTED WIRE IN HAIGH'S MILL AND OTHER ASSORTED WAREHOUSES.

MY BEST GUESS IS CLOSE TO TWO HUNDRED TONS HAVE BEEN ALREADY WORKED INTO THE BRIDGE CABLES.

GOOD CHRIST.

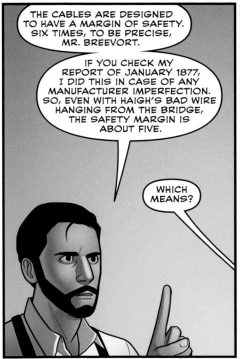

THE CABLES ARE DESIGNED TO HAVE A MARGIN OF SAFETY. SIX TIMES, TO BE PRECISE, MR. BREEVORT.

IF YOU CHECK MY REPORT OF JANUARY 1877, I DID THIS IN CASE OF ANY MANUFACTURER IMPERFECTION. SO, EVEN WITH HAIGH'S BAD WIRE HANGING FROM THE BRIDGE, THE SAFETY MARGIN IS ABOUT FIVE.

WHICH MEANS?

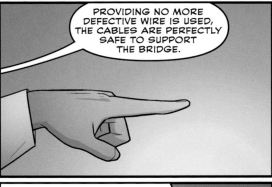

PROVIDING NO MORE DEFECTIVE WIRE IS USED, THE CABLES ARE PERFECTLY SAFE TO SUPPORT THE BRIDGE.

COLONEL, YOU KNOW AS WELL AS I THAT THE PUBLIC TRUST WOULD BE SHATTERED, NOT TO MENTION THE PROBLEMS OF NEW YORK PAYING THEIR JUST SHARE EXACERBATED BY THE—

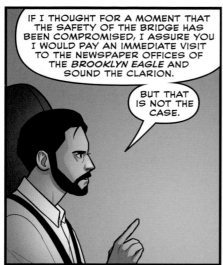

IF I THOUGHT FOR A MOMENT THAT THE SAFETY OF THE BRIDGE HAS BEEN COMPROMISED, I ASSURE YOU I WOULD PAY AN IMMEDIATE VISIT TO THE NEWSPAPER OFFICES OF THE *BROOKLYN EAGLE* AND SOUND THE CLARION.

BUT THAT IS NOT THE CASE.

WHAT *IS* THE CASE, COLONEL?

THERE'S AN EVEN BIGGER SCOUNDREL THAN HAIGH AT WORK HERE, AND IT HAPPENS TO BE THE ESTEEMED MR. HEWITT.

I'VE HAD QUITE ENOUGH OF THESE GAMES, ROEBLING, AND I WILL NOT—

I HAVE DOCUMENTS THAT WILL SHOW MR. HEWITT HELD A MORTGAGE ON HAIGH'S WIRE WORKS AND A DEAL WAS IN PLACE THAT MR. HEWITT WOULD NOT FORECLOSE SO LONG AS HAIGH TURNED OVER TEN PERCENT OF WHAT HE MADE FROM THE BRIDGE WIRE CONTRACT.

YOU WILL BE HEARING FROM MY ATTORNEY, ROEBLING.

I DOUBT IT.

HELL OF A "BOONDOGGLE," HEWITT, *hmm?*

167

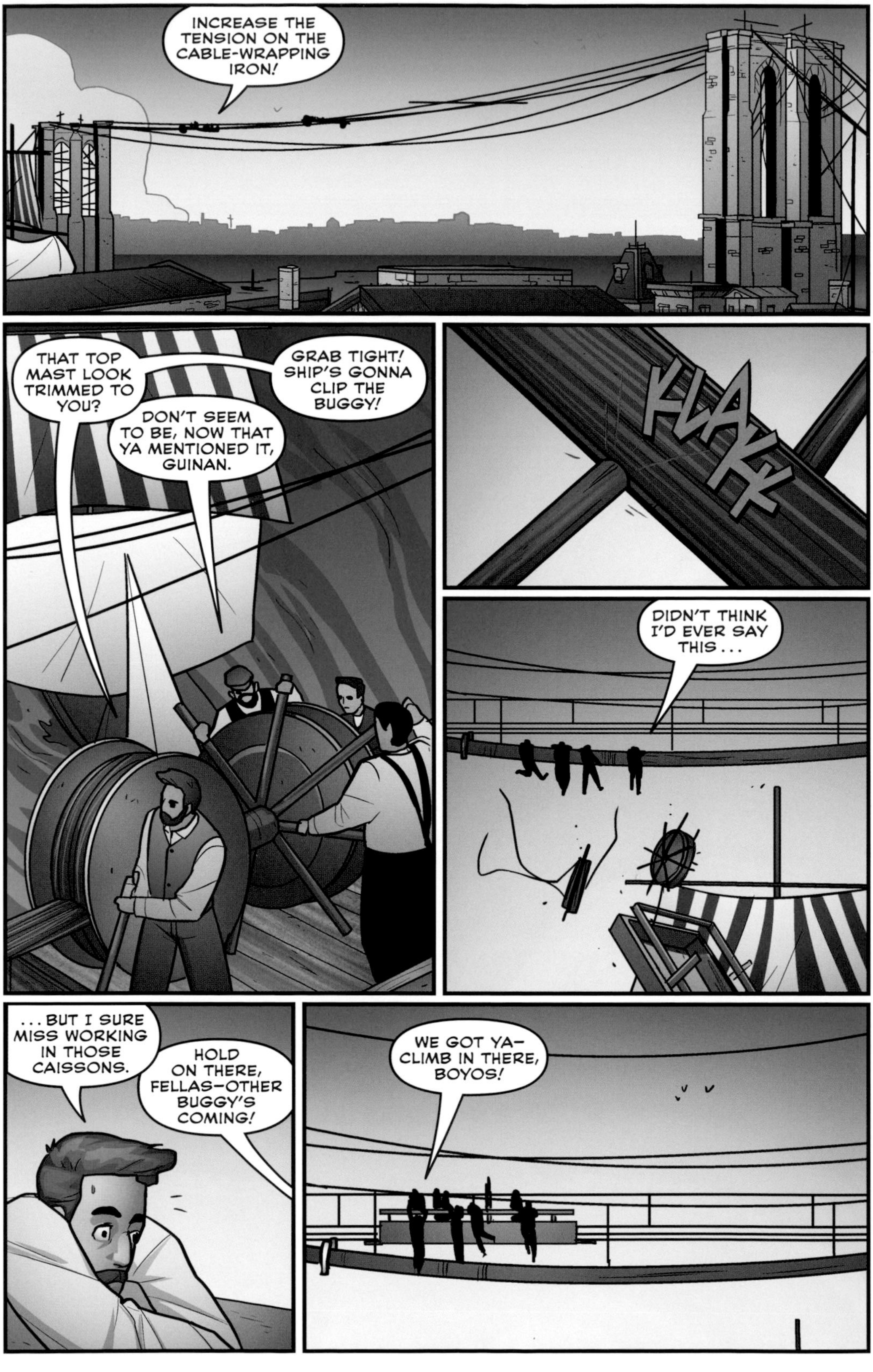
INCREASE THE TENSION ON THE CABLE-WRAPPING IRON!
THAT TOP MAST LOOK TRIMMED TO YOU?
DON'T SEEM TO BE, NOW THAT YA MENTIONED IT, GUINAN.
GRAB TIGHT! SHIP'S GONNA CLIP THE BUGGY!
KLAKK
DIDN'T THINK I'D EVER SAY THIS . . .
. . . BUT I SURE MISS WORKING IN THOSE CAISSONS.
HOLD ON THERE, FELLAS—OTHER BUGGY'S COMING!
WE GOT YA—CLIMB IN THERE, BOYOS!

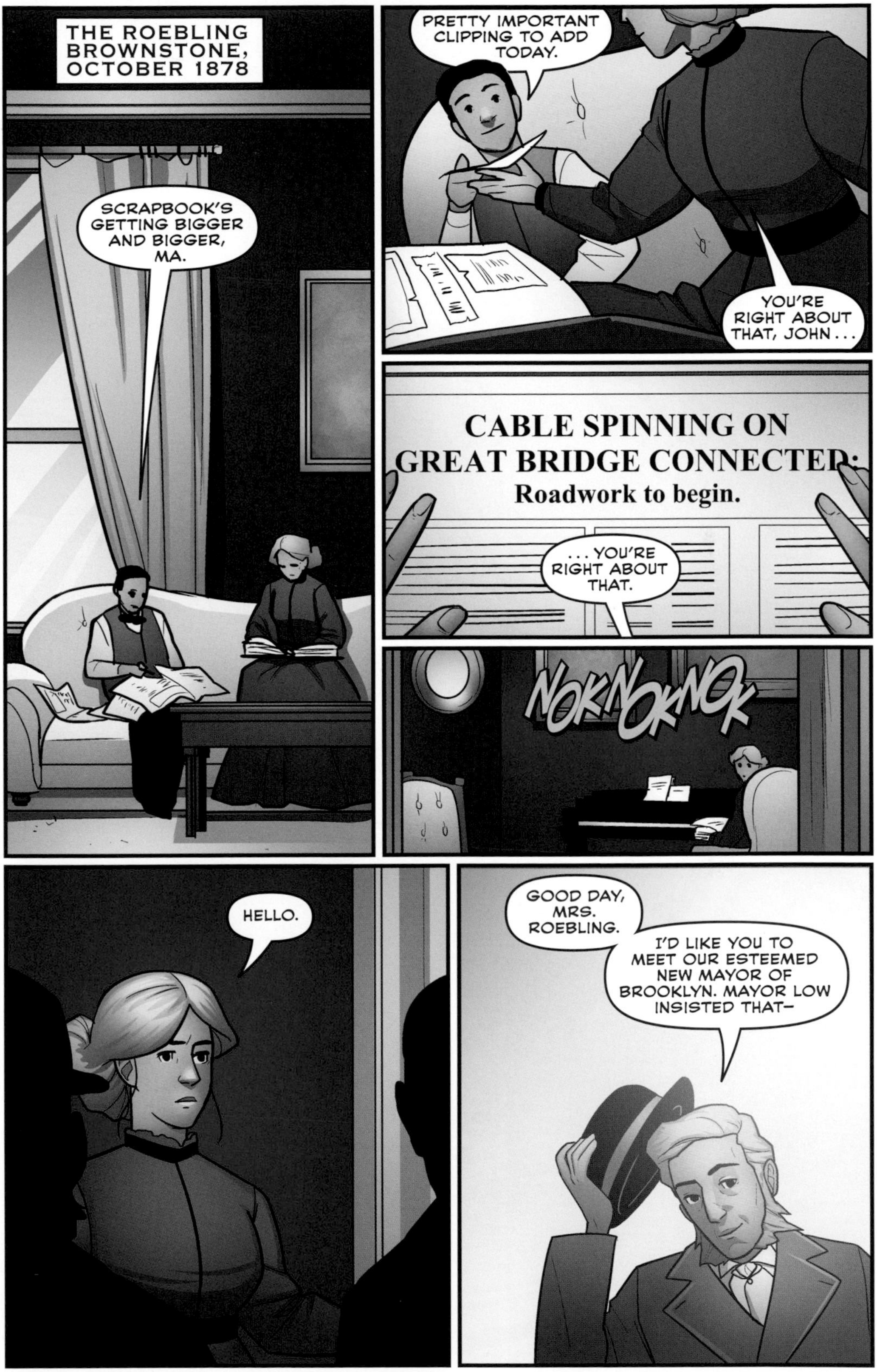
THE ROEBLING BROWNSTONE, OCTOBER 1878
SCRAPBOOK'S GETTING BIGGER AND BIGGER, MA.
PRETTY IMPORTANT CLIPPING TO ADD TODAY.
YOU'RE RIGHT ABOUT THAT, JOHN . . .
CABLE SPINNING ON GREAT BRIDGE CONNECTED:
Roadwork to begin.
. . . YOU'RE RIGHT ABOUT THAT.
NOKNOKNOK
HELLO.
GOOD DAY, MRS. ROEBLING.
I'D LIKE YOU TO MEET OUR ESTEEMED NEW MAYOR OF BROOKLYN. MAYOR LOW INSISTED THAT–

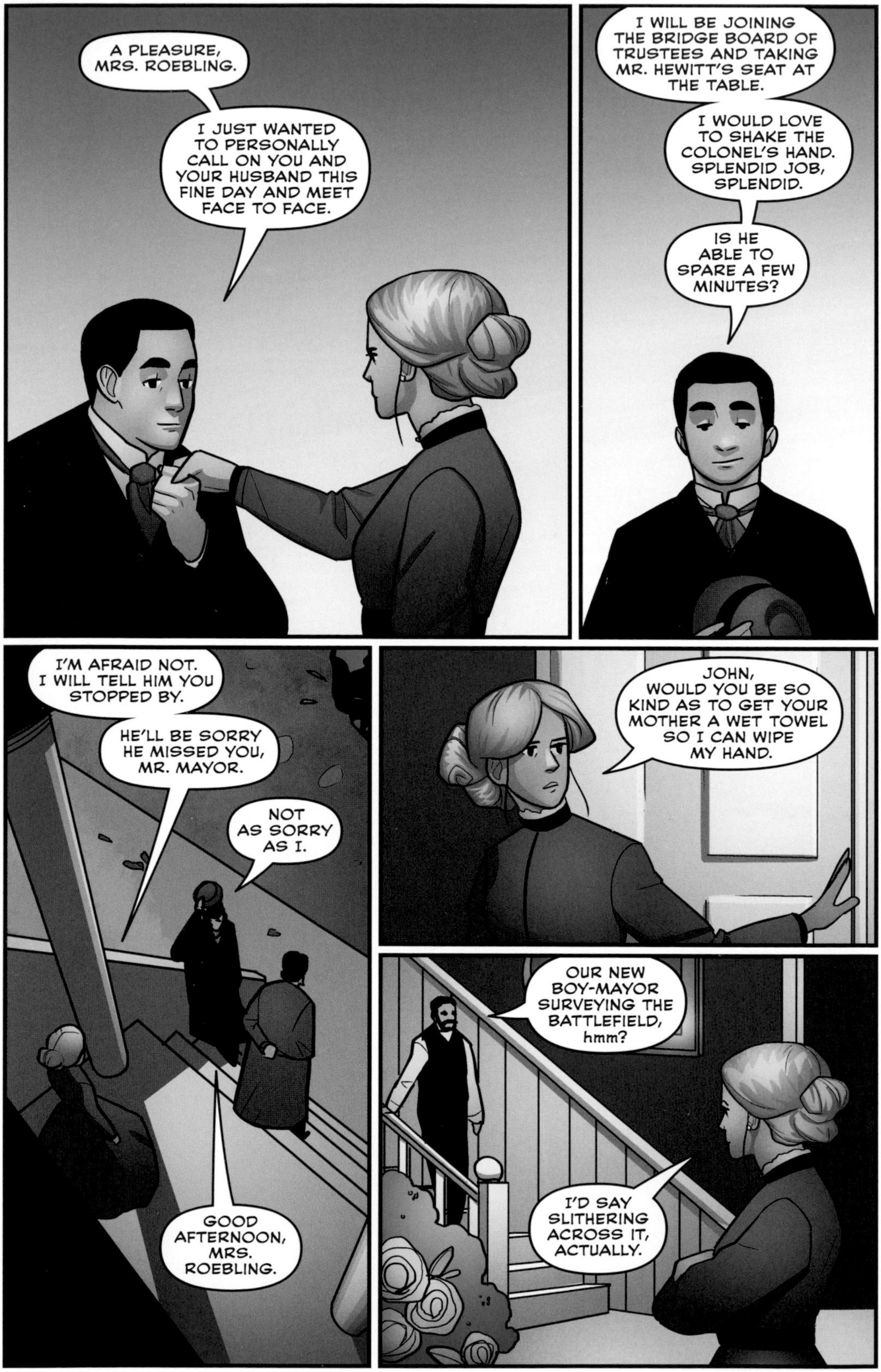

A PLEASURE, MRS. ROEBLING.
I JUST WANTED TO PERSONALLY CALL ON YOU AND YOUR HUSBAND THIS FINE DAY AND MEET FACE TO FACE.
I WILL BE JOINING THE BRIDGE BOARD OF TRUSTEES AND TAKING MR. HEWITT'S SEAT AT THE TABLE.
I WOULD LOVE TO SHAKE THE COLONEL'S HAND. SPLENDID JOB, SPLENDID.
IS HE ABLE TO SPARE A FEW MINUTES?
I'M AFRAID NOT. I WILL TELL HIM YOU STOPPED BY.
HE'LL BE SORRY HE MISSED YOU, MR. MAYOR.
NOT AS SORRY AS I.
GOOD AFTERNOON, MRS. ROEBLING.
JOHN, WOULD YOU BE SO KIND AS TO GET YOUR MOTHER A WET TOWEL SO I CAN WIPE MY HAND.
OUR NEW BOY-MAYOR SURVEYING THE BATTLEFIELD, hmm?
I'D SAY SLITHERING ACROSS IT, ACTUALLY.

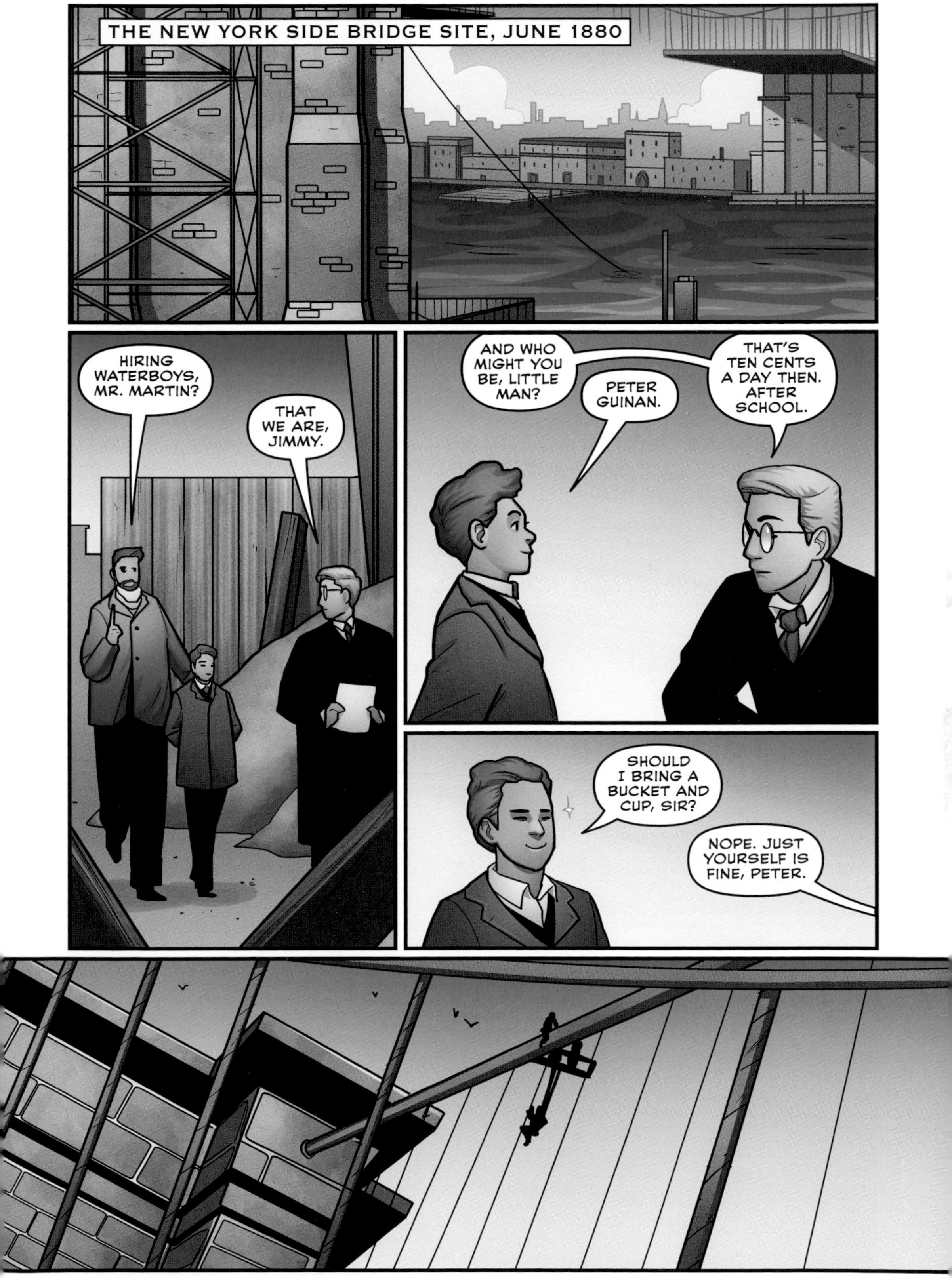
THE NEW YORK SIDE BRIDGE SITE, JUNE 1880
HIRING WATERBOYS, MR. MARTIN?
THAT WE ARE, JIMMY.
AND WHO MIGHT YOU BE, LITTLE MAN?
PETER GUINAN.
THAT'S TEN CENTS A DAY THEN. AFTER SCHOOL.
SHOULD I BRING A BUCKET AND CUP, SIR?
NOPE. JUST YOURSELF IS FINE, PETER.

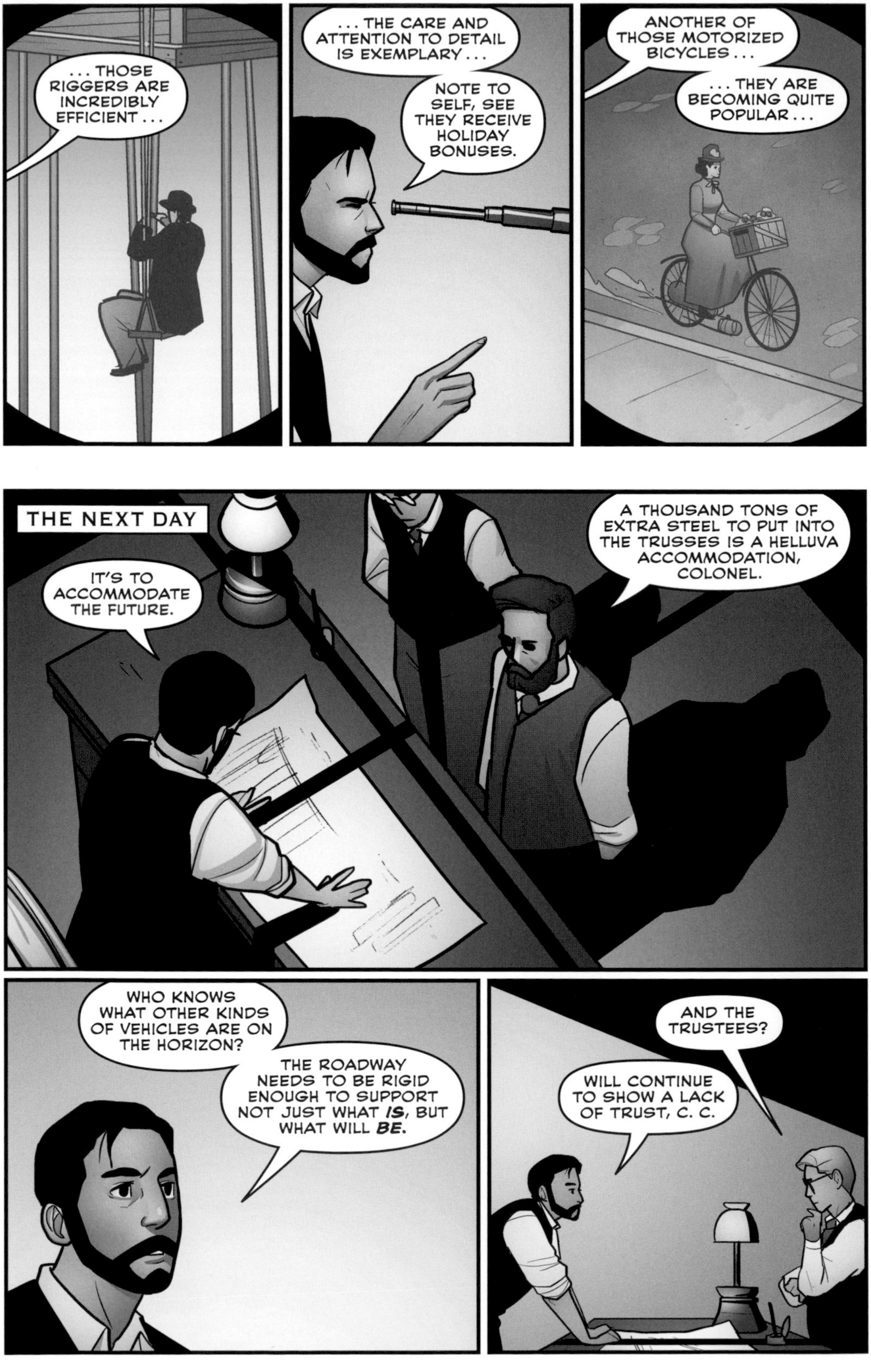
. . . THOSE RIGGERS ARE INCREDIBLY EFFICIENT . . .
. . . THE CARE AND ATTENTION TO DETAIL IS EXEMPLARY . . .
NOTE TO SELF, SEE THEY RECEIVE HOLIDAY BONUSES.
ANOTHER OF THOSE MOTORIZED BICYCLES . . .
. . . THEY ARE BECOMING QUITE POPULAR . . .
THE NEXT DAY
IT'S TO ACCOMMODATE THE FUTURE.
A THOUSAND TONS OF EXTRA STEEL TO PUT INTO THE TRUSSES IS A HELLUVA ACCOMMODATION, COLONEL.
WHO KNOWS WHAT OTHER KINDS OF VEHICLES ARE ON THE HORIZON?
THE ROADWAY NEEDS TO BE RIGID ENOUGH TO SUPPORT NOT JUST WHAT *IS*, BUT WHAT WILL *BE*.
AND THE TRUSTEES?
WILL CONTINUE TO SHOW A LACK OF TRUST, C. C.

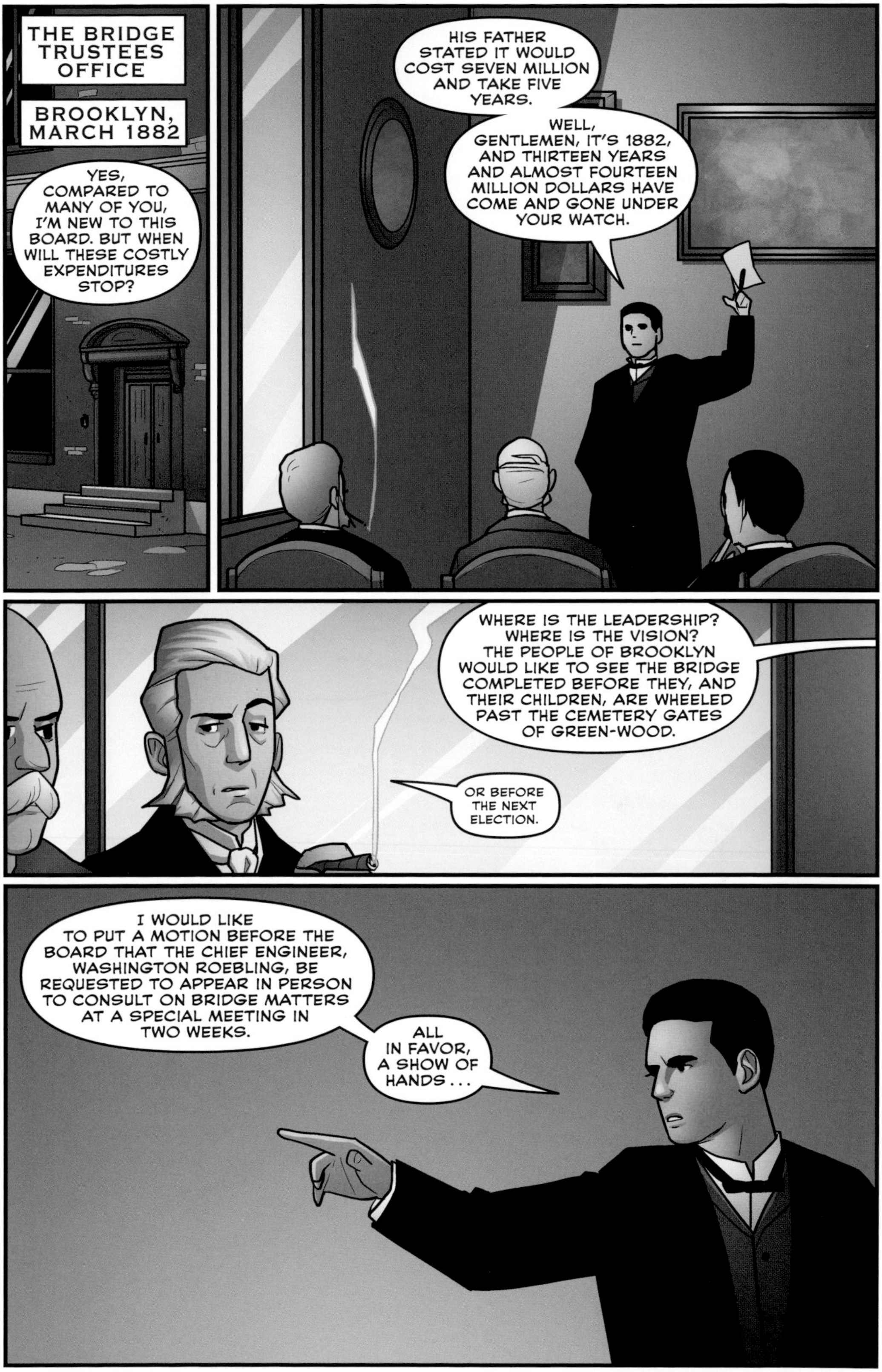
THE BRIDGE TRUSTEES OFFICE
BROOKLYN, MARCH 1882
YES, COMPARED TO MANY OF YOU, I'M NEW TO THIS BOARD. BUT WHEN WILL THESE COSTLY EXPENDITURES STOP?
HIS FATHER STATED IT WOULD COST SEVEN MILLION AND TAKE FIVE YEARS.
WELL, GENTLEMEN, IT'S 1882, AND THIRTEEN YEARS AND ALMOST FOURTEEN MILLION DOLLARS HAVE COME AND GONE UNDER YOUR WATCH.
WHERE IS THE LEADERSHIP? WHERE IS THE VISION? THE PEOPLE OF BROOKLYN WOULD LIKE TO SEE THE BRIDGE COMPLETED BEFORE THEY, AND THEIR CHILDREN, ARE WHEELED PAST THE CEMETERY GATES OF GREEN-WOOD.
OR BEFORE THE NEXT ELECTION.
I WOULD LIKE TO PUT A MOTION BEFORE THE BOARD THAT THE CHIEF ENGINEER, WASHINGTON ROEBLING, BE REQUESTED TO APPEAR IN PERSON TO CONSULT ON BRIDGE MATTERS AT A SPECIAL MEETING IN TWO WEEKS.
ALL IN FAVOR, A SHOW OF HANDS . . .

THE ROEBLING BROWNSTONE

I AM NOT SOME DOG TO BE SUMMONED TO ITS MASTER!

I WILL NOT FALL PROSTRATE TO MY KNEES BEFORE THE TRUSTEES—I NEVER DID IT WHEN I WAS WELL, AND I WILL NOT DO IT NOW!

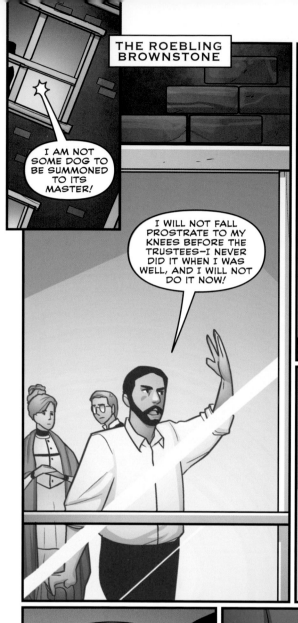

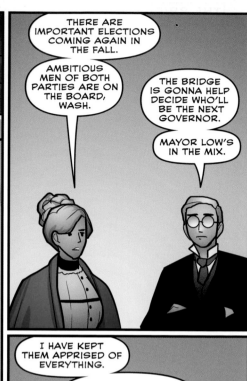

THERE ARE IMPORTANT ELECTIONS COMING AGAIN IN THE FALL.

AMBITIOUS MEN OF BOTH PARTIES ARE ON THE BOARD, WASH.

THE BRIDGE IS GONNA HELP DECIDE WHO'LL BE THE NEXT GOVERNOR.

MAYOR LOW'S IN THE MIX.

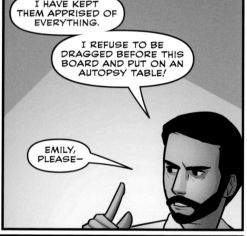

I HAVE KEPT THEM APPRISED OF EVERYTHING.

I REFUSE TO BE DRAGGED BEFORE THIS BOARD AND PUT ON AN AUTOPSY TABLE!

EMILY, PLEASE—

READY WHEN YOU ARE, WASH.

FIRE AWAY.

174

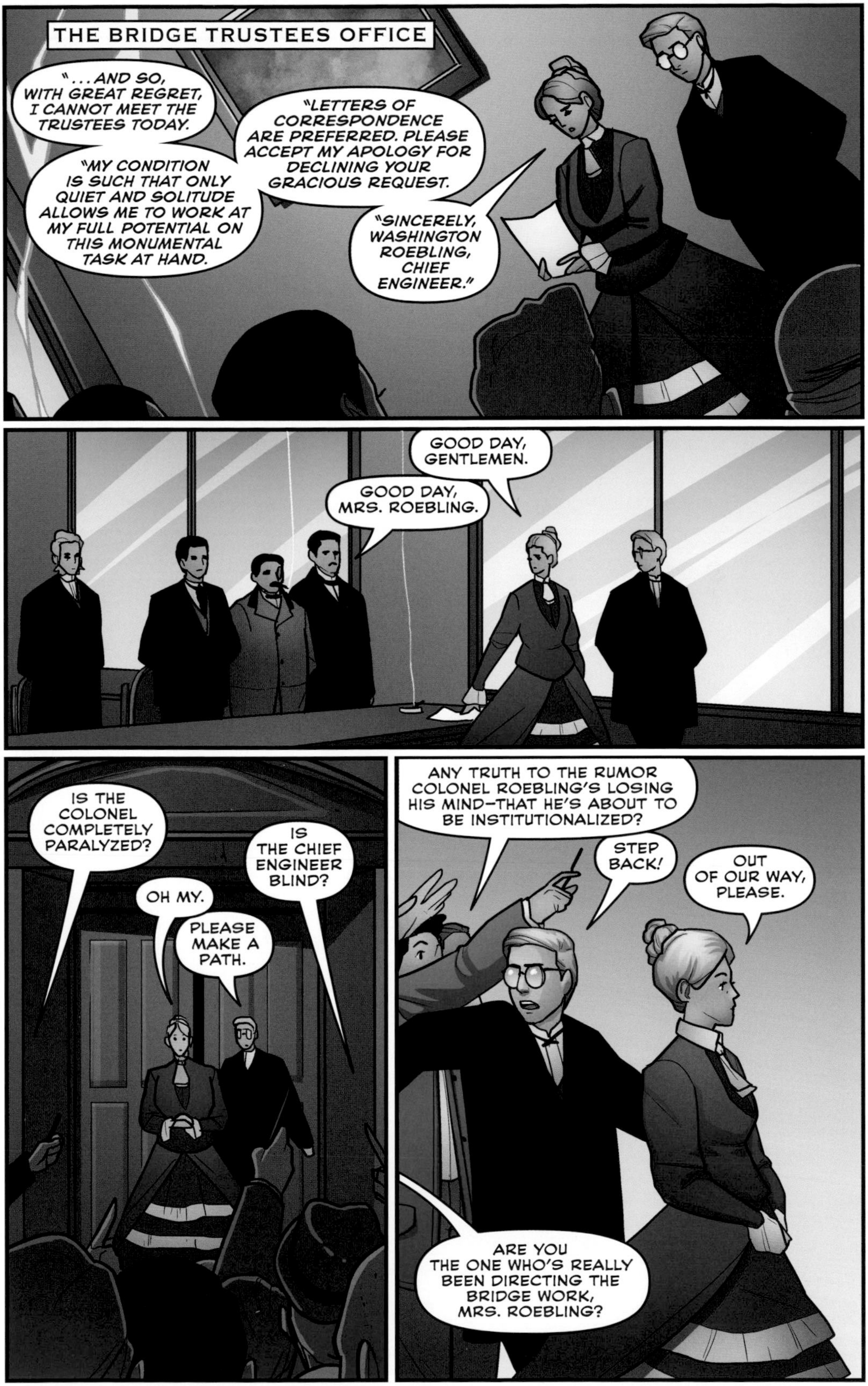
THE BRIDGE TRUSTEES OFFICE
"...AND SO, WITH GREAT REGRET, I CANNOT MEET THE TRUSTEES TODAY.
"MY CONDITION IS SUCH THAT ONLY QUIET AND SOLITUDE ALLOWS ME TO WORK AT MY FULL POTENTIAL ON THIS MONUMENTAL TASK AT HAND.
"LETTERS OF CORRESPONDENCE ARE PREFERRED. PLEASE ACCEPT MY APOLOGY FOR DECLINING YOUR GRACIOUS REQUEST.
"SINCERELY, WASHINGTON ROEBLING, CHIEF ENGINEER."
GOOD DAY, GENTLEMEN.
GOOD DAY, MRS. ROEBLING.
IS THE COLONEL COMPLETELY PARALYZED?
OH MY.
PLEASE MAKE A PATH.
IS THE CHIEF ENGINEER BLIND?
ANY TRUTH TO THE RUMOR COLONEL ROEBLING'S LOSING HIS MIND—THAT HE'S ABOUT TO BE INSTITUTIONALIZED?
STEP BACK!
OUT OF OUR WAY, PLEASE.
ARE YOU THE ONE WHO'S REALLY BEEN DIRECTING THE BRIDGE WORK, MRS. ROEBLING?

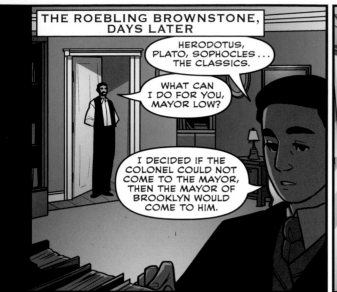

THE ROEBLING BROWNSTONE, DAYS LATER

HERODOTUS, PLATO, SOPHOCLES... THE CLASSICS.

WHAT CAN I DO FOR YOU, MAYOR LOW?

I DECIDED IF THE COLONEL COULD NOT COME TO THE MAYOR, THEN THE MAYOR OF BROOKLYN WOULD COME TO HIM.

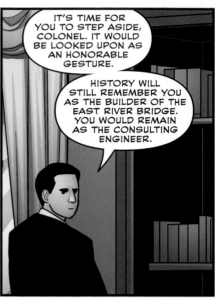

IT'S TIME FOR YOU TO STEP ASIDE, COLONEL. IT WOULD BE LOOKED UPON AS AN HONORABLE GESTURE.

HISTORY WILL STILL REMEMBER YOU AS THE BUILDER OF THE EAST RIVER BRIDGE. YOU WOULD REMAIN AS THE CONSULTING ENGINEER.

THE MORE THINGS CHANGE, THE MORE THEY REMAIN THE SAME.

SO, WHAT GAUNTLET DO I POSE FOR MAYOR SETH LOW AT THIS JUNCTURE?

PROGRESS.

HA! IS THAT RIGHT?

YOU ARE A SICK MAN, COLONEL.

YOU NEED TO WASH YOUR HANDS OF THIS DAILY BRIDGE BUSINESS.

THE GOVERNOR'S CHAIR AWAITS, *hmm?*

I AM GOING TO CROSS THE BRIDGE YOU STARTED AND THE BRIDGE THAT I HELPED FINISH, BECOME THE MAYOR OF NEW YORK, THEN THE GOVERNOR, AND WITH A LITTLE HELP FROM MY FRIENDS, THE REPUBLICAN NOMINEE FOR THE PRESIDENT OF THE UNITED STATES.

I LOOK FORWARD TO THE STATUE SURE TO BE ERECTED IN YOUR HONOR, ALONG WITH THE PIGEONS THAT WILL MAKE A MESS OF IT.

REST ASSURED YOUR DAYS AS CHIEF ENGINEER ARE NUMBERED, COLONEL ROEBLING.

HAVE AT IT, SIR.

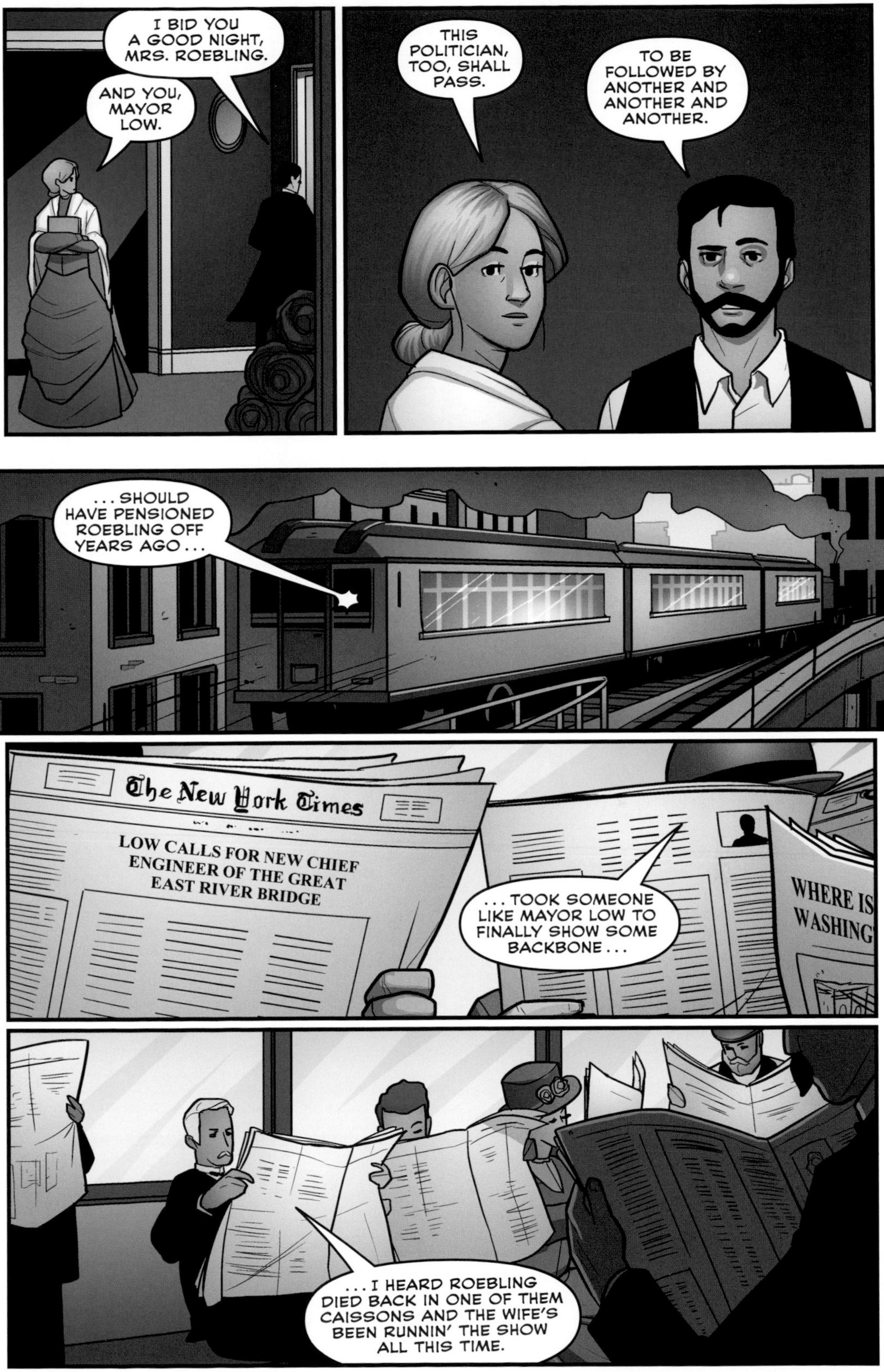
I BID YOU A GOOD NIGHT, MRS. ROEBLING.
AND YOU, MAYOR LOW.
THIS POLITICIAN, TOO, SHALL PASS.
TO BE FOLLOWED BY ANOTHER AND ANOTHER AND ANOTHER.
. . . SHOULD HAVE PENSIONED ROEBLING OFF YEARS AGO . . .
The New York Times
LOW CALLS FOR NEW CHIEF ENGINEER OF THE GREAT EAST RIVER BRIDGE
. . . TOOK SOMEONE LIKE MAYOR LOW TO FINALLY SHOW SOME BACKBONE . . .
WHERE IS
. . . I HEARD ROEBLING DIED BACK IN ONE OF THEM CAISSONS AND THE WIFE'S BEEN RUNNIN' THE SHOW ALL THIS TIME.

THE BRIDGE TRUSTEES OFFICE

HOW LONG IS THIS GONNA TAKE?

YA GOT ME.

AND NOW DOWN TO BUSINESS.

HERE ARE THE RESOLUTIONS THAT WE ARE VOTING UPON TODAY . . .

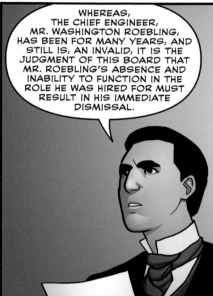

WHEREAS, THE CHIEF ENGINEER, MR. WASHINGTON ROEBLING, HAS BEEN FOR MANY YEARS, AND STILL IS, AN INVALID, IT IS THE JUDGMENT OF THIS BOARD THAT MR. ROEBLING'S ABSENCE AND INABILITY TO FUNCTION IN THE ROLE HE WAS HIRED FOR MUST RESULT IN HIS IMMEDIATE DISMISSAL.

I HAVE A SELECTION OF TODAY'S PAPERS TO PERUSE.

Um, THANK YOU. I'LL READ THEM LATER.

A CONCERNING DAY, I KNOW.

FAR FROM MY MIND. WHATEVER WILL BE WILL BE.

WORK IS ALL THAT MATTERS.

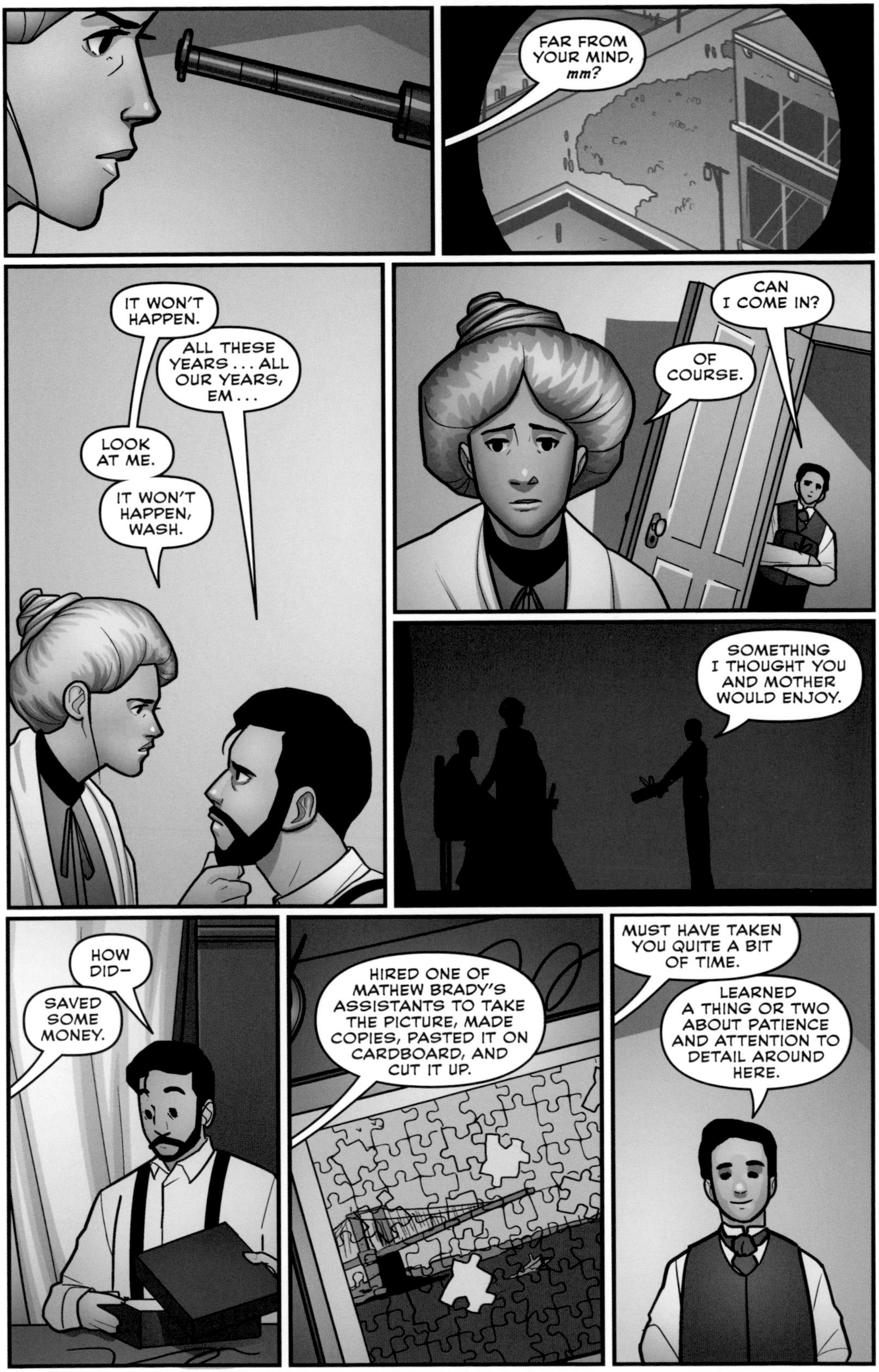
FAR FROM YOUR MIND, *mm?*
IT WON'T HAPPEN.
ALL THESE YEARS . . . ALL OUR YEARS, EM . . .
LOOK AT ME.
IT WON'T HAPPEN, WASH.
CAN I COME IN?
OF COURSE.
SOMETHING I THOUGHT YOU AND MOTHER WOULD ENJOY.
HOW DID—
SAVED SOME MONEY.
HIRED ONE OF MATHEW BRADY'S ASSISTANTS TO TAKE THE PICTURE, MADE COPIES, PASTED IT ON CARDBOARD, AND CUT IT UP.
MUST HAVE TAKEN YOU QUITE A BIT OF TIME.
LEARNED A THING OR TWO ABOUT PATIENCE AND ATTENTION TO DETAIL AROUND HERE.

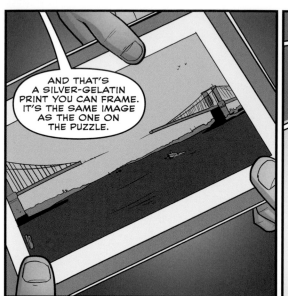

AND THAT'S A SILVER-GELATIN PRINT YOU CAN FRAME. IT'S THE SAME IMAGE AS THE ONE ON THE PUZZLE.

IT'S BEAUTIFUL, JOHN. THANK YOU.

HOW MANY PIECES?

AROUND TWO THOUSAND, I THINK, DA.

IT SHOULDN'T BE A PROBLEM.

BOTH OF YOU ARE PRETTY GOOD AT PUTTING THINGS TOGETHER.

WELL, MR. ROEBLING, I'D APPRECIATE IT IF YOU WOULD PLACE YOUR BUTTOCKS ON THE FLOOR HERE BESIDE ME.

MY PLEASURE, MRS. ROEBLING.

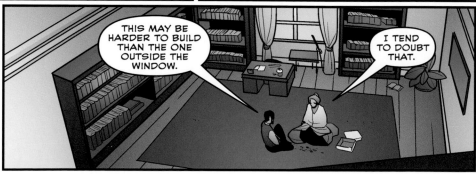

THIS MAY BE HARDER TO BUILD THAN THE ONE OUTSIDE THE WINDOW.

I TEND TO DOUBT THAT.

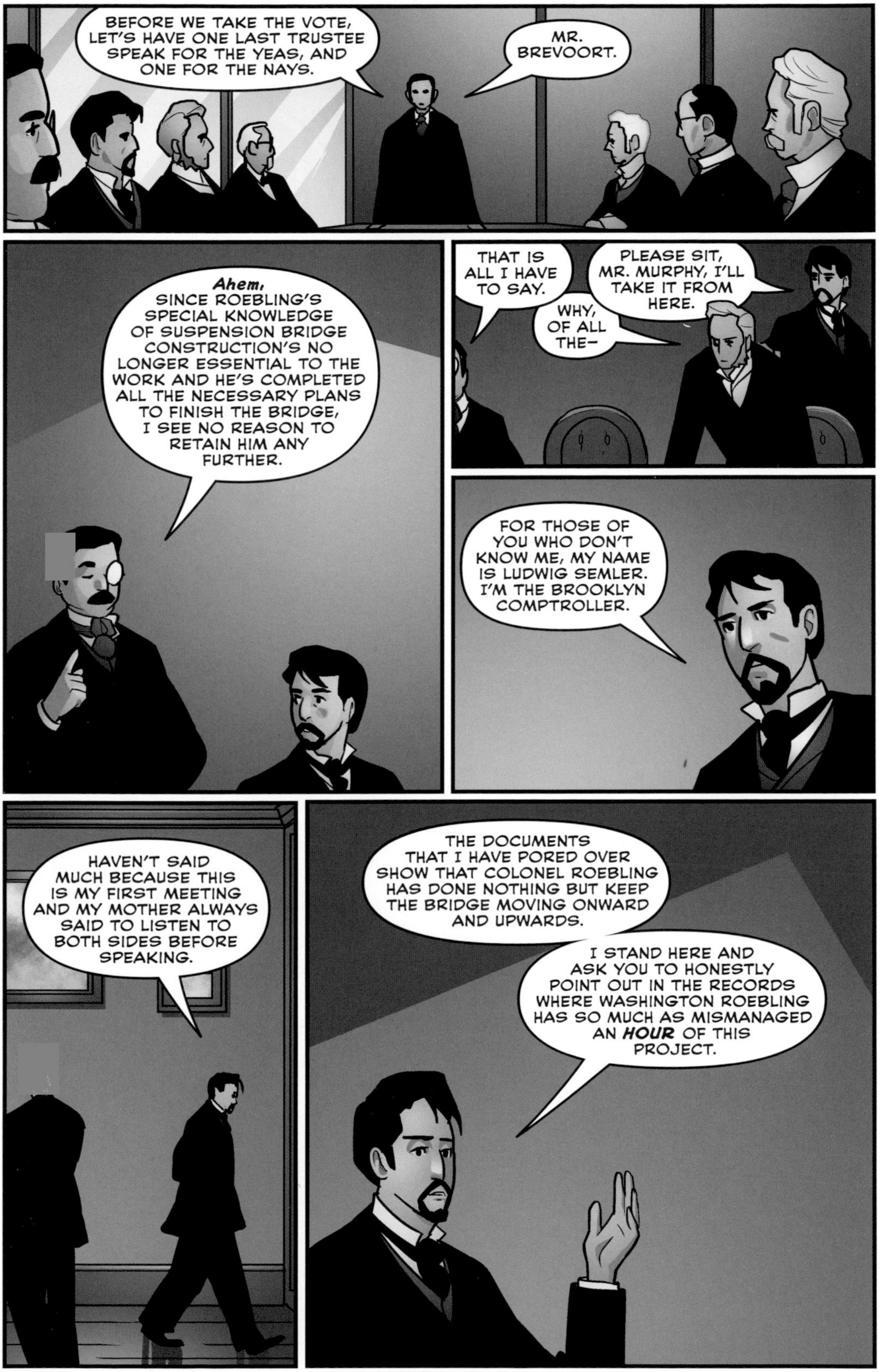
BEFORE WE TAKE THE VOTE, LET'S HAVE ONE LAST TRUSTEE SPEAK FOR THE YEAS, AND ONE FOR THE NAYS.
MR. BREVOORT.
Ahem, SINCE ROEBLING'S SPECIAL KNOWLEDGE OF SUSPENSION BRIDGE CONSTRUCTION'S NO LONGER ESSENTIAL TO THE WORK AND HE'S COMPLETED ALL THE NECESSARY PLANS TO FINISH THE BRIDGE, I SEE NO REASON TO RETAIN HIM ANY FURTHER.
THAT IS ALL I HAVE TO SAY.
WHY, OF ALL THE–
PLEASE SIT, MR. MURPHY, I'LL TAKE IT FROM HERE.
FOR THOSE OF YOU WHO DON'T KNOW ME, MY NAME IS LUDWIG SEMLER. I'M THE BROOKLYN COMPTROLLER.
HAVEN'T SAID MUCH BECAUSE THIS IS MY FIRST MEETING AND MY MOTHER ALWAYS SAID TO LISTEN TO BOTH SIDES BEFORE SPEAKING.
THE DOCUMENTS THAT I HAVE PORED OVER SHOW THAT COLONEL ROEBLING HAS DONE NOTHING BUT KEEP THE BRIDGE MOVING ONWARD AND UPWARDS.
I STAND HERE AND ASK YOU TO HONESTLY POINT OUT IN THE RECORDS WHERE WASHINGTON ROEBLING HAS SO MUCH AS MISMANAGED AN *HOUR* OF THIS PROJECT.

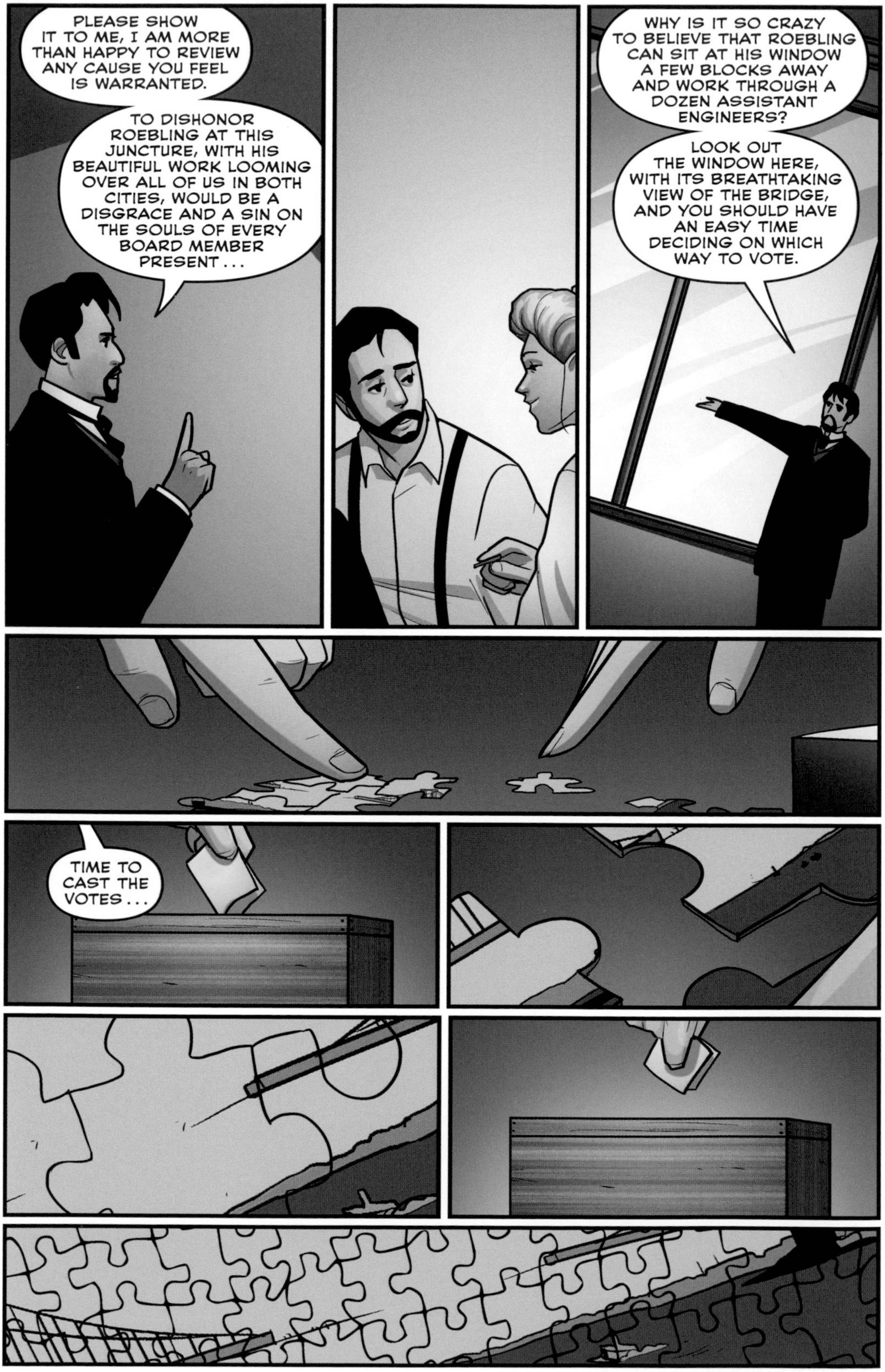
PLEASE SHOW IT TO ME, I AM MORE THAN HAPPY TO REVIEW ANY CAUSE YOU FEEL IS WARRANTED.
TO DISHONOR ROEBLING AT THIS JUNCTURE, WITH HIS BEAUTIFUL WORK LOOMING OVER ALL OF US IN BOTH CITIES, WOULD BE A DISGRACE AND A SIN ON THE SOULS OF EVERY BOARD MEMBER PRESENT . . .
WHY IS IT SO CRAZY TO BELIEVE THAT ROEBLING CAN SIT AT HIS WINDOW A FEW BLOCKS AWAY AND WORK THROUGH A DOZEN ASSISTANT ENGINEERS?
LOOK OUT THE WINDOW HERE, WITH ITS BREATHTAKING VIEW OF THE BRIDGE, AND YOU SHOULD HAVE AN EASY TIME DECIDING ON WHICH WAY TO VOTE.
TIME TO CAST THE VOTES . . .

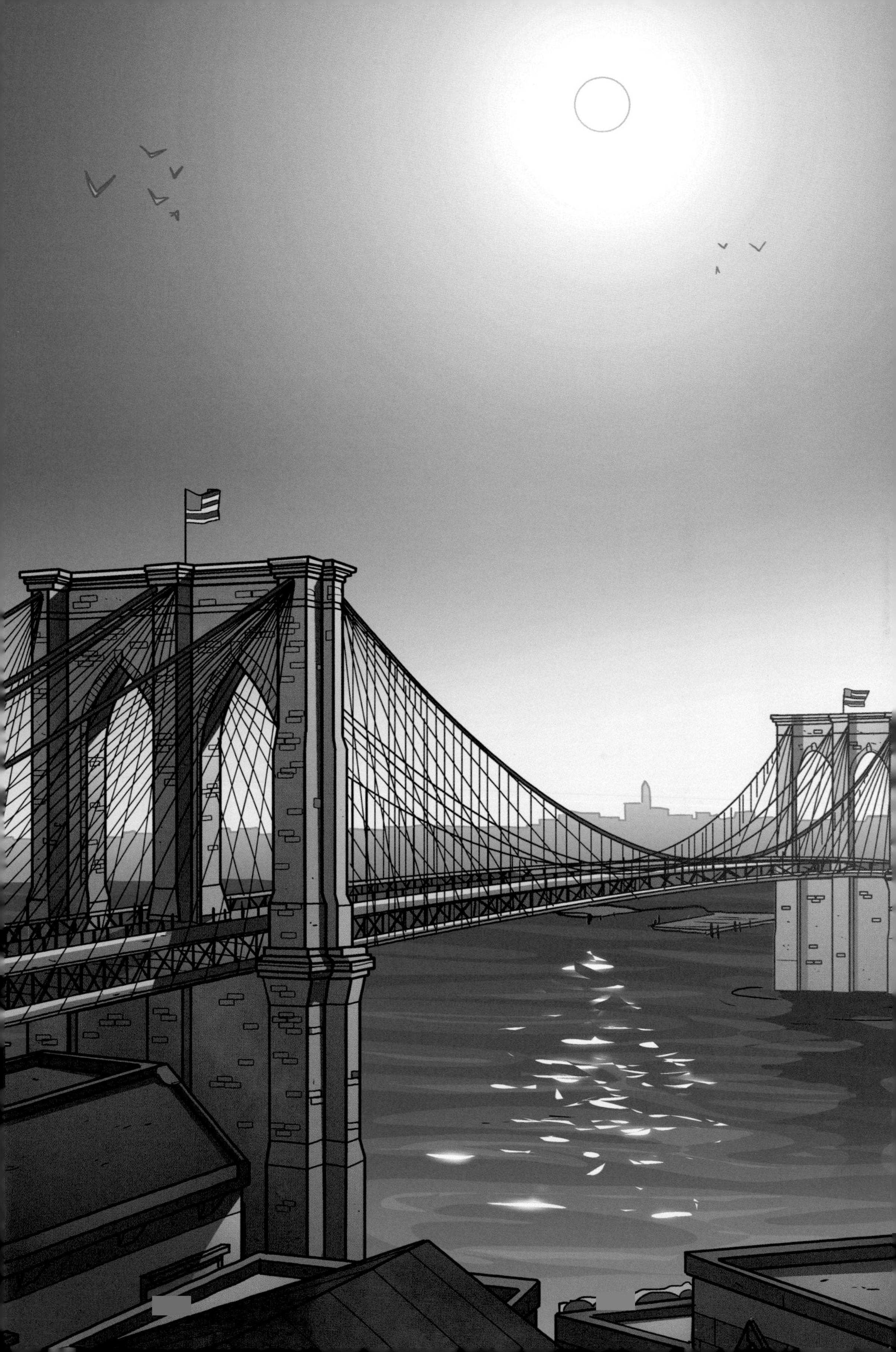

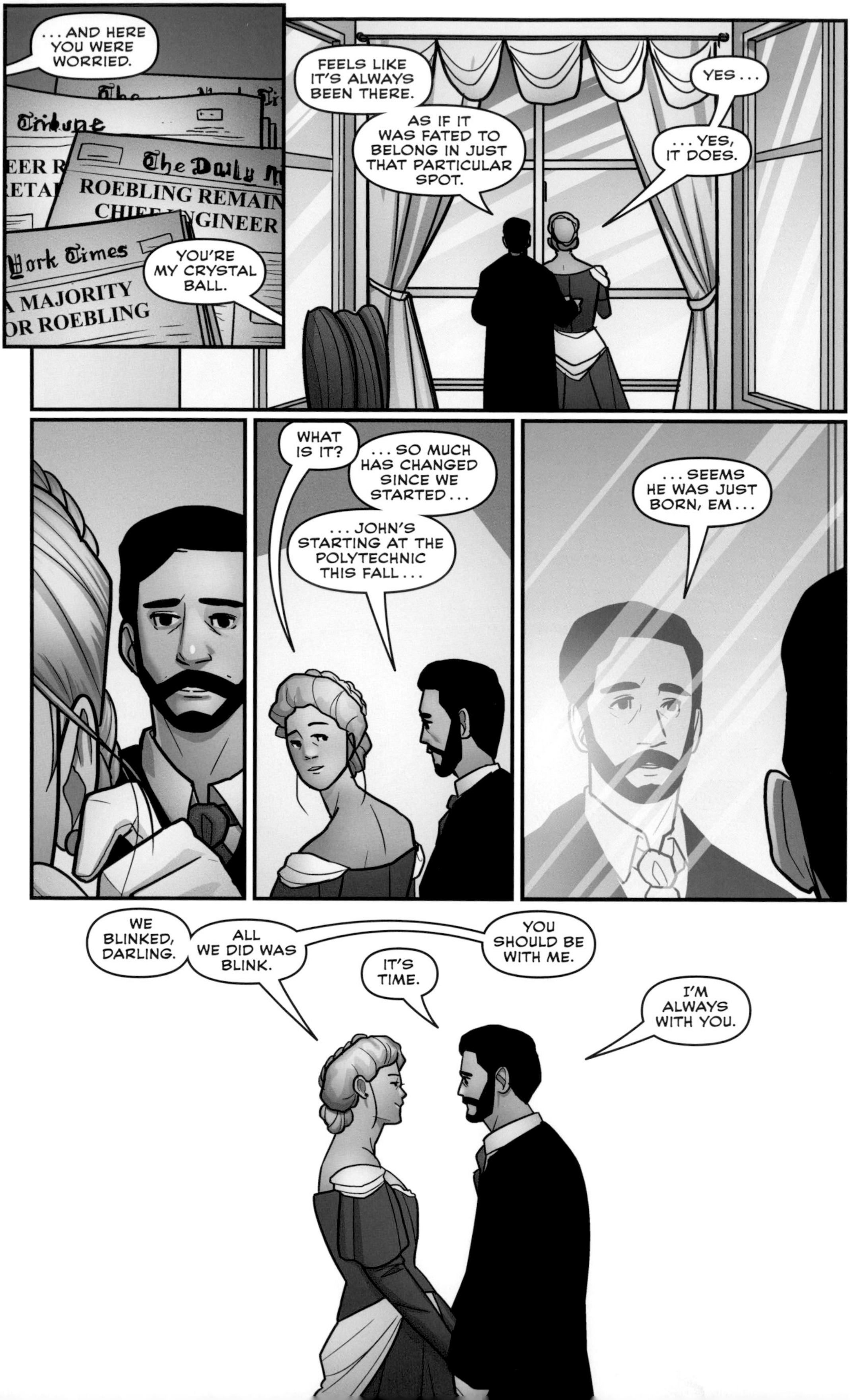
. . . AND HERE YOU WERE WORRIED.
Tribune
ROEBLING REMAIN
CHIEF ENGINEER
A MAJORITY
YOU'RE MY CRYSTAL BALL.
FEELS LIKE IT'S ALWAYS BEEN THERE.
AS IF IT WAS FATED TO BELONG IN JUST THAT PARTICULAR SPOT.
YES . . .
. . . YES, IT DOES.
WHAT IS IT?
. . . SO MUCH HAS CHANGED SINCE WE STARTED . . .
. . . JOHN'S STARTING AT THE POLYTECHNIC THIS FALL . . .
. . . SEEMS HE WAS JUST BORN, EM . . .
WE BLINKED, DARLING.
ALL WE DID WAS BLINK.
YOU SHOULD BE WITH ME.
IT'S TIME.
I'M ALWAYS WITH YOU.

YOU LOOK QUITE BEAUTIFUL, MRS. ROEBLING.

THANK YOU, MR. MARTIN.

AS YOU REQUESTED.

MR. SEMLER, COULD YOU PLEASE JOIN ME FOR A MOMENT?

GOOD DAY, MRS. ROEBLING.

HOW CAN I BE OF ASSISTANCE?

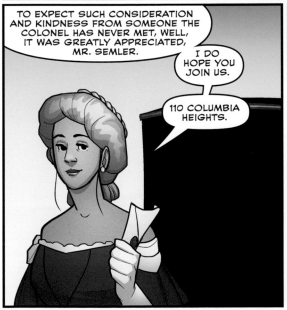

TO EXPECT SUCH CONSIDERATION AND KINDNESS FROM SOMEONE THE COLONEL HAS NEVER MET, WELL, IT WAS GREATLY APPRECIATED, MR. SEMLER.

I DO HOPE YOU JOIN US.

110 COLUMBIA HEIGHTS.

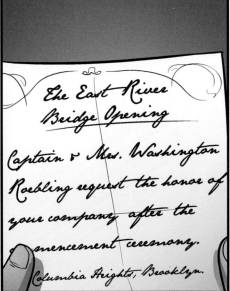

The East River Bridge Opening

Captain & Mrs. Washington Roebling request the honor of your company after the commencement ceremony.

Columbia Heights, Brooklyn.

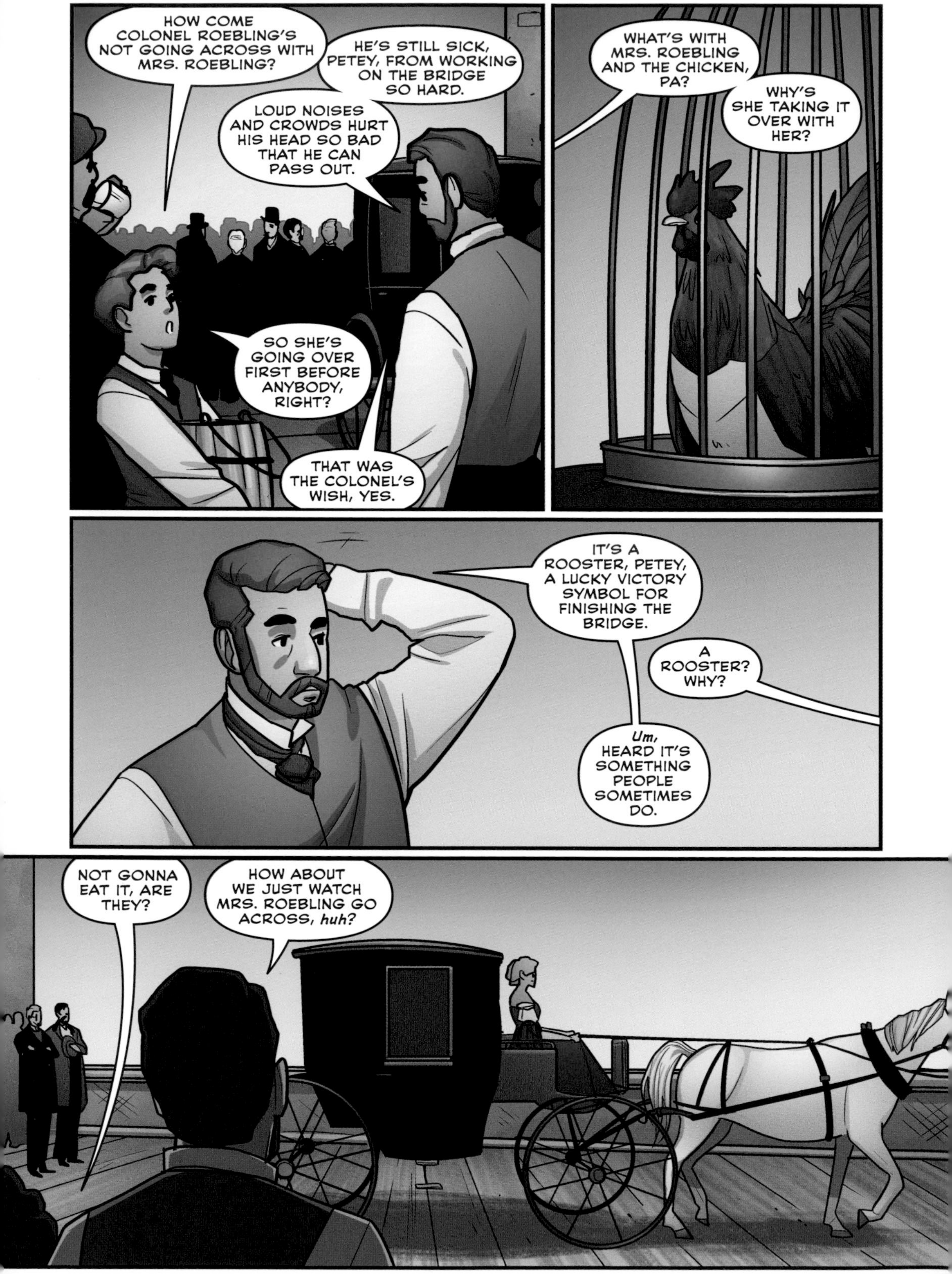
HOW COME COLONEL ROEBLING'S NOT GOING ACROSS WITH MRS. ROEBLING?
HE'S STILL SICK, PETEY, FROM WORKING ON THE BRIDGE SO HARD.
LOUD NOISES AND CROWDS HURT HIS HEAD SO BAD THAT HE CAN PASS OUT.
SO SHE'S GOING OVER FIRST BEFORE ANYBODY, RIGHT?
THAT WAS THE COLONEL'S WISH, YES.
WHAT'S WITH MRS. ROEBLING AND THE CHICKEN, PA?
WHY'S SHE TAKING IT OVER WITH HER?
IT'S A ROOSTER, PETEY, A LUCKY VICTORY SYMBOL FOR FINISHING THE BRIDGE.
A ROOSTER? WHY?
Um, HEARD IT'S SOMETHING PEOPLE SOMETIMES DO.
NOT GONNA EAT IT, ARE THEY?
HOW ABOUT WE JUST WATCH MRS. ROEBLING GO ACROSS, *huh*?

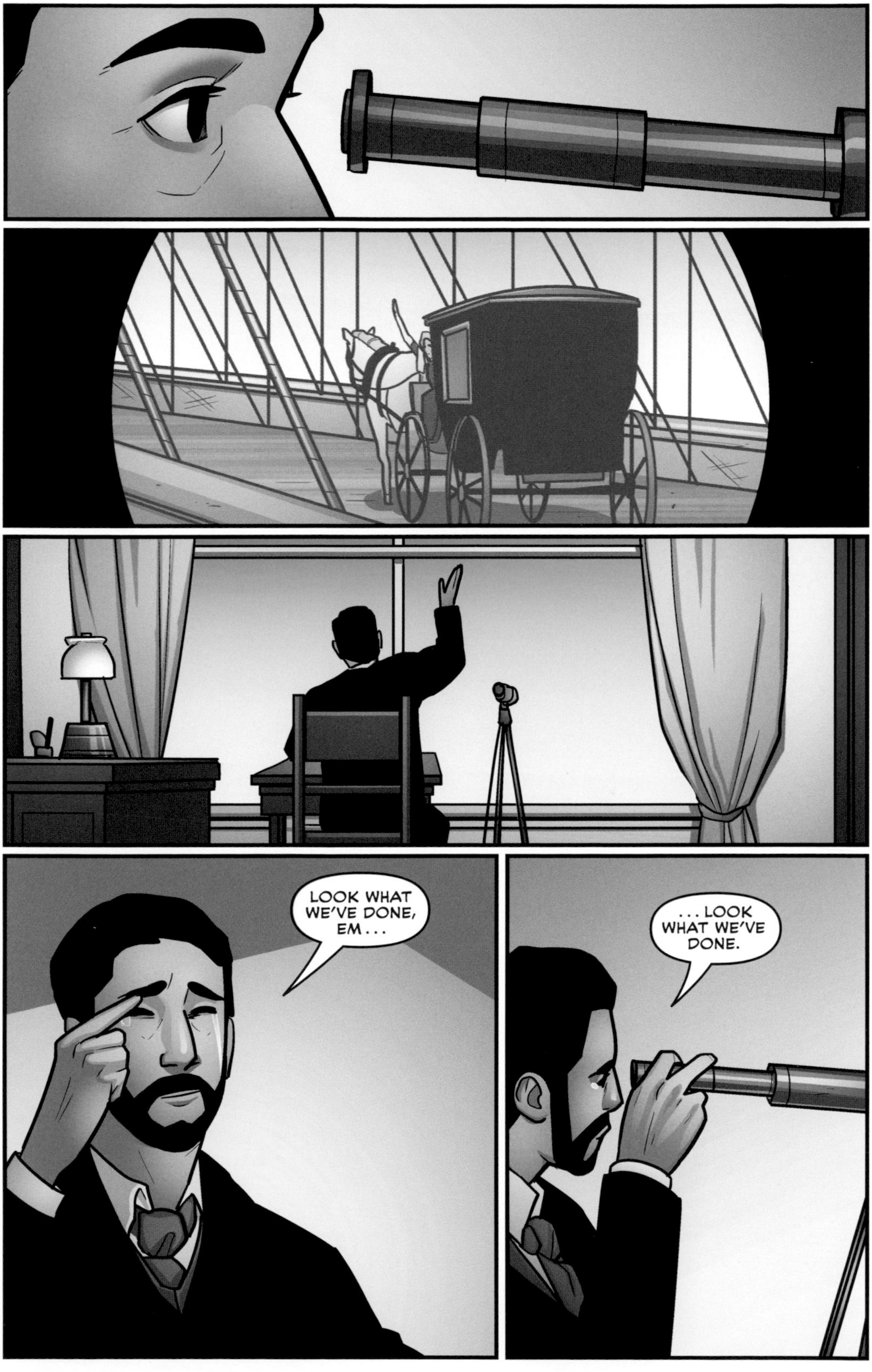
LOOK WHAT WE'VE DONE, EM...
...LOOK WHAT WE'VE DONE.

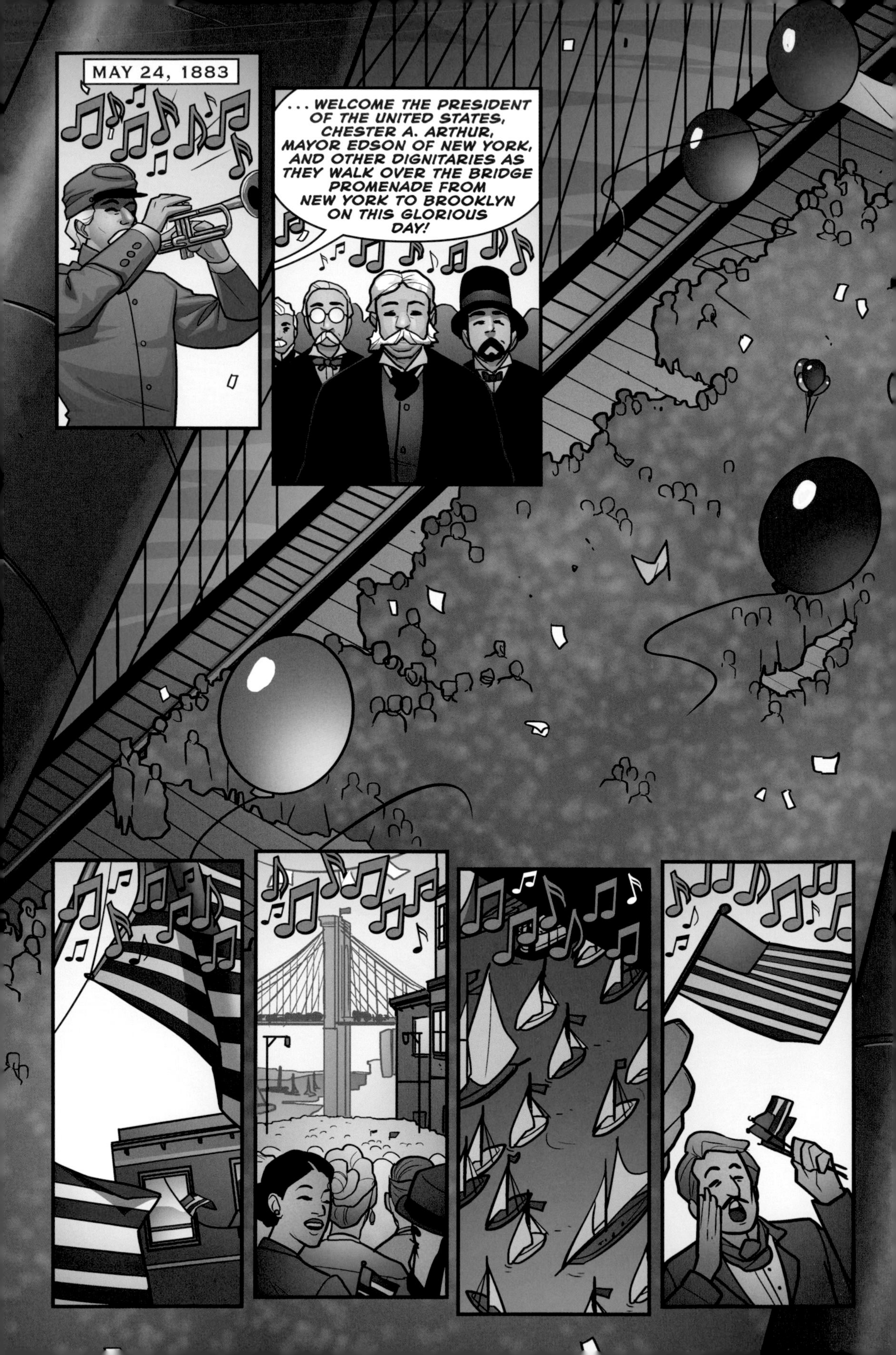
MAY 24, 1883
. . . WELCOME THE PRESIDENT OF THE UNITED STATES, CHESTER A. ARTHUR, MAYOR EDSON OF NEW YORK, AND OTHER DIGNITARIES AS THEY WALK OVER THE BRIDGE PROMENADE FROM NEW YORK TO BROOKLYN ON THIS GLORIOUS DAY!

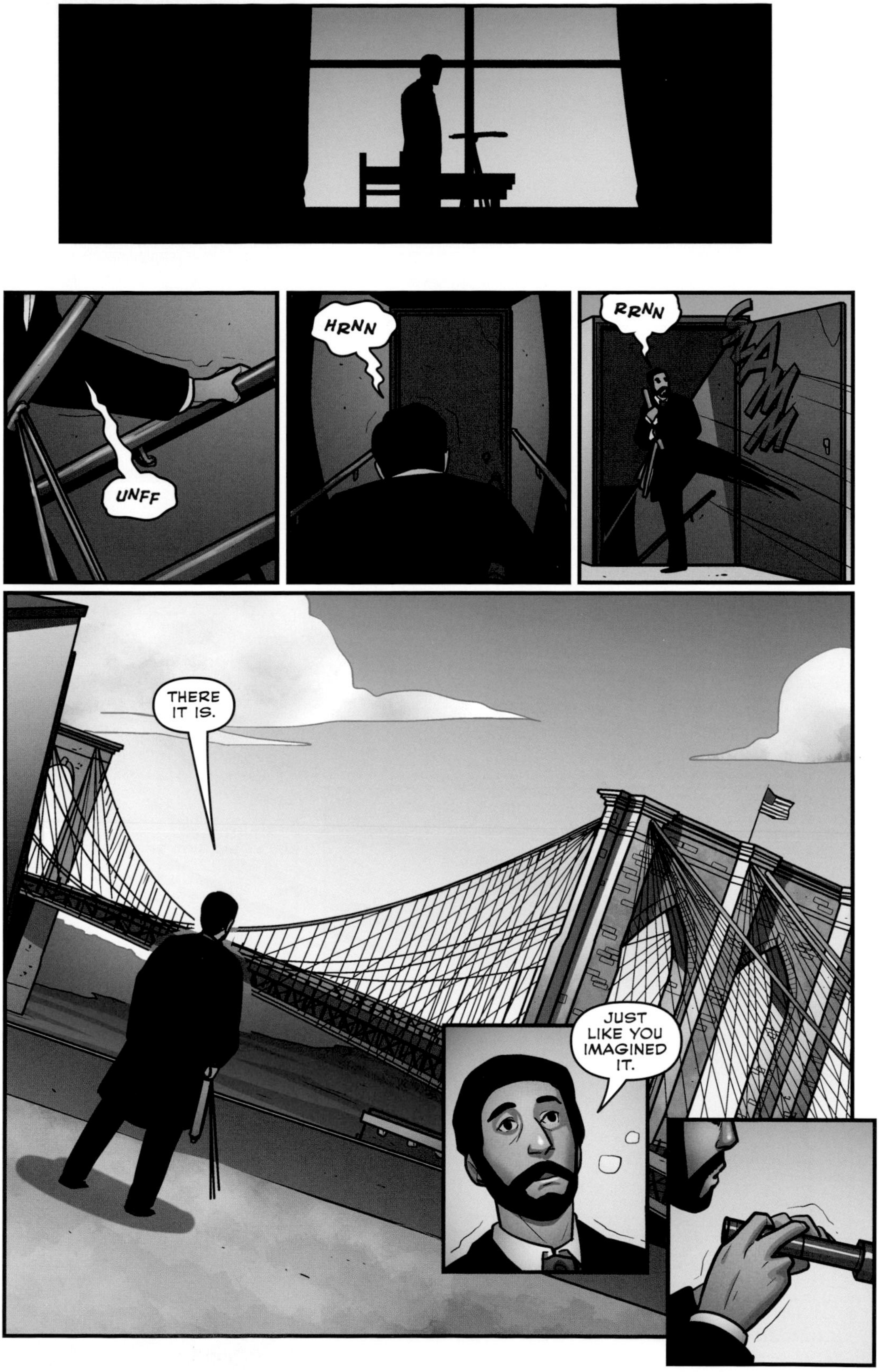
UNFF
HRNN
RRNN
SLAM
THERE IT IS.
JUST LIKE YOU IMAGINED IT.

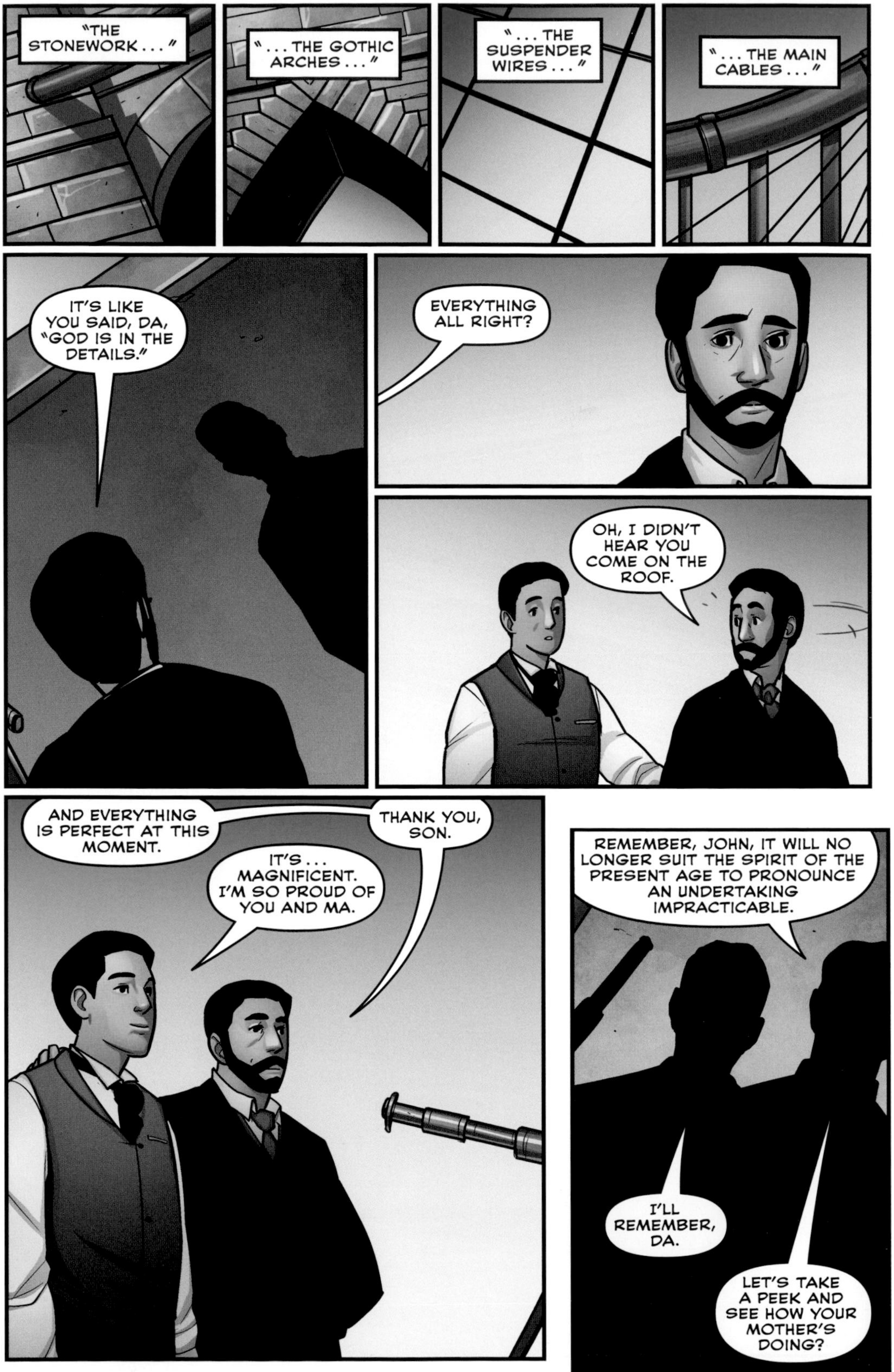
"THE STONEWORK . . ."
". . . THE GOTHIC ARCHES . . ."
". . . THE SUSPENDER WIRES . . ."
". . . THE MAIN CABLES . . ."
IT'S LIKE YOU SAID, DA, "GOD IS IN THE DETAILS."
EVERYTHING ALL RIGHT?
OH, I DIDN'T HEAR YOU COME ON THE ROOF.
IT'S . . . MAGNIFICENT. I'M SO PROUD OF YOU AND MA.
THANK YOU, SON.
AND EVERYTHING IS PERFECT AT THIS MOMENT.
REMEMBER, JOHN, IT WILL NO LONGER SUIT THE SPIRIT OF THE PRESENT AGE TO PRONOUNCE AN UNDERTAKING IMPRACTICABLE.
I'LL REMEMBER, DA.
LET'S TAKE A PEEK AND SEE HOW YOUR MOTHER'S DOING?

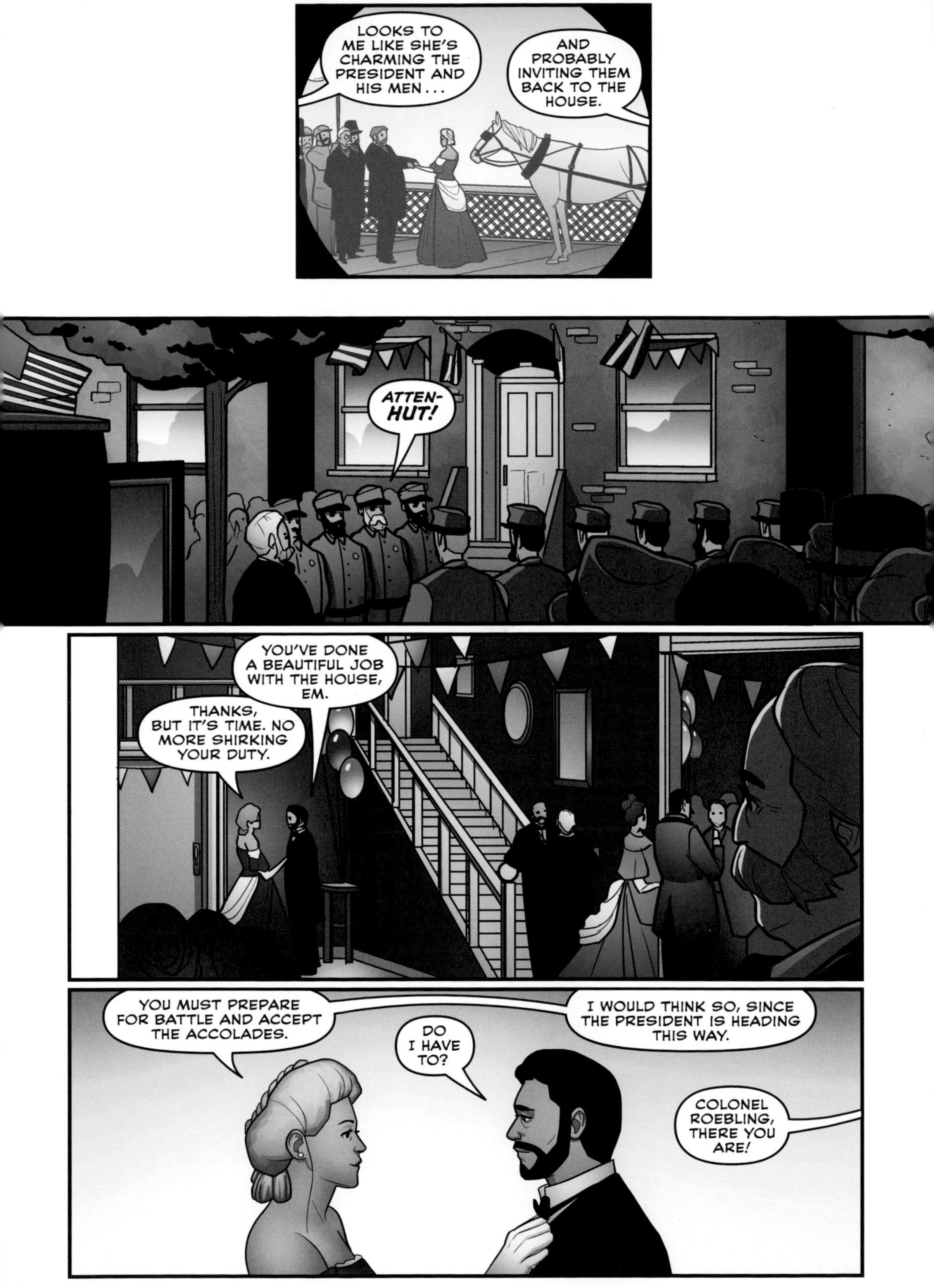
LOOKS TO ME LIKE SHE'S CHARMING THE PRESIDENT AND HIS MEN...
AND PROBABLY INVITING THEM BACK TO THE HOUSE.
ATTEN-HUT!
YOU'VE DONE A BEAUTIFUL JOB WITH THE HOUSE, EM.
THANKS, BUT IT'S TIME. NO MORE SHIRKING YOUR DUTY.
YOU MUST PREPARE FOR BATTLE AND ACCEPT THE ACCOLADES.
DO I HAVE TO?
I WOULD THINK SO, SINCE THE PRESIDENT IS HEADING THIS WAY.
COLONEL ROEBLING, THERE YOU ARE!

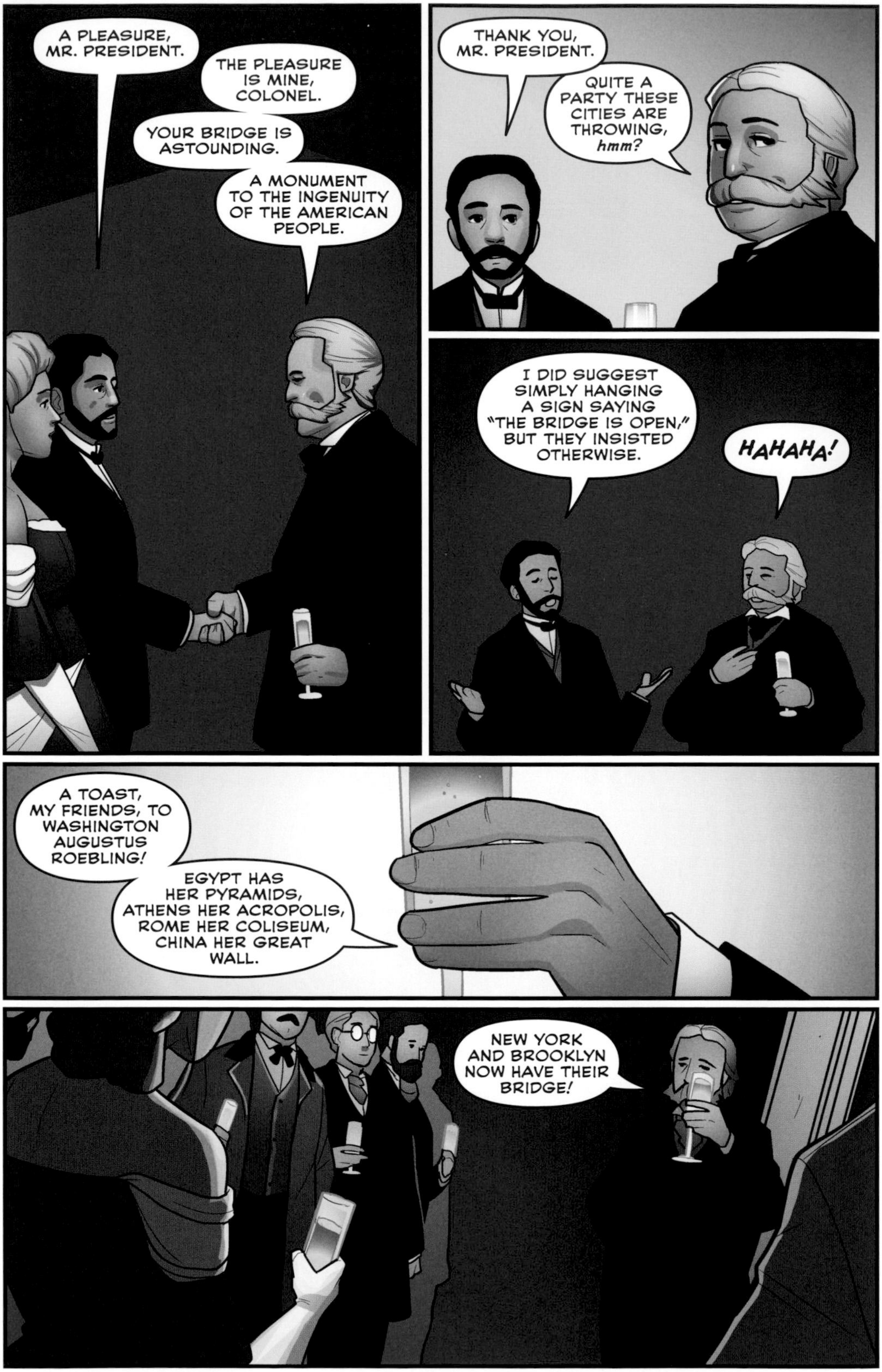

A PLEASURE, MR. PRESIDENT.
THE PLEASURE IS MINE, COLONEL.
YOUR BRIDGE IS ASTOUNDING.
A MONUMENT TO THE INGENUITY OF THE AMERICAN PEOPLE.
THANK YOU, MR. PRESIDENT.
QUITE A PARTY THESE CITIES ARE THROWING, *hmm?*
I DID SUGGEST SIMPLY HANGING A SIGN SAYING "THE BRIDGE IS OPEN," BUT THEY INSISTED OTHERWISE.
HAHAHA!
A TOAST, MY FRIENDS, TO WASHINGTON AUGUSTUS ROEBLING!
EGYPT HAS HER PYRAMIDS, ATHENS HER ACROPOLIS, ROME HER COLISEUM, CHINA HER GREAT WALL.
NEW YORK AND BROOKLYN NOW HAVE THEIR BRIDGE!

SPEECH, ROEBLING!
YES, SPEECH!
SPEECH!
TING TING TING
WELL, IF YOU INSIST.
AT FIRST, I THOUGHT I WOULD SUCCUMB TO MY INJURIES THOSE MANY YEARS AGO, BUT I HAD A STRONG TOWER TO LEAN UPON . . .
. . . MY WIFE, A WOMAN OF RARE BEAUTY, INFINITE TACT, AND WISEST COUNSEL.
EMILY ROEBLING.
CLAP CLAP CLAP CLAP
FOR FOURTEEN YEARS, I HAVE BEEN BLESSED TO WORK WITH A GROUP OF MEN WHO HAVE GONE ABOVE AND BEYOND ALL THAT I HAVE ASKED OF THEM.
FOR THAT I AM FOREVER GRATEFUL.
HERE'S TO MY ENGINEERING STAFF.
AND LAST, BUT NOT LEAST, OUR THANKS AND THOUGHTS TO THE MEN WHO WORKED AND DIED ON THIS BRIDGE OF THE PEOPLE.
THEIR NAMES MAY BE LOST TO HISTORY, BUT AS LONG AS THE EAST RIVER BRIDGE STANDS, THEY ARE IMMORTAL.
CLAP CLAP CLAP CLAP
TRUE HEROES, ALL.

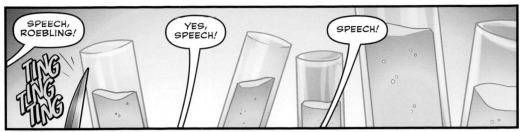

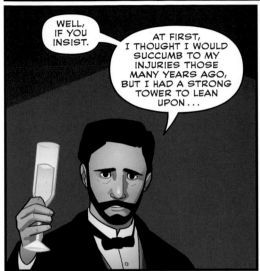

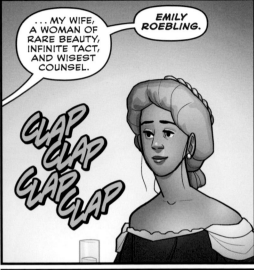

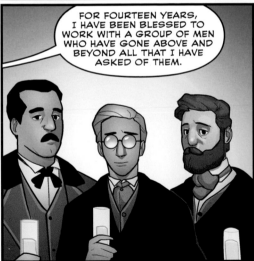

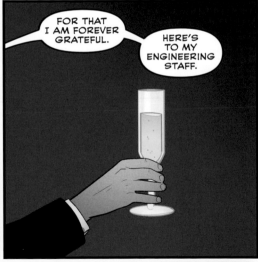

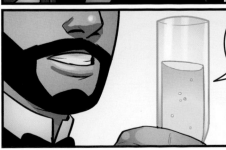

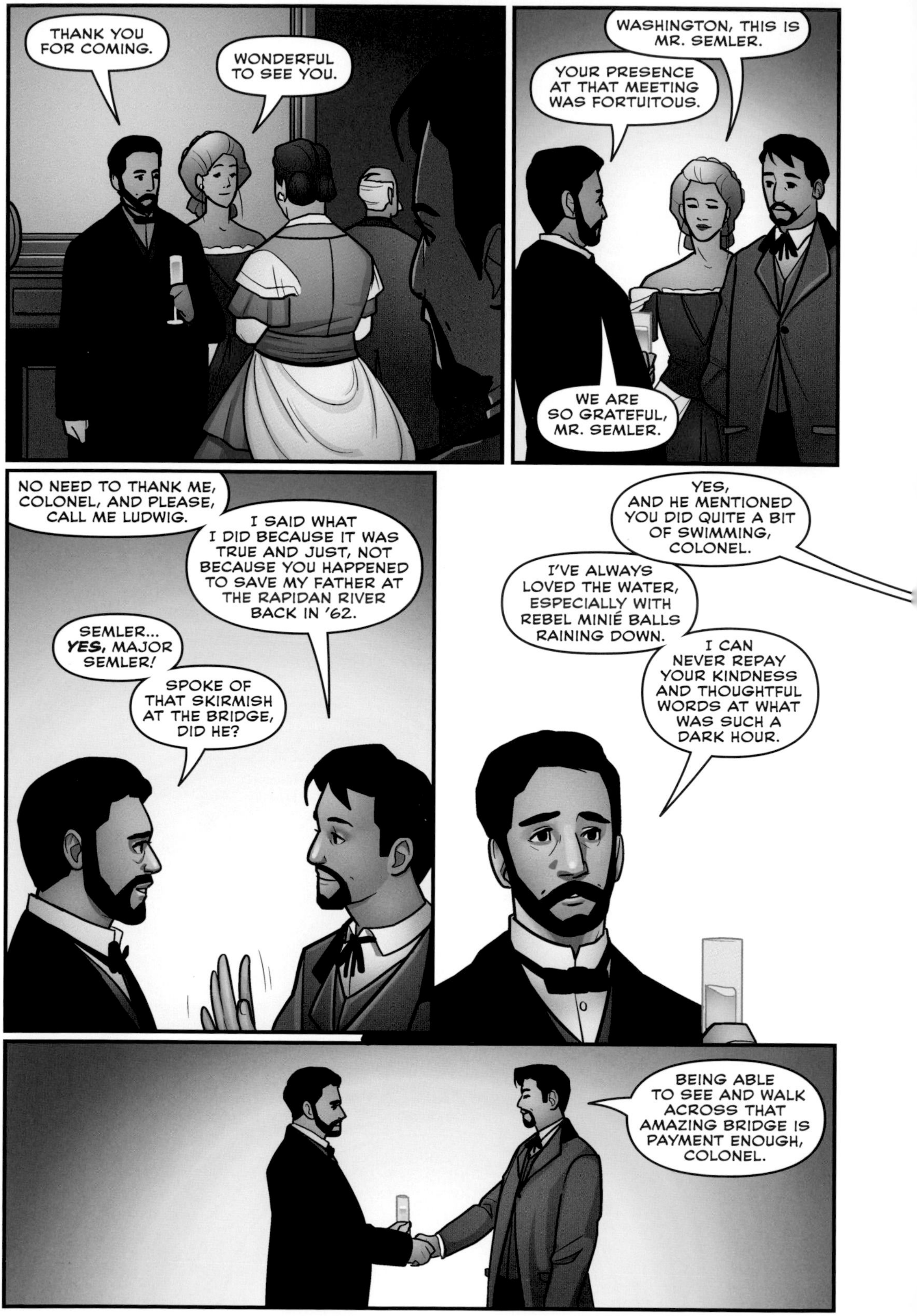
THANK YOU FOR COMING.
WONDERFUL TO SEE YOU.
WASHINGTON, THIS IS MR. SEMLER.
YOUR PRESENCE AT THAT MEETING WAS FORTUITOUS.
WE ARE SO GRATEFUL, MR. SEMLER.
NO NEED TO THANK ME, COLONEL, AND PLEASE, CALL ME LUDWIG.
I SAID WHAT I DID BECAUSE IT WAS TRUE AND JUST, NOT BECAUSE YOU HAPPENED TO SAVE MY FATHER AT THE RAPIDAN RIVER BACK IN '62.
SEMLER... **YES,** MAJOR SEMLER!
SPOKE OF THAT SKIRMISH AT THE BRIDGE, DID HE?
YES, AND HE MENTIONED YOU DID QUITE A BIT OF SWIMMING, COLONEL.
I'VE ALWAYS LOVED THE WATER, ESPECIALLY WITH REBEL MINIÉ BALLS RAINING DOWN.
I CAN NEVER REPAY YOUR KINDNESS AND THOUGHTFUL WORDS AT WHAT WAS SUCH A DARK HOUR.
BEING ABLE TO SEE AND WALK ACROSS THAT AMAZING BRIDGE IS PAYMENT ENOUGH, COLONEL.

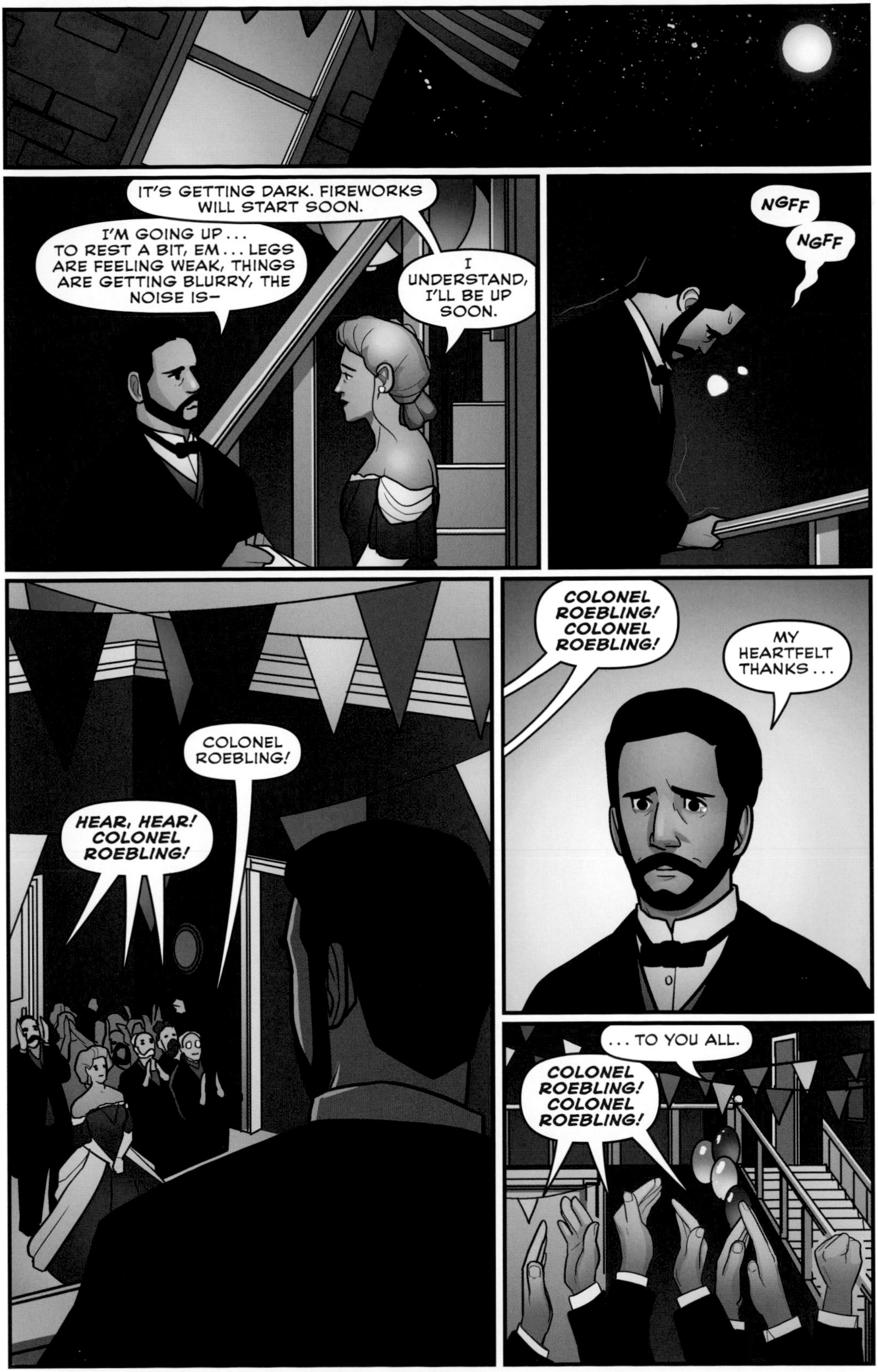
IT'S GETTING DARK. FIREWORKS WILL START SOON.
I'M GOING UP . . . TO REST A BIT, EM . . . LEGS ARE FEELING WEAK, THINGS ARE GETTING BLURRY, THE NOISE IS–
I UNDERSTAND, I'LL BE UP SOON.
NGFF
NGFF
COLONEL ROEBLING!
HEAR, HEAR! COLONEL ROEBLING!
COLONEL ROEBLING! COLONEL ROEBLING!
MY HEARTFELT THANKS . . .
. . . TO YOU ALL.
COLONEL ROEBLING! COLONEL ROEBLING!

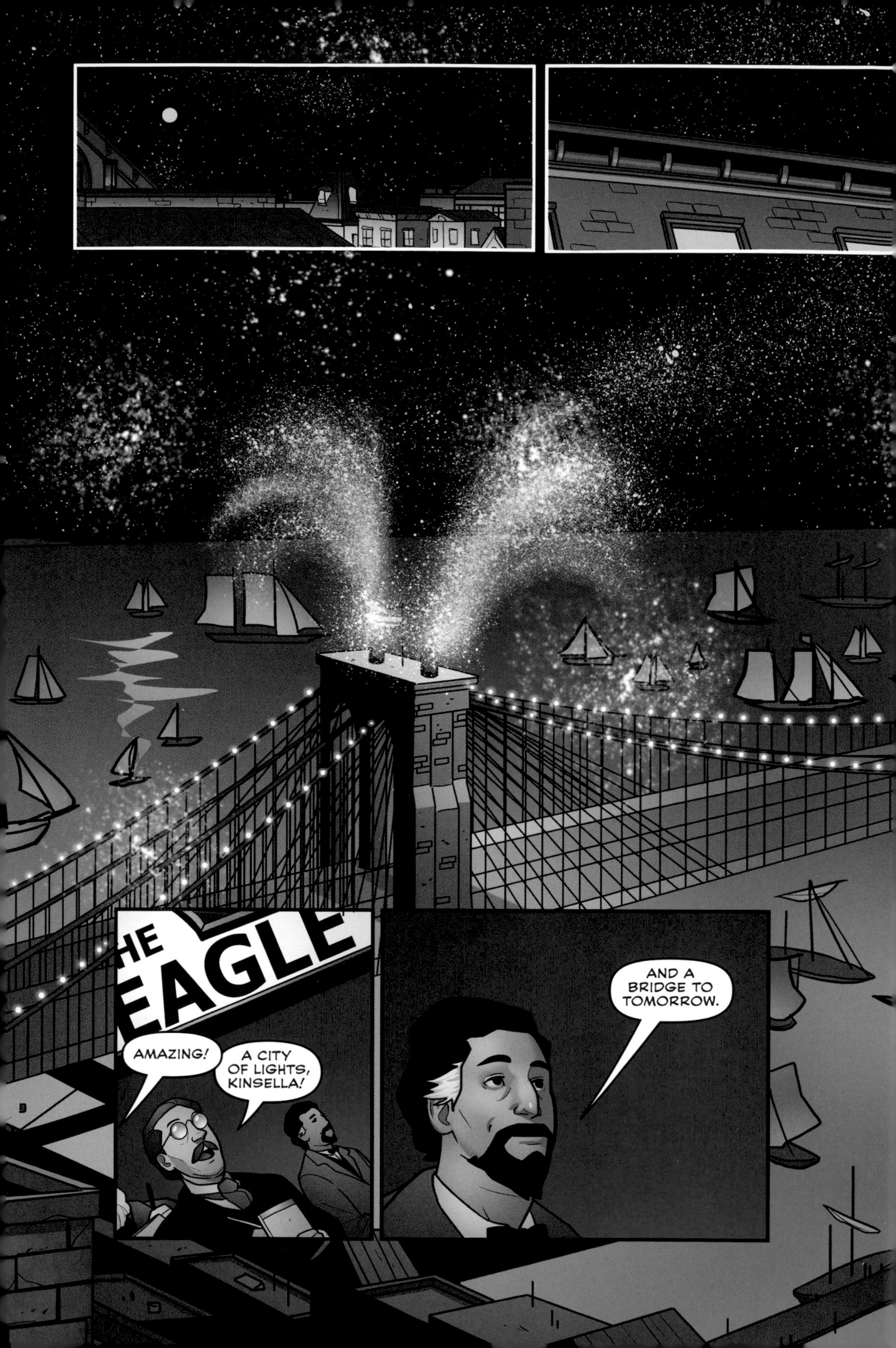
THE
EAGLE
AMAZING!
A CITY OF LIGHTS, KINSELLA!
AND A BRIDGE TO TOMORROW.

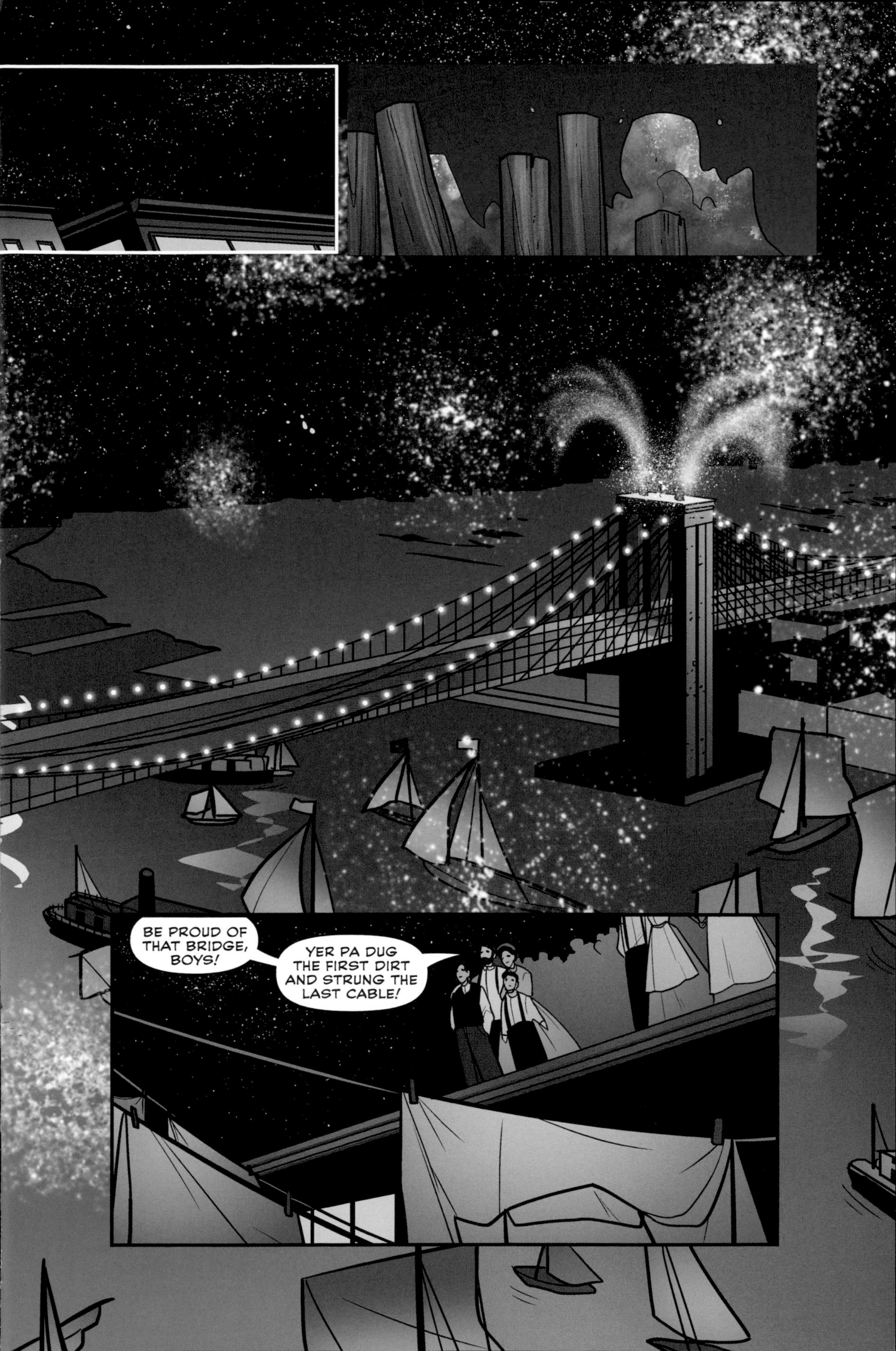
BE PROUD OF THAT BRIDGE, BOYS!
YER PA DUG THE FIRST DIRT AND STRUNG THE LAST CABLE!

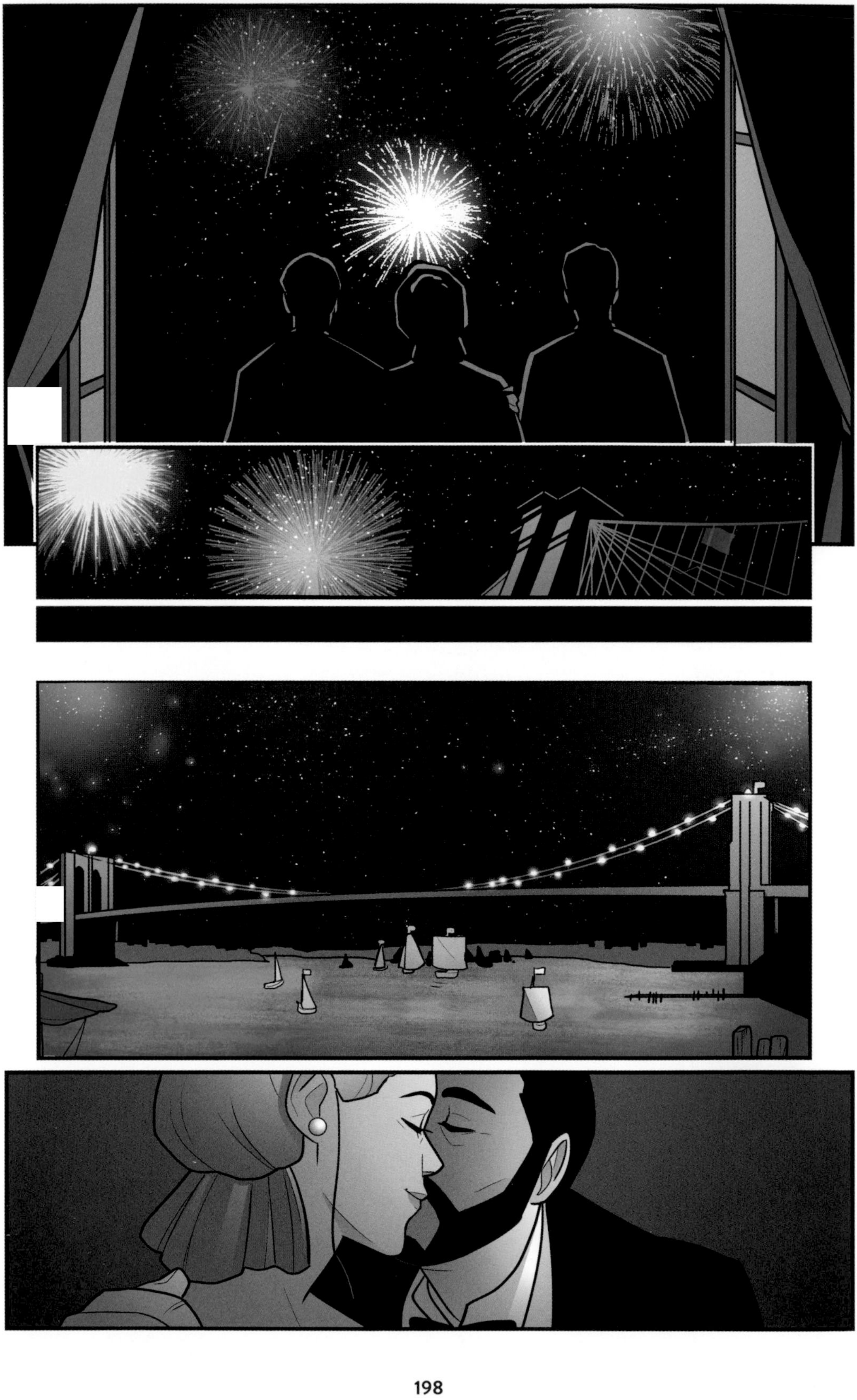

WEEKS LATER

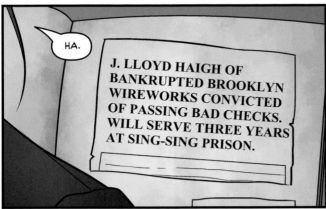

HA.

J. LLOYD HAIGH OF BANKRUPTED BROOKLYN WIREWORKS CONVICTED OF PASSING BAD CHECKS. WILL SERVE THREE YEARS AT SING-SING PRISON.

AND JUSTICE IS SERVED.

AFTER YOU'RE DONE, I DO BELIEVE THAT TODAY IS THE DAY YOU CROSS YOUR BRIDGE.

NEXT WEEK, EM.

I HAVE GARDEN WORK THAT—

WHAP

—I GUESS CAN WAIT TILL TOMORROW.

199

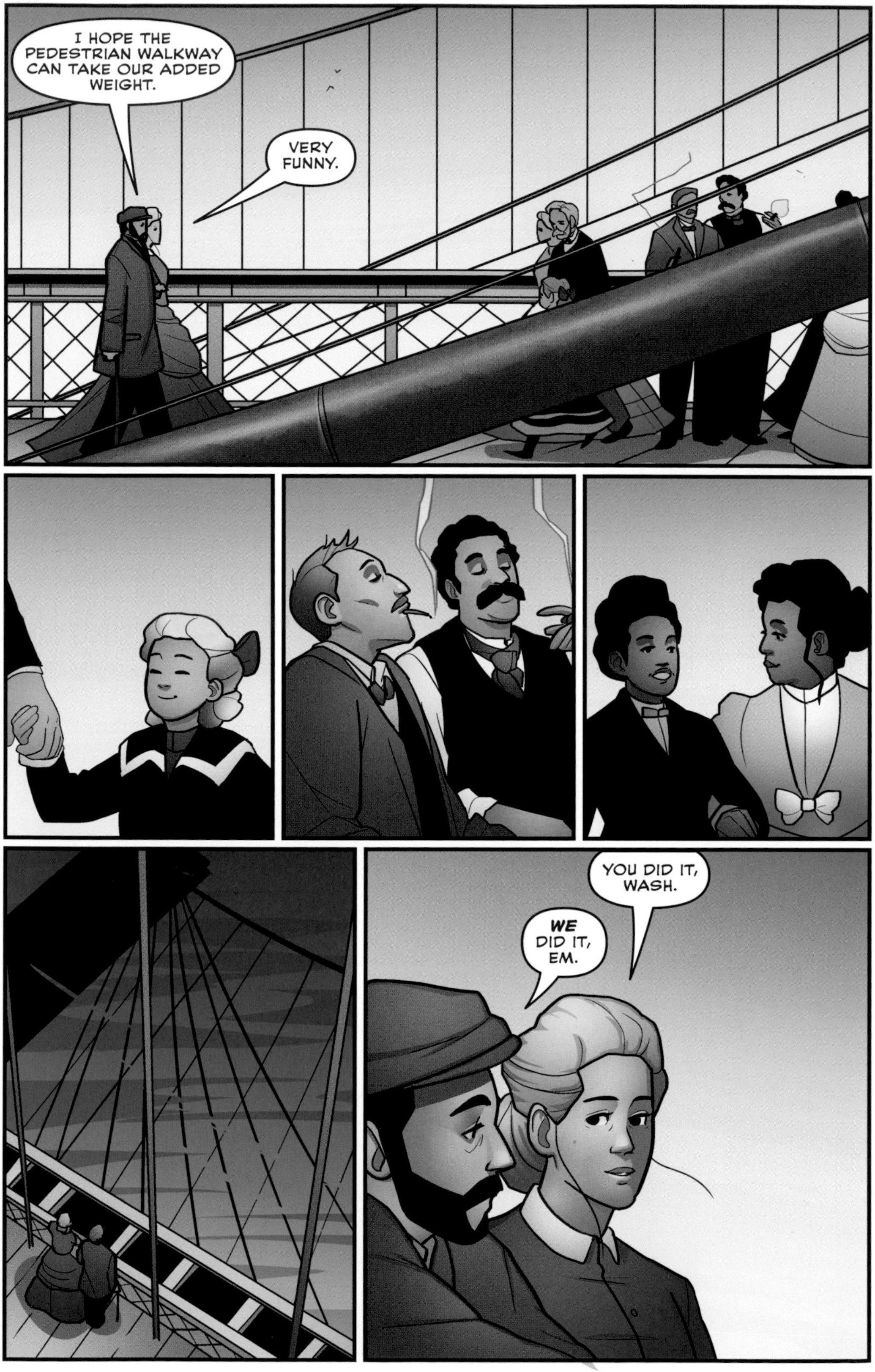
I HOPE THE PEDESTRIAN WALKWAY CAN TAKE OUR ADDED WEIGHT.
VERY FUNNY.
YOU DID IT, WASH.
WE DID IT, EM.

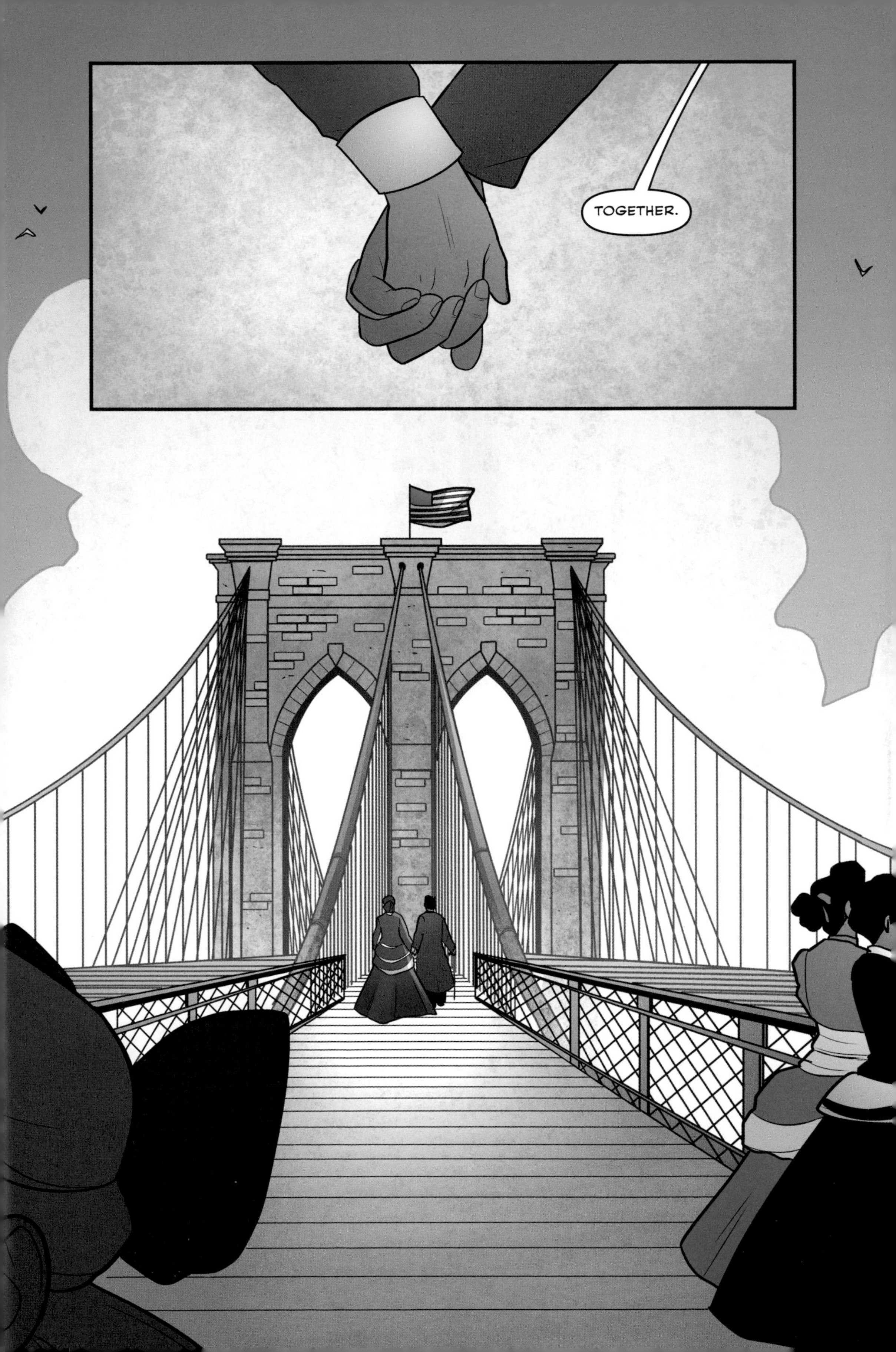
TOGETHER.

Selected Media

These are the books, articles, film, and archive collections that helped make this project as accurate as possible. By immersing myself in all this wonderful material, I couldn't help but be transported into the lives of the Roeblings and the building of the most iconic bridge known the world over.

Two hundred pages have allowed Sara DuVall and me to just scratch away at the full breadth of these amazing lives and times. Hell, there's a mammoth book waiting to be written just on Washington's father, John A. Roebling, and his creation of a whole town in Saxonburg, Pennsylvania, not to mention a book on Washington Roebling's Civil War years, where it's damn near incredible he survived to build the Brooklyn Bridge at all after having participated in almost every bloody battle.

My love of all things bridges springs from two men and one woman: Othmar Ammann, Hildegarde Swift, and David McCullough. I grew up in the shadow of the bare steel skeleton of the George Washington Bridge, which was designed by Ammann in Washington Heights (long before it was branded Hudson Heights by real estate marketers). Swift's wonderful children's book from 1942, *The Little Red Lighthouse and the Great Gray Bridge*, was burned into my DNA after countless readings. (In addition, the lighthouse literally existed only two blocks down the hill from our family's old apartment.) And the coup de grâce coming after a dog-eared copy of McCullough's *The Great Bridge* found its way into my New York history–hungry hands back in high school, taking hold of my imagination and leading me to walk across the Brooklyn Bridge for the first time at thirteen years old, where I would stare into the murky depths of the East River wondering how anyone actually worked in those caissons under the muck and set the stone for the towering gothic arches above. Years later, I was quite proud to stand on the bridge again for its Centennial Celebration on May 24, 1983, which I still have the program for.

It's obviously a no-brainer to say that Ammann, Swift, and McCullough's artistry put the hook in me forever. I am indebted to their masterworks and the fact that my mother never found out about my somewhat dangerous expeditions of discovery on the Gray Lady that spans the Hudson, or the many parentless trips on the A train down to Fulton Street, where I would walk across the Brooklyn Bridge and grab a slice and a chocolate egg cream before heading home.

Books and Library Archives

Board of Trustees of the *New York and Brooklyn Bridge. New York and Brooklyn Bridge Proceedings, 1867-1884*. Brooklyn Museum Libraries/Archives.

Bridge to the Future: A Centennial Celebration of the Brooklyn Bridge. Annuals of the New York Academy of Sciences, vol. 424 (1984).

Brooklyn Museum. *The Great East River Bridge, 1883-1983*. New York: Harry N. Abrams, 1983.

Brown, Francis William. *Big Bridge to Brooklyn*. New York: Aladdin Books, 1956.

Burrows, Edwin G. and Mike Wallace. *Gotham: A History of New York City to 1898*. New York: Oxford University Press, 1998.

Haw, Richard. *The Brooklyn Bridge: A Cultural History*. New Brunswick, NJ: Rutgers University Press, 2005.

McCullough, David. *The Great Bridge*. New York: Simon & Schuster, 1972.

Rodin, Richard. *The Brooklyn Bridge: The Official Illustrated History*. New York: Brooklyn Bridge Centennial Corporation, 1983.

Roebling Collection, MC 04. Institute Archives and Special Collections, Rensselaer Polytechnic Institute, Troy, New York, 1824-1926.

Roebling, Washington. *Washington Roebling's Father: A Memoir of John A. Roebling*. Reston, VA: American Society of Civil Engineers Press, 2009.

Roebling, Washington Augustus. *Washington Roebling's War: Being a Selection from the Unpublished Civil War Letters of Washington Augustus Roebling*. Newark, DE: Curtis Paper Company, June 1961.

Schuyler, Hamilton. *The Roeblings: A Century of Engineers, Bridge Builders, and Industrialists*. Princeton, NJ: Princeton University Press, 1931.

Steinman, D. B. *The Builders of the Bridge: The Story of John Roebling and His Son*. New York: Harcourt, Brace & Company, 1945.

Zink, Clifford W. *The Roebling Legacy*. Princeton, NJ: Princeton Landmark Publication, 2011.

Film

Stechler, Amy and Ken Burns. *Ken Burns America Collection: Brooklyn Bridge*. Florentine Films/ WNET Channel 13/PBS Home Video, 1982.

Periodical Archives

"Brooklyn Bridge: An Account of the Opening Exercises" (author unknown), *Harper's Weekly*, May 24, 1883.

"The Brooklyn Bridge—History of a Great Enterprise—Details of its Construction" (author unknown), *Brooklyn Daily Eagle*, January 2, 1898.

"Brooklyn Bridge's History—Story of Heroism and Sacrifice" (author unknown), *Brooklyn Daily Eagle*, May 24, 1933.

"A Builder of New York and His Bridge" (author unknown), *New York Times*, December 29, 1929.

Conant, W. C. "The Brooklyn Bridge: A History of the Bridge," *Harper's Magazine*, May 24, 1883.

"German Builds Homes and a Bridge" (author unknown), *Brooklyn Daily Eagle*, February 15, 1948.

"Glorification-No More Shall the River Divide" (author unknown), *Brooklyn Daily Eagle*, May 24, 1883.

"Heroic Story of Mrs. Roebling" (author unknown), *Brooklyn Daily Eagle*, June 22, 1952.

Hyman, Stanley Edgar. "This Alluring Roadway," *New Yorker*, May 17, 1952.

Kinsella, Thomas. "Dead," *Brooklyn Daily Eagle*, February 11, 1884.

"Mrs. Washington Roebling Dead" (author unknown), *Brooklyn Daily Eagle*, March 1, 1903.

"Rejoicing-Brooklyn Welcomes Her Many Guests- Colonel Roebling's Esteemed Visitors" (author unknown), *Brooklyn Daily Eagle*, May 25, 1883.

Schuyler, Montgomery. "The Bridge as Monument," *Harper's Weekly*, May 24, 1883.

"The Story of the Brooklyn Bridge's 50th Anniversary" (author unknown), *Brooklyn Daily Eagle*, April 19, 1933.

Trachtenberg, Alan. *Brooklyn Bridge: Fact and Symbol*. Chicago: University of Chicago Press, 1965.

"Two Great Cities United" (author unknown), *New York Times*, May 25, 1883.

Acknowledgments

Our lives are like bridges: One main span, then roadways spreading out across other lives and places, making stops, some shorter, some longer, never knowing which atoms are going to bounce against us and change us in so many subtle and distinct ways.

My parents, Hal and Georgia, nurtured my love of arts and history, and my younger sister, Maria, kept everyone spinning with her kinetic energy and amazing singing voice.

Then there are family and friends who joined the cast and crew that my buddy, Anthony Martinez, and I put together in the days of yore when Super 8mm was king and the Canon 1014 was as beautiful as a Panavision camera in the hands of a thirteen-year-old.

That storytelling focus continued thanks to teachers like Dennis Seuling and Irene Cascione at John F. Kennedy High School in the Bronx, and Nick Tanis and Jesse Kornbluth at New York University School of the Arts. After NYU I worked on film, TV productions, and music videos, watching other storytellers at work, then decompressed after fourteen-hour shoots by writing my own stories and screenplays before crawling under the covers to grab five hours of shut-eye before the next day's call time.

Over the years, my writing DNA was twisted and turned by great historians and writers like David McCullough, Alan Taylor, Stephen Ambrose, Cornelius Ryan, David Halberstam, Ron Chernow, Shelby Foote, Gore Vidal, John Steinbeck, and countless others.

Then came DC Comics, where I have honed my storytelling craft for over twenty years thanks to editors and fellow writers who have left behind something in their wake for me to chew on. Paul Levitz, Mike Carlin, Geoff Johns, Dan Didio, John Ostrander, Robert Kanigher, Len Wein, Frank Miller, Garth Ennis, Alan Moore, Grant Morrison, Denny O' Neil, Jeph Loeb, James Robinson, and so many more, including the late, great Archie Goodwin, who would let me bend his ear many mornings before the office hallway started humming to talk about characters and what makes a good story.

This book wouldn't be in your hands if not for a Brooklynite by the name of Charles Kochman, editorial director at Abrams ComicArts, along with the other passionate folks at Abrams I've worked with along the way: Orlando Dos Reis, Pamela Notarantonio, Anne Jaconette, Maya Bradford, and Samantha Hoback, and also Charles Olsen at Inkwell.

My greatest respect and admiration for the bridge-building crew, artists all, who brought this story to life: Sara DuVall, Gabe Eltaeb, Rob Leigh, and John Kalisz.

Finally, above all as always, this couldn't have been written without the love, advice, and support of my wife, Deborah, a rainbow surfer and true storyteller herself, and my son, Alexander, who should always remember the motto: Who Dares Wins.

Readers looking for true grit and indomitable spirit will find it by visiting the Brooklyn Bridge and thinking of the hands, hearts, and minds that made something from nothing.

Peter J. Tomasi

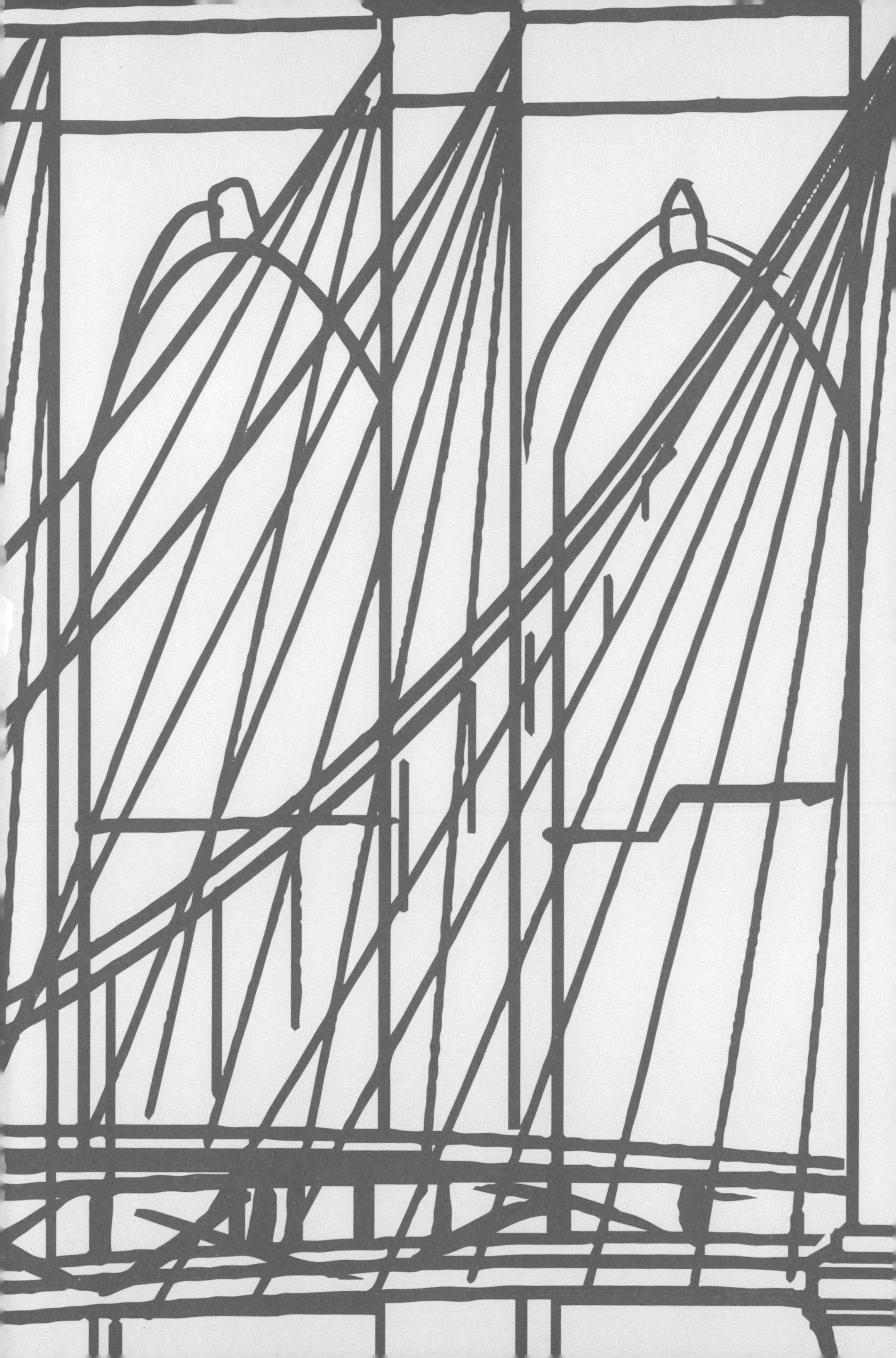

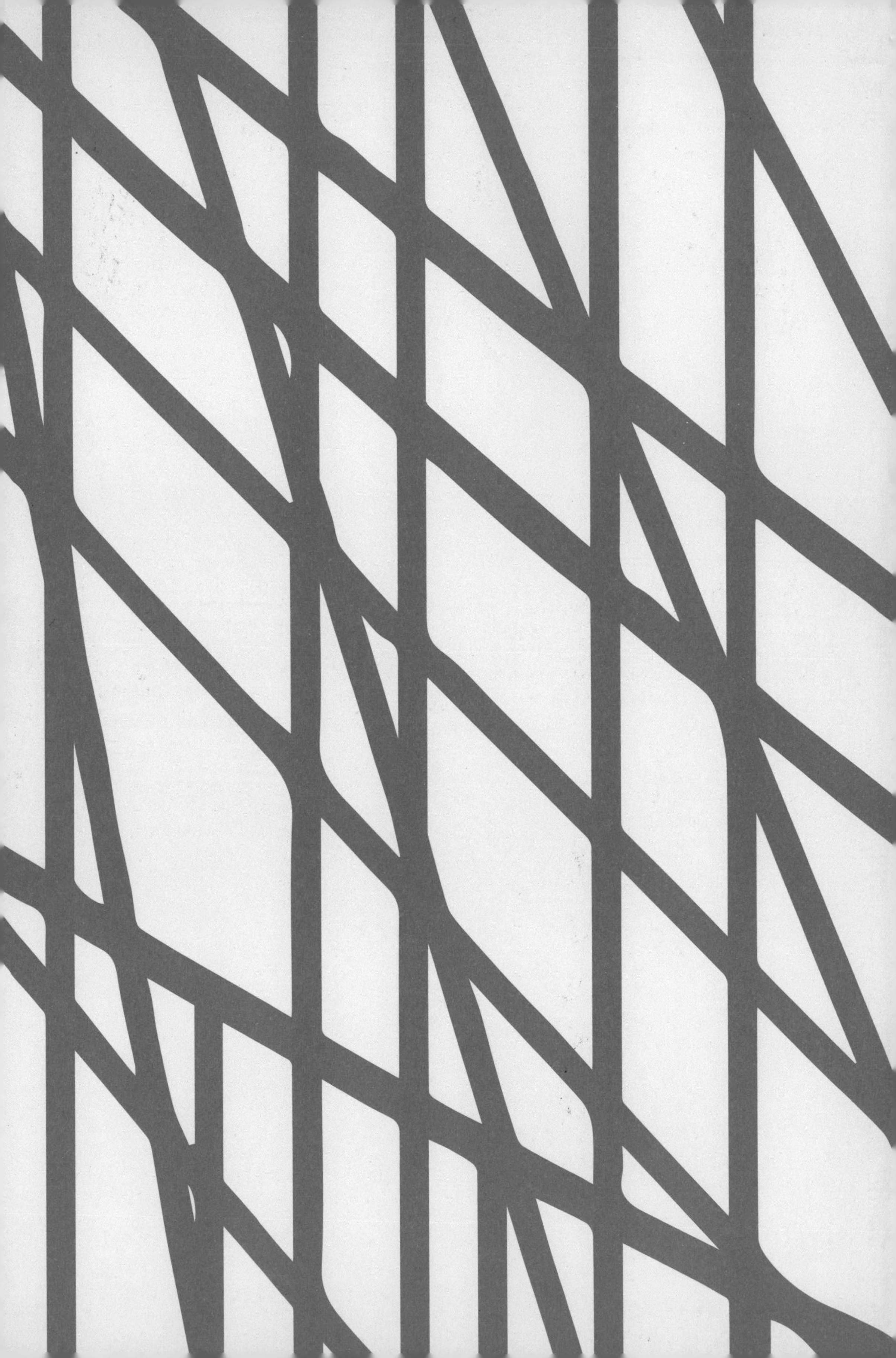